International Hospitality Management

International Hospitality Management

Concepts and Cases

Clarke and Chen

ELSEVIER

AMSTERDAM • BOSTON • HEIDELBERG • LONDON • NEW YORK • OXFORD
PARIS • SAN DIEGO • SAN FRANCISCO • SINGAPORE • SYDNEY • TOKYO
Butterworth-Heinemann is an imprint of Elsevier

Butterworth-Heinemann is an imprint of Elsevier
Linacre House, Jordan Hill, Oxford OX2 8DP
30 Corporate Drive, Suite 400, Burlington, MA 01803, USA

First Edition 2007

British Library Cataloguing in Publication Data
A catalogue record for this book is available from the British Library

Library of Congress Cataloguing in Publication Data
A catalogue record for this book is available from the Library of Congress

ISBN: 978 0 7506 6675 6

For information on all Butterworth-Heinemann publications
visit our web site at http://books.elsevier.com

Typeset by Charon Tec Ltd (A Macmillan Company), Chennai, India
www.charontec.com
Printed and bound by MPG Books Ltd, Bodmin, Cornwall, Great Britain

07 08 09 10 11   10 9 8 7 6 5 4 3 2 1

Contents

Preface

The development of hospitality and the issues with hospitality management have been growing rapidly. It is an area of study and practice which has emerged and established itself in Universities and Colleges around the world. Alongside these courses, there has been an explosion in text books and journals that explore the industry and the concerns with its development. We are now adding to that collection with this book.

We believe that the study and the practice of hospitality management is a significant area in contemporary lives and that it deserves serious consideration. Moreover we believe that hospitality is an area of activity that is sufficiently different to be considered separately from other aspects of management. This differentiation does not mean that hospitality has to discover everything for itself but it does mean that we have to look carefully at the translation of management studies into this field. There is a culture identifiable within hospitality that requires general notions to be translated, adapted and developed to fit the working conditions of the industry.

The focus of this book centres on the development of the hospitality industry in the context of international markets and operations. These also call into question the applicability of general notions as we believe that local cultural conditions, organisational cultural contexts and the processes of international management only make sense when these conditions are recognised. We are against simplistic universalistic applications and hopefully demonstrate our reasoning in the following chapters.

Our thoughts have been shaped in many ways and over many years. However, one simple message that comes through these experiences and which hopefully is borne out in the book is that we can never take anything for granted. Just because we are used to doing something in one particular way does not make that the right way or the only way. We would urge you to develop a critical approach to what you think you know and to question where the basis for that knowledge comes from. This will help you to explore your own cultural inheritance and question your expectations.

We began as you are now and would urge you to maximise your potential through your studies and your work in the industry. We share a wonderful experience of studying for our PhDs with supervisors who encouraged us to think and question our subjects. We owe them our thanks and our gratitude for giving us far more than the formal qualification. We hope that the approach taken in this book will help you develop that approach also.

We would like to recognise the contributions of some of our colleagues including Prof. Stephen Ball, Peter Spencer, Sue Horner, Dave Egan, Emma Martin, Mike Rimmington, Mike Mathews, John Swarbrooke, Kitty Wang, Jenny Wade, Jenny Cockill, Zhao Haolu, Li Gang, and Huang Rong. There are others, such as Stuart Hall and Raymond Williams, who inspired the questioning of culture and many more in Universities in Sheffield (both of them), North London, Milton Keynes, Derby, Nottingham and Veszprém who have given us ideas and questions that we continue to work with. Their friendship and their academic support continue to be important to us.

Further more over the years we have worked with students at Diploma, Undergraduate, Masters and PhD levels and learned more from these encounters than we knew before. A particular mention is due to all the Sheffield Hallam University Hospitality Business Management course students because it was thinking through their needs that gave rise to this specific project. It is a pleasure to see the growth of students and watch the responses to seeds of ideas that are taken away and developed. It is a source of great satisfaction to us to be involved in this process.

We have drawn widely from material that is available to any of you if you know where to look. We have done our best to identify copyright holders where ever possible, but particularly with some of the web sources this proved difficult. We have also raised the question with some who were not sure how to respond, so we apologise for causing alarm and grateful for their help in resolving the concerns. If an unknowing use of copyright material has been used please contact the authors, via the publisher, as every effort was made to contact the owners of the material. We are grateful for their work as it adds richness to our arguments and we would encourage them to keep up the work of monitoring and examining our industry.

Acknowledgements

We would like to thank the people who have made this book possible. We have benefited greatly from the supportive and critical dialogues with our friends and colleagues, both in the industry and in Universities around the world. We have met many people who gave us the belief that this was an important book – and some who asked why we were doing it. All of them kept us going. Special thanks has to go to our students, wherever we found them, who made the book possible with their constant questioning of what we thought we knew – they were and continue to be a constant source of inspiration. We have had wonderful support from Sally North and Francesca Ford at Elsevier and we hope that they feel their patience was worthwhile. Our wives must have sympathized with them, surely knowing how they felt and we are unbelievably grateful for their love and understanding as the book interrupted what passes for normal in our lives – thank you.

As usual we accept that we are indebted to many people for the sources and contacts that produced this book, but they also know that all the errors in the book are ours.

We dedicate this book to our children: Ruth, Jamie, Dan, Ben and Alex – they are the future of international hospitality.

CHAPTER 1

Welcome: an introduction to international hospitality management

Figure 1.1
An example of a multilingual welcome – this key holder was issued at the InterContinental in Budapest in 2006.

■ Introduction

As the illustration suggests, you are welcome! You are welcome to join us on a rapid journey through the ways in which hospitality can be managed within an international context. This book addresses a challenge that is becoming increasingly important as we move through the 21st century, namely how can we attempt to manage hospitality internationally. There have been many attempts and there are some which offer examples of good practice but there are also many examples of failure and underperformance that point to a lack of understanding of or an inability to meet the management challenge. We will draw on many examples in an attempt to explore the issues which we believe underpin the operation of the hospitality industry. For us we see the hospitality industry as the group of organizations providing hospitality services and products to the public, and we believe it has a very close relationship with the tourism industry. You will be introduced to the traditional aspects of the industry, with examples from hotels and restaurants, but we will also look at the ways in which the industry has been changing (though we stop short at giving full consideration to the underwater hotels and the space race!).

One of the tensions in the international study of any subject is how it is constructed in different countries – this is very true for our field. In the United Kingdom, tourism has overtaken hospitality as the centre of attention and research, with hospitality seen as a supporting sector. In the USA, the major focus has tended to be on hospitality with tourism emerging as a concern for the hospitality industry. In China, the phrase used is almost always hospitality and tourism or tourism and hospitality. This most clearly reflects our view that the two are interlinked and mutually dependent. The hospitality and tourism industries together are the largest and fastest growing industry in the world. The World Travel and Tourism Council (www.wttc.org) estimate that hospitality and tourism as a global economy are directly and indirectly responsible for 11% of gross domestic product, 200 million jobs, 8% of total employment and 5.5 million new jobs per year until 2010. This creates a wide range of management challenges and we will critically explore the developments within the industry in the book.

This chapter will introduce the aspects of international hospitality management that we will address in the book and explain the rationale for how we have divided it into 11 chapters, all of which deal with a major element of international hospitality management.

Our position has grown out of our experiences of living and working in international hospitality, both in our native countries and in other people's. This has sensitized us to the need to operate internationally in a way that facilitates exchange and growth. We have seen ventures based on a simple single culture being overwhelmed by the complexities of the world we live in and that they had chosen to operate in. We will look further at those issues by examining as a crucial example the introduction of the Disney brand and the Disney concept into the European and Chinese markets. These launches were not straightforward even for an organization as well developed and powerful as Disney.

Our position is an unusual one within hospitality management and that contributes to the challenging nature of this book. We have grown up in the debates in leisure studies and tourism studies, which have seen those areas move into critical debate. Jones (2004) has noted that hospitality research is still lagging behind those fields. He identified the principal schools of thought in hospitality as follows:

- Hospitality science model: Based on the natural and physical sciences such as chemistry, biology and physics. Studies of this type include research in diet, nutrition, ergonomics, equipment performance and so on.
- Hospitality management school: This is largely based on empirical and quantitative studies, often related to studies of hospitality marketing and consumption.
- Hospitality studies: This includes qualitative as well as quantitative research.
- Hospitality relationship: This is a recent school of thought and separate to, and distinct from, any management or industry association.
- Hospitality systems: Systems thinking accommodates both positivist and normative research.
- Hospitality pragmatics: This is an all inclusive position dealing with the realities of the industry.

We do not sit easily in any of these positions, deriving a concern for the practical from the hospitality management school whilst being informed by the concerns for the hospitality relationship. We hope this book brings together the grounded elements of the case studies we provide with the insights of the awareness of the dynamics of the relationships which are central to our understanding of the hospitality industry and the distinctive relationships which mark out our concern with the management of international hospitality. We believe it is important to acknowledge our roots in the different traditions in order to clarify where our perspective comes from and how it shapes our analysis. We draw on the critical social sciences, valuing a constructivist approach towards social research and our analytical frameworks seek a holistic interpretation. We are pragmatic in that we live, work, teach and holiday in the real world, but we are conscious of the importance of recognizing the power of the theoretical in framing and explaining those real world situations.

■ The roots of hospitality management

Hospitality is rooted in the relationships that develop between hosts and guests, a dynamic which has existed since the first human societies emerged. The early relationship was defined in terms of honour and respect within a reciprocal framework. It was an honour for someone to visit you and, as a good host, you treated your guest with respect and offered them comfort, security and entertainment. As a guest, you were aware of the honour that the host was bestowing upon you during your stay by welcoming you into the heart of their home and it was your duty to repay that kindness with respect for your host's values and customs.

Even when we look at the earliest origins of the hospitality industry we find a mixture of journeys, both near and far, but they are all set within the context of the honour of the host–guest relationship. In setting our book within the context of this debate, we realize that we are visiting, and indeed revisiting, a well trodden and yet still controversial corner of the hospitality field. The couplet has been much used and some would argue misused over the years in the study of tourism impacts and tourism development but the critical dimensions feature less strongly in hospitality. We are seeking to use it in the sense established in Smith's seminal work (1977), in order to explore the dynamics of international hospitality management.

We are adopting a holistic view of human society and a methodology of cross-cultural analysis within this book, and we agree with Smith's emphasis on the need to unveil the internal processes of change inherent in societies (see also Smith, 2001). She gives prominence to globalization and the shrinking distances as communication and transportation bring destinations closer and with it their connections to issues of time, authenticity, identity and ethnicity.

Guest expectations

We also want to engage with the notion of guest within that range of experiences.

Aramberri (2001) called his confrontational contribution *The Hosts Should Get Lost*. He contends that the host–guest couplet is based around a pre-modern formulation where there were three main features:

1 Protection extended by the host to the guest on the grounds of their common humanity.
2 Reciprocity with the guest returning their host's generosity.
3 Familial duties and obligation – with the guest becoming a part of the host's family and supported in the same ways.

Aramberri argues that the modern experience no longer contains these elements of exchange and obligation. His argument is based on the replacement of the pre-modern experience of covenant by the contract form of modern capitalist societies. "The point, however, is that the nonmaterial reciprocity of the old covenant is gone and that no amount of mourning will bring it back to life. If the covenant is gone, so are also the fuzzy codes of mutual rights and duties that spelled its details. Now the main tie that binds the contracting parties is the deliverance of services – commodities – on the part of the hosts, and payment in cash for the tab they have been running on behalf of the guests. In fact, the hosts are no longer hosts, just providers of services, while the guests are no longer guests, just customers" (Aramberri, 2001: 746–747).

The argument continues by suggesting that the hosts have deliberately constructed the context for the commercialization of the contract because of the opportunities to grow rich at the expense of the guests. We will elaborate many of the points surrounding the contract relationship during our discussions but rather than losing the host, we feel that they help to redefine and recognize the role of the host in what we are calling international hospitality management.

Because too much hospitality and tourism, or the wrong type of hospitality and tourism, can despoil a community and marginalize the residents it is necessary to develop hospitality and tourism with care. Ideally, hospitality and tourism development will permit hosts to cope with hospitality and tourism by providing some cultural space for the guests while simultaneously preserving other, more private space for the hosts. Smith (2001) advocates the use of the four H's – habitat, history, heritage and handicrafts – as key elements in an ethnographic assessment of hospitality and tourism. This book will show how these inform the practice and analysis of international hospitality (Figure 1.2).

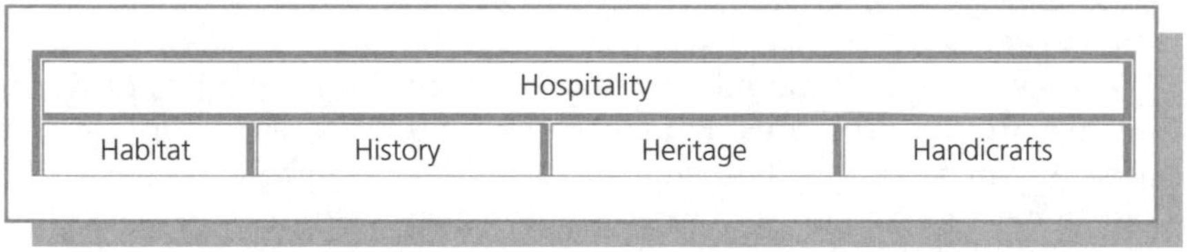

Hospitality			
Habitat	History	Heritage	Handicrafts

Figure 1.2
The four H's

We would suggest that this can be re-presented within hospitality service as shown in Figure 1.3.

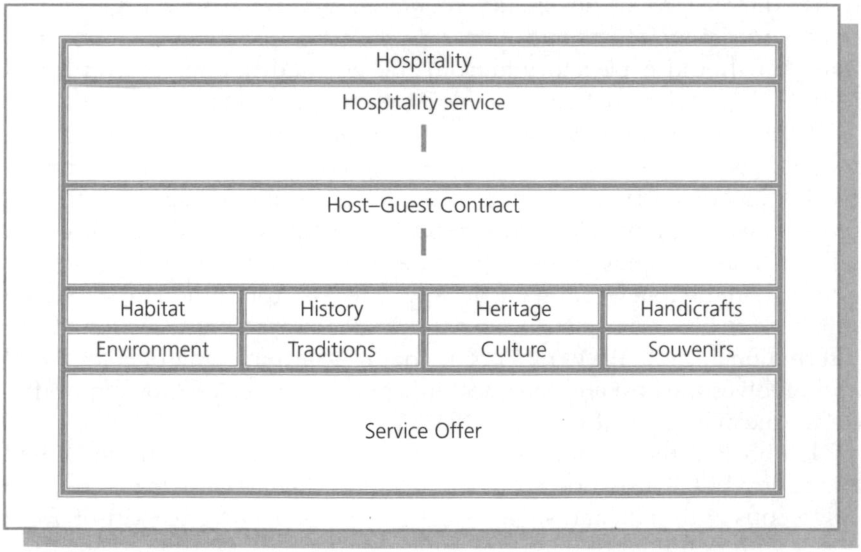

Hospitality			
Hospitality service			
I			
Host–Guest Contract			
I			
Habitat	History	Heritage	Handicrafts
Environment	Traditions	Culture	Souvenirs
Service Offer			

Figure 1.3
The hospitality context

These elements help to translate the anthropological approaches into the domain of the manager and the service provider that we will go on to explore.

■ The context of international management in the hospitality industry

The hospitality offer takes many forms, the hotel room, the coffee or should that be low-fat latté, the restaurant, the time share and so on. These offers share a common starting point in the relationship between the provider and the customer. However these relations are structured in many ways, by the expectations of the organization and by the cultural constraints of the hosts and the guests. If you do not believe that the offer is structured try ordering one of the top of the range sports cars from a car hire company if you are not 24 years old or hold a driving licence from a different country!

When you explore the relationship between the hospitality provider and the customer the constraints become more apparent. Moreover we become accustomed to the usual practices that we grow up with. The English have had a long and interesting history with the sale of alcohol, growing accustomed to licensing laws that impose strong restrictions over who can purchase alcohol, where and when. Travel outside those narrow national boundaries and one of the surprises is the way that alcohol is treated differently in other countries.

This simple example begins to raise the interest level in the international dimensions of hospitality management. We would urge you to open your imaginations and put aside the idea that there is a "normal" that you should expect to underpin the hospitality offer as you travel round the world or that you would impose on that offer.

We see the international dimension as more complicated than the simple trade between two countries. These commercial transactions can take place with any commodity, subject to international trade agreements and the willingness of the two parties to trade. In hospitality we are concerned with a more complex transaction, one where the hosts and guests are involved in the transactions at a variety of levels. You could argue that the purchase of a "tea" is a simple purchase and mirrors the transaction of any international trade. We would argue that it is far more complex than that and involves the host and the guest in a more complex relationship. What do we mean by tea? Also refer to Plate 1.

This book is the product of many sessions drinking tea in the United Kingdom, but it was not a traditional English breakfast tea, served in china cups with milk and sugar. Mostly it was a Chinese tea, drunk from mugs with nothing but the tea to interfere with the taste. Quite what the neighbours would have said if they had known remains the subject of

Plate 1
Source: Bettys Harrogate. Bettys is a well-loved Yorkshire institution, having a long history of serving fine quality tea, coffee and cakes

speculation. In Hungary we serve tea but with lemon not milk, but we do not go into the Turkish tradition of sugaring everything despite, or because of, the years of Turkish occupation. The offer of tea is therefore culturally a complex one, drawing on the specific cultural patterns of the hosts and may well challenge the conventional expectations of the guest (Plate 2).

Plate 2
An Asian tea house. Source: Author's photograph. This shows the entrance to an Asian tea house, which has traditionally been more important to the culture than coffee

We believe that such tensions are at the heart of managing international hospitality. How the specific and the different can be presented to the guest/customer as an exciting and satisfying experience, without reducing everything to a standardized commodity is at the heart of the challenge faced by the industry.

We believe that we need this book because the hospitality industry has moved into a position where any and all of its transactions could be set within this international context. We are aware from our experiences of hosting both in our native cultures and within foreign cultures of the challenges that these hospitality offers construct and that overcoming these interconnecting difficulties is never as simple as it first appears. Challenges and opportunities exist for the new generation of hospitality managers, even for a local hotel, where there is a frequent need to think outside the narrow confines of a local cultural construction and meet the expectations of an international market. This may not only be presented in the demands of foreign travellers but also in the worldwide influences that have come to work on the expectations of the local clients as well. It has been argued that the most famous café in the world is not a Starbucks or a McDonald's but "Central Perk", the café that kept the cast of characters from "Friends" fed and watered throughout the 10 series of the worldwide smash hit American television comedy. "Friends" influenced people in many ways – styles of dress, haircuts, names for their children and even what to ask for in a café! This worked both in terms of the menu and the style and décor of the space itself. Starbucks and their like influenced these trends but did not necessarily control them as they were also influenced by them. The cultural pressure derived from the media, and the huge success of the series, contributed to the growth of the internationalization of guests' expectations about hospitality. It was not an intended consequence of the series but the effect was felt nevertheless.

What we mean by international must therefore be seen in this broader and more culturally informed context. Rather than being contained in the trade between two countries, what we see as defining the international is the exchange of cultural values and expectations that underpin the host–guest relationship within any hospitality exchange. For us the focus is cultural rather than commercial and it is the cultural dynamic which is constantly changing and shifting that lies at the heart of the management challenge as we perceive it.

■ Interpreting the concept of international management

Most management texts assume that the concept of management is self-explanatory, it is after all about managing. We feel that the concept deserves slightly more consideration as our perspective will suggest that the ways in which management is interpreted is itself culturally significant and introduces a change into the operating environment of the organization.

One suggestion is that management is all about ensuring that the organization makes a profit – and certainly does not make a loss! In most cases, survival is not a preferred option as managers are required to show greater returns on the company's investment (Figure 1.4).

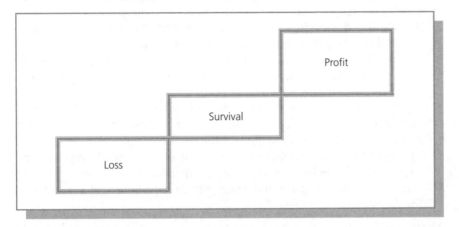

Figure 1.4
The peaks of management

This is a view of management that is based on the concept of the advanced capitalist firm, operating with a division of labour that separates the management of the organization from what happens within it. We do not see management as merely the mindless pursuit of profit as we see managers having a more open role in hospitality organizations. Whilst the concern for the bottom line and profit will be a factor, we believe that managers have a crucial role in the delivery of service quality and are vital to the internal and external image of the organization. Therefore we would suggest that the manager is involved in a process which involves taking the organization from where they are now, the current state, to where they want to be, the desired future state. The desired future state will encapsulate a more rounded view of the organization than simply its profitability (Figure 1.5).

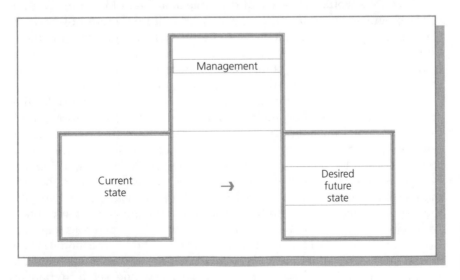

Figure 1.5
The management journey

Let us consider what the process of management involves and therefore what is required of the manager. We believe that there are six components of the managerial role:

1   Strategy: Determining the direction of the organization and establishing the ways in which it will be able to achieve its objectives.
2   Structure: Considering how the organization is patterned and ensuring that the structure facilitates the delivery of the objectives.
3   People: The management process will involve dealing with people inside and outside the organization, with a variety of roles from development to discipline.
4   Operating environment: Coming to understand the internal and external forces that influence the organization and the impacts they may have on the future performance of the organization.
5   The market(s) and marketing: How will the organization select and present itself to existing and potential customers.
6   Social responsibility: Demonstrating both a private and social profit for the company.

These are the elements that we see constituting what a manager should do – but we recognize that not all managers will do all of them all of time. However we do see an increased awareness about what is involved in these six areas as helpful in developing sensitive and informed managers for the hospitality organizations of the future. We would also stress that this management process does not operate in a vacuum. All organizations are set within the context of cultures and given that the focus of this book is on international management, we would have to address the role of international cultures in shaping the opportunities for organizations. This can be seen both positively and negatively, with some aspects of the cultural environment encouraging development – those we have termed enabling forces, whilst others are likely to present obstacles to challenge the development of the organization – which we have identified as resisting forces. We would also say that the same analysis holds for the culture of the organization itself or the management culture (Figure 1.6). Parts of this will be open to the challenge of international management but others will be more resistant. We would therefore ask you to share our model of how this international hospitality management is constructed.

There is one danger with this model, and indeed with all such models of management, which is that it presents an analytical framework for the study of international hospitality management but the very drawing of the model denies the interrelationships between the elements. Our model does not intend to prioritize any of the six elements in the centre, they could be presented in any order and the model would be just as coherent. Nor do we intend the sets of forces to be seen as separate from the elements contained by them. We see this as a dynamic relationship between the cultural forces, from both the organizational management and international dimensions, and the knowledge, skills and competences required to deliver the practice of management. Our conception of the model is one of analytical separation but we recognize that the separation is required for presentational purposes but in practice we would see a myriad of

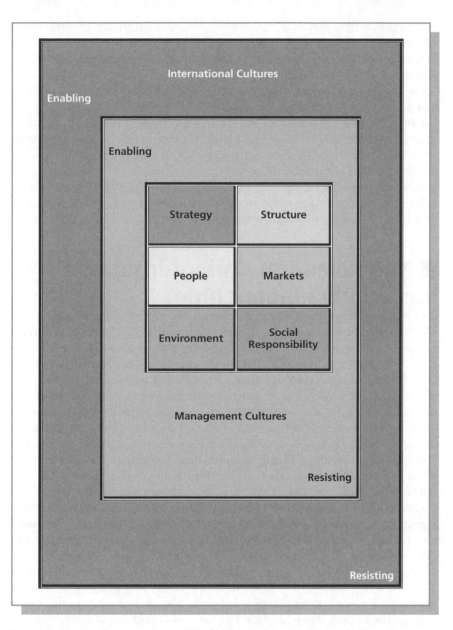

International Cultures

Enabling

Enabling

Strategy	Structure
People	Markets
Environment	Social Responsibility

Management Cultures

Resisting

Resisting

Figure 1.6
The cultural contexts of international hospitality management

interconnections, crossovers, reinforcements and contradictions between and within the elements and their settings.

This book is built around the central notion of culture and the way it constructs the hospitality industry, from design to offer, for both the developers and the guests. We therefore have to say something about the way that this notion of culture impacts on the ways in which management has been presented and written about in the past. It has been noticeable that management training and practice has been developed from a largely westernized base of knowledge. These theories and perspectives were developed to account for, explain and perfect the operations of business organizations. It has been recognized that there is a production bias to many of these approaches which makes the transition to services difficult in some areas. We would also note that the cultural specificity of these accounts in westernized, capitalist, modernist societies also creates issues for translation into other societies, with different traditions and historical contexts.

We see our challenge as authors as setting the issues facing hospitality management in a cultural context that allows for the recognition and valuing of a diversity of cultures. For us the practices of international management in different societies, with their different cultures and their own economic and political systems are not just about the implementation of the tried and tested knowledge of western management gurus. It is a practice that begins from the recognition of cultural diversity rather than adapting to it as a part of the process. It is an international management which is open to cultural dynamics rather than closed by checklists and guidelines.

■ Globalization and international hospitality management

Much of the work which is being done by academics in terms of the international situation has been talked about in terms of globalization (Dicken *et al.*, 1998, Wahab and Cooper, 2001). We must explore carefully what this term means, as it appears that there are different ways of using the same term, which have very different impacts on the way the issue is presented. As academics write about globalization, they appear to have two different models of the process open to them (MacLeod, 2004). One sees globalization as a distinct process – something which is happening to the world. The other sees globalization as an intensification of changes which are taking place in society as a result of other identifiable forces (Rosenberg, 2002).

The first model of globalization as a distinct process (De Beule and Cuyvers, 2005) is most powerfully seen embodied in the "disneyfication" argument, where it is seen that Disney is transforming the world. Everyone knows Mickey Mouse. Even in China, Mickey is recognized as much as Mao. This version of globalization sees a process where global corporations are producing and reproducing a world in their own image (Dunning, 1993). The businesses, and this would include hospitality and tourism businesses, are operating in a market which is no more than an extension of their own back garden, but that marketplace has been extended across the world and constructed in their own conditions (Davis and Nyland, 2004). One key factor involved in these accounts is the role of technology in facilitating participation in this global system (Roy, 2005). A critical account of this thesis can be found in Ritzer's accounts of McDonaldization (1993, 1998). Here globalization offers the promise of worldwide standards in service provision, with the promise of not disappointing the customers' expectations wherever they are.

The second model sees globalization as the summation of a range of other processes which are happening within the societies of the late 20th and early 21st centuries (Hoogevelt, 1997). There are processes which change the way that social life is lived – access to satellite and cable broadcasting networks opened up mass communications in a way which has revolutionized the way the broadcasting system works today (Hirst and Thompson, 1995). In the United Kingdom we have the institution of the BBC, with a public broadcasting rationale. It is the voice of the nation in the air and, with globalization, they are seeking markets throughout the world, under the slogan "nation shall speak unto nation". However with the diversification of the media, it is now possible to have a production – made by one person – and broadcast to an audience across the city, across the world – which might not be much more than two people in their own rooms. It is very different from the notion of mass broadcasting and conjures up a notion of narrow casting where specialist audiences can be accessed by minority interest programming. There are political processes which are taking place alongside this (Smiers, 2003).

There is a possible third view of the processes of globalization, which sees "globalization" as a discourse. The importance of discourse for this account is that discourses have a power in themselves and in particular they have the power to shape the "lived realities" of people's everyday life. These realities do not exist until they are constructed by people interacting in and through social processes (Jameson and Miyoshi, 1998). Moreover, those processes then assume a reality and you get to the really important point about what they have been creating. The more people buy into a discourse the more power those discourses have. You will find that the more people believe that the only products which can appeal anywhere are those which are acceptable in the global market, the more you will have people who only produce products which will appeal in that global marketplace. To oversimplify the argument to demonstrate the logic, if you believe that the only type of hospitality and tourism product that can appeal globally is a Disney style theme park, then you will only be prepared to invest in and develop that style of attraction. All tourists will then go to the new attractions because they have no other choice within this new Disney style theme park world. The closure of the discourse is demonstrated as attendance at the theme parks is up, tourists are choosing to go to them and you were right to join the global market and offer the tourists what they want in your own locale. Look at the example in France, where a great deal of the cultural capital of northern Europe can be found. Now they find that more visitors go to Euro Disney than the attractions in Paris.

These definitions of the globalization process must be questioned. However in asking the questions, it must be recognized that there are certain effects of the globalization discourse which are affecting hospitality and tourism on three levels. These levels are:

1 the expectations of the guests,
2 the expectations of the locals,
3 the opportunities which may exist because of these changing expectations.

The expectations are different for both the international guest and the domestic guest – What is the domestic tourism experience in the region? It is necessary to consider what has traditionally been the domestic tourism experience and what the expectations are now. How that is changing with the expectations that come with the global process is an important aspect of the cultural dynamic.

It can also be seen to bring about opportunities. Part of this globalization process is that opportunities are being created. There is a danger in presenting an argument such as this of being seen as being opposed to globalization but what ever our feelings about the trends it represents, it has to be recognized that it does create opportunities. We now have the opportunity – if we have the money – to stay in a three/four/five-star hotel almost all the way round the world. This did not exist before so that it is a new opportunity that has refined the way the host–guest relationship is constructed. Globalization also makes things available – it puts into place an international infrastructure which makes things possible. It is an infrastructure which makes the changing expectations realizable (Olds *et al.*, 1999). It changes the opportunities open to people and it changes the availability of those opportunities.

What is more important than studying the global at the global level is to look at the ways in which it impacts on people's lived realities (Whalley *et al.*, 2006). When you examine the way that people live their everyday lives, what you see is that discourse of the globalization processes cut right the way across everyday life. It constructs civil society in new ways, but it has to be recognized that the impact is differently experienced locally (Huaichuan, 2004). The changes are re-presented in many different ways depending on the local contexts upon which the processes are being mapped and the discourses read. It will be different in Hong Kong from Beijing, from Kuala Lumpur, from Manila and from Bangkok and Birmingham. It is different regionally as well as locally and it will be different between countries. There will be as many differences – if not more – than there are similarities – across regions and certainly across nation states.

If anyone suggests that there is a monolithic process called globalization and that, as a result, we will all be the same a few years down the line – do not believe them (Robertson, 1992). That observation is predicated upon a notion that the power of the economic is total and that it will be the force that determines the future. Economics is not the only social process involved (Gangopadhyay and Chatterji, 2005). Development theory introduced the notion of core and peripheral regions, centres that were the "core" of the civilizing and development processes and peripheral regions which supported the continued development of the core (Peet, 1991). In the good old days, the United Kingdom could be seen as a core with our colonies as the periphery. The same patterns of development can be seen across the Asia Pacific region, not only with colonial core periphery regional relations but also between strong national capitals and peripheral regions within the nation state. It is also possible to propose that there is a core for the Asia Tiger economies and then a periphery within the region which has supported that development.

If we place this argument within the context of a globalization process which is working towards a monocultural and monoeconomic system, you cannot have core and periphery systems. The relationships can be about dependence and supply, but they are not about core and periphery. The challenge for countries in the region is about repositioning the hospitality product(s) in a global market and you have to accept that some of the old positions which have been constructed are no longer tenable. The debate has moved on and the market has moved on – more accurately, the markets have moved on. The consumer, for that is what the guest is, has moved on.

The implication must also be therefore that the core no longer exists. Where are the claimants for the title of the capital of the global society? They do not exist. The capital of the global society does not exist. Capitals exist for nation states and globalization operates across the construction of the nation state, with no fear of borders at all. There would be no passport control, no immigration. There is no differentiation within the global. Yet there has to be a way of marking one place off from another, for creating and maintaining the concept of the destination (Turner, 1994). This increasingly becomes an issue of "image", of the images which the hospitality and tourism industry can create and maintain. For the consumer the only reality they have of the destination is the image that is constructed of that location. This is partially – the professionals would argue largely – informed by the brochure and the videos produced within the tourism industry. The decision to travel to a particular place is often taken before there is any personal knowledge of the place which could be used to inform the decision. In business, the decision of where to stay and where to eat may well even be taken by someone else in the organization. The image which has to be sold therefore has to be compatible with the customers' position within the forces of globalization.

ACTIVITY

Plate 3 is a photograph taken in a food court in a shopping plaza, only one of many throughout the world. Looking at the style of the catering units and the range of offer (Thai, Japanese/Sushi and Pizza) – Where do you think you are?

Plate 3
Where are we today?

There are not many clues! The format is very familiar – the Coca-Cola cups almost omnipresent. There are examples of French, Italian, Japanese and Thai characters but the actual clue is in the word "bufé". This marks the setting out as Hungarian and it is, in fact, the Balaton Plaza in Veszprém in Hungary.

Take this opportunity to look at your local high street. Note what sort of retail and cafés are available to you as a contemporary customer.

After doing this, talk to anyone over 50 years old or go to the local history archive and check out how this has changed over the years. Even if you only go back 15 years the changes will be obvious. If you go back further, they become even more apparent. The local library will have photographs that depict the changes you have been talking about. Find those and consider how unfamiliar the old photographs look to you because you know the contemporary version. Then remember that for other people the older photographs are more like the reality they remember.

The changes are a part of the processes we are talking about here. They do not just affect other people as your work demonstrates they affect all of us, no matter where we live.

There is a need to construct a strong local image, because there has to be a distinction – a difference. However this difference has to be constructed within the global forces of the hospitality marketplaces. There has to be an image of the region, the nation and the local which appeals to the market and moreover which outperforms the images constructed by other regions, nations and locales that are also competing within the marketplace. The globalization processes can be seen in the increasingly popular tourism quiz of cutting out the photographic images from the brochures and the travel magazines and inviting participants to state "where in the world is that?" It is such a good competition that during 2002, Silk Air could offer a prize of a free trip to the winner of such a competition in their in-flight magazine. What the globalization processes mean for the hospitality and tourism market is that the entrance to the market is already set at a very high level. There is a potential of a global market, but the individual "signatures" of destinations – be they regions, nations or specific locations – have to be read in the context of the global hospitality and tourism market constructed within the globalization processes. Again if the argument is exaggerated to demonstrate the logic of the globalization processes, it is possible to argue that the processes will eventually culminate in just one dominant touristic image or a register of agreed touristic images. One suggestion would be the – ubiquitous – white sand beach and palm tree image used to promote exclusive beach tourism. Players in the hospitality and tourism markets are therefore competing against this pre-given, pre-determined construct of the attractive tourist location. Even if you can match the image, what can be offered to the market to convert the interest in the image to an actual sale?

■ Implications for hospitality and tourism

The implications of this are felt all the way through the hospitality and tourism model and inform the analyses offered in the chapters that follow this introduction. Globalization fundamentally challenges the way in which hospitality and tourism are constructed. At its very basic, it impacts because some of the opportunities are no longer there. Some businesses have ceased trading and therefore their part of the hospitality and tourism offer is no longer available. Moreover the same is true for some of the guests. The guests may not be there because of the economic crises as some people are no longer able to afford the products. The global level of expectations has gone up, at exactly the time when the economic crises have threatened the ability of the destinations to provide for and to satisfy these expectations (Go and Pine, 1995).

The future for hospitality and tourism is not all bleak and an optimistic vision can be seen if the economic logics of crises and globalization are confronted and stood on their heads. The processes of globalization suggest a coming together of provision in the market but rather than looking to a single global culture, it is possible to argue that hospitality and tourism produces a distinctive culture of its own. The touristic culture binds the experience of hospitality and tourism with its own set of expectations. For hospitality and tourism development, there appears to be a rationale based within the touristic culture for differentiation rather than standardization.

There are some expectations which hospitality and tourism promotes itself. It argues that guests should expect high quality of service. This has been interpreted by the industry as having to improve service in a continuous way and it has been built into the hospitality and tourism industry in every sector. The satisfaction questionnaire is now found every where the guest goes. The responses are analysed and something is done about it. The problem about that is that if the industry continues raising the levels of service quality they can never satisfy the demand. They are bound to fail and they are bound to fail a challenge which they need not have taken on. What the industry needs to address is the appropriate level of quality and ensure that this level is met. If the offer is a three-star experience, the quality should be appropriate to a three-star expectation of quality. It should not be a four-star version of quality, because that is not what the demand was for. If the offer is of four-star quality, it should be offered to consumers demanding four-star standards. This has been taken out of context in hospitality and tourism, where the industry has gone in search of the holy grail of the perfect holiday.

When we say that the issue of guest safety is important, we have to recognize that we are talking about an issue which is as rooted in image and discourse at least as much as it is in any experienced reality for the majority of potential tourists. The more you talk about the problem, saying it does not exist and there is nothing to worry about – the more you confirm the discourse that there is something to worry about it. The experience of Jamaica is relevant here, as the introduction of all inclusive resorts to the island was in part designed to offset the sense of threat tourists were thought to feel from the increasing violence in the capital. However the discussions around the bars and the pools in the all inclusives furthered the sense of danger and discouraged the tourists from ever leaving the resort development. This had the consequence of seeing the tourism numbers being maintained, in more expensive resorts, but the figures for tourism expenditure declining in the Jamaican economy.

The concern for quality is a minimal standard in making a touristic offer in the global marketplace, but it cannot be the sole criteria for decision-making. The quality of the experience in any part of the region will be comparable; therefore the actual offer has to move beyond the boundaries of the definition of quality. The transcendence can come from the richness of the offer, still maintaining quality levels but offering an acceptable and attractive difference to the other offers. There is also a marketplace for the cheaper offer. The offer can undercut other destinations but such a policy has consequences for the type and style of the development which has been provided around the offer.

The future of hospitality and tourism is also going to be affected by the emergence of what Pearce (1982) has called touristic careers. This is a concept which seeks to understand the way tourists build their experience and levels of confidence into what will be called here touristic literacy. As the literacy levels rise so do the demands of the tourist for what they want – they will not all be demanding the same thing for some will demand more independent travel and others will seek more sophisticated packages but they will share a clearer set of expectations of what it is that they as customers are seeking. It is important to recognize that the tourist changes. Each touristic experience increases the level of the literacy of the tourist. What the industry must consider is what level of literacy it is demanding from the tourists it is seeking to attract. Can you target people who are first timers away from home, who want to sit in a bar which looks remarkably like their bars at home, who want to eat food which looks remarkably like their food at home and where the entertainment is provided in such a way as it looks like the entertainment they have at home? This requires hospitality and tourism which is designed for the illiterate tourists, but probably does not dare to call them that.

If the industry is aiming for a more literate tourist, then the package has to be altered. The tolerance of difference – in deed the expectation of difference will be greater. The menus will not have to have pictures of the food on the menu. The confidence will also increase the size – or perhaps puncture – the tourist bubble. For the illiterate the bubble includes the hotel and the beach – and possibly the next hotel because that will probably have tourists in it. The aim of the hospitality and tourism developers has to be to find ways of extending the safety of the hospitality and tourism bubble to encourage the usage of a wider range of resources. The more experienced guest will seek out local information to probe the area and discover the extra, the additional and the different within their chosen destination. They are independent and safe in their independence.

The prospect is that the industry will have to work increasingly hard at ensuring that the hospitality and tourism offer meets the expectations and the needs of their tourists. It will have to do that with the pretourism experience as well as the events in the destination. This will then ensure that the tourists who arrive in the destination leave as a satisfied customers and a hospitality and tourism ambassador for the region. The pretourism work is vital, especially where the uncertainty around the definition of the destination exists, and is primarily concerned with image. Image is constructed by the industry and those who know – or who we think ought to know.

The economic crises of the 1990s did not spell the death knell for the hospitality and tourism industry. There is no simple death sentence because hospitality and tourism is a resistant industry. It survives partly because it is a luxury product and as such is something people want to have. People may trade down but hospitality and tourism will survive. The implications for the region of trading down can be significant. Value for money will become increasingly important as a determinant. The industry will have to ensure a maximization of the return of the tourists' investment. Hospitality and tourism businesses expect a return on their investment, so why should they think their customers are any different. The prospects for the region will be determined by the ability to provide viable answers to the question of why should the tourist come here. The quality of the experience will come for the sectors of the industry working together with the best possible quality – including the taxi drivers. Who do the tourists see in your city? They see the front-line people in the hotels, the taxis – they do not see the highly paid hospitality and tourism planners. Education is therefore the key to improving the level of service and as there is no way of predicting who will be working in the front line of the hospitality and tourism offer, the education has to be made available to all as part of a national curriculum to help prepare the society for hospitality and tourism and the hospitality and tourism society.

We also need to educate our guests as well. The tourists require education before they set off and in their destinations. They need education which helps to explain the responsibilities of tourist within the societies they visit and how they should behave to avoid insulting and upsetting their hosts. This of course is a circular argument, for if you are learning to be a good host you are also learning how to be a good guest and vice versa. It is a big challenge but that is the one global consequence of extending hospitality and tourism as an international and domestic experience of quality and of difference.

■ The structure of the book

The book will now take you through a series of chapters that outline the parameters of the international hospitality industry, drawing your attention to the dynamics of the development through a series of international case studies. We have selected the case studies and examples from a wide range of contemporary sources to try and maintain the immediacy of the book but also to demonstrate the range of the industry we are concerned with.

The first part of the book deals with the importance of culture in shaping the industry and the expectations which drive it. These will be arguments that are presented and then critiqued from the perspective of our understanding of international cultural dynamics. This will take you through a critical discussion of cultures, national, organizational and touristic, and how they interact to create the context for international hospitality practice.

In Chapter 3, you will be asked to consider the definition of the industry, both in terms of its structure and of its organizations. This will include the development and the size of the sectors. For instance you will be taken through the Lodging industry, looking at the classification of hotels and the main niche markets. We will also explore the interconnections between different sections of the international hospitality industry by looking at the linkages between the gambling and accommodation sectors, in the form of casino developments. We will address the construction of the contexts within which the international hospitality industry operates. We will explore the international environmental issues that underpin the development of the hospitality offer. This will take forward our interpretation of the concept of international management and commenting on past and current influences to establish a view on future trends and developments. We will seek to develop an analytical framework that evaluates the general environment and can interact within the hospitality and tourism industry, cultural factors, political factors, legal factors, economic factors and technological factors.

The next part of the book will present several different international hospitality management issues and applications. These chapters are not intended as introductions to the totality of the subject but are written to focus on what is important for international hospitality management about, for instance, marketing, by developing the international issues. Our book cannot offer to be comprehensive about the elements we are discussing but there are huge texts available to you in the specific disciplines we address. The intention here is to present accounts that make you think about the issues we think are central to the practice of international hospitality management. Our chapters reflect the six elements we presented in the model of international management earlier in this introduction. You will encounter strategic management, marketing, human resource management and the roles of small- and medium-sized enterprises (SMEs) in global competition. You will also be asked to explore some of the business models commonly found in the international hospitality industry. These will include Franchising and the Issues to consider about international franchising, including the political environment and legal considerations; language, culture and traditions; and the availability of resources. This section will also explore the origins and the history of the management contract and its role in the future of the international industry. Lastly we will consider the role of consortia in the development of the international hospitality industry. Finally we will review the ethical dilemmas and social responsibility issues involved in the international hospitality management, with the adoption of a more sustainable approach to international hospitality.

The final chapter will offer the evaluation of a large international case study, elaborating the implications for now and for the future. This will give a concrete rehearsal of the arguments we have developed throughout the book, exploring issues (such as cultural/political/economic environments, international market development, emerging markets, international strategy, ethical marketing, risk management, local SMEs, human resource management and new technologies). This will be an integrative analysis of the one case of the Disney Corporation designed to show not only the various elements we have discussed but the interrelationships between them.

■ Review questions

1 What factors establish the context for the operation of international hospitality management?
2 Does the host–guest relationship mean anything in the modern world?
3 What are the opportunities that globalization promotes?
4 Why do we talk about international hospitality management rather than global or globalized hospitality management?

These are challenging questions and we would ask you to think through the arguments carefully. They will help you deal with the arguments that come later in the book. We are not providing answers here but would suggest you look at the discussions we have posted on the website. There you will find our opinions about the questions but remember they are only one set of opinions and other people see the relationships in hospitality differently to us. If you use any of the material to answer specific questions you have been set on your own courses, you will have to look further than our generalized opinions to be successful. By all means use what we say, but make sure it is justified in the context in which you are developing your own work and the requirements of your specific assignment.

So, we hope this welcome will encourage you to join us on our journey. We begin in the next chapter by looking at the role of cultures within international hospitality management.

CHAPTER 2

Cultures and the challenges of international hospitality management

Chapter objectives

After working through this chapter, you should be able to:

- Identify the context of international hospitality management
- Determine the roles of different cultures in international hospitality management
- Explore the cultural dynamic for organizations with national cultures, organizational cultures and touristic cultures
- Examine the processes used in managing cultural diversity
- Consider the implications of overlapping cultures in international hospitality management

■ Introduction

As we have seen in Chapter 1, anyone who travels, crosses boundaries not only of time and space but also of culture and the observant will recognize and react to a series of differences which confront them. We have already noted differences in language, lifestyle and rituals which in the context of hospitality become very important for the management of hospitality services. This book will explore the reactions that companies make to fit with the international dimensions of their markets. However in this chapter we will be more concerned with the cultural impacts on the operational environment of hospitality organizations. We will argue that cultural differences constitute a sufficient force for companies to actually consider different ways of organizing and communicating within their own organizations. This rejects traditional notions that organizations could operate in a culture-free environment, sometimes seen as "universalism" and urge you to consider that ~~international hospitality management is not only culture sensitive but also culture specific.~~ You may think that it is old history to consider the universal accounts of management, but there are close similarities between these accounts and those offered by the evangelists of globalization. It is not a big jump from the homogeneity of globalization to arguing that there is, or will be, a global cultural response which is appropriate for all hospitality.

In the 1950s and 1960s, there was a growing interest in studying management in different countries, but this work was still underpinned by a concern with how the ways in which we managed could be made to work in these strange places. In other words, the researchers set out to identify the benefits of the universal principles of management that underpinned sound management practice and would be applicable anywhere despite the specificities of local cultures. This was recognized as the convergence hypothesis and argued that all countries would come into line with the accepted best practices of Western capitalism. It was based on a similar assumption to that which we have identified in writings on globalization, that the logic of industrialization would have a homogenizing effect on business practice, eventually leading to the evolution of a universal type of business organization. The focus of this work shifted in the 1970s as the belief in convergence waned, perhaps with the emergence of the powerful Japanese models that almost led to a convergence with Eastern models rather than with Western ones.

The danger with emphasizing the importance of the cultural factors in the analysis of management is that we must remember that they do not operate in isolation. The work of culture is set in a context that is influenced by the changes in technology, scale of operation and even contingency factors that may well operate across cultures as well as within them. The complexity of international hospitality organizations means that we may find both convergence and distinctiveness factors at work within them. We are not denying that there are pressures towards convergence and homogeneity but would stress both the need to recognize the difference and the opportunities for resistance that local cultural options offer. Moreover Child (1981) noted that the forces may work at different levels of the organization. He saw the formal aspects of organization being shaped by the convergency factors of technology and industrialization. However significantly he recognized that the formal organization works alongside the informal organization (see Chapter 7) which would be more influenced by the cultural factors of distinctiveness. The interactions of leadership and the patterns of decision-making would be set within the local cultural contexts. However even this recognition may not go far enough according to some of the work we will consider next.

Culture is a difficult concept to define and has been the subject of many attempts. Some of the definitions use culture as a synonym for nation or country without seeking to give the concept any theoretical grounding (Child, 1981: 304). The problem with such a loose definition is that the concept becomes nothing more than a catch all or an omnibus variable representing social, political, economic and historical factors. What we can put forward is that culture is not a characteristic of individuals but of a collection of individuals sharing common concerns that may include values, beliefs, ideas and rituals. These groupings can be seen operating within organizations, but you can also track the cultural patterns at regional and national levels. These categories often overlap, reinforcing and challenging cultural values and establishing ways of behaving, thinking and perceiving that are common to all those who belong to the group and differentiate them from others who are not members of that particular group.

Defining culture

What has to be observed is that the cultural patterns we share are learned and continue to be learned. Culture is neither static nor fixed. It is a set of beliefs that we develop from childhood and throughout our lives, with some values becoming relatively fixed whilst others are more changeable. This process is recognized as socialization but we must reinforce that the process works differently in different regions and differently within different organizations. The process is grounded in the specific contexts which generate and are generated by the production of culture.

This means that the cultures we live are historically informed and shaped by our social environments. For instance, even the climate can have effects on the cultural patterns as lifestyles differ between warm and cold climates. This also includes the conditions in the organizations that we work for and are aware of (Figure 2.1).

What is Culture?

Culture comes from the Latin word "colere", meaning to build on, to cultivate, and to foster.
Culture is a set of accepted behaviour patterns, values, assumptions, and shared common experiences.
Culture defines social structure, decision-making practices, and communication styles.
Culture dictates behaviour, etiquette, and protocol.
Culture is something we learn. It impacts everyone, and influences how we act and respond.
Culture is communication. It is a way people create, send, process and interpret information.

Figure 2.1
What is culture?

Culture in general is concerned with beliefs and values on the basis of which people interpret experiences and behave, individually and in groups. Broadly and simply put, "culture" refers to a group or community with which you share common experiences that shape the way you understand the world. This has usually been seen at the national level and the organizational level. We believe that it is now possible to talk of a touristic culture which exerts pressure on the hospitality industry, that is to say the demands placed on the hospitality industry are themselves culturally determined. However the demands arise from a group – the tourists – that exist within and beyond national cultural boundaries and share the common experience of travel, thereby forming a distinct culture of their own.

The cultural minefield ... identifying yourself

ACTIVITY

Understanding and effectively interacting within the cultural groups to which we belong is like walking through a minefield. Being culturally aware means much more than just understanding the culture of other groups or countries. It means understanding who you are and your own cultural dynamic.
Consider the following "cultures", and the impact on your life:

- Where you were born.
- Your nationality and heritage.
- How you were raised and your family life.
- The schools you attended.
- Your religious preferences.
- Your profession.
- Your company and its corporate culture.
- Your gender.

Thus, the same person can belong to several different cultures depending on his or her birthplace, nationality, ethnicity, family status, gender, age, language, education, physical condition, sexual orientation, religion, profession, place of work and its corporate culture.

Culture is the "lens" through which you view the world. It is central to what you see, how you make sense of what you see and how you express yourself.

For example, consider what it means to say you are an American. A recent search in Yahoo for "American Culture" pulled up 56 categories! America, once considered a global melting pot, is now viewed as a salad bowl filled with a large variety of ingredients.

Example: The cultural iceberg

Culture is like an iceberg. As everyone who has seen *Titanic* knows the problem with icebergs is not the part that you can see, as this represents only some 10% of the iceberg. The other 90% is hidden below the waterline but is most definitely still there.

The tip of the cultural iceberg is easy to see. This includes the visible aspects and do's and taboos of working in other cultures. The remaining huge chunk of the iceberg hidden below the surface includes the invisible aspects of a culture such as the values, traditions, experiences and behaviours that define each culture. Venturing into different cultures without adequate preparation can be just as dangerous as a ship manoeuvring icy waters without charts, hoping to be lucky enough to avoid hitting an iceberg. The difference is that the ship will know immediately when it hits an iceberg.

Unsuspecting companies may never realize they hit an iceberg but they will, nevertheless, feel the impact. It appears in the form of delayed or abandoned projects, misunderstood communications, frustrated employees and a loss of business and reputation. The costs of cultural myopia and the inability to adjust can be staggering. By definition, cross-cultural awareness means not only becoming culturally fluent in other cultures but also having a solid understanding of your own culture.

Building trust across cultural boundaries

Research indicates that there is a strong correlation between components of trust (such as communication effectiveness, conflict management and rapport) and productivity. Cultural differences play a key role in the creation of trust, since trust is built in different ways and can mean different things in different cultures.

For instance, in the US, trust is demonstrated by performance over time. In the United States, you can gain the trust of your colleagues by "coming through" and delivering on time on your commitments. In many other parts of the world, including many Arab, Asian and Latin American countries, building relationships is a pre-requisite for professional interactions. Building trust in these countries often involves lengthy discussions on non-professional topics and shared meals in restaurants. Work-related discussions start only once your counterpart has become comfortable with you as a person and recognized your status as appropriate.

Cultural differences in multicultural teams can create misunderstandings between team members before they have had a chance to establish any credibility with each other. Thus, building trust is a critical step in creation and development of such teams. As a manager of a multicultural team, you would need to recognize that building trust between different people is a complex process, since each culture has its own way of building trust and its own interpretation of what trust is.

Harnessing the power of diversity

Diversity is a specialized term that describes a workplace that includes people from various backgrounds and cultures, and/or diverse businesses – and therefore it is a concept which we come across in international hospitality all the time. You can find a strategic competitive advantage in an organizational and cultural context by seeking to leverage, rather than diminish, what might appear to be opposing forces. An important but widely overlooked principle of business success is that integrating opposites, as opposed to identifying them as inconsistencies and driving them out, unleashes power. This can be demonstrated on both a personal and on an organizational level.

Cultures and standards

We are often tempted to take our own culture for granted and in fact, we are scarcely aware of it until we interact with another. Each culture has a worldview: a set of values and beliefs that allow its members to understand and interpret the world they live in and experience. This will be meaningful to its members but appear alien to others. As a consequence, we look at people from other cultures, see that their ways are different and often react to that by saying that their ideas are not normal and we end up disliking their ways even before we understand them. For instance, research on the food industry in the United Kingdom would uncover rather different variables to the ones that Johns *et al*. (2002) found in Hong Kong. Their study of 400 employees found that their relationships with customers were affected by saving "face", conservatism and the repayment of good/evil. These are the factors to be found in the local Hong Kong culture and therefore have a local power over the service offer. You would not necessarily expect them to emerge in a study set in the United Kingdom.

Employees who have cross-border responsibilities and/or cross-cultural relationships need to be prepared to effectively handle the inevitable intercultural tasks and challenges involved.

Six fundamental patterns of cultural difference

1 Different **communication styles**.
2 Different **attitudes towards conflict**.
3 Different **approaches to completing tasks**.
4 Different **decision-making styles**.
5 Different **attitudes towards disclosure**.
6 Different **approaches to knowing**.

There are differences that we experience not only **between** cultures but also **within** cultures. For example, Australian culture can be identified with that of the majority Anglo-Celtic population but the nation's culture also encompasses a number of distinctive subcultures. Hofstede argued that an individual's culture may have several levels: (1) national; (2) regional, ethnic, religious, linguistic; (3) gender; (4) generation; (5) social class; (6) organizational. We can see that this mixture provides an intriguing cocktail for anyone involved in organizational recruitment to attempt to disentangle for a performance assessor to misunderstand during an appraisal a management consultant or trainer to "correct". All in all, there is massive scope for a clash of cultures – and the emergence of prejudices.

The development of genuinely transnational business organizations therefore requires managerial approaches and systems which allow for variations recognizing and deriving from such diversity. This might be "national" cultural diversity between nations, races or ethnic groups (e.g. in a two-nation joint-venture), intra-national diversity involving the range of cultures within a single nation (e.g. in the United States or in China) or internal cultural diversity where managers need to deal with foreign-owned transnational companies in their own country. All this is well known, and there is indeed a burgeoning literature on the management of cultural diversity. But the problems go deeper than is often appreciated: it is not simply a matter of minding your manners or learning to deal with varying attitudes to punctuality. These are the surface manifestations of much deeper differences in mental structures and cultural acceptance.

The perception of time

Our cultures mean that we all have in-built standards, the origins of which we rarely question and which we interpret as "normal". This has profound implications for people management at the global level. Triandris (1972) pinpoints the perception of time as one element of cultural complexity. He argues that different cultures have different attitudes towards time and deal with varying attitudes to punctuality. Time-keeping is treated tolerantly in underdeveloped societies – with few things to do, one can do them in any order. But in industrialized countries there are many things to do and they must be coordinated with other people. Hence, time becomes more important and is regarded as something precise and highly significant. However even in Europe it is possible to identify differences in the attitude to time. Organizing a meeting with participants from the north of the Netherlands and from southern Italy reveals differences in the European attitude to time. The Dutch will characteristically arrive early to be ready for the starting time and not cause any delays to other participants. The Italians, on the other hand, will be happy to take another coffee before moving into the meeting even if the scheduled start time has already passed. (Please note that this presentation commits the sin of stereotyping at the national level – not all Italians are the same and therefore do not share the same attitudes to time. We will address the dangers of stereotyping later.)

Another significant time characteristic is that of short- or long-term orientation. Typically, it has been recognized that East Asians are considered to have a longer-time perspective than nationals of many other regions. The impact of short termism on business planning becomes apparent when the plans of different companies are considered and the demands for instant returns are minimized. These are the surface manifestations of much deeper differences in mental structures. A few examples will make this clear.

Human resources

The global operator obviously needs managers capable of working globally. Some European hospitality organizations are now recruiting "non-nationals" in order to resolve their problems quickly, but how does a human resource specialist trained in his own culture, who can make a rough assessment of a candidate's capabilities in a brief interview, deal with the problems of recruiting staff in other cultures? How valid is psychological testing when applied cross-culturally? How much do most human resource managers know about other school and university systems? Suppose a German manager needs to choose between, say, a Finn, an Italian and a Portuguese. That would require an awareness not only of the very different education systems in European countries but also the ways in which educational background influences patterns of thought and managerial style: how, for example, education underlies the way in which the same conflict might be addressed in France by seeking orders from a superior, in Britain by sending the people in conflict on a management course and in Germany by employing a consultant.

Assuming for a moment that these problems can be resolved, how might the issue of dual allegiance be tackled? For the employment of local managers necessitates the creation of loyalty on their part to a distant entity with culturally diverse norms and assumptions. Even a long-term expatriate who is nominally still of the same nationality but has in fact "gone native" might respond to an order in this way: "I'm sure my local employees won't like this, so I won't tell them and try to smooth over the issue in some other way". It can be much more difficult for the locally employed manager, especially under stress.

Roles

Triandris also relates cultural complexity to the way we define our working and other roles. In complex societies roles become increasingly specific – compartmentalized into separate mental boxes and hierarchical positions. We can be finance managers, parents and social club officials, and behave differently in each role. In less-complex societies, on the other hand, roles are diffuse, affecting every aspect of people's lives. Religion, politics and matters of taste are important in these more diffuse cultures. They are less important in role-specific cultures unless they become formalized into the specification of the role. Developed countries tend to be role-specific, avoiding role confusion. Recruitment practices in Northern Ireland used to say that there was no discrimination between Protestant and Catholic applicants, but research demonstrated that putting the name of your school on the application form could effectively reveal your religion and disqualify you from consideration by employers who justified their discrimination by arguing that they were wanting to maintain a cohesive workforce.

Theory and best practice in key human resource management (HRM) areas such as selection, performance measurement and development assume an equal opportunities approach in which people are dealt without favour or prejudice. However, this notion is alien to diffuse-role cultures, in which it is natural to favour members of one's own family or community.

Cultural training

Human resource managers have a considerable role to play in preparing staff for work overseas. Given the range and sensitivity of cultural differences, it is clear that people working in an international context can benefit from tuition in the business customs and social manners of the countries they will work in. Human resource managers can play a major part in developing programmes for sales and other staff whose behaviour must be fully acceptable in target countries. For instance, this type of training can often encompass language, social behaviour, local business, structure and practice and table etiquette.

Cultural training is essential to avoid potential conflicts and to improve the disastrous failure rate of joint-ventures in the recent past. In fact, most hospitality organizations with global ambitions now provide cross-cultural training in order to create genuinely international managers. This sometimes involves in-house training, and is also provided by consultants and business schools. Yet much of this training deals with the traditional, superficial problems without seeking to explore the deeper causes of underlying cultural differences. Another problem is that much of the research and background material is rapidly out-dated as the pace of cultural change accelerates.

Language

Language is one of the most obvious aspects of culture and therefore it can be readily recognized that the use of language has critical implications. It is not just the question of what is the correct literal translation but of observing what would be the appropriate translation for the specific context. If you are asking for quiet in a meeting saying "shut up" may be appropriate in the United Kingdom and the United States but translated into Hungarian it is a very rude thing to say and alternative ways of requesting silence should be found if you do not want to cause offence.

In appraisal feedback meetings or interviews, people managers must be aware of cultural differences covering for instance:

- **Directness**: Westerners may begin an informal meeting with a joke (well, some of us might). At this stage in a Japanese relationship such familiarity would be regarded as extremely offensive, expecting formality until each other's status and authority are clearly understood. Some cultures deem it appropriate to talk about family and friends before commencing the business of the meeting – to refuse to join in is not seen as being efficient or wanting to get down to business, it is interpreted as a lack of respect and becomes a barrier to building trust in the relationship.
- **Politeness**: All cultures employ polite forms of address which are expected in particular circumstances. Politeness is socially supportive behaviour which maintains harmony and respect between individuals. You need to understand the local culture in order to appreciate what is acceptable. In many languages there is a distinction between formal terms of address and the informal for friends and family – however your host may feel that you have become acceptable and shift to the informal terms even in business settings and you must be able to respond appropriately. To continue to reply in the formal terms would again be to show disrespect to your host. Similarly to greet them in the informal is to be presumptuous and also shows them a lack of respect they may feel is due to them.

Customs or rules

These patterns of behaviour are the product of historical evolution and establish standards that are embraced by the members of the society. The greetings example demonstrates how complex this is even at a simple level. A knowledge of the historical practices may also help managers to understand the different concepts of morality that condition the way in which business is conducted. Some key issues that are culturally conditioned include: bribery, nepotism, the giving of gifts (and when this should become the exchange of gifts), buying and selling, eating and drinking and, as we have seen, rules about time. We will return to some of these controversial issues in the Section on Social responsibility which comes later in this book.

Non-verbal behaviour

One of the most critical areas in multicultural settings is that of non-verbal behaviour. Stories abound of contracts being lost because of inappropriate expressions, overeagerness, unacceptable familiarity and general insensitivity. It is possible to detail a number of key behavioural features: proximity, touch and gaze; expressiveness; gestures; accompaniments of speech; symbolic self-presentation; rituals that have to be considered in international settings. Once again we behave normally at our peril, as our definition of what is normal may be alien to our proposed partners and may jeopardize any negotiations if it is thought to be too outrageous in the terms of the host culture.

Cross-cultural communication challenges

Culture is often at the root of communication challenges. Exploring historical experiences and the ways in which various cultural groups have related to each other is key to opening channels for cross-cultural communication. Becoming more aware of cultural differences, as well as exploring cultural similarities, can help you communicate with others more effectively. Next time you find yourself in a confusing situation, ask yourself how your knowledge of your culture and your knowledge of the host's culture may be shaping your own reactions, and try to see the world from the other's point of view.

Eye contact

In some cultures, looking people in the eye is assumed to indicate honesty and straightforwardness; in others it is seen as challenging and rude. In the United States, the cheapest, most effective way to connect with people is to look them into the eye. Most people in Arab cultures share a great deal of eye contact and may regard too little as disrespectful. In English culture, a certain amount of eye contact is required, but too much makes many people uncomfortable. In South Asian and many other cultures direct eye contact is generally regarded as aggressive and rude.

Culture shock

Failure to identify cultural issues and take action can lead to a culture shock. In order of priority, the most often found symptoms of culture shock are:

- feeling isolated,
- anxiety and worry,
- reduction in job performance,
- high nervous energy,
- helplessness.

Not coping with culture shock symptoms when they appear can lead to a very negative situation.

Respecting differences and working together

Anthropologists discovered that, when faced by interaction that we do not understand, people tend to interpret the others involved as "abnormal", "weird" or "wrong". Awareness of cultural differences and recognizing where cultural differences are at work is the first step towards understanding each other and establishing a positive working environment. Use these differences to challenge your own assumptions about the "right" way of doing things and as a chance to learn new ways to solve problems. Organizationally there is often conflict between the international culture of the management and the culture of the local people. Huyton and Ingold (1995) detailed the problems that the Ritz–Carlton group experienced in Hong Kong when they attempted to introduce the company's total quality management (TQM) programme. The implementation was hindered because the local workforce adhered to the Chinese value system, known as "guanxi" which is not necessarily compatible with TQM. Guanxi supports:

- Respect for authority: Employees would always do what they were told.
- Power relationships: Clearly defined, recognized and observed, totally deferential.
- Authority without responsibility: Doing things is important but the authority for the task is passed upwards within the organization.
- Face: Preserving one's status and reputation creates an unwillingness to be open about weaknesses or mistakes.
- Unwillingness to share information: Saying too much is seen as dangerous and a possible weakness.
- Forming informal social groups: Giving an alternative to the official organizational channels.

When we work together we hope for meaningful interaction but often find this difficult to achieve. One way of looking at this is the Hopes and Fears model:

Communication: hopes and fears

Hopes
- the possibility of dialogue,
- learning something new,
- developing friendships,
- understanding different points of view.

Fears
- being judged,
- miscommunication,
- patronizing or hurting others intentionally.

There are several suggestions to make the attempt at communications more meaningful.

Approaches
- Learn from generalizations about other cultures, but don't use those generalizations to stereotype. Use them rather to understand better and appreciate other multifaceted human beings.
- Practice, practice, practice.
- Don't assume that yours is the only right way to communicate. Keep questioning your assumptions about the "right way" to communicate. Communicate trust and build rapport by talking in your client's preferred mode.
- Search for ways to make the communication work, rather than searching for who should receive the blame for the breakdown.
- Listen actively and empathetically. Try to put yourself in the other person's shoes.
- Honour others' opinions about what is going on.
- Suspend judgement, and try to look at the situation as an outsider.
- Honest acknowledgement of the mistreatment that has taken place on the basis of cultural difference is vital for effective communication. Use this as an opportunity to develop trust.
- Awareness of current power imbalances is necessary for understanding each other and working together.
- Remember that cultural norms may not apply to the behaviour of any particular individual. We are all more complicated than any cultural norm could suggest.

Levels of cultures

It is also possible to identify different aspects of culture. One approach, developed from the work of Triandris (1972), notes the difference between objective and subjective aspects of culture. Objective culture is seen as the tangible aspects of culture, such as art and architecture. Subjective culture refers to the intangible aspects, such as ways of perceiving and belief systems. What is apparent in studying organizational culture is that the two are connected and are used to reinforce each other. Objective aspects such as the design of the hotel and the uniform are important in establishing the recognition of the brand and also serve to embody the value system the organization is advocating.

Another way of looking at culture was developed in the important work undertaken by Hofstede (1991). In the study of international culture, four layers of culture are identified ranging from the visible to the deeper meanings of the culture. The four layers are:

1 symbols,
2 heroes,
3 rituals,
4 values.

The symbols level refers to words, gestures and objects that carry a particular meaning to members of the group. If you think in terms of a national culture you will see obvious symbols in the national flag and the national anthem. However these can be amended to more local groups, for instance with the change to the national anthem always sung at the English football cup final, where "God save the Queen" becomes "God save our team" – producing a reference to the symbols relevant to the group of supporters attending the match (although both team's supporters may make the same change to the national anthem invoking God for both teams involved in the contest!).

Heroes refer to those people, living or dead, real and imaginary, who have a status in the group and may serve as role models for the group. Reading a history of a nation will make these characters apparent – although the Scottish may have mixed emotions about the invocation of Braveheart (William Wallace to the Scots) constructed by Mel Gibson and Hollywood! Within an organization, you can see attempts to use this level of culture in the award of prizes to the best worker(s) in the organization. These awards confer hero status on the holder and serve to motivate them and their colleagues to achieve the desired standards.

Rituals are those patterns of behaviour encouraged by a group, from simple forms of greeting to more complicated ones like weddings or organizational induction programmes. Even the simple form can be constructed differently, marking out the group members effectively from those who do not belong. A greeting in the United Kingdom is formally very easy – you meet someone and you shake hands. In Hungary the traditional greeting is to kiss on both cheeks (not the lips as that conveys other meanings). What happens when a Hungarian is introduced to someone from England becomes an unchoreographed dance – an English hand is extended as the Hungarian cheek is offered, but then realizing the mistake the hand is withdrawn and English lips are prepared only to find the Hungarian head withdrawing and a hand being offered in its place. Experience suggests that the way to avoid such embarrassment is to do both greeting rituals at the same time, thereby avoiding any awkwardness. The moral of this tale is to demonstrate the importance of difference, not to point to the right or wrong of either greeting. To assume one particular set of rituals is right is limiting and can be called ethnocentrism – in international collaboration such reactions can create increased likelihood of conflict in partnerships.

> **Example: Cultural distance and participation in cultural tourism**
>
> Bob McKercher and Billie Chow So-Ming's (2001) research looked at the concept of cultural distance, which refers to the extent to which the culture of the originating region differs from that of the host region. It is hypothesized in this article that cultural distance influences participation in cultural tourism, with visitors from more culturally distant source markets being more interested in cultural tourism than those from culturally proximate source markets. Through the comparison of visitor profiles, cultural tourism participation rates and activities pursued visitors to Hong Kong from three Asian and three Western source markets were examined and it was revealed that there were statistically significant differences between these two groups.

Hofstede maintains that values operate at the deepest level of culture, representing collective beliefs, assumptions and feelings. This allows group members to understand what is normal in their society without having to think consciously about it. It is important that these values do not have to be consciously recognized as they are deeply embedded. For instance, in most Asian societies it is common to accept the authority of the social elders and this carries through into relationships in the workplace.

Four cultural dimensions

Cultures – both national and organizational – have been studied among many dimensions in order to try and explain the differences. Four of the most important can be seen to be:

1 **Directness** (get to the point versus imply the messages);
2 **Hierarchy** (follow orders versus engage in debate);
3 **Consensus** (dissent is accepted versus unanimity is needed);
4 **Individualism** (individual winners versus team effectiveness).

The study for which Hofstede is justifiably famous involved research in 50 countries and 3 regions of IBM's operation, both in the parent company and its subsidiaries, involving a formulation of these four dimensions. The work recognizes the overall context of the multinational organization's own culture and was relatively controlled in terms of the age and gender of the samples in the different places. Hofstede claimed that the national differences explained more of the differences in work-related values than did the position within the organization, profession, age or gender. The research was designed to look at the four issues outlined below:

1 Power distance: how marked are the status differences between people with high and low power.

2 Uncertainty avoidance: a measure of flexibility and need for rules.
3 Individualism versus collectivism: is a culture focused on individuals or groups?
4 Masculinity versus femininity: aggressiveness (level of individual assertiveness and competition) as masculinity (Table 2.1).

Table 2.1 Scoring the four cultural dimensions

Country	Power/distance		Uncertainty/ avoidance		Individualism		Masculinity	
	Index	Rank	Index	Rank	Index	Rank	Index	Rank
Argentina	49	18–19	86	36–41	46	28–29	56	30–31
Australia	36	13	51	17	90	49	61	35
Austria	11	1	70	26–27	55	33	79	49
Belgium	65	33	94	45–46	75	43	54	29
Brazil	69	39	76	29–30	38	25	49	25
Canada	39	15	48	12–13	80	46–47	52	28
Chile	63	29–30	86	36–41	23	15	28	8
Colombia	67	36	80	31	13	5	64	39–40
Costa Rica	35	10–12	86	36–41	15	8	21	5–6
Denmark	18	3	23	3	74	42	16	4
Ecuador	78	43–44	67	24	8	2	63	37–38
Finland	33	8	59	20–21	63	34	26	7
France	68	37–38	86	36–41	71	40–41	43	17–18
Germany (FR)	35	10–12	65	23	67	36	66	41–42
Greece	60	26–27	112	50	35	22	57	32–33
Guatemala	95	48–49	101	48	6	1	37	11
Hong Kong	68	37–38	29	4–5	25	16	57	32–33
Indonesia	78	43–44	48	12–13	14	6–7	46	22
India	77	42	40	9	48	30	56	30–31
Iran	58	24–25	59	20–21	41	27	43	17–18
Ireland	28	5	35	6–7	70	39	68	43–44
Israel	13	2	81	32	54	32	47	23
Italy	50	20	75	28	76	44	70	46–47
Jamaica	45	17	13	2	39	26	68	43–44
Japan	54	21	92	44	46	28–29	95	50
Korea S.	60	26–27	85	34–35	18	11	39	13
Malaysia	104	50	36	8	26	17	50	26–27
Mexico	81	45–46	82	33	30	20	69	45
The Netherlands	38	14	53	18	80	46–47	14	3
Norway	31	6–7	50	16	69	38	8	2
New Zealand	22	4	49	14–15	79	45	58	34
Pakistan	55	22	70	26–27	14	6–7	50	26–27
Panama	95	48–49	86	36–41	11	3	44	19
Peru	64	31–32	87	42	16	9	42	15–16

(continued)

Table 2.1 (Continued)

Country	Power/distance		Uncertainty/ avoidance		Individualism		Masculinity	
	Index	Rank	Index	Rank	Index	Rank	Index	Rank
The Philippines	94	47	44	10	32	21	64	39–40
Portugal	63	29–30	104	49	27	18–19	31	9
South Africa	49	18–19	49	14–15	65	35	63	37–38
Salvador	66	34–35	94	45–46	19	12	40	14
Singapore	74	40	8	1	20	13–14	48	24
Spain	57	23	86	36–41	51	31	42	15–16
Sweden	31	6–7	29	4–5	71	40–41	5	1
Switzerland	34	9	58	19	68	37	70	46–47
Taiwan	58	24–25	69	25	17	10	45	20–21
Thailand	64	31–32	64	22	20	13–14	34	10
Turkey	66	34–35	85	34–35	37	24	45	20–21
United Kingdom	35	10–12	35	6–7	89	48	66	41–42
United States	40	16	46	11	91	50	62	36
Uruguay	61	28	100	47	36	23	38	12
Venezuela	81	45–46	76	29–30	12	4	73	48
Yugoslavia	**76**	**41**	**88**	**43**	**27**	**18–19**	**21**	**5–6**
Regions								
East Africa	64	(31–32)	52	(17–18)	27	(18–19)	41	(14–15)
West Africa	77	(42)	54	(18–19)	20	(13–14)	46	(22)
Arab countries	80	(44–45)	68	(24–25)	38	(25)	53	(28–29)

Source: Hofstede (1991).

Power distance

This aspect of national culture looks at how different societies have addressed the issue of social equality and how they have legitimized power relations in those societies. In the context of organizational development, high power distance – a high tolerance for differences in power – means acceptance of strong leaders and centralized organizations. For Hofstede power distance is the extent to which members of a society accept that power in institutions and organizations is distributed unequally. Inequality of power is traditionally to be found in formalized, hierarchical organizations with well established superior–subordinate relationships. The study found that there were large power distance values in Latin countries (both in Europe and in the Americas) and for Asian and African countries. Northern Europe and the English-speaking countries scored much lower on this dimension.

Uncertainty avoidance

This variable recognizes that the future is unknowable and therefore there is a degree of uncertainty in all our lives. How a society deals with these uncertainties is one of the defining aspects of its culture. What Hofstede was exploring here was the extent to which the society could tolerate uncertainty and how it would deal with ambiguity. Societies with formalized rules for such situations also tend to recognize absolute truths and respect expertise. The pattern of responses on this variable does not fit easily with the suggested link to economic wealth or development, as the top four countries are Singapore, Jamaica, Denmark and Sweden. High scores, indicating a high propensity to accept uncertainty, were found in Latin America, Latin European and Mediterranean, Japan and South Korea. The scores in German-speaking countries in Europe (Germany, Austria and Switzerland) were medium high. Scores of medium to low were found in Asian and African countries, and Anglophone and Northern European countries.

Individualism versus collectivism

This continuum reflects the degree to which individuals in a country feel a part of the society or experience life as individual actors rather than as members of cohesive social groupings. In individualistic countries, everyone would be expected to look to their own interests and their own families with an agenda of self-preservation. In countries where collectivism dominates the emphasis is on extended social ties between individuals, with commitments to an extended family, clan, tribe or community within the society and these ties help to secure social responsibilities.

On the whole, the developing countries were characterized as collectivist and the industrialized countries as individualist. Hofstede's study showed a high correlation between the wealth of the nation (GDP per capita) and the individualism of its people's attitudes. The richer the country, the more individualist were its people's values. It is worth noting that the exception identified in the study was Japan, where despite the wealth in the economy, there were still relatively strong collectivist values compared to most Western countries.

Masculinity versus femininity

The words are used by Hofstede in a deliberately stereotypical way. Hofstede took masculine values to be a strong work ethic linked to financial rewards and achievement recognition. There was a sense of "tough" or "macho" values such as performance, achievement, making money, showing off, glorifying power and success. Feminine values were taken to be those which demonstrated stronger concern for social well being and quality of life. Here caring values were emphasized, such as putting relationships first, care for the young and weak, protection of the environment and a concern for the "small is beautiful" ethos. Masculine dominant societies were seen to define male–female gender roles more strictly than feminine dominant societies. On the basis of the study Hofstede concluded that Japan and Austria were highly masculine, whilst the Scandinavian countries and the Netherlands were highly feminine.

These four characteristics are not the only ones that can be identified in the study of the effects of national culture on organizational performance, but they do offer an insight into structuring the analysis of different patterns of behaviours. We shall return to this in looking at motivation and leadership in the Section on International human resource management.

Given our definition of culture and the caveats we added about the importance of context and specificity, it is interesting to think through how the intervening 30–40 years since the study would impact on the findings. The attitude to feminism and the changing international political alignments may well have changed some of the attitudes and experiences which the original study was based on. Hofstede has recognized this and in a more recent work (Hofstede and Bond, 1988) added a fifth dimension to try and look at national values from a non-Western perspective. This was called Confucian dynamism and attempted to capture the values related to persistence, relationship definitions, thrift, shame, reciprocity, saving face and respect for tradition. We will refer to many examples of this dimension in looking at what is important in organizations as we focus on face and trust in other discussions.

Chapter case study: Tipping

Tipping is a sensitive topic in Asia, where breaches of social convention are taken more personally than they would be in the West. Tipping practices are widespread, and rewarding good service without causing anyone to "lose face" in Asia can be difficult. Tipping is not a Chinese custom, but with British influence came the practice of tipping. Though there is a 10% service gratuity added to most restaurant and hotel bills, tips are still expected. Dewald's research (2001) examined the tipping habits of tourists from six distinct countries – three Asian and three Western – while visiting Hong Kong. This study shows that even though there is a slight adaptation to local tipping habits, those who tip more often at home do the same while travelling abroad. Americans tended to tip more often and in relation to service whereas British and Australian tourists tipped less frequently. Mainland Chinese tipped the least often. Furthermore there seemed to be a relationship between the level of service quality and tipping frequency for some personal, one-on-one services (Plate 4).

This photograph taken recently in a five-star hotel in China underlines the differences in practices and cultures. Not only is the issue of tipping addressed directly, but also explicitly prohibited. Also of interest is the way that the tip is represented with a $ sign, underlining the cultural differences at play in this international meeting point.

Plate 4
Chinese attitudes towards tipping in hotels.
Source: Vonzerö 2005 bt.

Organizational cultures

Every organization will develop a culture of its own as it matures and draws on the beliefs of its original creators but reacts to the changing environment it finds itself in. It is difficult to move in the Marriott empire without finding some reference and even photographs of the founder of the international corporation, and those views still underpin the mission and operation of the company. This is a recognition of the espoused culture of an organization, but we must also be aware that cultures can emerge from other sources and that these other cultures can support or resist the views of the espoused culture.

Robbins (2001) suggested that there are seven elements that define an organization's culture. These elements will be more or less present in all organizations, but their specific alignment would allow you to explore the nature of the organization (Figure 2.2).

These dimensions would allow us to plot an organization and to explore these interesting elements, but it would not necessarily reveal the same depth of understanding about an organization as we have been considering in the early part of this section in terms of national cultures. To add that depth we would have to consider the values and beliefs of the organization as well as its expressed practices. One way to approach this is through Schein's (1985) classification (Figure 2.3).

You can experiment with the levels of culture outlined here and try to think through them with some examples. For instance the artefacts of airlines include the uniforms they design for their cabin crew and these uniforms carry messages about the company which we may or may not be

Innovation and risk taking

The extent to which employees are encouraged to take risks and to think through problems for themselves.

Attention to detail

Focuses on the expected precision and attention to detail that employees are expected to show. This also considers how much autonomy workers have within the system.

Outcome orientation

How far the organization focuses on outcomes rather than the processes involved.

People orientation

How far is management concerned with the effect of the outcomes on the people involved.

Team orientation

How is the organization structured and to what extent workers are expected to become parts of teams rather than remaining as individuals.

Aggressiveness

Considers the competitive nature of the organization and how this translates into its internal operation.

Stability

Considers the amount of acceptable change in terms of structure, objectives and personnel.

Figure 2.2
Elements of
organizational
culture

able to interpret. In the mid-1990s, Lauda Air was a low-cost carrier that dressed its cabin crew in tight black jeans, explicitly because this gave the crew ease of movement in the cabin and had nothing to do with the heightening of the sexuality of the hostesses that such a uniform created! A target market of middle-aged businessmen might explain one or other of these interpretations. If you look at many of the national flag carrying airlines, you can see that their designs have been set within a recognition of the traditional national costume and stylized into a fashionable, stylish uniform.

The values may be seen in such things as the name badges of staff and the information they contain. It says much about an organization if the title of the post is more important than that of the person in the position. Equally you might be able to draw conclusions about the organizational

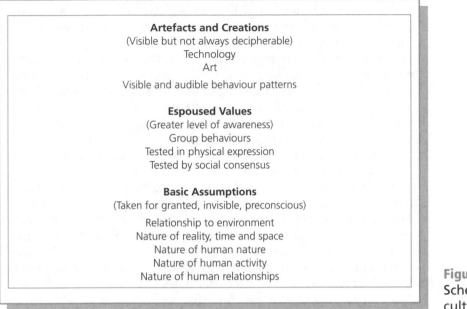

Artefacts and Creations
(Visible but not always decipherable)
Technology
Art
Visible and audible behaviour patterns

Espoused Values
(Greater level of awareness)
Group behaviours
Tested in physical expression
Tested by social consensus

Basic Assumptions
(Taken for granted, invisible, preconscious)

Relationship to environment
Nature of reality, time and space
Nature of human nature
Nature of human activity
Nature of human relationships

Figure 2.3
Schein's levels of culture

culture of a hotel where the lowly positions are named on a first name basis but the senior positions are filled by people with surnames.

The basic and tacit assumptions are those that are taken for granted in the organization and it is possible to identify both strong and weak cultures, although there may be some strong values in even a weak organizational culture. We will consider this later in the book in relation to absenteeism and the acceptance of absenteeism within certain cultures, but not others.

Many of the texts suggest that strong cultures come from a formal process of socialization within the organization, based on the assessment of induction programmes at places such as Disney and McDonald's. Strong norms – the implicit rules of accepted behaviour – can be very useful to the management as they avoid the need for managers to constantly manage. The workforce effectively subscribes to the values and beliefs that the managers would want to see voluntarily as part of their sense of belonging to the company. We would also urge you to consider the importance of informal groups within organizations and how these also generate norms, which can also be very powerful within the organization and follow an informal process of socialization.

Example: Everyday work

Then there is the nitty—gritty of everyday working together to consider, the problem of creating the rituals, the back-room humour and the "off-stage" relationships which are so vital to harmonious corporate life.

Company jokes and in-group stories, for example, are notoriously difficult to translate into other cultures: what sounds laudable to a Briton can seem risible to an Italian. Language is another problem. Although it might appear that the use of English as the common working language of the international hospitality community favours native English-speakers, this can turn into a disadvantage when one of them is unaware of the problems that a regional accent or rapid speech might create, and how linguistic confidence can be perceived as a manifestation of quasi-colonial arrogance. Non-conformity with what might be termed the "industry pidgin" can also generate unexpected tensions.

Worse still, behind the words on the surface, lurk centuries of cultural and ideological rivalries which have even often exploded into war. At moments of strain, when a minor conflict might have irreversible consequences, simmering stereotypes and prejudices boil up. Studies of cross-cultural teams indicate that often it is the most superficially similar cultures which in the end experience the greatest traumas: while differences such as those between the United States and Japan are obvious, serious problems often occur where they are least expected – say, between Britain and Denmark – and warning signals are neither perceived nor acted upon. In a world as competitive as that of international hospitality will be in coming decades, nothing may be taken for granted.

Touristic cultures

The final element in our presentation of the dynamic surrounding the cultural understanding of hospitality deals with the tourist or the guest, who we forget at our peril. It is becoming apparent that there are patterns of behaviour emerging that would allow us to consider them as a form of culture. There are codes of dress and behaviour which are manifestly different from the styles adopted by the same people in their own home or working environments. There are also sets of expectations about the quality of the service and increasingly of the experience as a whole that underpin the consumption of hospitality. It is certainly still possible to identify the national characteristics of groups of tourists, but within these national characteristics are some underlying elements that underpin the process. The level of demand is increasing and the knowledge base of the guests is increasing. As we noted in the introduction, Pearce's notion of touristic literacy looks at the way in which tourists move through a continuum from inexperienced to more experienced. Inexperienced travellers would have little knowledge of what to expect from the hospitality offer and seek safety in familiar experiences. The greater the experience of travel becomes so does the knowledge of what to expect and how to ask for it. The sense of consumption is heightened and highlighted. This experience becomes a challenge to the hospitality industry as the response must be well judged not only in terms of the local offer but also of the touristic culture.

We can see this touristic culture consisting of four characteristics:

1 Touristic culture is not innate, but learned – through travel but also done through every day living and interaction at home, school, work or in the church with other travellers and non-travellers.
2 Various aspects of touristic culture are interrelated – meaning that certain aspects of touristic culture will connect with aspects of other cultures that can influence the experience such as religion and diet.
3 Touristic culture is shared – when people visit there is an exchange, no matter how limited, with the other elements of culture in a region or organization, such as religion or language.
4 Touristic culture defines boundaries of different groups both within and without the tourist experience – such as the distinction between the host and the guests or the paying customers and their servants.

It is the touristic culture that makes sense of the growth in the number of Irish pubs found around the world. As a matter of curiosity, this example can be found in the midst of Schipol International Airport in Amsterdam! There is an expectation that travellers would like to drink in the style of an Irish pub even in the Netherlands. You can play an interesting game as you travel by playing "I Spy the Irish Pub". They tend to come with English sports on television and English breakfasts on the menu and have few similarities to the authentic Irish pub that they are trying to recreate (Plate 5).

Plate 5
Outside an Irish pub.
Source: Vonzerö 2005 bt.

The final case study in this chapter is a little unusual. It is the notes from a discussion at a World Tourism Organization (WTO) meeting in which leaders of the tourism and hospitality industry came together to discuss the role of cultural diversity in the future of their industries. There are many interesting and challenging observations that you need to consider carefully.

Example: Section case – Tourism, cultural diversity and sustainable development

"Tourism is like a fire: it helps us cook our food but it can also burn the house down" Fox. The extensive setting which opens this phrase, cited by the Director of the Dialogue, Tomás de Azcárate, was where the theses and proposals of all the speakers of the session came together.

The incredible growth which tourism has experienced on a global level, in terms of the number of travellers or destinations available, has shown just how ill prepared we are to take on such developments. Handallah Zedan, the Executive Secretary for the Convention on Biological Diversity, was the first to cite the threats for society that the deficient management of the growth in tourism has created during the last few years. The last speakers also put forward their own contributions in this line, adding information and facts which were summed up in the arguments of Eugenio Yunis Ahués, Head of Sustainable Development of the WTO: "Few states have preferred to optimise the arrival of tourism and preserve a certain social, environmental and economical stability in this way". According to Yunis, "tourism must never squander that off which it lives".

That is to say, culture and indigenous culture must never be adversely affected in order to favour the tourist.

This is lamentably an exception. Administrations have believed that the more tourists who arrive, the better, something which has led to a low-quality tourism which has specifically contributed to the deterioration of the tourist destination itself. Zedan and Yunis also coincide in stating that the solution is in the hands of the administration and the private sector working together. The former have to take on the responsibility for establishing a legal framework and, through constant evaluations, ensure that the regulations are strictly adhered to. Businessmen, for their part, should manage their own activities in a more rigorous manner. On this point, Joan Gaspart, President of the Executive Committee of Tourism in Barcelona, not only urged businessmen to lose their fear of a possible regulation of the sector, but also encouraged the administration to "do whatever has to be done to preserve heritage", as "the sacrifice of today's businessmen will be sure to bring in profits in the future". According to Gaspart, one of the examples to follow is the city of Havana, where part of the heritage has been recovered thanks to the investments of hotel chains. This case was explained earlier by Eusebio Leal Spengler, Director of the Historian's Office of the Cuban capital. The reconstruction plan allowed the recovery of 33% of land and created some 11,000 jobs. However, according to Leal Spengler, the most important element was that achieved "by making the culture of the country the flagship of the project". Apart from the statistics, the greatest success was that visitors respected the local identity. What is the magic formula for achieving this? "We have to make the visitor feel emotion. Only emotion can create the type of link which is needed to convert rubble into beauty".

The importance of achieving this kind of respect by the tourist was also underlined by the Deputy Assistant Director General for Culture in UNESCO, Milagros del Corral. In her view, a way of not losing the soul of the city is by promoting those specific traits which differentiate it from other cities. This is what she calls cities with vocation or creative cities: cities which learn to make the most of their distinctive characteristics and so convert themselves into new tourist destinations.

To sum up, although tourism is a factor which ensures peace and allows developing countries to have a considerable source of income, the future is a black one if more emphasis is not placed on the management of tourism itself. The cooperation of the administration and businessmen is as important as the cooperation between hosts and tourists. Once again, dialogue, comprehension and respect are presented as being as essential as written regulations.

■ Conclusion

Cultures are like underground rivers that run through our lives and relationships, giving us messages that shape our perceptions, attributions, judgements and ideas of self and other. Though cultures are powerful, they are often unconscious, influencing decisions and attempts to resolve issues in imperceptible ways. Cultures are more than the explicit signs of language, dress and food customs. Cultural groups may share race, ethnicity or nationality, but groupings also arise from cleavages of generation, socioeconomic class, sexual orientation, ability and disability, political and religious affiliation, language and gender – to name only a few of the factors that may contribute to the distinctiveness of cultures.

Two things are essential to remember about cultures: they are always changing, and they relate to the symbolic dimension of life. The symbolic dimension is the place where we are constantly making meaning and enacting our identities. Cultural messages from the groups we belong to give us information about what is meaningful or important, and who we are in the world and in relation to others – our identities. Cultural messages, simply, are what everyone in a group knows that outsiders do not know. They are the water fish swim in, unaware of its effect on their vision. They are a series of lenses that shape what we see and do not see, how we perceive and interpret and where we draw boundaries. In shaping our values, cultures contain starting points and currencies. Starting points are those places it is natural to begin, whether with individual or group concerns, with the big picture or particularities. Currencies, in a cultural sense, are those things we care about that influence and shape our interactions with others.

How cultures work

Though largely below the surface, cultures are a shifting, dynamic set of starting points that orient us in particular ways and away from other directions. Each of us belongs to multiple cultures that provide us with messages about what is normal, appropriate and expected. When others do not meet our expectations, it is often because our cultural expectations are different. We may mistake differences between others and us for evidence of bad faith or lack of common sense on the part of others, not realizing that common sense is also cultural. What is common to one group may seem strange, counterintuitive or wrong to another.

Cultural messages shape our understandings of relationships, and of how to deal with the conflict and harmony that are always present whenever two or more people come together. Writing about or working across cultures is complicated, but not impossible. Here are some complications in working with cultural dimensions of conflict, and the implications that flow from them:

- Culture is multilayered: What you see on the surface may mask differences below the surface. Therefore, cultural generalizations are not the whole story, and there is no substitute for building relationships and sharing experiences, coming to know others more deeply over time.
- Culture is constantly in flux: As conditions change, cultural groups adapt in dynamic and sometimes unpredictable ways. Therefore, no comprehensive description can ever be formulated about a particular group. Any attempt to understand a group must take the dimensions of time, context and individual differences into account.
- Culture is elastic: Even knowing the cultural norms of a given group will not always allow us to predict the behaviour of a member of that group, who may not conform to norms for individual or contextual reasons. Therefore, taxonomies (e.g. "Italians think this way", or "Buddhists prefer that") have limited use and can lead to error if not checked with experience.

Culture is largely below the surface, influencing identities and meaning-making, or who we believe ourselves to be and what we care about – it is not easy to access these symbolic levels since they are largely outside our awareness. Therefore, it is important to use many ways of learning about the cultural dimensions of those involved, especially indirect ways, including stories, metaphors and rituals. Cultural influences and identities become important depending on context. When an aspect of cultural identity is threatened or misunderstood, it may become relatively more important than other cultural identities and this fixed, narrow identity may become the focus of stereotyping, negative projection and conflict. This is a very common situation in the development of international partnerships.

It is useful for people to have interactive experiences that help them see each other as broadly as possible, experiences that foster the recognition of what is shared as well as those that are different (Figure 2.4).

Figure 2.4
Patterns of cultural interaction in international hospitality management

Since culture is so closely related to our identities (who we think we are) and the ways we make meaning (what is important to us and how), it will always be a factor in international hospitality management. The dynamics can be read from the figure above, where we have attempted to represent the coming together of the cultures that we have discussed in this chapter. Cultural awareness suggests that we ought to apply the Platinum Rule in place of the Golden Rule. Rather than the maxim "Do unto others as you would have them do unto you", the Platinum Rule advises: "Do unto others as they would have you do unto them".

No comprehensive solution to the problems of cultural diversity in the context of the hospitality industry has yet been conceived. Yet it is clear that preparation for the successful management of such diversity in all its ramifications will be a vital component of long-term success in the global market. For while business is already global, management remains culture-bound.

■ Review questions

1 Can you describe the levels of culture involved in international hospitality management?
2 How can cultural differences be made into positives for an organization rather than being seen as problems?
3 Explore the tensions generated by intercultural communications in at least one international setting.
4 Why do you need to do more than understand other cultures?

CHAPTER 3

The international hospitality industry

After working through this chapter, you should be able to:

■ Define the hospitality concept in global business environment
■ Describe the structure of international hospitality industry
■ Chart the international operating environment of hospitality organizations
■ Recognize and understand the critical issues and trends in hospitality industry that are likely to impact on the future of hospitality

■ Introduction

This chapter sets out to describe the international hospitality industry and the ways in which it can be seen to be structured. The nature of the industry has changed considerably in the past decades and this explains why we think it is important to examine the underlying trends in the industry. Key issues like the internationalization of hospitality enterprises and chaining will be discussed. One of the primary tasks of this chapter is to analyse the market segmentation practiced by the major international hotel companies and the ways this structures their competition.

■ The elements of hospitality

What is hospitality and hospitality industry? Jones (2002: 1) explains "in essence, hospitality is made up two distinct services – the provision of overnight accommodation for people staying away from home, and the provision of sustenance for people eating away from home or not preparing their own meals. Both of these services meet very basic human needs – the need to sleep and need to eat." He is borrowing from the work of Maslow in making this comment, but we believe he does not go far enough in thinking through the use that the analysis of the hospitality industry can make of the concept of needs. Maslow's hierarchy of needs is one of the most famous of all management diagrams and has been much debated since it was first proposed in the 1950s (Figure 3.1). The basic model (1954) suggests that people have five levels of need in their lives but can only fulfil those needs once they have satisfied the lower level needs. Maslow himself revisited the idea (1968) adding several more layers to the analytical framework (Figure 3.2). However, the diagram is normally presented as a pyramid looking something like shown in Figure 3.1.

The suggestion is that satisfying the basic needs at the base of the pyramid is of paramount concern and that other needs will only be considered

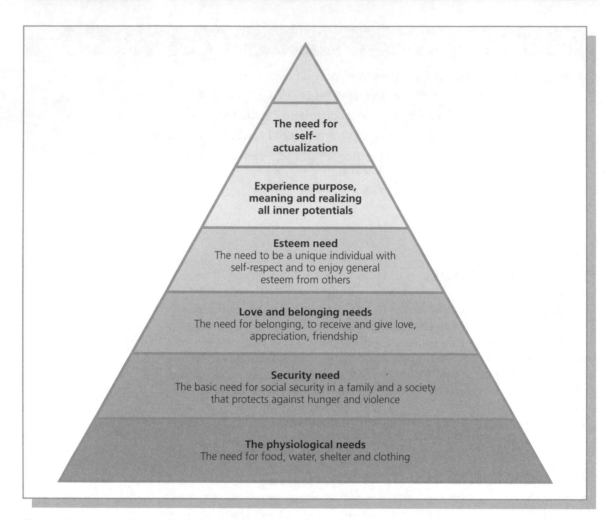

Figure 3.1 A version of Maslow's hierarchy of needs

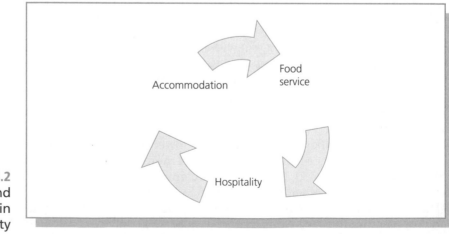

Figure 3.2
The elements and
linkages in
hospitality

once that concern has been satisfied, so once the need for basic food and shelter has been met individuals will begin to think in terms of security and then feel comfortable in thinking about more abstract concerns. We believe that this provides an interesting way to look at the structuring found in the hospitality industry as the offers target different markets and aim to satisfy different levels of needs. We will work through this in more detail, but to make the point clear the difference between a one-star hotel and a five-star hotel is not just summarized by the star rating classifications but also in the nature and spirit of the offer. The five-star hotel will provide shelter and security but it does more than this and its customers expect that the experience they will have will allow them to satisfy higher level needs.

■ International hospitality industry overview

As we are discussing the management of the international hospitality industry, we need to understand the general situation of the industry. The international hospitality industry is characterized by an industry structure composed of a relatively small number of large multinational enterprises (MNE) and a large number of locally operated small- and medium-sized enterprises (SME).

The industry is heterogeneous. It has been split up into many different identifiable sectors, each with its own specific needs. Geographically, the hospitality industry is very widespread and dispersed, from metropolitan cities to remote rural areas. The industry is also a very large employer in most countries and offers a wide range of job opportunities and employment categories (Jones, 2002). The globalization of the hospitality industry has accelerated under the pressures of the advances in technology, communication and transportation, deregulation, elimination of political barriers, socio-cultural changes, and global economic development, as well as growing competition in a global economy (Teare and Olsen, 1999). Table 3.1 shows large hotel companies have been fully involved in global competition.

A fundamental question for senior managers of all large hospitality enterprises is why hospitalities companies have gone international. Hospitality companies become multinationals for a number of reasons and there are internal and external demands for international expansion. Some of the reasons are:

● A growing world market for their services and product. North America, European Union (EU) and Japan are traditional major markets. India, China, Russia, Brazil and other emerging markets now generate huge business opportunities for international hospitality companies.
● A desire to protect themselves from the risks and uncertainties of the domestic business cycle, for example Japanese companies tried to keep their profitability through their global operation during its domestic

Table 3.1 Numbers of countries present of multinational hotel groups

Hotel group	Number of countries present
InterContinental	100
Accor	93
Best Western	85
Starwood	83
Hilton Group plc	74
Marriot	66
Carlson	66
Le Meridien	55
Golden Tulip	45
Hyatt	44

Source: Companies' websites, 2006.

economy downturn during 1994 to 2004. McDonald's future business growth depends not on the domestic market, but on the international market.

● A desire to reduce costs. Through global outsourcing and acquisition, most companies can gain from national economic advantages and develop their unique competences in the industrial competition.

● A response to increased foreign competition. Even hospitality companies focus on their domestic market; they cannot avoid the risks of foreign companies invading their traditional markets.

Example: Accor to invest R$43 million in Brazil in 2005

French hotel chain Accor plans to open another three units of its Formule 1 hotel in Brazil by the end of the year – two in Sao Paulo and one in Curitiba, capital of Parana state. The investment is estimated at R$43.8 million. The group has been in Brazil since 2001 and it plans to invest another R$120 million over the next 2 years in the opening of more Formule 1 hotels throughout the country.

Source: www.accor.com

ACTIVITY   Why is Accor making a direct investment in Brazil? Would they not have made more profit by putting these funds into a new France-based unit?

Because foreign markets appear to be more risky, companies have tended to expand their operations abroad incrementally and cautiously. Setting up a wholly owned subsidiary is usually the last stage of doing business abroad. A typical internationalization process for a hospitality company producing a standardized service or product might begin with a licensing or franchising agreement: a contractual arrangement in which one company provides access to some of its management know-how and brand to another company in exchange for a fee or royalty. This is typically followed by foreign direct investment. International market entry modes will be discussed separately in detail later.

There are two major sectors in the hospitality industry, the accommodation sector and the food service sector. We will discuss these main segments in this chapter.

■ The food service sector

The international food service industry is gigantic and complicated. It is a typical fragmented industry in most countries, which means it is hard to get any accurate data to present a global overview. We will mainly draw upon the United States and Britain as examples in this review.

In America, more than 10 million people are employed in food service and there are more than 835,000 food service facilities that operate in the United States. According to a restaurant customer study from Scarborough, published in July 2006; 96% of US adults dine out at a restaurant at least once per month. Two-fifths (40%) of the population visited a Quick Service Restaurant, such as McDonald's, Wendy's or Subway, six or more times during the previous month. About one-fifth (19%) of US consumers visited a sit-down restaurant (such as TGI Friday's or Chili's) six or more times during the previous month.

Between 2000 and 2004 the British market grew by around a fifth, with further growth (5%) anticipated in 2005, pushing the market to £28 billion. Once the effects of inflation are taken into account, the growth over the 2000–04 period is estimated by Mintel (2005b) to be around 5%.

There are important areas of overlap between the two sectors of the hospitality industry, most noticeably in the catering within hotels. In 2005 it was estimated that £4.1 billion would be spent on dining in hotels, out of a total eating out spend of £27.6 billion. Whilst the hotel catering market has grown from £3.8 billion in 2000, once inflation has been factored in, there has been a decline over the period of around 6%. However, the proportion of overall hotel revenue generated by food and beverage activity has risen over the period 2000–05 from 35.8% to a forecast 38.9%.

During the last few years the budget hotel sector has experienced considerable growth, as have those hotels that provide an upmarket product. These two types of hotel are almost at the opposite ends of the accommodation spectrum and this develops a polarity within the hotel catering market, with budget hotels paying little or no regard to catering, whilst the full-service hotels often develop their hotel around a signature or branded restaurant.

◼ Hotel food and beverage strategy: an evolving form

The traditional hotel restaurant remains a dominant feature of mid-market hotels, whereby food and beverage facilities and services are provided as a valued-added incentive for in-house guests. However, some hotels have sought to also attract walk-in customers, primarily through the provision of all-day casual dining outlets. Also a number of luxury or premium hotels, particularly in London, now feature signature outlets, which are managed and marketed as separate entities to the hotel.

Other hoteliers have decided to outsource their food and beverage operations, contracting third parties to manage some or all food and beverage facilities and services. Notably, there is now a blurring of the lines between signature and outsourced outlets as renowned chefs develop partnerships with contract caterers to set up hotel restaurants.

Outsourcing is a growing trend and will increase alongside more innovative developments. The number of hotels outsourcing their food and beverage facilities are set to increase in the next few years, in particular in London, as establishments become more attracted to a secure revenue stream, and also to avoid the costs and expertise required to run a restaurant. The intense competition within the eating out market has restrained the growth of the hotel catering market, and it is likely that the market will continue to decline in real terms in the short term. It has been noted that a key factor holding back future developments in the hotel catering sector is the lack of food service specialists, who are able to drive the market forward, manage food and beverage operations efficiently and to develop effective marketing initiatives.

The contracting out of food and beverage services to third parties will continue to be a major trend in the hotel catering sector over the next few years, although this will be much stronger in London than in the provinces. As many hotels continue to remain sluggish owing to evolving consumer demand for food and beverages and intense competition from the high street, the attraction of outsourcing food and beverage services will become increasingly appealing.

Vertical integration between many hotel and restaurant groups has meant that the outsourcing decision is often not such a radical step to take for many hoteliers, as costs and revenues remain within the group. Most outsourcing is agreed on either a flat fee or percentage basis and this is expected to remain unchanged.

Outsourcing is not always a straightforward option for hotels to make however. To attract walk-in customers, a hotel ideally needs to be located where there is easy street access to the restaurant itself, and the location of the hotel itself (city centre, countryside, etc.) needs to fit with the clientele that are being targeted – that is the product must be attractive to the passing trade. Despite these constraints, the number of outsourced restaurants is expected to increase considerably over the future.

■ The accommodation sector

In the past century, with fundamental developments in transportation and communication, the demand for accommodation as part of the international travel experience has increased dramatically for both business and leisure travellers.

Modern concepts of the accommodation (hotel) business developed from America from the beginning of 20th century, reinterpreting the older traditions of ad hoc development seen previously. These differentiated hotel products were first developed in the US market which is characterized by fierce competition, but which also offers the advantage of economies of scale to hotel companies. Europe still enjoys the largest hotel capacity of any region in the world, although capacity growth has considerably lagged the rest of the world. Europe claims about 36% of the total worldwide lodging capacity, which is still slightly more than that of North America (Marvel, 2004). Total room capacity in European hotels and similar establishments can be roughly estimated at 6.3 million, with the majority (over 60%) concentrated in five principal countries: Germany, France, the United Kingdom, Italy and Spain (Table 3.2). While hotels are different across the world, a majority of US hotel properties are purpose-built in conformity with strict market segmentation criteria, whereas in Europe hotel structures are typically older and not amenable to transformation to meet the standards of particular branded concepts. In fact, the hotel stock in Asia, Australia or the Middle East more resembles that of North America, as the units are generally larger and newer than those in Europe.

Table 3.2 Number of rooms in hotels and similar establishments worldwide, 1998–2002 ('000)

Region	1998	1999	2000	2001	2002	% of 1998–2002 Total
Americas	5,164	5,450	5,750	6,010	6,161	35.5
Asia/Pacific	3,487	3,680	3,865	4,004	4,124	23.8
Europe	5,935	6,050	6,150	6,240	6,300	36.3
Middle East	221	236	262	285	305	1.8
Africa	425	435	445	455	465	2.7
Total	15,232	15,851	16,272	16,894	17,355	100.0

Source: Mintel (2004).

Chapter Case Study: Case: Olympic Games and Hotel Accommodation

London's hotel chiefs have joined forces to back the capital's 2012 Olympic bid and have agreed to provide 40,000 affordable rooms for the event. Speaking at the HCIMA's London Conference on 6th September 2004, Charles Wijeratna, Director of London 2012, the capital's bid vehicle, confirmed a deal had been struck after 9 months of dialogue with the major chains.

The International Olympic Committee (IOC) views provision of reasonably priced rooms as extremely important for new bids, after hoteliers in Athens doubled rates during this year's Olympics. As a result, many international tourists boycotted the games on cost grounds, leaving some events only half-full.

Using the Internet: Please check London Olympic Website (www.london2012.org) and other relevant websites to find information about accommodation for the 2012 Olympic Games. Compare it with the accommodation information for 2008 Beijing Olympic Games (www.en.beijing2008.com/) and think about the business opportunities created by Olympic Games for hospitality companies.

Source: www.london2012.org

■ Chaining

The degree of hotel chain penetration worldwide varies considerably according to the region you are looking at (Table 3.3). Smith Travel Research (STR) estimates that 67% of hotel rooms in the United States are branded, mainly through franchise contracts. Estimates for other parts of the world are far less certain due to the lack of a centralized information source the equivalent of STR. Mintel (2005a) currently estimates that roughly 25% of European hotel rooms are branded. Similar figures can be estimated for other regions of the world. However, since hotel capacity in South America and the Middle East has been expanding at a rapid rate in recent years, mainly led by international hotel chains, it is quite possible

Table 3.3 Chain penetration, by region in % of total hotel stock, 2004

Region	Branded rooms as % of total
North America	65
East Asia	25
Middle East	>25
South America	>20
Europe	25

Source: Mintel (2005).

that the degree of brand penetration in those regions will be higher than estimated at the time of this study.

As shown in the table, hotel chain penetration in Europe remains well below that of North America, and is probably somewhat less than that to be found in the Middle East and South America, where hotel expansion is being primarily led by hotel chains. France and the United Kingdom have the highest proportion of branded rooms amongst the major European economies, estimated at 37% and 32% respectively (Mintel, 2005a). Accor is by far the number one operator in Europe, according to MKG Consulting, controlling 29% of all branded capacity in the core 15 European Union (EU) countries.

■ Market segmentations

In an increasingly competitive global business environment, companies are obliged to target clearly defined niche markets with specialized products and services. The hotel industry is no exception. The last two decades have witnessed a proliferation of differentiated hotel concepts designed to serve specific market segments. Business hotels, budget hotels, airport hotels, boutique hotels, conference centres, convention hotels, condo hotels and casino hotels are some examples. Each one of these hotel categories offers particular features and services which allow it to meet the customer needs of a specific market segment.

We want to approach these offers from within the perspective of a critical usage of Maslow's model. We believe that the model would look something like this and will work through the categories in the subsequent pages.

Rather than provide a detailed account of all the different types of food service and accommodation available, we want to focus on how the offer has been shaped and structured by the industries attempt to identify and satisfy what it sees as a market need. In order to do this, we are adapting the hierarchy of need model that we introduced earlier and will comment on the variety of offers that proposes to match these categories. Fuller details about the categories and the definitions can be found on the book's website, where you will find more extensive discussions of all of the categories and more case studies demonstrating the differences between the types of offer.

■ Level 1: The basic offer of shelter and sustenance

Roadside catering

This may not appear to be the most exciting area of the international hospitality industry to begin our analysis with, but it is still a significant and distinct part of the food service sector. Moreover it is a significant market, in the United Kingdom alone it was projected to be worth £491 million in 2004. It can be divided into two segments – motorway service areas (MSA) and off-motorway roadside outlets. The market is still dominated by three main players, Compass, Welcome Break and Roadchef, who have on the whole struggled to grow the profitability of their operations in recent years but are still the leading players in the sector.

Plate 6
Beach catering Lake
Balaton Hungary.
Source: Vonzerö
2005 bt.

All the beaches on the Balaton have versions of these catering outlets. The langós is a deep fried circular bread dough, served with a choice of toppings. Authentically this would be garlic oil but we have seen Bolognese and Chilli con carne on offer! This is catering done in small kitchens, contained in the hut, and produced by seasonal staff or members of the family. Everywhere will also sell cold drinks, including alcohol.

Budget hotels

Compared with the traditional forms of accommodation, budget hotel is a relative new concept in most countries. It is difficult to define the term budget hotel precisely. Logically a budget hotel could be any hotel below four-star level. It normally has a minimum of 50 rooms, and will be branded by a major chain. Such hotels typically have a standardized appearance and offer a no-frills service, with limited food and beverage facilities. The budget hotel sector can be further divided into at least three subsegments: "discount-budget", "middle budget" and "super-deluxe budget", or "upper economy" (Mintel, 2003).

Budget hotels were first developed in the United States with the creation of the interstate highway system. Quality hotel was founded in 1939 by seven southern motel operators; Holiday Inns was founded by Kemmons Wilson in 1952. In 1951, it was estimated by *Fortune Magazine* that there were 30,000 motels as compared to only 20,000 "true" hotels. In Europe, France is the most mature budget hotel market in Europe and the two major French operators, Accor and the Groupe Envergure control about two-thirds of the total European branded budget rooms. The second most developed budget hotel market is the United Kingdom, where two domestic mid-market budget brands, Whitbread's Travel Inn and Compass' Travelodge control 53% of the market. Express by Holiday Inn, the sub-brand of the InterContinent is only ranked 10th in Europe but is the third largest in the United Kingdom. The third budget market in Europe, Germany, is dominated by the Accor brands, especially Ibis and Etap. Budget hotels are known to be a particularly profitable sector of the hotel industry. A brief analysis of corporate strategy and accounts, as well as construction costs would seem to support this assertion. A glance at Whitbread's 2000 results reveals that Travel Inn generated a 44% EBITDA margin as opposed to only 28% for the Marriott/Swallow operation. A key factor driving high margins in the budget hotel business is low labour costs and low land cost. A 100-room branded budget hotel can be run efficiently with a full-time staff of 20 (Mintel, 2003). Assuming an occupancy rate of 75% and an average daily rate of £36, an un-leveraged return of equity of greater than 12% should be achievable. In normal situation, an investor could reasonably expect a 20% return on equity and an internal rate of return of more than 30%.

Read the following two cases and present your view of the future of budget hotel ACTIVITY

Case 1: Corporate Enthusiasm for Low-Cost Airlines and Budget Hotels Appears to have Peaked, the Barclaycard Business Travel Survey Indicates

Currently, nearly one-third (30%) of all flights taken for business purposes are with low-fare airlines. EasyJet was ranked as the second favourite airline – after British Airways – for business trips, and is rated far and away the best low-cost airline.

However, looking ahead to 2015, Barclaycard boffins say: "Low-cost air travel is not expected to increase further, with the level of business travellers who have used these services staying at the 2004/05 level of 74%. Similarly, budget hotels are falling out of favour. This year, 58% of business travellers used budget accommodation, against 61% last year. And 42% of those who have avoided low-cost hotels have done so because of the lack of 'extras' and facilities. Tellingly, 15% of those polled say staying in cheaper hotels 'doesn't reflect my position'".

The average spend on overnight hotel accommodation has gone up from £93 last year to £99.60 in 2005/06. Londoners, perhaps used to generally higher prices, spend an average of £115.70 per night.

Case 2: EasyHotel, the budget hotels division of easyGroup, is to open a second franchised outlet in Paris. Although the Premiere Classe and Formule 1 chains have hundreds of one-star hotels across France, easyHotel is confident in its central location and en-suite bathrooms will prove a success.
Source: Travel Industry Monitor by Mintel 16-02-2006 and Evening Standard 30-01-2006.

Fast food

The share fast food has of the total eating out market is forecast to grow marginally between 2000 and 2005, accounting for about 27% of total sales. The shifts in market share in the restaurant sector will be relatively small as well, with only pub catering gaining any significant share in addition to value.

Plate 7
Derbyshire pub food.
Source: Vonzerö 2005 bt.

Burger outlets such as McDonald's and Burger King still characterize the fast food sector and indeed the burger sector makes up around a third of fast food sales. Ethnic takeaways are the second largest category but tends to be characterized by numerous independents which are usually family owned businesses with no major national brands, although there are small chains concentrated within certain regions (e.g. Harlequin Group, Bombay Bicycle Club and tiffinbites). The pizza and pasta sector is characterized by a number of large chains including Pizza Hut and Domino's whose rapid expansion of outlets is helping to drive this sector forward.

The burger bar market has experienced phenomenal growth over the last few years, increasing in value by 31% between 2000 and 2004. This rapid expansion was due in part to the ambitious expansion plans of its market leaders McDonald's and Burger King.

Burger bars will no longer experience the rapid growth that characterized this market throughout the 1990s. Nonetheless, despite the slowdown in consumer demand, it is still poised for growth, although this is more likely to be through product innovation rather than through rapid outlet expansion.

McDonald's was the first player within the burger sector to respond actively to the changes in consumer preferences, and it initiated a radical programme to overhaul its menu and image in 2003 by introducing healthier options. McDonald's now offers a vastly different menu to 2 years ago with healthy alternatives such as porridge, bagels, fruit and an extensive range of salads being sold alongside traditional staples.

... but it is changing.

Increasing consumer concerns regarding the healthiness of fast food and rising awareness of diet issues have steered consumers away from the traditional exponents of the fast food concept such as McDonald's and Burger King towards newer brands such as Nando's, who have capitalized on the demand for fresh and healthy meals. This shift in public opinion has led to a radical rethink, and traditional fast food purveyors are now in the midst of redesigning their menus and recalibrating their brand image. The rapid opening of outlets has ceased as operators look to their food offer to build like-for-like sales (Mintel, 2005b).

Pub catering

Pub catering is the largest sector within the eating out market (23%) and is responsible for driving much of the growth. Between 2000 and 2004 pub-catering sales grew by 23%. When the effects of inflation are stripped out, the market had grown by 8%.

Despite the decline in the number of pubs, pub catering will continue to be a key force behind the growth in the restaurant sector. Although other eating out concepts may be gaining ground, pubs will continue to hold their place as a popular eating out destination. Consumer research for this report found that 53% of UK adults or 26 million people have visited pubs in recent months.

The major players with an extensive catering offer include Greene King, Mitchell's and Butler, J.D. Wetherspoon, The Sprit Group, Whitbread and Wolverhampton and Dudley.

The pub industry is in the midst of change, with the sector shifting away from the overt theming and homogeneity of branding that characterized the trade in the 1990s. Instead, there is now an emphasis on creating individuality by cultivating a distinctive ambience and food and drink menu.

Food has become an increasingly important part of the pub trade as drink sales decline. The trend towards selling a higher proportion of food is set to continue, particularly in suburban and rural areas. The catering share for the average pub has now reached 26% (compared to about a fifth in 2000) and there seems to be no evidence of this trend weakening. Meanwhile, the advent of "gastropubs" which feature restaurant quality meals in a pub setting has helped to raise pub-catering standards.

■ Level 2: Security

Airport hotels

With the growth of air travel, especially the boom of budget flights, the airport hotel has become an increasingly distinct segment offering specific features to travellers whose length of stay in the hotel is usually very short. These hotels generally have smaller rooms and reduced common areas. However, Chon and Sparrowe (2000) point out that increasingly the airport hotels have come to recognize the need to reach larger markets and have begun a process of adding guestrooms as well as banquet and meeting facilities. They target local business customers and large organizations hosting regional conferences, offering good-sized, quality facilities that save participants precious travel time between the airport and a convention centre. Such a marketing strategy puts airport hotels in direct competition with convention facilities and traditional downtown business hotels.

Airport hotels generally adapt their service offering to their target market. For instance, check-in and checkout times are often very flexible. The laundry and dry cleaning service is accelerated to accommodate clients who only have a few hours to spare. Most airport hotels offer a shuttle service, which can constitute a significant operating expense for the property.

According to Mintel (2003) airport hotels generally enjoy stable year-round occupancy and usually have better weekend occupancies than urban hotels targeting business travellers. Even in the aftermath of September 11th and with the ensuing slowdown in air travel, airport hotels have maintained above-average occupancy levels.

The following two examples demonstrate the success of the chain restaurant, which we would argue is built around the safety of the brand recognition.

Example: Chain restaurants growth

The food service consultancy Technomic found that US systemwide sales for the Top 500 rose to an estimated $199.9 billion in 2005, up $13 billion over 2004 on a same-chain basis. The 500 largest US restaurant chains registered solid performance, posting 7% sales growth in 2005, outperforming the restaurant industry at large, which grew 5.6%. Growth continues to be driven by leading chains. The Mexican category was led by Taco Bell's 8.4%

sale growth and quick–casual standout Chipotle, which grew an estimated 27.1%. The doughnut category continues its growth with Dunkin Donuts' 13.8% sales and the category's increased sales of specialty coffee. Limited-service chains within the Technomic Top 500 accounted for 82% of all US fast food restaurants. As a whole, this group grew at an impressive rate of 7%. Other limited-service sub-segments with sales growth above the segment average include bakery café (27.8%), beverage (19.8%), Mexican (12.4%), other sandwich (12.0%), donut (11.5%), and chicken (9.4%). The Mexican, steak and Italian categories all posted strong results with sales growth of 8.3%, 7.6% and 6.6%, respectively. Family style restaurants continued to struggle, but remained static (Technomic Information Services, 2006).

Seeing Double? Hooters Opens Second Restaurant in China Thursday May 25, 2:50 pm ET

ATLANTA, May 25 /PRNewswire/ – Hooters of Pudong, located in Shanghai, hosted the grand opening celebration on May 19th. This is the 2nd Hooters location in China, of the 4 slated to be open by this year's end including one in Beijing and the other in Hang Zhou. "The original Hooters location in Shanghai is doing very well, and we expect the same out of the new Pudong location," explained John Weber, EVP of Franchising for Hooters of America. "Ex patriots are enjoying a taste of home and the Chinese are enjoying our fun, casual themed concept."

International expansion has been a focus for Hooters and by the end of this year the concept will be introduced to seven new countries. These new countries include Australia, Columbia, Japan, Greece, Panama, Puerto Rico and Spain, bringing the grand total to 57 international Hooters restaurants in 25 countries.

The first Hooters location opened its doors 23 years ago, and today there are over 425 locations. It did not take long for the concept to catch on in the United States followed by successful international expansion. Hooters is well known for its brand of food and fun, featuring a casual beach-theme atmosphere, a menu that features seafood, sandwiches and Hooters' signature spicy chicken wings, and service provided by the All-American cheerleaders, the Hooters Girls.

Source: Hooters of America, Inc.

■ Level 3: Belonging

Conference centres and hotels

The conference market is a huge business. In 2000 alone, there were an estimated 1.3 million conferences in the UK generating sales revenues of

£6 billion. Conference centres are facilities including hotel accommodation which are specially designed to accommodate groups and meetings. Unlike ordinary commercial hotels with adjacent conference space which serve all market segments, conference centres concentrate on the meeting or exhibition market, sometimes even going to the point of excluding other business segments which might distract the conference groups (Mintel, 2003). Conference centres have the clear objective of providing an environment for successful meetings and training courses. Therefore, the properties are generally located in relatively isolated surroundings. Normally the conference centre should be within reasonable distance to a major airport and should be accessible by efficient transport links, like the Birmingham NEC. Conference centres also often include a full range of recreational facilities, such as gym, swimming pools, tennis courts, golf courses and fitness rooms which provide meeting participants with the opportunity to unwind. This begins to demonstrate the interconnectivity of sectors within the industry.

Conference hotels are designed to accommodate customers attending conferences or exhibitions. Common areas are extensive, with meeting space per guestroom, and typically include facilities such as ballrooms and break-out areas for meetings and conferences. Exhibition space for trade shows, sample and display rooms for sales meetings, 24-hour business centre, and extensive restaurants and lounges are necessary. Guestrooms are normally larger than in an average hotel and are equipped for work, often broadband, two telephone lines, speakerphone. The meeting rooms are equipped with the latest in the way of audiovisual and computer features. Typically, a conference package will include meeting planning services, accommodation, coffee breaks and meals. Banqueting is a very important service in conference hotel and should be running efficiently all year around with high standards. On the other hand, conference hotels should offer all the same recreational facilities as any ordinary commercial hotel.

Business hotels

Jones (2002: 49) points out this market is so valuable to hotels not only because business customers can afford high average room rates but they have high food and beverage spends, which will bring in greater margins of profit to the hotels than other markets. Moreover business demands are also concentrated on different times to leisure travellers. Normally business customers use hotels during the working week, with March to May and September to December being their peak seasons, which is a very different profile from that of leisure customers.

The business traveller market is recognized as having particular needs, and bedrooms are being upgraded to provide better work areas, and facilities for laptop computers connected with broadband Internet (Jones, 2002: 49–51). Some business customers require their rooms with an executive style lounge with an area for meetings, a business secretarial service and complimentary refreshments. Fast check-in and checkout is a crucial service for business hotels and ample parking space, free of charge, is a basic while necessary feature if the hotel is close to a motorway. For many executives, the lines between business and pleasure are blurring. According to a 2005 Deloitte Survey, some two-fifths of respondents claimed to be combined business and leisure travels. This is a significant trend, which can bring new opportunities and reshape the business hotel sector in the near future, especially when the Generation Xers become the main business travellers.

In most business hotels there are special corporate rates for company bookings, including a travel agent corporate rate for reservation through Thomson or American Express (Jones, 2002). There is also a local privileged rate for those local companies, which use the hotel regularly. In order to manage costs and maximize the value of hotel stays, corporate travel departments have been negotiating extra perks such as free breakfast and free high-speed Internet access in their contracts with hotel chains. Some companies have also attempted to fix rates with hotel chains for the next 2 to 3 years (Chon and Sparrowe, 2000).

During the recent economic downturn, corporate travellers and buyers traded down to mid-priced hotel chains to alleviate costs. As the hotel industry has strengthened, luxury and upper upscale properties, as well as mid-priced establishments without food and beverage facilities, made dramatic comebacks, outstripping the average rate of US growth in hotels by some one and half times (Mintel, 2005). However, despite these positive developments, the corporate world is no longer so generous with travel expenditure as it was in the past, with cost savings and tight travel policies now being the order of the day and the hospitality sector must look to react accordingly.

Themed resorts

A themed resort is one that has a strong distinct identity, often one tied to some other place and time (Mancini, 2005). For example, the Venetian Resort Hotel in Las Vegas recreates the legendary elements of the city it takes its name from, by being equipped with canals and gondolas. Disneyland is the most famous themed resort and it creates different themes in the park, such as "The future", "Wild West" and "Snow White". The Disney hotel has become an important part of the Disney group. For example, there are two brands in Disney Resort Tokyo, the economic hotel brand – Ambassad or (www.disneyambassadorhotel.com) and Luxury hotel brand – Miracosta (www.hotelmiracosta.com). Children and adults can continue their Disney experience in the hotel after spending a whole day in the theme park.

Casino resorts

Casino resorts feature extensive gaming facilities in a destination where gambling is legal. Casino hotels are a huge growth area in the hospitality industry. Casino hotels are exemplified by the huge properties in the major

US gaming centres such as Las Vegas and Atlantic City. These hotels can have thousands of rooms and are accessories to the casino to which they are attached. For instance, the average size of Harrah's 23 casino hotels is 644 rooms, and the average space devoted to gaming areas is about 6,000 square metres. Most of their properties have convention centres too, which are very important for corporate customers. An important feature of casino hotel management is a detailed segmentation of the clientele, according to their gambling profiles (Mintel, 2003). Many different client profiles can be defined, separated into group and individual clients. Since the main profit generator is the gaming operation, the hotels can afford to be flexible with room rates, offering special discount to heavy gambling segments of their customer base. According to Harrah's market research, 27% of the US population gambles in casinos every year. In terms of age segmentation, the ageing "baby boomer" cohort, those in the 52–66-year-old age range, have an even higher participation rate at 31%. Also those in the above average income (over $95,000 per annum) group are also more likely to gamble (35%). In Britain, there has been a huge debate about giving the permission for Las Vegas style super casino hotels. According to the BBC news in July 2006, London, Glasgow, Newcastle and Sheffield were the top four cities in the competition to host the first mega casino hotel in Britain. In Asia, Macau and Singapore will be considered to be the main destinations with mega casino hotel. Especially Macau, where it was thought that it had the potential to overtake Las Vegas to be the number one Casino destination when we began this book and it has achieved that target by the time we are going to press!. This will be discussed further in Chapter 10.

Example: Macau to overtake Las Vegas Strip as world largest Casino market

Macau's booming economy, based primarily on gambling, is set to overtake the Las Vegas strip as the world's leading casino market by 2007, according to Globalysis, cited by Agence France-Presse (AFP). The company predicted that Macau would generate US$8 billion dollars by 2007, with more than US$20 billion currently committed to the construction of 25 new hotels and casinos over the next 5 years. However, Globalysis emphasized that the Special Administrative Region was still some way from eclipsing all of Las Vegas's hundreds of casinos, which brought in a total of US$9.1 billion dollars last year. The island's casino and gaming revenue is expected to be driven next year by substantial growth in non-casino amenities, in the form of new convention-centre venues and innovative entertainment facilities, which will be integrated into resorts to make the territory "a holistic leisure tourism destination". Most investments are to reportedly being directed at the Cotai Strip a gaming district currently being constructed by the Las Vegas Sands Corporation.

Massive US investment has helped to spur growth in the sector after the opening of the successful Sands Macau resort in 2004. The growth of the gambling sector has also been helped by the relaxation of travel restrictions on Chinese tourists, boosting visitor numbers to a record 18 million in 2005.
Source: World Markets Research Limited August 04, 2006.

■ Level 4: Self-esteem status

Resort hotels

Resort hotels accommodate primarily leisure customers. Traditionally resort hotels have been known in the British hotel market as those hotels located in seaside resorts such as Blackpool, Scarborough and Brighton. Such towns have been dominated by small independent hotels. The resort hotels discussed in this chapter cover a wide range of types of accommodation. Internationally they are generally found in following environments: tourism destinations, ski resorts, beaches and theme parks. A ski resort hotel usually has many facilities for recreational activities, such as swimming pools, pubs, tennis courts and a golf course. It normally includes dining facilities as well.

Increased leisure time, the growth of the short-break market and annual weekend breaks, the increased demands of the grey market, and a great interest in sport, health and fitness activities have all contributed to the new popularity of resort hotels (Jones, 2002). Low-cost airfares mean that the leisure travellers in developed countries can now take their main holiday overseas, in destinations where there are better weather conditions and lower prices. British tour operators recognize the need to fight the British climate and have therefore invested in large-scale all-weather facilities, such as "Center Parc's swimming paradise".

Check the website of Center Parc's (www.centerparcs.co.uk) and list the facilities and service Center Parc's provides. Compare it with a business hotel, such as Sheffield Hilton Hotel.   **ACTIVITY**

Chapter Case Study: Case: Rosewood Hotels & Resorts Seeks Global Growth

Dallas-based Rosewood Hotels & Resorts, the premier manager of ultra-luxury hotels and resorts throughout the world, announced the global expansion of its premier portfolio in June 2006. Dedicated to upholding the highest standards of service and offering guests one-of-a-kind amenities and experiences, Rosewood has announced plans to open, manage and build a host of new hotels and resorts around the world. The new properties will join Rosewood's present collection of 15 extraordinary hotels and resorts.

Internationally, Rosewood is building on the success of Las Ventanas al Paraíso, A Rosewood Resort in Los Cabos, Mexico and will open The Rosewood Mayakoba, in Mexico's Riviera Maya in 2007. The stunning resort will offer an earthly paradise of white sand beaches, 120 state-of-the-art over-water and lagoon-nestled suites, a world-class spa perched on its own island and a nearby championship Greg Norman-designed golf course. Rosewood is also building its third Saudi Arabian hotel, Corniche, A Rosewood Hotel, located in Jeddah, opening in late 2006. Joining Rosewood's renowned Middle Eastern properties, Hotel Al Faisaliah and Hotel Al Khozama, Corniche will offer spectacular views of the Red Sea, an incredible roof-top pool and an array of exceptional dining.

Rosewood's development pipeline is the strongest in its history and includes several world-class hotel projects in Telluride, Costa Rica, Tahiti, Barbados and Fiji.

Source: www.rosewoodhotels.com

■ Country resort hotels

Country resort hotels tend to be located outside main cities or in the country with extensive leisure facilities. They enjoy not only a peaceful rural atmosphere, but also provide extensive and often exclusive recreational and leisure facilities. Jones (2002) argues that they have a very clear profit

Plate 8
A different lake-side dining experience.
Source: Vonzerö
2005 bt.

motivation compared with the traditional country house hotel. Now international chains have moved into this sector and operate on a large scale. They could operate in a converted country house or purpose-built new buildings. To generate more income, these country resort hotels use their comprehensive facilities to appeal to different customers, attracting the business and conference markets as well as leisure travellers. For example, there are 11 Marriott Country Club Hotels in United Kingdom, each has its own swimming pool, gym, sauna, and a health and beauty salon. There are also 18-hole championship golf courses in some hotels.

We would also stress that the categorization of need satisfaction is not an equivalence of price.

There are many restaurants around Lake Balaton offering excellent dining experiences, such as this one at Tihany. They are a far more expensive and exclusive offer than the beach bars and bufés that we pictured earlier!

■ Level 5: Self-actualization

Boutique hotels

It is generally accepted that boutique hotels date from 1981 with the opening of the first two properties: Anouska Hempel's The Blakes Hotel in South Kensington and The Bedford in Union Square, San Francisco, which was to become the first in a series of 35 hotels operated by the Kimpton Group. Boutique hotels are a mysterious segment of the accommodation industry but also one of its sexiest (Sangster, 2002). Various names are bandied about such as boutique, townhouse or design-led. There are no commonly understood definitions and when dealing with this type of offer the normal star ratings, the traditional yardstick of the industry, appears to have little meaning.

Boutique hotels attempt to offer the guest an alternative to the standardized international hotel chain brand formats which have increasingly dominated the hotel business since the 1970s. Boutique hotels differentiate themselves through architecture and design, which seek to create an intimate and distinctive atmosphere (Mintel, 2003). Personalized service is another hallmark of the boutique format. Customers are addressed by name and some hotels make an effort to anticipate guests' special needs, for example supplying the room with their favourite drinks and snack foods on arrival and prepare their favourite music.

It looks that boutique hotels do have a bright future in the long term. According to Sangster (2002), there are two important factors which are likely to support growth of the boutique segment. Firstly, the Internet is facilitating access to boutiques. Rather than depending on traditional channels for accommodation information and booking, such as travel agents and global distribution systems (GDS), customers can search hotel properties themselves if they want to. Secondly, big hotel companies are themselves opening boutiques. Starwood, Rezidor and Park Plaza have already started their business in this niche market. Other operators entering the field include the Hilton Group with the opening of its Trafalgar in London and Marriott International through its joint venture with jeweller Bulgari.

Example: Kimpton Hotels announce the launch of Global Business Programme

Founded by Bill Kimpton in 1981, San Francisco-based Kimpton Hotels & Restaurants is a unique collection of boutique hotels coupled with chef-driven, destination restaurants. While all Kimpton Hotels are thoughtfully appointed and managed to help guests maintain and enrich their lifestyles on the road, each is individually designed to reflect the energy, personality and pulse of its distinct location, history and architectural style. Featuring highly personalized guest services, comforting in-room amenities, and one-of-a-kind specialty rooms and suites, Kimpton Hotels provide travellers with welcoming atmospheres that embrace its signature elements of care, comfort, style, flavour and fun. Kimpton takes pride in its social responsibility, supporting select like-minded partners and is a leader in ecological practices. Kimpton currently operates 39 boutique hotels with restaurants throughout the United States and Canada. This includes 70 park avenue hotel, the first Kimpton in New York City, Hotel Solamar in San Diego, the renovation and relaunch of Mayfair Hotel & Spa in Coconut Grove, Miami and the newly acquired Caleo Resort & Spa in Scottsdale, Arizona. Kimpton will debut the Hotel Palomar, Washington DC in mid-2006 and the Hotel Palomar, Dallas in June 2006. Several additional projects are currently underway in New York, Texas, Florida and Virginia.

In May 2006, Kimpton Hotels announces the launch of its Kimpton Global Business(TM) Programme, an innovative programme geared towards acknowledging smaller- and mid-sized companies, associations and clubs, with specialty rates and exclusive benefits typically reserved for large-scale corporations. Membership in the Kimpton Global Business(TM) Programme is free of hassles, negotiations, contracts and volume caps. As a member of the programme, companies receive exclusive rates at all Kimpton Hotels, starting at 10% off the best available rate, 7 days a week. Additionally, guests enjoy signature Kimpton Hotels' amenities and services, such as complimentary Internet access and a late checkout (subject to availability), all without any membership fees. Rates and amenities are available across the Kimpton brand and will be offered to members at all hotels as Kimpton expands nationwide.

Source: www.kimptonhotels.com

If you doubted that the food service sector could contribute to self-actualization, we would ask you to read through the following two examples. The first comes from a press release:

El Bulli is voted best restaurant in world – again

11 April 2006

BARCELONA – El Bulli, the haute cuisine eaterie run by chef Ferran Adriá, has been voted the best restaurant in the world again.

An international jury, selected by the British magazine Restaurant, said El Bulli was the best place to eat on the planet for the second time.

El Bulli, which only has 50 places and is permanently booked out with up to 400,000 applications for a place from all over the world each year, was opened in 1981 at Roses, near Girona in Catalonia.

Adriá says of El Bulli: "It is not a restaurant, it is place for investigation."

For the Catalan chef, the restaurant is a way of "seeing how far we can take cooking".

The restaurant is only open for 6 months of the year and an average meal costs from €150.

Adriá said one way to reduce demand would be to raise the price to €1,000 per person.

But this would be against his principles because he does not want haute cuisine to be considered elitist.

Adriá has worked with 20 charities to spread the use of haute cuisine ingredients to the Third World.

He says he only gets angry when he is attacked for charging €200 per meal while people are starving in the world.

Adriá, who, has been awarded three Michelin stars, spends 6 months of the year dreaming up new recipes at his "laboratory" in Barcelona.

Source: EFE with expatriots www.expatica.com/

But even that is not as convincing to us as the second example and we make no apology for the disappointments that you will experience when you dine anywhere that offers less of an opportunity to self-actualize than our final example.

Example: Lunch at the world's best restaurant

We would urge you to read the full review of a visit to the Fat Duck in Bray in May 2006 (www.in.rediff.com/news/2006/may/29spec.htm).

It was enough to make us feel we had been there as the reviewer lovingly recounts the delights of eating in the best restaurant in the world. It is not just a meal but a phenomenon. Heston Blumenthal was not just a chef but a "culinary alchemist" producing miracles in the kitchen and the restaurant. Our summary cannot do justice to the passion evoked by the writer as he describes the tastes and textures of this ultimate eating experience. As the reviewer salivates … "Besides that are the wonder, awe and drama of its creation. Blumenthal has set the stage for the next 3.5 hours of delight, intense flavour, surprise and sheer joy." Read the review and we guarantee you will want to understand how liquid nitrogen at minus 193 degrees Celsius, a smoking silver flask, a silver bucket and a silver pump-type foam dispenser combine into a tea infusion with lime and vodka mousse!

This is what Maslow was thinking about when he talked about self-actualization both for the chef and the diner!

■ Limitations to the framework

We have used the above analysis to introduce some of the range of provision in our industry in a relatively unconventional and we believe interesting manner. What we have to acknowledge is that the adaptation of Maslow's hierarchy of need does have certain limitations. We would like to address two of them now. Firstly, our presentation cannot handle categories which are multifaceted. We were on safe ground using categories which were clearly defined and narrowly delimited, such as boutique hotels. However other categories have been created that are broad and all encompassing, such as the small establishments clustered together as Small Hotels, B&Bs and guest houses. These can cover the whole spectrum of properties from those offering shelter to social security claimants to magnificent individual properties, providing a service and an experience to challenge the five star. Secondly, we consider other forms of accommodation which are also multifaceted and which do not fit easily into the grid, such as serviced accommodation, Suite hotels and timeshare developments. Finally, we have to acknowledge that the framework cannot respond rapidly to change in the markets and we have relied upon the historically built sense of the category in making our decisions about where to locate various types of offer. However we recognize that our industry is subject to rapid change and would seek to explore this with a brief examination of the cruise sector. Traditionally this was seen as very exclusive, staking a claim for level 3 social or level 4 esteem rankings, but recent changes have challenged this image as we shall see and the nature of the offer has shifted (Figure 3.3).

Maslow's hierarchy	Food service	Accommodation	
5	The world's best restaurant	Boutique hotels	Self-actualization
4	Leading restaurants	Resort hotels	Status privilege
3	Themed restaurants	Business hotels	Belonging
2	Chain restaurants	Airport hotels	Security
1	Fast foods Roadside catering	Budget hotels	Shelter and sustenance

Figure 3.3
Applying Maslow's hierarchy to the hospitality industry

■ Small hotels, B&Bs and guest houses

Although most industry and academic research focuses on the multi MNE, SME constitute the backbone of the international hotel industry. SMEs are generally defined in terms of the number of employees, with small enterprises having between 10 and 49, and medium, between 50 and 249 employees. In Europe, in general, and in Switzerland in particular practically all individual hotel units could be considered as SMEs by the above definition. Most chain hotels under franchise or management contract are still in reality SMEs to the extent that they represent individually owned units (Mintel, 2001). There are almost twice the number of SMEs in tourism (22.5%) as compared to the European average among all business enterprises (13%). More than 6% of the GDP of the EU is derived from tourism. Within the sector, the hotel, restaurant and café sector is the largest single component, generating more than 50% of all tourism turnover and employing more than 6 million people or 4% of all employment in Europe. The great majority of SMEs could be characterized as micro-enterprises employing less than 10 people.

There has been a growing awareness of the role of SMEs in the economy in recent years, which has resulted in a number of studies as to how governments could help in their creation and management. The European hotel industry is highly fragmented, and the hotel stock is often older and smaller than in North America and Asia Pacific. Small hotels typically lack resources and advanced management and marketing skills, particularly in inherited, family run businesses. According to Mintel (2001), this situation is further exacerbated by a lack of opportunities for economies of scale, both from the marketing/distribution point of view, as well as from the operating expenses side. Although technology could be seen as widening the gap between the small independent hotels and the multi-nationals, it could also ultimately help the smaller operators to access a far wider range of distribution, purchasing and financial management possibilities than before.

In general, it is difficult to be optimistic about the future competitive position of SMEs with less than 50 rooms and which are neither affiliated nor particularly well located. They will find it difficult to attract the customers, while at the same time they will need to find the investment to maintain their position, which will be difficult unless they can focus on some special niche for themselves, with a unique identity.

■ Other accommodation sectors

Suite hotels

Suite or all-suite hotels are designed to serve individual business or leisure travellers. Hence, a distinguishing feature is a reduced common area (i.e. restaurant, lounge, meeting rooms and lobby areas), which allows more space to be allocated to the guestrooms. Thus, the individual units usually include a sleeping area and a separate living room space, which typically contains armchairs, a coffee table, a dining table, TV and a couch convertible into a bed. Most offer a kitchen with at least a microwave oven and a small refrigerator. The bedrooms are smaller than standard hotel rooms, but have the same furnishings.

Serviced apartments

Serviced apartments or "extended stay" accommodation, as they are called in America, are a relatively new addition to the hospitality sector. These lodging facilities are designed for the guest whose stay is counted in weeks or months rather than days, as is the case for a traditional hotel. Typically, where the primary focus is on the business traveller, a property typically consists of one-bedroom units and studios. Each unit has a small kitchen, bathroom and living area. Serviced apartments need not be located in a central or prime position as would be the case for a full-service hotel. Nevertheless, proximity to central business districts, business parks, or at least transport connections is generally desirable given the primarily business traveller orientation of such establishments.

The concept was first developed in the United States in the early 1980s when Marriott introduced its Residence Inn brand which dominated the market for years thereafter. It was only in the mid-1990s; however, that growth in the segment accelerated to a rapid pace. According to STR, room capacity in the United States quadrupled between 1994 and 1999.

Timeshare

Timeshare or "interval ownership", as some developers prefer to call it, has been without a doubt the fastest growing segment of tourist accommodation in the world for the last two decades. Starting from a base of $965 million in worldwide sales in 1981, total unit sales reached $9.4 billion in 2002, which represents an annualized growth rate of 11%. North America accounted for $5.4 billion of sales, with Europe and Latin America making up most of the rest. The number of resorts has mushroomed from 631 20 years ago to some 5,425 with 325,000 units, as the number of interval owners has expanded from 230,000 to 6.7 million, who own some 10.7 million weeks of timeshare accommodation. Currently, about 1,700 resorts (31%) are located in North America and 25% in Europe, although due to the larger average resort size (80 units per resort, as opposed to a worldwide average of 60), 41% of all accommodation units are found in North America.

The basic timeshare product consists of the right to inhabit a resort apartment, villa, chalet or bungalow for a week every year. Timeshares have an average duration of about 40 years, although some are for perpetuity. Such rights are usually transmissible to heirs. Thus each timeshare property is divided into 52-week-long tranches, although typically some of the weeks are not sold, either for seasonal reasons, or to allow for a maintenance period during the year. The classic product consists of a fixed week every year. However, greater flexibility has become the rule and timeshare promoters increasingly offer a floating week within a season, or operate on a points-based system. In fact, points-based systems have continually gained acceptance and now account for 43% of all purchases from developers in the United States. Normally, a timeshare resort will segment its offer into three different seasons, high, low and shoulder, and the weekly units will be priced accordingly. Globally, the average price of a timeshare unit in 2002 was $10,600 per week-long unit.

Timeshare resorts are for the most part located in warm climates that have a minimum of seasonal variation, thus rendering a maximum number of weeks in the year attractive to timeshare purchasers. Therefore, it is not difficult to understand why the bulk of North American resort capacity is to be found in Florida (636 resorts), California (125 resorts) and South Carolina (119 resorts). In Europe, the number one location is Spain, especially the Canary Islands, which have an even, year-round temperature. Attractions and entertainments are the number one drawn for American timeshare purchasers, cited by 56% of survey respondents. Indeed, Orlando, home to Disney World and the Epcot Center, can rightly be labelled the capital of timeshare in the United States. Ocean beach and mountains are also high up on the list cited by 47% and 29% of respondents respectively. In Europe, the profile is similar, but the order is reversed with beach being cited by 59% and attractions/entertainment by 36%. Mountains are in the fourth place after history and culture cited by 26% and 29% of respondents respectively. The seasonality of Alpine locations, however, has proved a stumbling block for development of the concept in Switzerland or Austria.

From the point of view of seasonality, urban timeshare would seem an attractive possibility. Although a few units do exist such as Marriott's Boston, Paris and Mayfair properties, the concept has never really taken off due to the stiff competition from other profitable uses (office space, luxury apartments, full-service hotels) of prime central locations in major cities.

Timeshare owners in a mixed hotel/timeshare resort are generally good customers for the hotel's bars and restaurants, as well as any other service or leisure activities offered by the hotel such as fitness, golf, tennis, boating, horseback riding, spas, etc. Market research has demonstrated that timeshare guests are psychologically prepared to spend money on additional activities and meals, because their lodging is by definition already paid for when they depart on their holiday. Indeed, the average timeshare visitor party in the United States in 2002 spent $1,459 on bars and restaurants, $447 on entertainment and sports activities, $253 on sightseeing tours and $217 on gambling. In Europe the equivalent figures were somewhat lower but still significant at €464 on food and beverage, €53 on entertainment and sports and €60 on sightseeing tours.

There are also synergies in terms of operating costs. Once in operation, timeshare units require most of the same services as the rooms division of a hotel. A front desk is necessary to receive arriving guests and to distribute keys. Housekeeping services are also needed, at least once a week on the changeover day, although some resorts offer maid service 6 to 7 days a week. Another source of revenue for the hotel operator is maintenance fees, which are levied on a yearly basis to the timeshare unit holders to defray the cost of cleaning and upkeep. A difference between hotel-managed timeshare properties and those sold by independent developers is that the hotel company's property management infrastructure usually remains in place post-sale, whereas in the latter case, the promoter typically retires from the scene once the project is sold and a residents' association takes over the task of assuring cleaning and maintenance. Indeed, this situation can also lead to customer disappointments, since independent developers might keep maintenance charges artificially low, whilst selling off the units, leaving them to rise significantly once the owners' association takes over. Marriott realises about 10% of its timeshare-related revenues from maintenance fees.

Marriott's timeshare sales passed the $1 billion mark for the first in 2001, and rose by 20% in 2002 to $1.2 billion which means that the hotel group accounts for almost 13% of total industry-wide sales. Indeed, 32% of the firm's operating income in 2002 was generated by timeshare activity, which has proved far more resilient in the current economic and political climate than the traditional hotel business.

Most other upscale North American hotel chains have followed in Marriott's footsteps by entering the timeshare business, but usually with a lag of at least 8 years. Hilton's Grand Vacations Company timeshare product dates from 1992, and embodies many of the same features as that of Marriott. Purchasers of timeshares are awarded an annual allotment of HGVC points which can be used to purchase cruises, air travel or stays in the 2,400 Hilton hotels worldwide, which include those of Hilton Group, the British-owned entity which has worldwide rights to the Hilton brand outside of the United States. Hilton has developed seven resorts, two in Orlando, three in Las Vegas and one each in Hawaii and Miami, which it markets as timeshare properties. Hyatt entered the timeshare business in 1994 and has just opened its 10th resort, the Hyatt Pinon Point in Sedona, Arizona, famous for its red rocks. The Four Seasons offers interval ownership in its four "Residence Clubs", but has also developed "Private Residences", that is to say they offer vacation properties for sale. Cendant, the leading hotel franchiser in the world, whose activities extend to car rental (Avis) and real estate brokerage (Century 21) has committed substantial resources to the timeshare business.

Timeshare has developed outside the United States, but at a slower pace. In Europe the sector encounters several obstacles beginning with the bad reputation the business acquired in the 1970s and 1980s.

■ Condo hotels

Condominium hotels represent an increasingly popular way of financing lodging developments, and the sector has experienced explosive growth in the past few years, especially in the United States (Mintel, 2006). Strictly speaking, a condo hotel is a property with units (apartments or guestrooms) that are managed centrally, like any other type of hotel. The difference is that, these units are owned by individual investors. The concept originated in Europe in the late 1950s, and then travelled to the United States. Now condo hotels are making a reappearance in Europe, as well as in the Caribbean. The condo hotel idea is gaining momentum due to declining hotel investment returns, and rising residential real estate prices. Especially prominent in prime resort areas and major cities, condo hotels combine investment features with those of second homes.

Condo units may or may not be operated by a major chain, although the current trend is towards branding by major upscale to luxury brands such as Fairmont, Sheraton, Trump International Hotel & Resorts, Four Seasons, Ritz Carlton, Kempinski, etc. Also, condo owners may or may not be restricted as to their individual use of the property. Marketing activities in the United States, where most condo hotel development has occurred so far, are severely restricted by SEC (Securities Exchange Commission) regulations. Condo hotel management contracts (between developers and hotel chains) may differ significantly from those involving traditional hotel properties.

The development of condo hotels have given the chains a new supply of properties with which to expand their brands and to generate fees from the management and franchising of the operations. In the past, management companies have been the developer or a group directly related to the developer. However, increasingly, the management company is a third-party hotel operator, such as Fairmont, Westin, Hyatt or Four Seasons, amongst others, which the developer and unit owners agree should manage the guestrooms and facilities for unit owners (such as F&B outlets, recreational amenities and meeting space). The industry is currently shifting its management strategy towards the outright sale of the hotel management opportunity to nationally affiliated hotel companies, operating these properties similarly to that of a conventional hotel operation. The chains may also earn additional fees from renting out the units placed in the hotel rental management programme and for managing various condos. They may even participate in royalty fees, derived from licensing their names to the condominiums, and collect a percentage of the sales price of units sold.

These markets are varied and appeal to a variety of motivations from both the business and the leisure traveller.

Cruises: re-establishing and repositioning

According to the Seatrade report, 25 million people will be taking cruises annually by 2015 (Travel Trade Gazette, 2006) which makes this a significant sector in the industry but it is one which has traditionally received little attention (Table 3.4).

Table 3.4 Worldwide cruise supply/demand real/projected to 2015

Year end	Berths	% increase	Passengers	% growth
2006	368,000	5.7	14,329,000	4.5
2007	395,000	7.3	15,260,000	6.5
2008	415,000	5.1	16,023,000	5.0
2009	438,000	5.6	17,064,000	6.5
2010	460,000	5.0	18,173,000	6.5
2011	487,000	5.9	19,263,000	6.0
2012	517,000	6.2	20,400,000	5.9
2013	549,000	6.2	21,582,000	5.8
2014	579,000	5.5	22,661,000	5.0
2015	614,000	6.0	23,839,000	5.2

Note: there is allowance here for loss of berths through service withdrawals/scrapping.
Source: Mintel/TTI 2005.

It is only a conservative estimate to suggest that the last 5 years of the decade (to 2009) will produce more than 90,000 new berths. With most new ships now averaging 3,000 total berths, just 8 ships a year means 24,000 extra berths, and history suggests that industry demand will increase at approximately the same rate as capacity.

At the beginning of 2000, projections for the industry suggested there would be nearly 20 million worldwide passengers annually by 2010. In the immediate aftermath of 9/11, projections were revised downwards to just 17.25 million. There were many, both inside and outside the industry, who said that even this was far too bullish. Yet, despite the problems that have followed with wars on terrorism, and the situation in Iraq, Mintel revised those estimates upwards to more than 18 million by 2010, with the 20-million mark reached in 2012.

Beyond 2015, there is the prospect of even greater emphasis on building ships of increasingly large capacities if the Panama Canal goes ahead with its plan to widen its locks, and so increase the Panama limit.

■ Main markets

North America remains the number one source market and continues to show impressive growth. In 2004, there was an 11.1% rise to more than 9.1 million. In fact, in the 3 years since 2001 – generally accepted as being the most difficult in the history of the cruise industry – numbers have grown by nearly one-third (32%).

It is a similar situation in the United Kingdom, where numbers for ocean cruising rose by nearly 7% to top 1 million (1.03 million) for the first time in 2004, although, if river cruise passengers are included, it went above 1 million in 2003. This meant that the number of ocean cruise passengers had doubled in 7 years, and quadrupled in 10 years.

It has also meant a steady increase in cruising's share of the overall outbound tourism sector in the United Kingdom, especially as it has coincided with the recent decline in the package holiday market. Cruising's share of the UK's inclusive tour market has nearly trebled in 10 years, with 2004 showing a substantial increase to 5.2% from 2003s 4.9%.

The largest single market in Europe, Germany, maintained its recent healthy growth but the largest advance was made by Italy, which added 13% more passengers. This occurred despite the loss of Festival, for which Italy was the major market, underlining the rapid expansion of Carnival-owned Costa Cruises as well as the emergence of Mediterranean Shipping Company's (MSC) Cruises. Owned by the cash-rich Mediterranean Shipping Co, MSC is just as ambitious as Festival. However, unlike Festival, MSC has the financial resources to achieve its aim of becoming the industry's fourth major player.

Although Spain's rapid growth appeared to stall in 2004, this was a statistical anomaly as the new Spanish cruise lines, which have fuelled its recent rapid growth, are continuing to add capacity.

Elsewhere, Asia cruise numbers fell again as the main player, Star Cruises, reduced capacity. A resurgence is expected from 2006 as Star Cruises grows again and a Carnival brand for Asia is expected to emerge. There are signs of growth in the nascent Indian and Chinese cruise markets, too.

Australia's passenger numbers are growing through a combination of home grown and international products, whilst Dubai's substantial investment to attract ships to its homeport appears to be on the point of finally paying off with several lines close to deciding on an Arabian Gulf programme.

The two leading cruise companies generated US$14.3 billion of revenue in 2004, suggesting the value of the worldwide industry is now more than US$19 billion. This is because, between them, Carnival Corporation and Royal Caribbean Cruises (RCC) carried nearly three quarters (9.7 million) of the world's 13.4 million passengers.

Their combined profits also reached record proportions – at more than US$2.3 billion – as yields through the industry arrested the decline that had set in since they peaked in 1999/2000 – a decline that had been exacerbated by 9/11 and the war in Iraq. With yields improving once more in 2005, record profitability is again predicted.

There was an 8.4% increase in worldwide cruise passengers in 2004 and, although there has been some slowdown in new ship ordering, which will slow passenger growth in 2005/06, capacity increases will start to accelerate again from 2007.

■ The changing offer and market

The trend which 9/11 stimulated for US-based cruise lines to increase their ex-North American port sailings continued in 2004. Known generically now as "homeland cruising", its impact can be gauged from one statistic: in 2004, 90% of CLIA member lines' 10.5 million passengers embarked their cruise at a North American port, compared with about 70% in 2002. It has also had several key side effects, notably the emergence of many more homeports as non-cruise ports and their surrounding communities recognizing the potential economic impact of attracting this growth sector of tourism. These have generally developed around the Gulf of Mexico in states like (northern) Florida, Texas, Louisiana and Alabama.

Homeland cruising has also helped turn Mexico into the world's most popular country cruise destination, with 7.6 million visits in 2004 (+15%) and the Mexican port, Cozumel, into the most popular cruise port of call, with 2.9 million visits (+7%). Mexico's cruise visitor numbers have doubled since 2001.

There was also an initial impact on destinations away from North America, with the Mediterranean (2002/03) and then Northern Europe/ Scandinavia (2004) seeing their share of worldwide capacity drop.

Although homeland cruising appears here to stay, the lines now recognize it as a new business generator as it brings the cruise product within range of a broader public, both geographically and socio-economically. They are now simultaneously returning more ships to the Mediterranean and Northern Europe in their new policy – delayed by 9/11 – of sourcing more business from emerging source markets in Europe.

Then we have to consider the impact of new players in the sector, with the questions remaining as to what the offer and the target markets will be. The first is likely to be more traditional than the second example.

Example: Disney Cruise Line to sail Europe in 2007!

Summer 2007, a big time in Europe as Disneyland Resort Paris turns 15!

But wait! What is this? For the first time ever the Disney Cruise line will be sailing the Mediterranean Sea! 10- and 11-day cruises aboard the *Disney Magic* will depart from Barcelona, Spain. Also Disney is offering two 14-day trans-Atlantic cruises.

Carnival Freedom will debut in March 2007 with new 12-day cruises that include Carnival Cruise Lines' first visit to the Greek Isles and Turkey, as well as extended calls at a variety of Mediterranean ports.

Example: EasyCruise to add two new vessels

EasyCruise has signed a letter of intent with Greek shipbuilder Neorion Holdings for two 500-passenger ships and an option for a further two.

Source: Travel Weekly 12-05-2006.

It is also possible to examine other sectors that would only be subject to definition if the context in which they were operating could be established as the services and products they offer will be determined by their relations with other providers. We are here thinking of contract catering which could prove to be one of the major expansion opportunities in the future. The contract catering market has seen numerous changes, with the focus now shifted upon developing more commercialized and retail inspired concepts. This market is in the midst of consolidation. Although there are only a handful of very large companies in the contract catering business there are a plethora of small-to medium-sized businesses. The size of a business is therefore quite easily and radically altered by the acquisition of one or two large contracts.

Furthermore gains can be made by merging or purchasing similarly sized rivals. Companies have therefore not only been taken over by the giants of the business but by medium-sized operators seeking to gain scale. Over the past year there have been a number of changes of ownership namely the acquisition of Caterlink by Wilson Storey Halliday and on a larger scale the acquisition of the Eaton Group by ISS, Everson Hewitt by Compass and Catering Alliance by Aramark.

The business and industry sector is by far the largest sector of the contract catering market despite the fact that it has not been growing as fast as other sectors in recent years. In-store catering has been steadily expanding for some time, fuelled both by the growth in outlets and by the consumer's increasing desire for casual dining. Historically confined to supermarkets and departments stores, there is now a diverse range of retail outlets offering in-store outlets. However contracts are very important in health care. The National Health Service (NHS) in the United Kingdom alone serves 700,000 meals a day or 300 million per annum at a cost of £500 million across 300 NHS trusts and 1,200 hospitals. Contract caterers serve approximately 4.7% of hospital outlets and only around 14% of meals so there is still considerable scope for growth.

Attitudes and behaviour with regard to eating out on the high street are also being identified within the contract catering sector. Often contract caterers are competing with high street rivals especially in the business and educational sectors. Shorter lunch breaks curb the propensity to sit down for a hot cooked meal and eating patterns are now intermittent and no longer fixed to specific periods. Snacking and on the go have become the norm amongst the UK's workforce. Contract caterers have had to adapt their offering to be available often throughout the day and to offer quick and filling snacks in preference to plated meals.

The provision of such an offer has called for a rethink not only in menu items but in the staffing and equipment requirements as well. Initially the loss of sales from a higher value main meal could have caused concern but the cost savings and better volumes from delivering what the customer wants has helped some contracts become more profitable.

There is still considerable potential for further growth within the contract catering industry, particularly for larger caterers. In many sectors of the market, most notably the public sector, contract caterers only make up a small proportion of the overall food service operators within the sector.

With changes in local authority and government procurement practices there has been considerable scope for development within sectors such as education, the prison service and other areas of public catering yet the majority of supply is still through direct service organizations (DSO). Public sector contracts often require substantial investment in equipment or infrastructure and hence only the bigger players will benefit from this opportunity.

■ Conclusion

This chapter provides an overview of the international hospitality industry and enables students to gain an appreciation of the changing nature of the industry. We have presented the components of the international hospitality industry in terms of the sectors and what they seem to offer to the market. The new features such as international chaining, niche products development and multiple brands play an important role in the industry's evolution and it is clear that the international hospitality industry is moving from being characterized as a fragmented industry towards appearing as a consolidated industry.

In this chapter, we have explained:

- Definition of hospitality industry and its latest changes.
- The structure of international hospitality.
- Accommodation sector, including business hotel, resort hotel, budget hotel, boutique hotel, timeshare, etc.
- Food service sector, including restaurant, fast food, hotel catering and contract catering.
- Other hospitality business sectors, such as cruise lines and contract catering.

This is more that a traditional description as it attempts to offer an analysis of both motivation and market that you would not find elsewhere.

In Chapter 4 we will address the techniques for exploring the operating environment in the industry and will further unpack some of the sectors we have considered in this overview.

■ Review questions

1 Do you think that satisfying needs is an appropriate basis on which to catalogue the international hospitality industry?
2 Can you draw up a map of the range of the international hospitality offer that is comprehensive and meaningful? Explore the difficulties in undertaking such a task.
3 How would the different offers be seen in different cultures? Explain the differences with at least two examples.
4 Do you think the traditional cruise operations will feel threatened by the introduction of new competitors such as Easycruise? Please explain your reasons.

CHAPTER 4

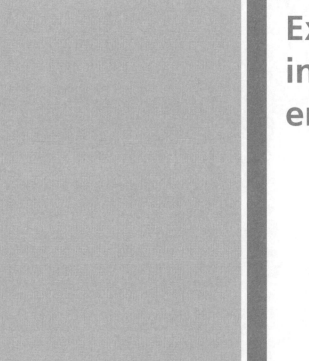

Exploring the international environment

After working through this chapter, you should be able to:

- Chart the international operating environment of hospitality organizations
- Undertake situational analyses of the internal environment of companies
- Undertake PEST analyses of the external environment
- Recognize and understand the critical issues and trends in hospitality industry that are likely to impact on the future of hospitality

■ Introduction

This chapter introduces you to the ideas of exploring and assessing the wider environment in which organizations operate. We are concerned to explore the play of resisting and supporting forces that can be found and suggest two techniques for identifying them accurately. Without accurate identification, the rest of the management function would be flawed and recommendations based upon inadequate data. We make no apology for presenting the two most popular techniques for you to consider, partly because they are the ones you will come across most frequently when you look at the industry and partly because they perform their job very well. We will highlight some thoughts about their future prospects and what may affect the industry's development over the next decade will be identified and discussed. Having considered the structures of the international hospitality industry, we will also focus on the environment in which those organizations operate. This means looking at the conditions behind the companies and the factors which influence their performance and set the context for their decisions. This will mean considering a number of factors and looking at examples of the way these factors can impact on future developments. You will be introduced to two models that allow you to explore the working environment of a company, both internally and externally.

■ External environment analysis

The reasons for wanting to undertake analysis of the operating environment should be fairly clear if you have followed the arguments in the previous chapters. For readers joining us at this point, we can summarize the major arguments for looking at the external environment in the following points:

- International hospitality operates in an environment of constant change and often these changing forces are completely beyond the control of the destination.
- Events in neighbouring countries, other regions or even worldwide can have profound effects on the level and nature of tourism demand.

- It is crucial to anticipate threats and attempt to minimize them, and identify opportunities and capitalize on them through the use of available resources (destination strengths).
- A situational analysis is the process of combining internal examination (resource analysis) and external information gathering (environmental analysis), and this is usually conducted along the lines of a SWOT analysis, which examines the strengths, weaknesses, opportunities and threats pertaining to any product (Kelly and Nankervis, 2001).
- Planning strategically and managing proactively in such an environment is daunting but necessary.

■ Situational analysis

Any planning relies upon accurate and thoughtful analysis of both the current state of the environment and the desired future state, that which the organization is aiming to achieve. Without understanding the forces at work in the environment, any planning or decision-making is at best guess work. We would also argue that understanding the complexity of the international hospitality environment is important in shaping the direction of the organization. Moreover we would argue that standing still is almost never an option that leads to strategic success as perhaps this example demonstrates. Examine the following example and note the problems that would be encountered by stasis.

Example: The ethnic sector is the most vulnerable to changes

Although there are some operators within the ethnic sector (most notably the Indian food sector) who have developed their offer, it is generally the lack of dynamism within this area that has seen its share being eroded. Intensifying competition means that the ethnic sector will continue to lag behind if key changes are not initiated. Meanwhile, this sector faces a clear challenge from the ready meal sector, which now boasts an array of ethnic options. Multiple grocers are attempting to emulate the take-away experience by packaging their products in a similar manner to that traditionally found on the high street.

This is one of the most popular aspects of the food service industry in the United Kingdom and strongly based on the entrepreneurial activities of small businesses, the sector still finds itself threatened by changes in the market and the competitive environment. The wide range of these threats underlines the importance of undertaking analysis and being open to the consideration of issues which may traditionally have been out with the scope of the core business. Here, for example, restaurateurs will have to consider the challenges from within the retail food sector.

The most common of all approaches to the analysis of the competitive environment is what is usually referred to as the SWOT analysis, although some people call it TOWS – which is exactly the same thing but with the elements in a different order!

SWOT stands for Strengths, Weaknesses, Opportunities and Threats and should be compiled for a specific organization at a given point in time as changes in the environment may change the content of the SWOT. It is often described as a snap shot of a particular moment and this accurately captures the static nature of the analysis offered through a SWOT. The strengths and weaknesses come from the consideration of the internal position of the organization with opportunities and threats coming from a consideration of the external environment. One of the most important distinctions between strengths and weaknesses and the opportunities and threats is the degree of control that managers within an organization can have over them. Strengths and weaknesses derive from internal conditions and therefore, theoretically at least, are within the control of the organization managers. For instance, if the analysis reveals that there is a skills gap in the organization then the problem can be addressed immediately by the management. However if the threat to the organization comes from the prospect of international terrorist attack then the response of local managers may only go part of the way to presenting a solution to the problem. Addressing internal security measures may seem to address the threat but will not deal with the root causes of the threat which will remain even if the likely impact has been reduced (Figure 4.1).

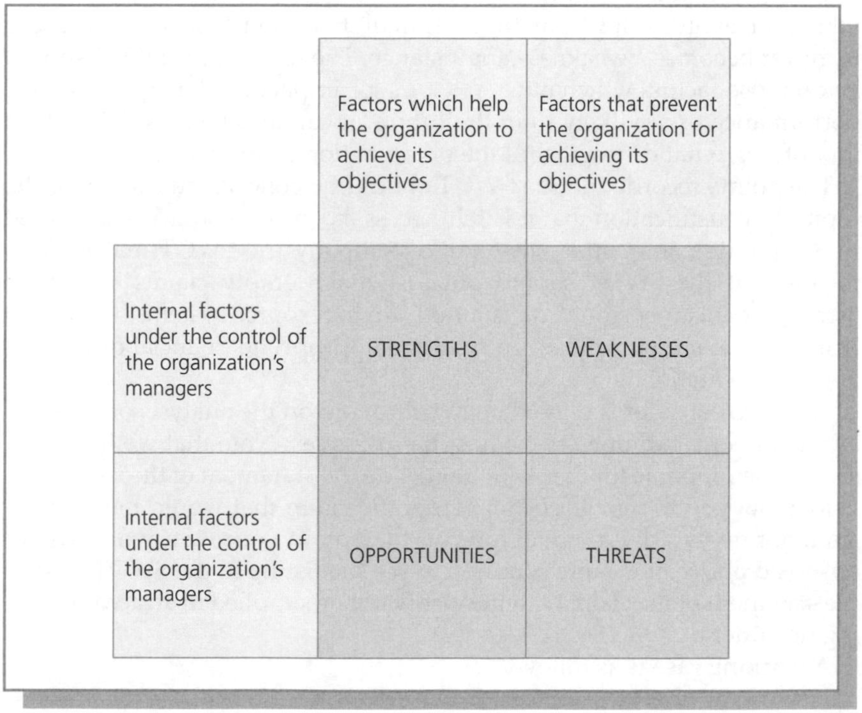

	Factors which help the organization to achieve its objectives	Factors that prevent the organization for achieving its objectives
Internal factors under the control of the organization's managers	STRENGTHS	WEAKNESSES
Internal factors under the control of the organization's managers	OPPORTUNITIES	THREATS

Figure 4.1
Building a SWOT analysis

You may notice some similarities here with the idea of enabling and resisting forces that we identified in the model for this book. In traditional approaches to SWOT these are characterized as helping or preventing an organization but we would encourage you to think about the wider constructions and include cultural factors in developing your approach to SWOT analyses.

The value of the SWOT will only ever be as high as the quality of the data and opinions collected to complete it. Asking an organization about its own performance is subject to the problems of interpretation – some managers are naturally optimistic and err on the side of exaggeration whilst others are more pessimistic and underestimate the situation. Both errors impact on the validity of the SWOT and every effort must be made to check the data that you are using are reliable. We were commissioned to compile a SWOT for a city in the United Kingdom where the responses indicated that the floral displays in the city were either a strength or a weakness. The opinions of the respondents were based on the assessment of the same flowers – but were interpreted differently because of their expectation levels. It is also not impossible for them both to be correct assessments – the floral displays could be very good but at the same time they could be improved. In looking at the SWOT it is worth considering whether some of the points overlap or repeat issues raised already – combining them makes the SWOT easier to read and may give a clearer impression of the priority that should be given to the issue.

There should be a clear point in undertaking the analysis – assessing strengths and weaknesses and opportunities and threats are relative judgements and the point of comparison has to be clear for those undertaking the analysis. It is sometimes difficult to establish at what level staff turnover becomes a weakness, for instance. The focus of the SWOT should be on those factors which have had a major impact on the organization's performance or are likely to in the future. It can also be a useful tool for identifying what distinguishes the organization from others.

The points recorded in the SWOT should be concise indications of the topic. Any justification that it is felt necessary to add should be provided in a separate commentary that can accompany the SWOT matrix. This means that the SWOT should not just make empty claims – such as "strong financial position" or "sound human resource systems" – without being able to support the claim from the appropriate financial or personnel documentation.

A case to consider is offered below, drawing on the analysis of a destination but concentrating on the hospitality issues. Note that we have presented the rationale for the claim alongside the statement of the issue. This is to allow you to see the sort of evidential claim that would merit inclusion, not necessarily a model for you to copy in your own work. As we observed above, it is more common to see the listing in the SWOT as simple statement of the claim with the justifications supplied in an accompanying document.

A working case is as follows.

Dubai's Strengths and Weaknesses

Strengths		Weaknesses	
Strategic location	Dubai's strategic location midway between Europe and Asia makes for easy accessibility, with London a mere 7 hours away by air, Frankfurt 6, Cairo 4 and Hong Kong 8. Great potential as a short-break stopover destination.	Exploitation of migrant workers	Although they benefit from jobs, the poor conditions and wages have resulted in revolts. These revolts may be targeted at tourists in an attempt to gain recognition.
Support from local government	The Dubai government offers a great deal of support to the tourism industry and enlists the help of other public and private sector organizations.	Rapid population growth, potential of overcrowding	The influx of young workers, its cultural preference for large families coupled with its improved medical care have all contributed to the large and rapidly growing population, the majority of which are young people. The young migrant working population is growing rapidly due to the lack of labour force among the UAE citizens.
Attractions: A variety of attractions showcasing its history and culture	Forts and museums (e.g. Dubai museum reportedly the oldest building, or Sheikh Saeed Al Maktoum's House) Heritage and diving villages Archaeological sites at Al Ghusais, Al Sufooh and Jumeirah Burj Nahar (Dubai towers) The Godolphin Gallery Gold and diamond park Spectacular desert scenery	Pollution: Noise, environmental and aesthetic	Noise, environmental and aesthetic pollution as a result of the ongoing building works taking place in the city, which could affect people's holidays.
Events: Renowned in the region for its sporting events and facilities which are among the best in the world	Emirates International Trophy for rugby The Rugby Sevens The Desert Classic Golf Tournament Dubai Tennis Championship		

(continued)

Strengths		Weaknesses
Shopping: Dubbed the shopping capital of the Middle East shoppers can buy in comfort and style	Arabic market stalls Mall of the Emirates with 350 shops and ski slope BurJuman mall for designer labels Dubai Shopping Festival (DSF) in January Dubai Duty Free's reputation	
Accommodation: Some finest hotels in the world	Large luxurious beach front hotels mostly five-star standard and above	
Accommodation: Some finest hotels in the world	Large luxurious beach front hotels mostly five-star standard and above	
State of the art infrastructure: Continuous development	The Dubai International Airport Island resorts (e.g. the palm and the palm jumeriah) Numerous landside developments (e.g. Palazzo Versace Resort and the Jumeirah beach residence)	
Meeting facilities: A prime conference destination with several state-of-the-art venues	Dubai World Trade Centre Airport expo Dubai cruise terminal	
Dining and entertainment: Remarkable variety of food and beverage outlets (F&B)	With an inherently multicultural environment and a melange of nationalities, it is only natural that the choice of food in the emirate should be wide and varied	
Numerous transport links	There are approximately 115 scheduled flights from the United Kingdom to Dubai every week. Source: TTG (Travel Trade Gazette).	

Dubai's Threats and Opportunities

Threats		Opportunities	
Congestion	Arising from the growing population of migrant workers into the city seeking jobs in construction. More transport networks have to be created to deal with the capacity. This leads to a vicious cycle as more workers will be needed to do so, which will in turn compound the congestion issue.	Jobs	The creation of jobs in the city and environs has provided a livelihood for many families of workers in neighbouring countries and regions. These people hopefully live a better standard of life.
Terrorist attacks	At present Dubai enjoys a politically stable environment and is virtually crime free, other countries in the Middle East are experiencing political unrest and war which may eventually extend to Dubai and damage its tourism industry.	Short-break stopover market	Due to its strategic location and the combination of city and beach makes Dubai a great destination for a short break whilst on route to or from another destination. It's a great opportunity to break the monotony of long-haul travel from destinations in the Far East or Australasia. Dubai shouldn't only invest on capturing this market but also establishing the destination for longer stay tourists.
Erosion of culture/values as Dubai becomes a cosmopolitan city	Dubai is attracting residents and expatriate workers from nearby regions due to the relaxed attitudes towards alcohol and partying. This may be taken advantage by the migrant workers, thereby eroding their culture, with the potential to filter down to the young UAE nationals thus causing controversy.	Developing the spa tourism niche market	The exceptional spa facilities available in Dubai are being capitalized on by the DCTM as they have released a brochure encouraging this type of tourism in 2004.

(continued)

Threats		Opportunities	
Competitors (e.g. Abu Dhabi, Qatar, Jordan, Oman and Egypt)	Dubai operates within an environment of strong competition posed by its neighbouring emirates, neighbouring countries and other destinations offering similar products. Hence the need to differentiate itself from its competitors (similar Strengths).	Bad weather in other countries (e.g. Western Europe)	This poses a great opportunity for Dubai as they benefit from 365 days of sun, sea and sand, and is therefore an alternative for those seeking to escape bad weather.
Culture	The culture of other destinations may appeal to a wider range of travellers; this may be a deterrent to some who wish to visit Dubai.	Liberalization of visas	The liberalization of visas in 2001 which has afforded Dubai the opportunity to capture a wider market. This seems to be responsible for generating an increment of up to 475,000 visitors per year during the period 2001–2003.

The restaurant sector

This sector is normally seen as being made up of three main segments in the restaurant business:

1 Fine Dining, such as El Bulli (which we considered in the previous chapter). The fine dining restaurant is characterized by a high level of attentive table service, expensive-looking furnishings and decorations, and fine cuisine. Sometimes, this category of restaurant is referred to as "white tablecloth" but now that might not accurately describe some of the furnishings. Prices lie at the high end of the market, with guests paying $50 to $100 or more.

2 Theme restaurants take a different approach to providing a distinct dinning experience. These restaurants seek to provide diners with an experience that evokes other times, places and people. The Hard Rock Cafe chain is a good example.

3 The third one is Casual dinning restaurant, such as FGI Fridays. Casual dining restaurants seek to attract middle-income customers who enjoy dining out but wish to avoid high prices and the formality they feel may characterize the fine dining restaurants.

Think through the SWOT analysis for these three variants within the restaurant classification. You will find that there are many similarities but also some very important differences in your presentations. This will help you to recognize the need for specificity in the preparation of your analyses.

Could you see the reasons for Hard Rock's decision to open a Cafe in Mumbai?

Example: Hard Rock Cafe opens first restaurant in India

January 26, 2006 – Hard Rock Cafe International, Orlando, Fla, has opened its first restaurant in India – a 6,000-square-feet, 169-seat cafe in Mumbai, India. "India has meant so much to rock music over the years that I couldn't be more excited to finally open Hard Rock Cafe in Mumbai", said Hamish Dodds, President and CEO of Hard Rock International, in a statement. "Hard Rock was actually founded on principles from Indian culture. 'Love All, Serve All,' the motto on the wall of each and every Hard Rock, is derived directly from our founder's long love affair with India. So, in a sense, the opening of this new Hard Rock Cafe feels very much like coming home."

Could your SWOT help to justify this decision to promote Middle East expansion?

Example: Macaroni Grill heads to Middle East

Casual dining leader Brinker International Inc. is confident that its brand of pasta, brick-oven pizza and tiramisu will win over Middle Eastern taste buds.

The second-largest casual restaurant operator in the United States, behind Florida-based Darden, has signed an agreement to take its Romano's Macaroni Grill to the Middle East.

The deal will put Macaroni Grill eateries in Egypt, Jordan, Kuwait, Qatar and the United Arab Emirates, among other countries.

Most importantly, it will bring the casual dining giant closer to its goal of quadrupling its international revenue to 20% of its total revenue in less than 5 years, says Charles Sonsteby, Chief Financial Officer for Brinker International Inc.

"Just as we pioneered casual dining, we intend to be pioneers in other parts of the world that will generate growth for a long period of time", Sonsteby said.

Since opening its first restaurant outside this country in Canada in 1991, Brinker's international revenue has grown to 5% of the company's total revenue. Brinker generated revenue of $3.9 billion in 2005, up from $3.7 billion in 2004.

In addition to 238 Macaroni Grill locations, including locations in six foreign countries, the company owns, operates or franchises a total of 1,130 Chili's Grill & Bar outlets, 141 On The Border Mexican Grill & Cantina locations and 37 Maggiano's Little Italy stores.

Of its more than 1,550 restaurants, 119 are in foreign countries. "Our international strategy has definitely evolved", Sonsteby said.

The Dallas-based restaurant operator (NYSE: EAT) is stepping up its international efforts "based on the incredible success" of franchise partners in the Middle East and Latin America and in Pacific Rim countries such as Taiwan, Japan and South Korea, Sonsteby said. The fact that some of Brinker's international restaurants are experiencing double-digit same-store sales growth also caught the company's attention, Sonsteby said. The company plans to double its number of global outposts in the next 2 years. In 2008, it plans to open 80 new restaurants outside the United States. Through the Middle East agreement, Brinker will have three franchise partners for 14 Macaroni Grill stores to be completed by 2009.

■ Environmental analysis

When we begin to look at the operating environment, we rapidly become aware that we are dealing with a complex context. In order to deal with this complexity, the analytical framework has been subdivided to facilitate the analysis. However it should be remembered that this is an analytical separation and the elements are constantly involved and interact across the categories. The division proposed here is that of a traditional PEST analysis – Political, Economic, Social and Technological. We recognize that more sophisticated tools have been proposed, such as SCEPTICAL – Social, Cultural, Economic, Physical, Technical, International, Communications and infrastructure, Administrative and institutional, and Legal and political. However we feel that the elaboration into nine components (some of which are actually combination of forces that could be further divided, for instance legal and political could well be treated separately) adds to confusion rather than precision. This is especially true where the analysis comes to reintegrate the elements. As you will see it is difficult enough to reintegrate a four-way separation, let alone attempt a nine-way reunion. Further we feel that we can use the PEST categories to good effect if we reinforce the context of this book throughout the four areas, that is to say all the analytical factors are constituted in terms of an awareness of international culture.

One other note has to be registered before considering the operation of the categories and that has to do with the broad nature of the hospitality field. There are potential changes in legislation (part of the political consideration) that would affect the food industry but would not affect the whole of the hospitality sector. To make the analysis relevant, the key operational objectives must be clear and inform the selection of factors for the analysis. Some changes would clearly affect the whole of the hospitality sector and so would be common to any PEST analysis but in order to make the analysis relevant, the specific factors affecting the case must be addressed within the framework (Figure 4.2).

Benefits	Dangers
Increased awareness of environmental changes	Limited by availability of information
Increased understanding of the context in which hospitality organizations operate	Static picture in a changing world
Increased understanding of multinational contexts	Closed to new sources of data
Increased sensitivity to changes in the environment	May be disconnected from the rest of decision-making
Prioritizes factors	Uses the past to inform the future but is that always reliable?

Figure 4.2
Environmental analysis: benefits and dangers

We were taken by the optimism shown in the following report by Kim Sengupta about investment plans for Iraq. Do keep reading as the final sentence contains a vital piece of information that may not have been properly factored into the decision-making process.

Example: Iraq plans hotel and theme parks for a tourism boom

By Kim Sengupta in Baghdad, 7 November 2005

A £48 million, five-star, 23-storey hotel rising in the city centre; an opulent palace complex being turned into a theme park; cheap flights to the picturesque "Venice of the East" all the trappings of a country gearing up for a tourist boom.

Except the country in question is Iraq. With a new constitution and elections in the offing, officials insist there is a new beginning. The tourist board has 2,400 staff and 14 offices. There has been a rise in the volume of travellers, with Iraqis either leaving or expatriates returning for visits. And there is also the continuous and steady number of foreigners, mainly contractors, coming in for the huge wages they can now command for working in such a risky environment.

The planned hotel is very much at an embryonic stage. The land "in the heavily guarded Green Zone" has been donated by the Iraqi government, and the finance is being provided by an Iraqi businessman.

Thair Feeley, of the Iraqi Commission for Investment, insists everything is in place. "It is not true that it will be a five-star hotel", he says with a flourish, "but a seven and half stars one".

The hotel is intended to have the usual accoutrements: plush suites, business centres, conference halls and a golf range. However, this is Iraq and Mr Feeley is not keen to make more details of the structure public for "security reasons". Nor is he willing to reveal the name of the businessman, again for "security reasons".

The building will have to be built to withstand mortar and rocket attack, just as the one major existing hotel in the Green Zone, Al Rashid, was built to do. Despite the carnage outside and its shabby appearance, the Rashid can still charge $150 (£86) a night.

Another plan is to turn Saddam Hussein's former palaces at his home town of Tikrit into a themed tourist destination. The complex, which contains 18 palaces and 118 other buildings, is surrounded by rolling gardens overlooking the Tigris.

Mohammed Abbas, a Regional Official, said: "Ordinary Iraqis were never allowed into these palaces. It will be an opportunity for them to see how their money was spent. International visitors will also be able to see the kind of lifestyle Saddam enjoyed."

Basra in the south has already officially declared itself open for tourism. But, says an official: "Tourists should dress like locals and maybe dye their hair. And they should have armed guards and they should be always vigilant."

PEST

In the beginning the consideration of a PEST analysis, is often useful to take stock by outlining the factors that have impacted on the organization in broad or general terms before going on to explore the issues more thoroughly. This overview can often provide a feel for the position of the organization and help to provide a focus for the analysis that follows.

As with the SWOT analysis, we provide a worked case of a PEST to outline some of the features that you would expect to see in the presentation. There are other fuller examples provided on the website but this brief PEST for McDonald's is illustrative.

The broad environment

In recent years, McDonald's has faced two major types of threats from the broad environment: socio-cultural forces and political forces. Socio-cultural forces are related to social responsibility and health, while political forces are related to issues of obesity, trans fat labels, and – after 11 September – to issues related to bad corporate practices.

The changing international environment has proved to be a constant threat to the public image of the company. Marketing, future strategies and public relations initiatives have all aimed to counteract public opinion from the issues described.

Political factors cover the range of governmental, party political and legislative issues that affect our industry. This will consider the Government system, its bureaucracy, and the rules or laws that society's members must follow. Consideration will also be given to the level of political stability, within the country and within the region.

However increasingly this category must also include consideration of non-democratic politics – historically the concerns over labour relations would be debated here but in these days of security threats and terrorist alerts, we have to recognize the political reality of these tensions as well. In some countries, governments also own businesses in the hospitality industry and these would have to be considered in terms of the political influence on their future developments. There are also countries where there are restrictions or limits on local ownership of business operations.

Again this section used to focus on domestic legislation but increasingly we must be aware of supranational bodies that intervene in hospitality – be it the World Tourism Organization (WTO) or the European Union. Equally, if we are operating in different countries we must be as aware of likely changes in policy in those countries (markets) as are in the domestic one. Similarly government policy used to be a narrowly focused area of concern for the hospitality industry but now alongside domestic regulations and taxation policies, there must be a concern for international policies such as exchange rate issues (even within the Euro zone), international trade policies and also foreign policies, which may generate impacts either in the domestic or foreign markets the organization is operating in.

Even apparently obvious events in the operational environment may not have the effect that one would expect. For instance the political analysis of a city affected by widespread and long lasting riots would normally suggest that hotel accommodation would become less popular and bookings would decline. However as the report below shows, things are not always as the analysis would suggest.

Example: French riots haven't hit bookings so far

This is based on a report by Aude Lagorce, for MarketWatch

Current situation
Eleven nights of rioting in France have yet to affect travel bookings, a leading European operator said on Monday. "We are seeing normal booking conditions", said a spokesman for Tui AG, a German tour operator that sells trips to Paris, Nice and Strasbourg. Although he noted that the agency had received calls from guests enquiring where their hotels were located.

International positioning
The US State Department on Friday issued a cautionary statement against travel to some parts of the city.

"Americans should avoid the affected areas that include the northern suburbs and also Trappes in the southwest of Paris, and should move quickly away from any demonstrations that they may encounter", it said. But despite the recent warning, the impact is still expected to be mild.

"We believe the terrorist attacks in the UK and Spain had much more of an impact", said a spokesman for Travelpress.biz, the world's largest publisher of travel news. "The recent riots may hurt France's image a little bit, but it's such a powerful tourist destination that we don't expect a real impact. Of course the events are still enfolding, so it's hard to predict what the ultimate impact will be", he said.

The overall economic impact
Marc Touati, an economist with Natexis Banques Populaires, said the news hasn't hit the Euro zone's second-largest economy – as yet. "There's nothing to panic about right now, but if things continue this way, there'll definitely be cause for concern. Unfortunately, this is happening just as we were seeing a slight pickup in investment due to the lower Euro", he said. "A climate of fear and pessimism could stop the recovery dead in its tracks if the situation continues to worsen", he added.

The head of France's main business group, Laurence Parisot, on Monday warned of the consequences of the violence for the French economy, notably on tourism and investment. "France's image has been deeply damaged", Parisot told Europe 1 radio.

Political response
President Jacque Chirac made his first public address on the riots on Sunday, in an attempt to reassure the population. "The law must have the last word", Chirac said after a security meeting with top ministers. France is determined "to be stronger than those who want to sow violence or fear, and they will be arrested, judged and punished".

The belief in Paris seems to be that the image of stability and civility that the French capital has long enjoyed will offset the short-term effects of the rioting. This is a very good example of having to undertake the analysis of elements in the specific context in which the events have to be understood. Few other destinations would have a strong enough image in order to position themselves in this way to resist the negative publicity.

Health

Another major political issue in the industry concerns health issues, which is expressed both in terms of an active lifestyle agenda but also focuses on healthy diet and nutrition. This has become a big issue for contract caterers in the public sector. The issue of health and healthy eating has permeated every aspect of food preparation and menu development. Healthy eating is a big political issue and of late, meals served in schools and hospitals have been subjected to much criticism and scrutiny. In the United Kingdom, even the celebrity chef, Jamie Oliver, has entered the debate-making a television series about school meals and trialing new menus in the schools, which he claimed remained within the existing budget but offered an improved nutritional and dietary balance for the school children. Contract caterers are at the forefront of this issue. Changes are being made not just within the commercial sector but also within the education and healthcare sectors where action is being made whereby caterers are introducing more organic and locally produced food. On a wider scale the incidence of saturated fats and salt in processed foods is of concern and again these are often products that are offered by contract caterers in both public and private contracts. As well as government pressure to act, consumers are realizing for themselves the importance of healthy eating and are looking for caterers to offer the appropriate products.

However this is not just an issue of governmental concern and demonstrates the way politics is also being shaped by extra-parliamentary pressure groups. This next example not only highlights the issue of concern to the pressure group but also demonstrates the power they have, as it highlights the way in which the group may or may not initiate legal action against other firms.

Case: KFC Gets Fried. Is Starbucks Next?

Kate DuBose Tomassi, 21 June 2006, 1:10 PM ET

When KFC was hit with a lawsuit last week over its use of partially hydrogenated oil, the question on many lips was "Who's next?" But despite a flurry of reports pointing at Starbucks, the Center for Science in the Public Interest (CSPI) says it has no immediate plan to sue the ubiquitous coffeehouse.

That's not to say that CSPI, a consumer action group that describes itself as an "advocate for nutrition and health, food safety, alcohol policy and sound science", isn't eyeing Starbucks. It is. Michael Jacobson, CSPI's Executive Director, says Starbucks is one of a number of other major chains the centre is looking at for their use of partially hydrogenated oil, such as Burger King Holdings, McDonald's, Applebee's International, Denny's and Darden Restaurants' Red Lobster. Partially hydrogenated oil is a so-called trans fat, which has been linked to heart disease.

So why is the coffee seller among the more often demonized fast food chains on CSPI's hit list? Jacobsen says Starbucks sells an apple fritter that has 12 grams of trans fat, almost the healthy limit for an entire week, and almost as much as a three-piece chicken combo meal at KFC. He says people don't necessarily expect to be consuming something so unhealthy at Starbucks, which, he notes, bills itself as "socially responsible".

But CSPI's plans may be just so much hot foam. The legal barrier to such suits is high, and Starbucks is already taking steps to eliminate the problem fat.

"CSPI has enormous legal hurdles in this type of litigation", says Jane Thorpe, a partner in the Atlanta office of Alston & Bird in the firm's product liability group.

First, these plaintiffs can't show they've suffered any actual injury from eating a fried chicken leg or apple fritter, Thorpe says. And even if they were to get over this fundamental hurdle, they'd have to show, under most state consumer statutes, that the restaurant had engaged in an unfair and deceptive practice, which could be tough, since most people know that fried foods aren't healthy – be it a fritter or a drumstick.

"What CSPI is trying to do is enter an area which is the proper jurisdiction of the experts and the government", says Thorpe. And CSPI doesn't necessarily disagree. Jacobson says that if the US Food and Drug Administration (US FDA) were to act by "revoking its acceptance" of partially hydrogenated oil, the centre wouldn't need to sue company by company. Since the FDA hasn't acted, litigation and threatened litigation have become part of CSPI's strategy to force companies to practice what it deems honest labelling and marketing.

On 13 June CSPI filed a complaint against KFC (formerly known as Kentucky Fried Chicken), owned by Lexington, KY-based Yum! Brands The class-action litigation, filed in a superior court in the District of Columbia, is part of the consumer group's multipronged strategy to get KFC and the entire restaurant industry to stop using partially hydrogenated oil, said Jeff Cronin, a spokesman for CSPI, in a phone interview last week.

In an e-mail statement, KFC said, "This is a frivolous lawsuit completely without merit, and we intend to vigorously defend our position. All KFC products are safe to eat and meet or exceed all government regulations, and we take health and safety issues very seriously."

Whether Starbucks is next to be slapped with a lawsuit remains to be seen. In an e-mail, a company spokesman noted that "At Starbucks, we have always offered a wide variety of options, for both beverages and food, which meet the needs of our diverse customer base. For example, we offer more than 73,000 beverage combinations to our customers." Specifically, the company says, it offers reduced fat and fat-free baked goods, and lower-fat and -calorie Frappuccino drinks.

The company also pointed out that nutritional information is available in stores and on its website, and that the company is in conformance with FDA packaging requirements, which have required the inclusion of trans fat amounts since 1 January.

And it's important to note that at least for Starbucks, its targeting may become moot. In its e-mail statement, the company said it's working with regional bakeries "to help them focus on reducing and removing trans fats" from baked goods, and has committed to eliminating all trans fats in its national promotional offerings by this fall.

There are very interesting lessons to be drawn from this case. Firstly, the legal challenge has a legal force, with the chances of CSPI winning its case being determined by the judicial process. The consequences could be very severe for the whole industry if the case was successful as the precedent set would be binding throughout the sector and would have international repercussions as other governments came to review standards on the issue. However the political significance does not end with the judicial process. It is clear that the case is being presented as much outside the court in the public arena of the mass media as within the legal arena. The consequences of this are much more open and are not necessarily dependent upon the outcome of the judicial process. The raising of concerns and the making of allegations is sometimes enough to create the effect that the campaigners were hoping to achieve. This is an area of the political aspect which is very important in maintaining and enhancing the reputation of the organization and its products and services.

McDonald's political

The company is suffering from political threats from wars between countries where the company operates, as well as from governments now adding legislation to force them to put health warnings on their products. They have also become a symbol of capitalism and Americanism – meaning that they have now become the target of terrorist groups and attacks. McDonald's has no control over these political factors which are making the company suffer greatly. They can only leave war stricken countries, or places where terrorism is a threat. This means a loss in revenue, as well as the company becoming smaller and therefore weaker.

Economic
This section identifies the factors in the economic environment that will impact on businesses and their customers. You will want to be uncovering data about the predicted economic growth rates (usually given as percentage changes in the gross domestic product or as GDP per capita), levels of income in the economy and the likely movements in exchange rates and any indications of currency instability. Levels of unemployment and inflation may also be considered as they impact on the market's ability to purchase services along with wage rates for those in employment. When considering international investments, the balance of payments of the countries involved may be important and concern may be expressed for information about the levels of productivity in the destination. This would also cover questions of income elasticity, income inequality, and the availability of substitute products and cultural factors. These are relative factors and the analysis would have to be grounded in such a way as to recognize the local and the international significance of the figures being considered.

Some attempt should be made to map the potential in the market using notions such as market size, market intensity and market growth. These could be addressed with general economic data but it is also worthwhile looking for hospitality specific data such as average occupancies, achieved room rates and yield, visitor arrivals and visitor spend. The fast food sector seems to offer good examples of the sort of trends the analysis should highlight. Chicken outlets have benefited from the downturn in the popularity of burgers and new menu and product developments, which have helped to rejuvenate brands. This segment is dominated by takeaway sales, which accounted for 80% of the £908 million sales in 2004. The sector is expected to continue to grow faster than the overall eating out market largely due to the development of mobile or small-scale outlets such as takeaway kiosks and drive thru' restaurants.

Generally, this sector has been looking to broaden the appeal of its products by making them more portable and to compete directly with sandwich and coffee shops as well as supermarkets for the lunchtime trade. For instance, KFC re-introduced the "Mini Fillet", a snack-sized chicken burger, in early 2005.

Like the burger bar market, this sector is also trying to appeal to the more health conscious consumer by offering grilled as well as fried chicken options. The main player in the United Kingdom, KFC, is currently planning to introduce grilled chicken concept outlets called "Grillz" that will appeal to consumers looking for healthy and convenient eating options. The concept was tested in Japan during 2004, and in March 2004, Yum! Brands, the owners of KFC, registered the brand name in the United Kingdom, with the group anticipating a rollout either in 2005 or 2006. KFC's standard menu has expanded to include healthier alternatives such as salads as well as a chicken rice bowl.

Nando's, the Portuguese chicken restaurant is now one of the fastest growing chicken eat-in restaurants within the United Kingdom. It currently operates 103 outlets within the United Kingdom compared to just 23 in 1999, around half of which are located in London. Seven more outlets are in the pipeline at the time of writing.

Over the last 4 years, growth in the fast food sector, especially burgers and fried chicken bars, has outstripped that of the restaurant sector, which encompasses pubs, in-store outlets as well as hotel catering. Indeed some sectors of the eating out market have actually declined or remained static since 2000. This includes hotel catering, roadside catering and ethnic restaurants.

The market is increasingly competitive and continues to offer an ever-broadening choice of outlet types, yet the number of restaurants in the United Kingdom has remained fairly similar since 2000. This is indicative of an active turnover rate of restaurant types as a new cuisine takes hold or as consumers grow tired of a concept that does not adapt quickly enough to consumer trends. Mintel estimates, based on current government data, show that there are around 26,000 restaurants within the United Kingdom in 2005, a rise of just under 2% over 2000.

The British Hospitality Association (BHA) estimates that around 70% of restaurants are still owner operated and therefore despite the presence of a number of chains, the restaurant market is still characterized by numerous small businesses.

As the competition intensifies, operators are finding it difficult to widen their profit margins. According to the BHA, the average mark-up for restaurants is now 2%. Wages are rising, not only because of inflation, but also because of the increase in the minimum wage. Alongside this, food costs are also rising as operators seek to improve the quality of supply and to meet all the necessary regulations. There is little scope for prices to rise as consumers can readily demonstrate their resistance to price rises by going elsewhere. At the same time, consumers are looking for the right levels of ambience and service, therefore leaving little scope for widening profit levels.

Using the analysis internationally also causes complications. For instance, there is criticism of the wage rates paid to some levels of employee in the hospitality sector but when these rates are transferred to developing countries the wage scales in hospitality can begin to look very attractive to the local labour force. In fact one of the impacts rapid hospitality can have on local economies can be seen in the shift of employment within the economy as more traditional forms of employment are rejected in favour of the hospitality industry.

When you are considering economic factors, you have to be careful not to double-count issues that you may have addressed in other areas of the PEST analysis. For instance, a government's decision to protect its currency or to let it float against other currencies is an economic consideration but the rationale for the government's decision may well be a political one. In one sense it does not matter where you locate the factor in the analysis but if you do place it in two areas, it may appear to have greater significance than you would want to ascribe to it.

One other comment about this aspect is that it is sometimes too easy to concentrate on the limits and the restrictions that apply here. The use of the concept economic almost suggests a review of what is in short supply and cannot be afforded. However shortage of resources is not the only source of problems, the opposite – an embarrassment of riches – should also be considered in this category. Following on from the SWOT we worked through on Dubai, it is possible to see the abundance of wealth as a potential problem as there appear to be few limits on the developers' imaginations as they struggle to meet the increased tourism demands. Dubai's programme of rapid hotel construction has seen it become a building site. During 2002 the construction industry was undoubtedly booming and in the hotel sector alone there were plans to build 150 more hotels over the next 5 to 7 years, thus taking the number of hotel rooms from 20,000 in 1990 to 55,000. Source: AME info Online. Although Dubai's modern infrastructure has made it popular, the environmental and aesthetic pollution that accompanies it may also disadvantage the destination as some travellers may be deterred from visiting.

McDonald's economic

McDonald's are experiencing economical problems. They have found a recent slump in sales from its fast food business, suggesting customers want more freedom of choice, something which they may not get at McDonald's. To combat this McDonald's have bought out other companies, such as Prêt á Manger. By diversifying the company they aim to increase sales again by offering the customer more variety, as this seems to be what consumers are demanding. The Prêt á Manger chain does not benefit from McDonald's company name, or reputation, and therefore must rely on its own brand name and image.

Social factors include both objective and subjective elements about the socio-cultural forces such as language, work habits, customs, religion and values. The factual data about social trends, including demographic details, would be considered here. However this element also includes the more subjective questions of how values and beliefs will impact on the organization. This is the obvious place to explicitly address cultural issues and to look at the multicultural aspects we considered earlier. The shift towards social responsibility is one aspect of this element which has come to have great significance for the hospitality industry as we shall see in the penultimate chapter of this book.

Demographic trends are important for projecting targets not only for customers and market niches but also for looking at the potential workforce. We can identify measurable characteristics of populations: income, population size, age distribution, gender, marital patterns, family size, educational attainment and occupation for example. These demographics may be supported by studies of psychographics (values, attitudes and lifestyles) and behavioural characteristics. The size and age structuring of the populations will determine the scale of particular segments in future periods. This may influence the selection of target markets in particular countries or influence the way international marketing appeals to potential customers. It may also cause concerns in human resource departments as particular categories of recruits may become scarce (or vice versa). For instance, graduate recruitment relies on the adequate supply of graduates, which in turn presumes a higher number of students entering higher education and by looking at the demographic trends it is possible to anticipate peaks and troughs in the labour supply.

The "grey pound"

The most obvious example there is for us to consider here is the inevitable "time-bomb" of an ageing population, which will be composed of Baby Boomers who have grown up in the era of eating out regularly, and who will look to continue this habit in appropriate places, making informed choices about hotels and restaurants for instance. Third agers, in particular, are becoming increasingly more active during this stage of their lives and are likely to intensify their impact on the eating out market going forward, resulting, for example, in more all-day dining options as well as lighter meals.

Sexuality

Social values are changing everywhere. For example, consider the public's view to homosexual, which has become much more open now.

Example: Holiday firm ends ban on gay couples

A holiday company which turned away gay couples from its resorts unexpectedly lifted the ban last night in the face of a campaign by an ex-government minister and sexual equality groups.

Sandals, the Caribbean resort company, announced it was lifting its ban on same-sex couples from 13 resorts, just before a spokesman was due to appear to defend its policy with the former minister, Barbara Roche, on BBC Radio 4's Today programme this morning. The company has resorts in Jamaica, St Lucia, Antigua and Bahamas.

Sandals was under commercial pressure from London's Mayor, Ken Livingstone, who had banned its advertisements from the tube because of its homophobic attitude to clients.

Think about the cultural impact to the industry. Is it opportunity or threat?

Source: *The Guardian* (12 October 2004).

Social structure is one part of demography but is concerned with the way in which social groups are organized in the society. Patterns concerning education, employment and social acceptability have all changed over recent years and are continuing to change. One of the changes to have impacted on the hospitality is the shift in the social structure that allows and accepts change in traditional patterns of employment in developing countries. The pattern of agricultural employment, the shift to two-job economies (helping with agriculture but employed in hospitality) and the presence of women in the workforce are all significant changes. They contribute to the changing patterns of employment in hospitality that would not have been found in traditional societies 30 years ago.

McDonald's social

McDonald's has faced a number of difficult charges from consumers, governments and other groups in recent years. The Environmental Protection Agency took on McDonald's in 2003 for the "Fluorinated telomeres" in their packaging material which were deemed to be indestructible pollutants. Other issues – ranging from the use of antibiotics in livestock to animal welfare – have also been raised with the company. In an attempt to reduce the terrible publicity and to alter the public's perception of the company as a bad corporate citizen, McDonald's have taken the following steps. The following statements are from the company's "2003 Social Responsibility Report".

- In 2002, McDonald's purchased more than $460 million of recycled packaging materials reducing packaging by an additional £35 million.
- McDonald's entered into a new collaboration with the Centre for Environmental Leadership in Business, a Division of Corporation International, to promote conservation and sustainable agriculture in global food supply chains and address issues related to sustainability in the fishing area.
- McDonald's announced new global healthy lifestyle initiatives, including the commitment to develop new Happy Meal options and to help educate consumers about the role of nutrition and fitness in maintaining good health.

ACTIVITY   Lifestyle issues are included in this section of the analysis but they are notoriously difficult to predict and to analyse. We offer a simple, but telling example to demonstrate with two extracts dealing with one of the lifestyle trends that is a major concern to the industry at the meeting. Consider the two reports carefully and think how you would use them to support your recommendation to a hospitality company.

On the one hand:

Summary: Healthier Eating Out Is the Main Trend to Watch

This survey of opinion, combined with the other consumer research findings earlier in this report, means that the eating out market will continue to drive the market going forward. The obesity issue will continue to be the dominant trend curbing fast food trade and influencing children's menus in general, food miles, provenance, fresh and locally produced and seasonal grown ingredients will remain influencing factors for the restaurant market. The growing healthy eating trend of the last 10 years has now reached a point where the quality of food consumed has now been reinstated as the most important aspect of eating out, whether it is as a fast food option or a formal dining occasion.

On the other:

Health Is Not the Only Future Trend

While healthy eating will continue to have a large influence over some sectors over the next few years, many customers come to a restaurant to escape from the day-to-day considerations about watching waistlines and taking exercise.

Innovation will become increasingly influential as the eating out market becomes more and more competitive, with customization, lighter meal options and sharing plates cementing themselves as "must-have" menu formats within the mid-market sector in particular.

The next 10 years will also see further developments being made between the Internet and eating out venues becoming increasingly mainstream as an advertizing medium. As most operators already show case menus and nutritional information on websites, in the future this may well extend into online bookings, pre-order meals or even choice of table through seating plans, generally culminating in more interactive websites.

More attention to the drinks component of the meal is also likely to be an increasingly important component for both operators and consumers as the range of soft drinks and premium alcoholic beverages widens. This also includes a growing trend for operators and waiting staff to offer consumers more knowledge of drinks choices (e.g. local bottled spring water, adult soft drinks, real ales or ciders).

The two comments are not actually mutually contradictory and can be taken together to inform a recommendation about the need for quality and difference within the offer. Customization and information can also be applied to the fast food sector and may be a way for that sector to move forward. And it is worth remembering that health concerns may not dictate all customer choice on every occasion.

But eating out is still a luxury

Although healthy eating is a dominant trend within the industry, at the end of the day eating out is still essentially a treat, be it a break from washing up or to celebrate a birthday for example and this is unlikely to change in the future even though eating out is now a regular lifestyle choice. As such some operators are now finding a balance by offering indulgent main courses with the option of a wide range of side dishes so that consumers can increase their intake of vegetables if they choose. Examples of these more diverse and innovative dishes include roasted vegetables, French beans and shallots or artichoke hearts. However, in other areas of the market venues will continue to choose not to follow the healthy eating trend as although Middle Eastern, Japanese or Italian cuisine easily lend themselves to lower-fat options, cuisine such as French fare is dominated by more rich and often cream-based flavours. Furthermore, as consumers increasingly concentrate on eating a balanced diet within the home, it almost becomes more desirable to indulge in less wholesome fare when they do choose to eat out.

French fries and milkshakes

Elsewhere in the burger market, albeit on a much smaller scale, there is evidence that consumers are trading up to premium burgers. Premium burger chains include the Gourmet Burger Kitchen (GBK) and the Fine Burger Company, both of which are concentrated in London. The Clapham House Group, a private equity firm, purchased GBK in November 2004 for £2.6 million, with plans to expand the number of GBK outlets. The number of premium burger bars is expected to grow in the near future, albeit on a small scale.

Sources: Adapted from Contract Catering, UK, December 2004 and Hotel Catering, UK, September 2005.

We would also remind you that we said that we took the role of international cultures and concern for the natural environment as part of all of the categories. However whilst we have drawn on a number of cultural examples, we have not addressed the natural environment as such. It has become such a strong feature of debate that we could argue that we now see there being a "green consensus" that informs these debates. This is not to say that everyone has subscribed to these views and certainly not that everyone has acted upon them but that the questions are now being asked of developments. We shall say more about this in the chapter on Social Responsibility towards the end of the book. However, there is now a sufficient movement for organizations to recognize a lifestyle force towards environmentally friendly policies. This social force can be realized within politics (through pressure for regulation and intervention to protect the natural environment) or economics (through the consumer decision-making process giving greater weight to green issues). The natural environment is a great asset for the hospitality industry and therefore its protection is also important.

Another point to remember in putting together the analysis is that innovation is also relative. What is "old hat" or taken for granted in domestic markets may look like innovation when introduced to a different market. Consider this example from KFC.

Example: KFC expansion: New Delhi, May 11 (Xinhua)

KFC, the world's largest chicken restaurant chain, Thursday announced its expansion plan to have up to 28 outlets in the country by the end of 2006, Indo-Asian News Service reported.

"We plan to expand to wherever our customers are and there is no limit to our expansion. By the year-end we will have anywhere between 25 and 28 outlets", said Sandeep Kohli, Managing Director (Indian subcontinent) of Yum! Restaurants International (YRI), whose flagship brand is KFC.

The fast food giant had opened its first restaurant in Bangalore, capital of south India's Karnataka in 1995 and now has 15 outlets, including five in Bangalore, three in Delhi, two in Pune and one each in Mumbai, Kolkata, Chandigarh, Ludhiana and Hyderabad.

Each outlet has handled round 2,000 customers every day in the country, Kohli said in Mumbai.

With global sales of US $13.2 billion, company officials view India as a key strategic market with immense potential for future growth.

But the company's expansion plan has roused protests of animal protection activists in Mumbai.

Activists of the People for Ethical Treatment of Animals (PETA), a non-government organization, demonstrated against KFC's maltreatment of chickens in front of the new restaurant in Bandra, a suburb of Mumbai.

KFC today has more than 12,300 restaurants in more than 80 countries.

Source: KFC (2006).

One example which links to our final aspect of the PEST as well will suffice here. The old tried and tested method of disposing of waste from ships was to dump it off the ship and into the water, be it river, lake or ocean. This practice still continues in many places but pressure on companies has brought a design innovation, made possible by advances in technology, but enacted to answer growing customer pressure. The P&O cruise ship, the Oriana, contains no fewer than four sewage plants on board, to ensure that as much waste material as possible is processed and returned to port where it is disposed of safely into containers.

Technological

The growth of the Internet has been a worldwide phenomenon, in the United States alone in 2001 there were an astounding 95 million users. Access to the web is spreading and expanding rapidly and produces a range of opportunities and threats that make it impossible to ignore. The technological environment has been a particularly significant area within the development of hospitality as many have seen the industry to be at the forefront of technology, both in terms of development but also in terms of implementation (Zongqing, 2004). Clearly, hoteliers have an interest in promoting the Internet channel, as it is far cheaper, especially where there is the facility for direct booking on the hotel's own website. A WTO report on e-commerce estimated that the cost of direct reservations by traditional means could be as much as 300% more than processing the same reservation through the global distribution systems (GDS). Furthermore, most reservations, passing through the GDS, are generated by travel agents who charge an average fee of 10%. Bookings via a chain central reservation system cost the hotel $6 to $10, while the cost of a direct online reservation on a hotel property's own site is only about $1.50.

For analysis purposes, the scoping should include operational processes, information and communications technology (ICT), logistics, products and services, and the social context in which these developments are taking place. Information technology (IT) has been taken into the heart of the industry with computer reservation systems (CRS) and global distribution systems (GDS) becoming indispensable parts of the hospitality system. There are of course still significant challenges ahead, such as the utilization of ICT and the developments in personal computing.

We have seen IT presented as a way of driving down costs and increasing value to both businesses and consumers. At the heart of the hospitality industry there has been a debate about the role of traditional intermediaries, such as travel agents, in a world where access to the Internet has increased so rapidly. When this was first considered it was thought that it could spell the death sentence of traditional high street travel agents as their customers took to researching and booking their own journeys. However, the reality has seen a slightly different future emerge, which may better be described as re-intermediation. What we see with re-intermediation is a redrawing of the roles and an extension of e-services. The travel agents still have an important role in promoting trust and face between the destinations and the customers, even though their customers may have briefed themselves by searching the www before venturing to the high street. Some business has been transferred directly to the Internet, but this has largely been offset by the increases seen in the marketplace. Re-intermediation also occurs on the e-commerce sites as well, with the linking of sites of hotels with car rentals, insurance and other additional services. We are looking at the development of value-added service chains created through e-commerce, with a dynamic that allows both service delivery to the traveller at point of demand as well as service information updates for the businesses.

Case: Fewer Consumers Using Internet to Make Travel Plans in 2006

Read the case and think about the link between travel plan and external economic factors.

US consumers are still largely satisfied with making travel plans online, but fewer are using the Internet to meet their travel needs than 2 years ago, according to the latest Consumer Internet Barometer, released on June 2006. The Barometer is the world's largest custom research company, covers 10,000 households across the country.

Only 28% of all men and 25% of surveyed women plan to research airline rates and availability online over the next 3 months, compared to 41% of all men and 25% of women in 2004. More men are using the Internet to make travel arrangements, with more consumers going online to research travel options and opportunities than to actually book trips.

"Vacation plans may have fallen victim to higher gas prices, rising travel costs and an increasingly uncertain economic outlook", says Lynn Franco, Director of The Conference Board Consumer Research Center. "The latest consumer confidence survey shows consumers' vacation intentions are at a 2-year low and this slowing in the rate of travel-related activity online only adds to overall concerns."

Source: The Conference Board (2006).

For instance this review of British Airlines demonstrates how a technological change available to everyone in the industry led BA to specific innovations. It is widely recognized that the CRS has played a very important role in the provision of airline services. Late in the 1990s, the CRS was integrated with a revenue management system and car rental and hotel booking systems were introduced with some other added functions (Chang *et al.*, 2003). The entire system has thus turned into a global distribution system (GDS), which is still the main idea behind current travel websites on the Internet. These systems have not only reduced airline operating costs, but also represented the globalization of the air transportation industry (Chang *et al.*, 2003).

For these reasons, British Airways upgraded and enhanced *ba.com* in order to encourage e-ticketing by providing simplicity and richer customer experience throughout the website. According to *Innovations for Our Customers* (Park-Smith, 2004, he was the Head of e-Commerce for BA), British Airways strategic priorities were based on simplicity.

BA set out on a programme called *Customer Enabled BA*, and the point of the programme and the vision that British Airways strive for is to make BA, an easy company to deal with. It also stated that this strategy for simplification and a richer customer experience would simplify the way BA do business. It would provide a cross-functional programme that covered the end-to-end customer experience, bringing consistency to BA delivery and removing duplicate processes. It was forecast that this would help to deliver at least £100 million savings within the organization, created by the simplicity and by the self-service.

In order to make their presence in the international market effective, the company instituted the following principles and actions:

1 British Airways have targeted the simplification of their online fares.
2 BA have provided an enhanced fare explorer.
3 BA e-ticketing is end-to-end self-service experience (e.g. research and book → pay and get ticket → follow-up and pre-airport queries → check-in and fly → arrive home and check miles).
4 BA has improved the facility for customers to change and update bookings on *ba.com*.
5 The website allows BA to do more up-selling.
6 BA have launched a new way of manage bookings.
7 *ba.com* provides a popular facility to select seats.
8 BA have launched home-printed boarding passes for Internet check-in.
9 BA have renewed their estate of self-service kiosks.

Already 50 % of BA's UK short-haul leisure business was booked on *ba.com, with an* e-ticket facility. This has contributed to a reported 50% reduction in the number of fares being delivered to their customers and it has seen a doubling in usage of e-tickets since the e-mail facility was delivered.

E-commerce strategy could be said to be a strategy that promotes the use of the Internet to join together all the elements in the business – linking the suppliers with the companies and the companies with their customers. From within the hotel industry, Hyatt offer a good example of what IT can do for an international organization and demonstrate the benefits of implementing a global e-commerce strategy

Hyatt's E-Commerce Business Strategy

Hyatt uses a business to customer (B2C) e-commerce business strategy. They use a combination of selling tangible and intangible products and services on a global scale. Hyatt has identified the need to use global e-commerce strategy to reach out to their customers worldwide. "Customers expect interactive capability wherever possible, in their own language and culture and adapted to their own environment" (Doole and Lowe, 2004: 424). The affect on Hyatt's marketing has had a promising influence. They strive to provide in-depth information to their consumers; this includes information on their resorts, what offers they have and about the company itself.

Hyatt as innovators

Hyatt sees themselves as innovators when it comes to technology. Mintel (2003) argued that recent examples of this included the introduction of "E-Folio" (an expense management tool for the business traveller) and the installation of high-speed Internet in all their hotels' meeting rooms.

The main website offers a range of information to the customers that visit the website. This has been designed to keep their customers interested in the website and the company. It focuses on informing and offering customers the chance to visit every hotel, at any location with the click of a button.

Hyatt also uses this e-commerce strategy to sell rooms wherever possible and helps to inform customers of the other services they provide.

Hyatt customer expectations

The opportunities for exploiting e-commerce by companies are truly international and this favours global players. So for Hyatt this innovation allows them to meet what they see as their consumers high expectations of service quality and image from the ways in which they conceptualize, sell and deliver their products and services.

Therefore they have recognized the need to constantly update their website and to constantly review how they sell their products and services. Hyatt has identified the needs of its consumers and has implemented this on every hotel page they operate, even offering the guest a number of things including the option to download a hotel brochure for themselves. Using the latest techniques for selling through the Internet, Hyatt are ensuring that their customers can find them, get to know them and purchase products and services that are relevant to their needs whenever and wherever at the click of a button.

The next set of examples may seem to come from an unlikely source for high-technology solutions, but the report serves to demonstrate how far reaching ICT has become and the multitude of areas in which it can be applied.

28 March 2006, 7:53 AM EST

New York (CNNMoney.com) – New technology innovations could soon force the restaurant industry to rejigger an often-used acronym – *QSR*, or quick-service restaurant – to *SSR*, or self-service restaurant, instead.

Self-service kiosks and computerized table-top ordering screens are just two of the trends that will be on display at the National Restaurant Association's (NRA) upcoming industry show this May, an annual event that showcases the latest offerings in technology, menu items, uniform fashions and restaurant designs.

"The restaurant industry is the most labour-intensive industry in the country", said Hudson Riehle, Senior Vice President of research with NRA, adding that it currently employs about 12.5 million workers in over 925,000 restaurants and is projected to grow by 2 million workers over the next 10 years.

"When you introduce technology into restaurant operations, whether these are fast food operators or family dining chains, you are able to get above-normal productivity increases", he said.

For example, industry insiders said franchisees of fast food leader *McDonald's* (*Research*), sandwich chain subway and restaurant operator Arby's have tested self-service kiosks.

Juan Perez, President of Adusa Inc., said his company, in partnership with IBM, has developed kiosks that allow consumers to self-order in grocery stores (Kroger is Adusa's biggest customer) and restaurants.

Said Perez, "Our kiosks are already in the pilot tests in grocery stores. A customer walks up to the kiosk and places an order to the deli or the bakery. They can pick up the order after they're done with the rest of their shopping." Moreover, customers can also use the kiosk to get information on wines or look up recipes, he said.

Customers in QSR will use the kiosks to order food and pay with a credit or debit card, Perez said, avoiding both misorders and long lines at the counter.

"It lets consumers feel more in control because they're getting exactly what they ordered. Businesses can deploy the staff elsewhere and refocus on speeding up order delivery", said the NRA's Riehle.

Likewise, casual dining order systems are undergoing an evolution of their own. Chosen Media will debut a table-top touch screen order system at the show.

"Customers can place their menu order through the system, they can ask for refills, call the waiter to their table and pay for their meal using a credit or debit card", said company manager Calvin Watkins. The system also acts as a personal jukebox.

McDonald's technological

McDonald's technology trials over the past few years have resulted in big failures. The company has made a variety of technology investments with mixed results, some of the results costing the company billions of dollars like the "Innovate" scheme designed to allow McDonald's management, at some point in the near future, to see just how many billions of burger patties, buns and chicken nuggets were being consumed at any or all stores at any time of the day. This real time digital network represented the most expensive and extensive IT project in the company's history as well as McDonald's corporate website – a glossy, expensive attempt to counter McSpotlight but many complaints have been received that there is no e-mail address for visitors to send in their opinions. To date, McDonald's attempts to use technology to put its products in the hands of hungry consumers faster have been largely unsuccessful. The company's failure to find a way to improve customer service is compounded by a lack of creativity like these there are other McDonald's technology experiments that have been more low key.

Having considered the elements, it is important to note that the analysis may not produce a simple and obvious answer that can be operationalized with a guarantee of success. So many of the variables considered can change so quickly that it is difficult to predict outcomes with any certainty.

We also hope that we have given you a clear idea about the purpose of analytical separation, whilst underlining the need for a synthesis of these factors in the final presentation. They are separable but they are also interconnected.

The scanning and reporting process is generally seen as consisting of five stages:

1 Scanning and monitoring of the operational and competitive environments for possible changes in the PEST areas.
2 Assessing the relevance of this information in the context of the international market for the organization.
3 Evaluating the changes and working through the relevant ones in detail.
4 Constructing relationships between the areas and evaluating the cumulative assessment of the environment.
5 Assessing the potential impact for the organization and its competitors.

Outcomes of PEST

The sorts of report that can be presented vary from those produced for specific in-company developments to ones that attempt to portray the picture for the whole of the industry. We have taken the highlights from two of the latter to demonstrate to you the scope of such exercises.

For instance, Poon (2003) split the report to the Berlin International Travel Show about the future of the international hospitality industry into supplier, consumer and destination trends, and suggested the likely outcomes of the trends they presented.

- Supplier Trends
  1 Cheaper, Shorter, Faster
  2 Closer to Home
  3 Information Technology is IT
  4 Increased Polarization
  5 Travel Agents Reinvent Themselves

- Big > Bigger
- Small > Niche Players
- Middle > Disappearing
- Mass Tourism > Mass Customization

- Consumer Trends
  1 Maturing Travellers
  2 Independent Travellers
  3 Rise of the Bourgeois Bohemians
  4 Body, Mind and Soul
  5 Value for Money is King

- Bargain Hunting > Value-Seeking
- Long and Expensive > Cheaper, Faster, Shorter
- Long-Haul > Short-Haul

- Hippies and Yuppies > Bourgeois Bohemian
- Baby Boomers > Ageing Travelers
- Physical > Spiritual
- Early Booking > Late Booking
- Group Tours > Independent Travel

- Destination Trends
  1 Enough is Enough
  2 From Products to Experiences (Poon, 2003, The Berlin Report)

- Mass Destruction > Enough is Enough
- Products > Experiences

Further research into the hospitality sector suggested a range of key issues that should be considered in looking at the future of the industry.

Key issues influencing the hotel industry

The hotel industry operates in a complex international environment, and is subject to most of the same trends that affect business and the economy in general. The following key issues influencing the industry's development have been identified:

- hotel grading standards,
- trends in marketing and distribution channels,
- guest loyalty programmes,
- in-house design and technology,
- spas and wellness,
- environment and sustainable development.

Hotel grading standards

Hotel grading standards seem to be largely taken for granted by both guests and the industry. Yet, they serve as a first indicator to the prospective client or travel intermediary of the level of service and comfort to be expected whilst staying in a hotel. Indeed, given the importance of hotel classification as a marketing tool, it has received scant attention. The hotel industry faces a fundamental problem: guests are sometimes disappointed by their stay in a particular hotel because their expectations are not met. These expectations may derive from experiences obtained in another hotel with the same number of stars.

However, the organization did qualify its position by noting that if the idea of an EU-wide system is pursued, consideration should be given to a scheme which would limit itself to establishing equivalences amongst national and regional classification norms. In such a case, the EU or international classification system would adapt itself to what already exists. Nevertheless, according to Ms Marguerite Sequaris, Secretary-General of HOTREC, there is no plan for a Europe-wide classification of hotels at present, as discussions continue as to the desirability and feasibility of such a project.

Besides the problem of the lack of uniform standards, there is the major question of whether grading criteria measure the features that guests appear to value most, such as employee attitude, check-in and check-out efficiency, or enhanced security, which is particularly desired by the increasing number of lone women travellers. Typically, existing grading standards are largely based on physical attributes of a property, such as the number of restaurants, or the size of guestrooms, which admittedly are objectively verifiable criteria. Intangible, service-oriented attributes are often subjective in nature, and hence more difficult to evaluate fairly.

At the high end of the accommodation business, particularly, clients are not buying just a bed in a room. The intangible service aspect is also highly important, especially for winning client loyalty. Therefore, to better meet customer expectations, grading standards must become more comprehensive so as to monitor the service aspect more effectively. Leading Hotels of the World (LHW) is a private independent marketing affiliation, regrouping some of the world's most prestigious upscale establishments. It provides a clear example of how to approach the evaluation of a hotel's attributes, putting maximum emphasis on service delivery.

Distribution channels

The predominant distribution channel for hotels remains direct contact with the property (via telephone, fax or e-mail), which, according to the last edition of Horwath's *Worldwide Hotel Industry Study*, accounted for 34% of all advance reservations in 2002, but which is down from 38% in 1995. This proportion varies between 27.5% for hotels in Africa and the Middle East and 40.5% for hotels in Europe. Even in the United States, about 70% of reservations for most hotels are still made directly to the hotel location, compared with the 30% that is now split between toll-free call centres and Internet reservations, according to Don Farrell, Founder and Chairman of Signature Worldwide, a consulting and training company. The world's leading franchisor, Cendant, estimates that 70% of its room nights are generated by walk-ins.

Indeed, according to KPMG's recent "Global Hotel Distribution Study 2004", the most efficient channel, overall, in terms of time taken to complete a booking remains calling the hotel direct. However, the time necessary to complete a call was found to vary significantly according to region.

The KPMG study found that generally by calling the hotel direct, the customer receives an accurate picture of availability and is able to get detailed information about the hotel and its facilities. The property-based reservation agent was more knowledgeable and proactive than call centre employees, and therefore better able to negotiate other options for the customer's stay at the hotel. One regional difference noted was the high level of automation when calling some hotels, particularly in Canada.

Hotels' in-house or outsourced central reservations offices (CROs) represent approximately one-quarter of advanced reservations (including call centres and hotel representatives). The KPMG study found that the service provided by CROs varies depending on the brand rather than the region, and that the level of automation and availability varies considerably globally. Several advantages to CROs were noted, such as availability, friendly and fast service, the ability to offer alternatives if the first option is not available and good product knowledge. Nevertheless, several drawbacks of CROs were identified by the study: agents generally are not from the country of the caller (e.g. some Europeans indicated that they had to speak English when calling the CRO); slowness in retrieving information (e.g. agent put the caller on hold to call the hotel to obtain information); systems problems (e.g. the caller was advised to check the hotel website or to call back later); and in some cases, incorrect CRO telephone numbers had been posted on the chain's website.

Nevertheless, there seems to be a trend towards consolidating property-based reservation desks into centralized units. According to an April 2005 report in *The Guardian*, Hilton Group (UK) has announced a £26.4 million investment in a central reservation system, which is to replace the reservation function at the front desk of the chain's roughly 400 properties. A network of centralized call centres will handle all calls from customers with operatives able to offer the caller another hotel within the Hilton group if the customer's first choice is unavailable. Hilton estimates that cross-selling between hotels would be a bigger boost to the bottom line than the cost savings. Tim Davis, Hilton's head of distribution and online, has suggested that such a centralized system could improve revenues by 9% at a hotel which lost its in-house reservation desk.

Traditional high street travel agents and tour operators are becoming increasingly redundant, both in the business and leisure travel segments. A survey by management consulting group, Accenture, of more than 550 business travellers in the United States found that 71% book their business travel primarily online, a trend that has been increasing in the 3 years since Accenture began fielding the survey. In contrast, only 22% of respondents reported that their preferred booking method is by telephone with a live agent, down from 36% in 2003. A similar study that polled 450 business travellers in the United Kingdom, confirmed the trend. In 2004, 53% booked their business travel primarily online, up from 47% in 2003. Only 27% said their preferred booking method is by telephone with a live agent, down from 41% in 2003. The greatest number of respondents in the United States (33%) and 31% in the United Kingdom ranked proximity to meetings or office as the top requirement in their choice of hotel rooms. In addition, in the United Kingdom, even more respondents (42%) ranked price as the most important hotel selection criterion. Only 15% of the US and 19% of the UK respondents cited the availability of high-speed or wireless Internet as a main criterion.

Hugh Morgan, Overseas Purchasing Director for the British tour operator, Cosmos, stated at a conference in April 2005 that by the summer of

2006, Cosmos would have stopped negotiating guarantees with Spanish hoteliers. Whereas 6 or 7 years ago, 80–85% of the group's Spain programme would have been on guarantee, Cosmos' accommodation-only site (www.somewheretostay.com) is currently providing beds for 100,000 passengers a year, although its stock does cover other city and beach destinations not located in Spain. Lowcostbeds, which was launched in October 2003 by Paul Evans, formerly Head of retail sales at First Choice, the British tour operator, currently provides beds to 3,500 UK travel agents and wholesalers, and also sells direct. Whilst the website currently focuses on beach destinations, it will add long-haul, ski and city properties, bringing its number of directly contracted hotels from 1,500 to 3,500.

According to TravelCLICK's eMonitor, room nights booked via third-party electronic channels (GDS as well as Internet intermediaries) increased by 7.5% worldwide in 2004. This year-on-year growth was fuelled by a 10.6% increase in Internet room nights booked through third-party websites powered by either GDS or Pegasus (which powers several of the top third-party hotel booking sites, such as Hotwire, Expedia.com, ebookers.com, Orbitz and Travelweb.com).

Further analysis reveals that travel agents' online bookings remained the dominant source of GDS and Pegasus hotel e-business in 2004, representing 80.6% of total room nights. In addition, the travel agent component of 2004 GDS bookings was responsible for driving a 6.6% increase in ADR over 2003 rates, confirming that travel agents continued to be a key driver of higher-rate business for hotels. The average rate for room nights booked through travel agents was 31.2% higher than room nights booked online by consumers. These statistics confirm the ongoing relevance of online bookings by travel agents. Internet (consumer online) room nights for 2004 grew by 10.6% over the 2003 level, as ADR rose by 10.2%, thus leading to a 21.9% increase in revenue for 2004. Whilst third-party website bookings rose by 10.6% in 2004, as noted above, Internet reservations received at the CROs of major hotel brands grew by 31.9%, or almost the triple rate of increase, according to TravelCLICK's eTRAK report. Indeed, in 2004, branded websites gained substantial share, compared to third-party merchant and opaque websites. eTRAK data show that branded websites were the source of 71.4% of the brands' centrally booked Internet reservations, compared to 66.5% in 2003. Merchant websites, such as Expedia, Orbitz, Travelocity, etc., were the source of 8.6% of Internet reservations. Merchant web operators buy hotel rooms outright and then offload them for the highest price they can get, thus pocketing the difference. Bookings via these channels grew by 9% over 2003. Opaque websites, such as Priceline and Hotwire, increased by 16% and sourced 7.5% of the brands' centrally booked Internet reservations in 2004.

Guest loyalty programmes

A February 2003 study conducted by InterContinental Hotels (then Six Continents) found that loyalty programmes are the most important driver of repeat customer business. In any case, whatever the merits or demerits of loyalty programmes, hotel chains that wish to remain competitive have no choice but to offer such incentives to their regular guests, especially given the present difficult market environment with hotel chains fighting desperately for market share.

Preferred treatment for long-standing guests, particularly of prestigious palace hotels, existed well before hotel chains appeared on the scene. Formalized loyalty programmes in the travel industry, however, were first developed by airlines and are widely used by retailers. Indeed, guest loyalty programmes are extremely popular in the travel and tourism industry and almost every travel business nowadays has some sort of frequent guest programme. From redeemable points to gift certificates to partnerships with airlines and car rentals, guest loyalty programmes can take many different forms. And, now, in view of technological advances, some observers tout these programmes as an excellent source of information about a hotel chain's client base. For instance, the programmes can be used to target market-specific demographic segments of the clientele.

In early 2004, InterContinental introduced its first two local-language Priority Club websites – in French and German – which allow members access to all online services in their own language. These sites include the following functionality:

- Quick enrol: Issues a membership number instantly upon signing up, enabling a member to immediately earn points on his first booking.
- Ability to redeem rewards online.
- View an account and review current reservations.
- Store personal information, preferences such as favourite destinations, room rates, room type and credit card information.
- Change points or miles earning preference – change earning preference from points to miles or vice versa.

In August 2004, in recognition of the huge growth potential of the Chinese travel market, InterContinental has created a third local-language Priority Club website in Chinese.

In-house technology and design features

Technology is not only important for hotels at the distribution level – Internet, GDS, etc. Technological advances and trends in design also have a big influence on the basic hotel product, including customer Internet access, PMS (property management systems), entertainment, rooms, bathrooms, F&B outlets, etc.

In 2002, Hotel Technology Next Generation (HTNG) was formed as a self-funded, non-profit organization association, whose mission is to develop technology solutions for the hospitality industry. HTNG comprises members from hotel and hospitality companies, technology vendors to hospitality, and other industry members, including consultants, media and academic experts. HTNG's executive board represents a "Who's Who" of leading hotel companies including: Hyatt, Four Seasons, Wyndham,

Mandarin, MGM Mirage, Destination and Marcus. HTNG's members participate in focused workgroups to identify solutions for specific business problems for the hospitality market. Currently more than 150 companies and individuals from across the spectrum are active HTNG members.

By using Internet-based technologies, hotels will, in many cases, be able to leverage the scale of the Internet to drive down the price points of technologies and services that are used in both hotels and in other industries – such as PABXs (private automatic branch exchanges), access control/locking systems, handheld devices, CCTV security systems, pagers, life safety and building management systems. Furthermore, the HTNG workgroup has the objective of identifying a set of fundamental hospitality features for telephony, including both Voice-Over-IP and other IP-based services.

This team will examine opportunities to integrate not only fixed devices provisioned to the room (such as entertainment systems, telephones, energy management systems, locking systems and minibars), but also devices carried by the guest, such as notebook computers, mobile phones, PDAs, Portable Media Centres, iPods, MP3 players, video cameras and portable DVD players.

For example, many hotel guests now have Personal Video Recorders (PVRs) in their homes, such as TiVo, and have become accustomed to being able to replay live broadcasts. However, there is no such device that addresses the unique requirements of a hotel guest, whose programme preferences can change every night, and where the desired viewing content may have been aired whilst a prior guest was still occupying the room. Similarly, the workgroup noted the need for simple, elegant IP-capable telephones appropriate for a bedside or bathroom, which do not currently exist.

The new SMS|Diplomat technology provides for interoperability between vendors. Instead of one vendor sending a message and waiting for a response, vendors have direct access to both data and business rules in other systems, and can proactively access what they need. Not only does this make it much easier and more efficient to communicate between systems, but it also allows guests and users to interact directly with SMS|Host system through in-room devices like telephones and televisions.

General Dynamics Interactive (GDI), the leading provider of digital video-on-demand for the luxury hotel market, deployed its Intrigue® Multimedia System entertainment-on-demand solution on Mandarin Oriental's high-definition LCD televisions. Thus, Mandarin Oriental guests are welcomed by name on the customized Intrigue television user interface from information provided by the SMS|Host Hospitality Management System. If the guest expresses a preference, Intrigue will turn the television on automatically in the guest's favourite language. If the guest has a voicemail or a fax message, a notification is displayed on the guest's television screen, and the guest can retrieve it from Percipia Networks, and either play the voicemail in "surround" sound through the Intrigue entertainment-on-demand system or view the fax on the television. A parallel interface with Intrigue's entertainment-on-demand feature allows guests to review all of their voice, fax and text messages from a single convenient web page accessed from Mandarin's in-room TV system.

Even as traditional an area as F&B services has felt the winds of change brought by technological evolution. "Smart" equipment and networked kitchens that speak multiple languages contain recipe files and can alert chefs to maintenance issues before they become a problem – these are some of the new features in this domain. Early adopters of the technology are seeing the biggest ROI (return on investment) with food safety issues. To maintain safety standards, traditionally an employee walks around with a clipboard and a pencil and manually records and monitors temperatures – what temperature food is cooked at, stored at, etc. Now equipment is there that will alert kitchen staff to a problem and maintain HACCP logs. (Hazard Analysis Critical Control Points, the HACCP is a system that was developed to ensure the safety of food for US astronauts nearly 30 years ago.) This can add up to better efficiency and some significant labour savings. The network also helps managers better monitor their equipment, by alerting the manager immediately if, for example, there is a repair issue or a cooler breaks down.

Spas and wellness

One feature that hoteliers and their guests increasingly see as a necessity, especially in upscale resort properties, is a spa or wellness centre. The word "spa" has evolved from its traditional meaning, which signified a resort with mineral water springs or therapeutic mud. In a modern hotel context, the term can mean anything from a small fitness room to an elaborate facility with pools and waterfalls. The most common industry definition is a facility including exercise equipment, a pool, whirlpool, steam room, sauna and treatment rooms offering massages, facials, manicures and pedicures. The majority of hotel spas occupy from 900 to 3,600 square metres.

In a survey of 30 resort-based spas in 1999, Health Fitness Dynamics (HFD 2001, "The Impact of Spas on Resort Occupancy"), a Florida-based spa consulting group, general managers and directors of operations were asked whether spas enhance or increase the following items listed below. The percentages of "yes" answers were as follows:

● Marketing advantage: 97%
● Revenue/occupied room: 83%
● Occupancy: 73%
● Perceived value for room rate: 70%
● Room rate: 57%
● Length of stay: 43%
● Number of people/occupied room: 27%

According to Judith Singer, HFD's President, the future of the spa industry will be in the creation of the "hybrid spa" – the resort/hotel spa that caters to lodging guests who want something as simple as taking an *à la carte* treatment to those who want to spend a few days on a special, spa-specific, multiday getaway. In order to maximize the revenue and profit-generating capability of the spa, the local community should be invited to use it on designated days. Some spas may even have a membership component.

Environment and sustainable development

So far, most hotels and major chains have done little more than pay lip service to the objectives of preserving the environment and promoting sustainable development, but three factors are making hoteliers sit up and take notice. First of all, it has been demonstrated in numerous cases that environmental practices can save money at an operational level and in the short term. The second point is that hoteliers, especially those in prime leisure destinations, are realizing that they must preserve their principal demand driver, which is the physical environs of the property. Finally, there is growing awareness that consumers and travellers are starting to use evidence of environmentally sound behaviour as a selection criterion for their holidays and lodging facilities.

In order for the industry to move forward in this domain, collective action is necessary. With this in mind, the International Hotels Environment Initiative (IHEI) was created in 1992, as a non-profit organization when a group of chief executives of 12 multinational hotel companies joined forces to promote ongoing improvement in environmental performance by the hotel industry worldwide.

IHEI focuses exclusively on hotels and how to improve their environmental management. Over the years this has been done through the development of industry-specific tools such as benchmarkhotel (www. benchmarkhotel.com), publications and a quarterly magazine called *greenhotelier* (www.greenhotelier.com). IHEI has also forged partnerships with other environmental bodies and associations, and provides a speaking platform where members have the opportunity to attend and speak about their experiences and achievements.

In recent years, hotels have broadened their perspective on environmental issues to include notions of community service and social responsibility.

India, interestingly, in February 2003, the government promulgated measures to encourage eco-friendly practices and facilities for the handicapped as a necessary requirement for all approved projects and classified hotels. Under the rubric of eco-friendly practices, the following points were noted:

- Energy conservation: It is necessary that all star-category hotels should have energy conservation lamps. The use of solar energy, timers, etc. is desirable.
- Water conservation: Water-saving taps and showers are necessary for five-star and five-star deluxe hotels, and desirable for one- to four-star and Heritage hotels.
- Waste management: Solid waste management and recycling of garbage should be undertaken. Garbage should be separated into wet and dry elements that which can be recycled or re-used. The wet garbage areas must be air-conditioned for three- to five-star deluxe categories, and is desirable for one- and two-star hotels. The aim should be to achieve a "zero garbage policy", by utilizing all the organic waste.

Potential for cost savings:

- Water accounts for 15% of total utility bills in many hotels.
- Most hotels pay twice for the water they consume – initially to purchase fresh water, and then to dispose of it as waste water.
- Many hotels pay to heat a proportion of their water, and so a water management programme will bring energy savings.
- Hotels pump fresh water and add chemicals to it, so, again, a water management programme will reduce these costs.
- A hotel that has a good water management programme will use as little as half the volume of water per guest per night than a hotel that has few manual or automated controls on water usage.

Evidence is gathering that consumers are demanding more environmentally friendly practices from tourism service providers, including hoteliers. A working paper, published in January 2004, entitled *Consumer Demand and Operator Support for Socially and Environmentally Responsible Tourism* (prepared by Zoë Chafe, and edited by Martha Honey of the Center on Ecotourism and Sustainable Development (CESD) in The International Ecotourism Society in Washington DC) recorded the following survey results:

- In the United States, more than three-quarters of travellers "feel it is important their visits do not damage the environment", according to a 2003 study. This study estimates that 17 million American travellers consider environmental factors first when deciding which travel companies to patronize.
- A separate study found that over 80% of American travellers believe it is important that hotels take steps to preserve and protect the environment, but only 14% ask hotels they are using if they have an environmental policy.
- In Britain, 87% of tourists interviewed in 2002 stated that it was either "very important" or "fairly important" that their holiday did not damage the environment; this was up from 85% in 2000. Additionally, 66% of British travellers said that they had placed importance on trips specifically designed to cause as little damage as possible to the environment.
- In a 1997 survey, 18% of British tourists said that a hotel's lack of concern for the environment would prevent them from returning to the same place again.

A 2002 survey found German tourists were expecting environmental quality, 65% want clean beaches and water, 42% "think that it is particularly important to find environmentally friendly accommodation" and 19% "would welcome it" if these accommodations were clearly listed in catalogues and guidebooks.

Chapter case study: Shangri-La Hotel

Introduction

Shangri-La Hotels & Resorts is the largest deluxe hotel group in the world, providing a wide range of business and recreational facilities and services, such as business centres, function rooms, Internet broadband and tea- and coffee-making facilities throughout the Asian region. It is also considered as one of the best hotel management companies with a high reputation all over the world. Nowadays, the Shangri-La group owns 44 deluxe hotels and resorts with more than 20,000 rooms in key cities of Asia and the Middle East and some famous leisure destinations. There are about 23,500 employees working for the group. Read the following account and try to develop your own situational analysis of the company and evaluate the descriptions you will find about what they are doing.

The history of Shangri-La

The first deluxe Shangri-La hotel was established in Singapore in 1971 by the Kuok Group (owned by a Malaysian Chinese family), a multinational conglomerate and was managed by Westin until 1983. Additionally, the company's name was changed to Shangri-La International Hotel Management Limited in 1983. In 1989, it developed its sister brand – Traders Hotels, which was first established in Beijing, and this was designed to deliver high value and quality accommodation to the business traveller at reasonable prices. In 1997, Shangri-La Hotels & Resorts (as it was then known) was bought by Shangri-La Asia.

Ownership

Shangri-La Asia Limited is a Hong Kong-based company, and it is the parent company of Shangri-La Hotels & Resorts which is a public company listed on the Hong Kong Stock Exchange (with subsidiaries also listed on the Singapore, Thailand and Kuala Lumpur exchanges). The Kuok Group also holds a controlling share in Shangri-La Asia Limited.

Vision and mission of Shangri-La

Shangri-La wants to be "The first choice for customers, employees, shareholders and business partners." To achieve this, it determines to "Delight customers each and every time." "Expanding the Shangri-La brand globally and exploring opportunities to operate hotels in gateway cities and key resorts around the world under management, equity participation or ownership" are Shangri-La's strategic objectives.

Shangri-La corporate culture

Shangri-La has clear corporate vision, mission and philosophy. It has 23,500 employees altogether. They all believe in one philosophy – "Shangri-La hospitality from caring people", "people" here includes customers, employees, shareholders and suppliers. Its core value also indicates that Shangri-La will devote itself to developing good relationship with people, maximizing customers' satisfaction, upholding shareholders' and suppliers' benefits and creating a prospective environment for employees. Moreover, the most important characteristics of Shangri-La are based on the Asian of style hospitality and this is combined with the local special culture in each and every Shangri-La Hotel & Resort. According to Tang Xiaoyao (2005) who is the CEO of Dalian Shangri-La Hotel, Shangri-La hopes all their employees will take pride in the achievements that this organization has earned in the industry, but they should be modest in their performances and provide the best services to every customer with sincere and warm attitudes.

There are some weaknesses of Shangri-La. First of all, it has a limited market. Shangri-La focuses its business on Asia, especially in the mainland of China. On the one hand, it has not followed the trend of globalization. Global business and global awareness may require Shangri-La to extend its global market, and this may reinforce its competitive advantage and brand influence, and increase market share in the global hotel market. On the other hand, China is the primary target for other big international hotel groups, such as Marriott, Hilton and Accor. Even though Shangri-La has had relative market share in China, its market may become smaller with the increase of other international hotels and the change of consumer's various demands. On the whole, Shangri-La should base on Asian market and extend globally. Secondly, it has single hotel type. There are 32 luxury hotels and only 5 traders hotels in Shangri-La Hotel group. As the development of tourism and global business, there is a variety of consumer demands. Especially the economic type – mid-level and budget hotel is dramatically growing. For Shangri-La, it is necessary to develop diverse hotel types. It may attract more customers, meet their demands and then improve it competitive advantage. In mainland China, it may reinforce its competitive position if it develops more hotel types.

Shangri-La's external context

After the financial crisis in 1997, the economy of Asia Pacific has gradually recovered. Most countries' GDP keep increasing trend. In 2000, South Korea grew 8.3%, following by Singapore, Malaysia, the People's republic of China and Taiwan whose growth rates were above 6%, and Thailand, Indonesia and Hong Kong's rates were between 4% and 5%, finally the Philippines was 3%. In 2005, most East and South Asian countries have achieved even better GDP growth, such as 7.5% in India and 9.5% in China. Although the 9/11 in 2001 and SARS in 2003 dramatically hit this region's economy, the global business development and booming exports encourage the regional economy upturn. Moreover, in order to stimulate economy recovery many countries have changed to relaxed monetary policies in the form of lower interest rates and relaxed investment policies for foreign investors. A good case in point is the People's Republic of China which has changed the limitation of direct investment by foreigners in 2002. These kinds of preferential policies may greatly encourage more and more international hotel groups to invest in this region.

In addition, every country in Asia Pacific experienced an increase in tourist arrivals from 1998. According to the Pacific Asia Travel Association (PATA), the average increase of this region was 9% from 1998 to 1999. Especially in 1999, the People's Republic of China increased 18.76%, followed by Hong Kong (11.5%), Singapore (11.4%) and Thailand (10.3%). In spite of the sharp downturn in 2001, the tourist arrival sustained increase in this region. As a result of the development of tourism, the demand of hotel may have significant increase.

Main market

There is evidence of an oversupply of hotels in some cities. Overbuilding is a current phenomenon in their hotel industry. Take China as an example, Beijing and Shanghai had negative growth in revenues per available room (revPAR), which were −14% and −17% (Andersen,

1999). This is because the Chinese market is the fastest developing market in this region, and being the capital city and financial centre cities – Beijing and Shanghai are the primary choices of global hotel chains. The supply of hotel has been over the demand. However, Shangri-La has 37 hotels in Asian region, and more than half (18) hotels are in China. Chinese market is Shangri-La's most important market. The negative growth may influence its hotel performance in these two cities.

Main competitors in China

Moreover, as the opening market and relaxed foreign investment policies in China, the entry limitation is greatly decreased, so more and more international hotel groups will enter Chinese market and reduce Shangri-La's market share. Firstly, Six Continental has the most hotels in China with the number of 36, following by Marriott (26) and Accor (23). Six Continental and Marriott focus on luxury hotels, and Accor cover both luxury and economic hotels. They are the close rival of Shangri-La. Consequently, the increasing hotel suppliers may enhance hotel consumer's bargaining power; meanwhile, the suppliers of hotel may also raise their bargaining power because of the increasing number of hotels. Secondly, due to the development of global business, there is an increasing demand of economic and mid-level hotels by business travellers. However, most Shangri-La hotels are deluxe hotels. There may be the threat of substitutes like mid-level and budget hotels. A case in point is Accor in China; its marketing strategy is focusing on the development of mid-level and budget hotels, such as Mercure and IBIS.

Shangri-La performance

At the end of 2002, Shangri-La owns 37 hotels including 18 in China, with total 19,109 rooms in China, Singapore, Malaysia, Indonesia, Philippines, Thailand, Fiji and Myanmar. The majority hotels are under the Shangri-La brand, with five hotels flagged as Traders brand. The brand of Shangri-La in hotel industry is equal to the luxury and top service quality, and it is Shangri-La's best competitive advantage. Every Shangri-La hotel has splendid decoration and elegant environment. It is regarded as one of the finest hotel group in the world.

Additionally, Shangri-La has stable positive profit. Even though with the influence of 9/11 event, the global downturn, Shangri-La's turnover was 58.3% and operating profit increased by 49.8% from 1998 to 2002. Besides, although it was affected by the SARS in 2003, Shangri-La conducted a plan and some useful measures for preventing the virus, and they were considered as a model for the hospitality industry. This implementation encouraged the hotel industry to conquer the shade of the SARS.

Shangri-La's strategies

Functional strategies
Human resource strategy
Shangri-La has extensive training programmes to improve service skills of its line staff and professional skills of other employees. Its in-house training programmes emphasize service attitudes, organizational values and job enrichment. The majority of Shangri-La's managers are from western countries or having western education background. The CEO of Shangri-La

Group (2005) said that the success of Shangri-La is focusing on the quality of service. The group considers the training of employee is the chief task. It invests a significant number of fees on training professional employees from knowledge and skills. As a result, Shangri-La becomes one of the most popular employers.

High service quality is the most important asset of the hotel. It is not easily copied by competitors. Hotel can keep longer competitive advantage with excellent service quality provided by loyal employees. Shangri-La is well known for providing cordial and considerate services.

Technology strategy

Shangri-La initiated an upgrade of its hotel reservation system to a state-of-the-art central reservation and information system (Merlin) in 2003, which was supplemented by strategically located voice reservation centres serviced by free-phone numbers.

Technology is more and more concerned as the development of computer techniques and the popularity of family computers. It is also seemed as an important competitive advantage for a hotel. Nowadays, online booking is widely adopted by customers. Shangri-La should not only provide multichannels of reservation, such as by Internet, by telephone, by fax and by post, but also improve the technology to reduce the booking time and procedures.

Renovations

Shangri-La has implemented an extensive renovation programme for its major hotels to ensure that they are in excellent condition to retain their competitive advantage and preserve the integrity of the group's brands. In 2004, it constructed the state-of-the-art spa facility in the Shangri-La Hotel, Bangkok. The group constantly strives to new concepts.

Business level strategies
Marketing strategies

In relationship marketing, Shangri-La has a loyalty programme called Golden Circle, which offers a series of rewards in three levels – Classic, Executive and Elite according to customer's accumulated stays in hotel including targeted programmes such as the current (up to 40% discount) "Rate Break" promotion. It operates 12 sales and marketing offices in Guangzhou, Shanghai, Beijing, Hong Kong, Singapore, London, Los Angeles, New York, Melbourne, Sydney, Tokyo and Dubai. Besides, it has established partnerships with almost 30 airlines.

Loyalty programme is a helpful and extensively used relationship marketing measure in hotel and airline industries. It helps retain old customers and attract new customers. However, it is easily imitated by competitors. Therefore, it requires Shangri-La to segment its market and conduct accordingly loyalty programme. For examples, Hilton Hotel has the senior loyalty programme which is only for the old market (age above 62 years). Marriott separates the governors and military as a segmented market and offers special discounts for them.

Management strategy

Shangri-La segments its business into three types: hotel operation, which relates to the ownership and operation of hotel business; hotel management, which means providing hotel management and related services; property rentals, which having the ownership and lease office, commercial and service apartments. In addition, Shangri-La has developed management contracts in its hotels owned by third parties, and in 2006, based on contracts executed to date, there will be 16 hotels operated by the Shangri-La group but owned by the third parties, comparing with 3 hotels in 2003.

Using diverse business and management strategies may reduce the business risk and save the cost of labour. Renting the property will add to the income of the company. However, the profit of Shangri-La will decrease because of not having the full ownership. Sometimes a hotel's reputation may be negatively affected because of the failing business of the owner(s).

Focus strategy

According to the chairman's statement (2004), Shangri-La will continue to invest, expand and build its brand strength in mainland China and continue to see it as their most important market. It will add seven new hotels in China (Figure 4.3).

Hotel	City	Country	Opening
Shangri-La Hotel	Zhongshan	China	December 2003
Shangri-La Hotel	Zhengzhou	China	2004
Shangri-La Hotel	Fuzhou	China	October 2004
Traders Fudu Hotel	Changzhou	China	July 2004
Shangri-La's Sunny Bay Resort	Sanya	China	January 2005
Pudong Shangri-La (extension)	Shanghai	China	May 2005
Jingan Shangri-La	Shanghai	China	2007

Figure 4.3
Shangri-La Hotels, pipeline growth, 2003–2007
Source: Mintel (2003)

The Chinese market is undoubtedly a market with great potential and given the readings of the international tourism and business trends, Shangri-La should be active in its global market development and exploring new products to satisfy various demands and expand its market.

Global strategy

Shangri-La also plans to expand the Shangri-La brand globally, reviewing opportunities to operate hotels in gateway cities and key resorts all over the world by management agreements, equity participation or ownership. Additionally, it will continually to develop the Chinese market. It is reported that Shangri-La Hotels & Resorts has opened a training centre in Beijing for staff working at its Chinese hotels. It plans to increase its presence in China from 17 sites to 32 by 2007.

As the market in China becomes more and more open, more and more international hotel brands will enter China and also attempt to enlarge their Chinese market. This situation may be a big threat for Shangri-La, which has always focused on the Chinese market and has the majority of its properties in China. It demands that Shangri-La group should extend global market to sustain its competitive ability and long-term development.

Shangri-La's future challenges

China's entry into the World Trade Organization in 2001, the awarding of the 2008 Olympic Games and the 2010 World Expo bring great opportunities for Chinese economic growth and for tourism and hospitality development. With its primary focus on the Chinese market, the Shangri-La group is optimistic about the future of the hotel industry in Mainland China and its share of that market.

Nevertheless, Shangri-La may face to some challenges in future. Firstly, the more relaxed market brings both advantages and disadvantages for the Shangri-La group. Shangri-La might extend its Chinese market share with less limitation, for example, it may be allowed to have single venture in China as a foreign company. However, the easier entry opportunities for the Chinese market may attract a significant number of international hotel brands to start or expand their Chinese operations. Most of them focus on the luxury hotel, such as Hilton, Marriott and InterContinental. As a result, Shangri-La meets more close competitors and it may hinder its Chinese market development. Secondly, Shangri-La has the awareness of global development. However, it mainly operates deluxe hotels and pays special attention to the Asian market. It might be difficult for it to extend into the global market, especially the European and the US markets where economic and budget hotels are very popular and have different cultures compared to the Oriental culture. Moreover, Knowles and Egan (2002) point out that there are some weaknesses of the hotel market in Asia Pacific Region. For example, hotels do not tend to use the data about customers very well and hotels are very reluctant to share knowledge. They suggested that hotels should pay more attention to the overall performance of the hotel, develop effective distribution and revenue management practices, undertake positive good relationship management and share business knowledge with each other.

In conclusion, Shangri-la should consolidate in the Chinese market and explore the global market more fully; meanwhile, it will need to develop effective strategies and consumer relationship programmes, and create new products and hotel types to keep its competitive advantage and expand into new markets.

■ Summary

- The hotel business worldwide recovered from 2004, and the outlook is positive for the next 10 years.
- There is widespread selling of hotel property by the major chains, while private equity funds have emerged as the most important buyers of major hotel properties, portfolios and chains from 2002. Most large hotel groups are focused on franchising and management contracts. Hotel chains are continuing to grow at a more rapid pace than independents.
- East Asia and the Middle East continue to have the most rapid expansion in capacity of any region, especially China, India, Vietnam, Hong Kong, Dubai and Egypt. Gaming centres, such as Macau and Las Vegas, are also preferred locations of hotel expansion.

● Internet distribution is growing rapidly but electronic travel agencies are losing share to the hotel chain branded sites.

■ Conclusion

In this chapter we have outlined the ways in which it is possible to analyse the internal and external environments of international hospitality organizations. The basic tools are simple but the effective use of the techniques requires a great deal skill and knowledge. Not everything is knowable but the greater the complexity of the analysis undertaken the less the impact of the unexpected should be on the conclusions drawn from the analysis. We hope that the practical examples we have given will help to contextualize the processes we have outlined and make them more meaningful for you and easier for you to use in your own work. The complexities of the international hospitality industry complicate such analyses but also make them more important if we want to fully understand the ways in which we can deliver improved performance. This is a theme we will take up in the next chapter which looks at international marketing.

■ Review questions

1   Do you consider companies make full use of situational audits and environmental analysis in their decision-making?
2   How far can companies respond to changes in the operating environment?
3   What sorts of information would make you advise against developing a hotel in a new country that you have no direct experience of?
4   Why do we strive to know all we can when we know we cannot know everything and can control even less?

CHAPTER 5

International
marketing

■ Introduction

In this chapter, you will be introduced to the key concepts of marketing in the international hospitality industry. We will start by explaining the differences between marketing and international marketing, and then discuss the applications of international marketing strategies in hospitality businesses. This chapter explores how marketing managers analyse country market potential in order to develop effective international marketing mix strategies. It reviews the adaptation versus standardization debate and also considers the rationale for selecting nationally responsive and globally integrated marketing strategies. Finally this chapter discusses very important issues of branding in the hospitality industry from an international perspective.

■ The marketing concept

There are hundreds of definitions of marketing available in the literature. Early definitions of marketing focused on the exchange or transaction process, which can generate first-time buyers. Now more academics suggest that customer satisfaction is the key to successful marketing, which is closely linked with the development of relationship marketing.

The following three definitions of marketing probably are widely accepted by both academics and industry management:

1 "Marketing is a social and managerial process through which individuals and organizations satisfy their needs and objectives via the exchange process" (Kotler, 2003).

2 "Marketing is the management process responsible for identifying, anticipating and satisfying customer requirements profitably" (Chartered Institute of Marketing, UK).

3 "Marketing is the process of planning and executing the conception, pricing, promotion, and distribution of ideas, goods and services to create exchanges that satisfy individual and organizational objectives" (American Marketing Association).

According to Rugman and Collinson (2006: 312), international marketing is "the process of identifying the goods and services that customers outside the home country want and then providing them at the right price and location". In the international marketplace this process is similar to that carried out within the domestic market, but with some important modifications to adapt the marketing efforts to the needs of the specific country or geographic location. International marketing involves a range of activities which are more complex than domestic marketing, such as marketing research, product design, pricing and branding.

International hospitality managers cannot assume that the foreign markets are the same as their home country and thorough investigations of the specific country before making major marketing decisions that are essential for successful international market development. International marketing is closely linked to international strategic management because it includes the process of deciding which markets to operate in, issues of international entry modes and decisions about whether to expand or contract operations. International marketing is vital if a company competes in a global industry or the industry is beginning to move towards globalization.

■ The concepts of marketing orientation

Marketing is about serving customers, fulfilling the needs of society and achieving the goals of the organization. Through customer satisfaction, marketing creates the customer loyalty necessary to reach an organization's objectives. In the past century, the approach to marketing has gone through different stages. In the new century marketing will be influenced by ethics, natural environments, cultural diversity and changing technology and innovation. Also for a prospective marketer, more stakeholders in the society now need to be considered in the process of marketing (Figure 5.1).

Production orientation

A production orientation indicates a company is more concerned about production variables, such as capacity, efficiency and quality than anything else in marketing. Companies assume customers want lower prices and higher-quality goods and services. Such an approach is still used internationally for selling commodities and service. For example, when the first McDonald's restaurant opened in Moscow, more than 30,000 customers waited outside to get in and taste the burgers. In the first year, 5 million customers came to eat and drink in this restaurant. To provide good quality

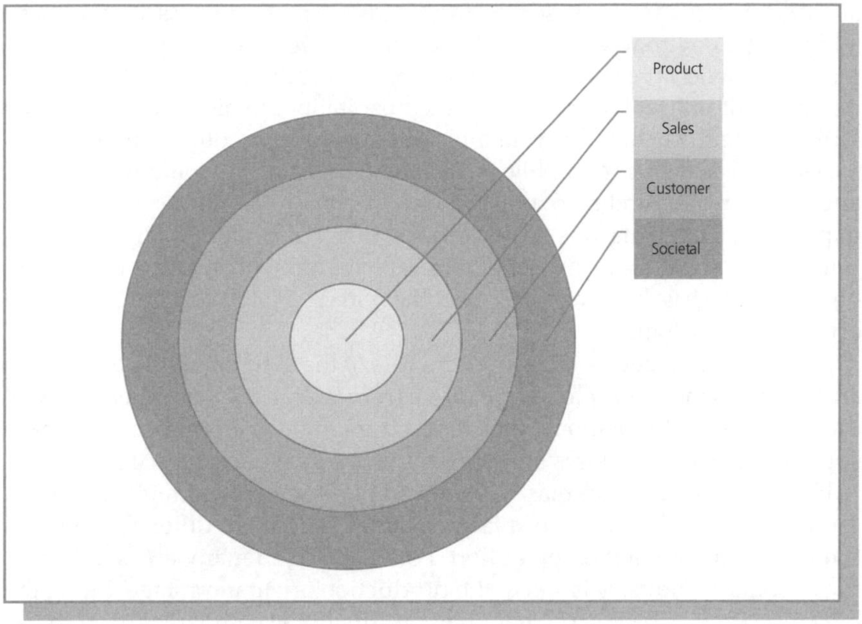

Product
Sales
Customer
Societal

Figure 5.1
Building the
concepts of
marketing
orientation

food efficiently has been the main objective of McDonald's Moscow for quite a long term because of unsatisfied demands. KFC is another example of production orientation. KFC started to develop business in China from 1990 and currently serves 1 billion customers in China alone in 2005.

Sales orientation

Demonstrating a sales orientation indicates that a firm assumes global customers are reasonably similar and it can therefore sell into foreign markets with the same goods or services it sells at home. Hospitality multinationals use powerful public media, or sponsor mega sport events to promote their products and services worldwide.

Customer orientation

A customer orientation indicates a firm is sensitive to customer needs, as it thinks in terms of identifying and serving the needs of the customer. Given a particular country market, what products are needed? In the auto industry, there is not a car for all the countries; in the restaurant business, there is a dish for every customer.

Societal marketing orientation

The societal marketing orientation indicates that a firm recognizes it must conduct its activities in a way that preserves or enhances the well-being of all its stakeholders. As it serves the needs of its customers it must also address the environmental, health, social and work-related problems that may arise when producing or marketing its products abroad. Customers may present unhealthy demands in the hospitality premises, some of which will be illegal, such as drug taking and prostitution, others merely anti-social, such as the use of mobile telephones. Hospitality should have a legal and ethical responsibility to inhibit these activities and even to prevent them happening. Following this societal marketing orientation, many organizations want to contribute to a better natural environment and now we are seeing many hotels beginning to use the Green Hotel concept to attract eco-friendly customers.

As Figure 5.1 suggests, the scope and role of the marketing function grows and becomes more complex as we move from the inner to the outer circles of the diagram. It also demonstrates that although the concept becomes more sophisticated, it never loses the elements of the former constructions.

Hospitality companies may have mixed marketing orientations in certain foreign market. For instance, a large country may be in different stages of the marketing orientation evolution. For example, in many areas in China, the hospitality industry is still in the production orientation stage. But in the big cities, such as Beijing or Shanghai, multinational companies need to use marketing orientation or societal orientation to reach the more sophisticated customers.

■ International market research and assessment

Marketing research is necessary for major hospitality companies when they plan to move into foreign markets. This presents unique problems because of the cultural, social and technological differences between countries (Usunier, 2000). These issues include:

● Language and translation difficulties. English-speaking or French-speaking researchers cannot use their questionnaires or conduct interviews in many foreign counties.
● Different cultural responses are found to the idea of market research surveys. The research findings may be biased by these different responses.
● Difficulty in obtaining comparable samples, especially in developing countries.
● Different cultural backgrounds and product knowledge.
● Differences in infrastructure.

According to Bowie and Buttle (2004), hospitality companies carrying out international marketing research need to be aware of these difficulties, and should employ specialist local research agencies to provide appropriate advice.

The beginning of the practical process of international marketing is to assess market conditions in the various possible countries in which multinationals may choose to enter. Rugman and Collinson (2006) suggest this assessment typically involves a series of analyses aimed at pinpointing specific offerings and geographic targets.

- The first step in this process is the initial screening. It is the process of determining the basic need potential of the multinational's goods and services in foreign markets. Marketers need to ask the question: Who might be interested in buying our services and products? Once a company decides to enter foreign markets, it must carefully collect and analyse data in order to determine specific country product-market potential and the marketing mix required to achieve its objectives. Total market potential represents the total potential sales of all the relevant competitors within a given market. To determine potential demand for its own product, a hospitality company must first estimate the potential sales of the total market and then estimate its current and desired market share. The major indicators, as we identified in the previous chapter's discussion of PEST analysis, for potential sales of most service and products are population and disposable income, plus the rate of growth in each. Other variables to be considered include income elasticity, income inequality, the availability of substitute products and cultural factors. For example, the total market potential for the hotel business in India will be enormous, as it has the biggest middle class in the world, and India's GDP growth reached 8% in 2005.
- At the second stage, screening is used to reduce the list of market prospects by eliminating those that fail to meet the necessary financial and economic considerations. According to Rugman and Collinson (2006), there are three important market indicators: market size, market intensity and market growth. (1) Market size is the relative size of each market as a percentage of the total world market. (2) Market intensity is the degree of purchasing power in one country as compared to others. (3) Market growth is the annual increase in sales. These data are usually analysed using quantitative techniques, such as trend analysis, regression analysis and cluster analysis.
- For hotel businesses, the essential data, which help companies to forecast operating performance in a new country, include industry average occupancies, achieved room rates and yield, visitor arrivals, visitor spend and other economic statistics. Bowie and Buttle (2004) suggest that the attractiveness of a different country market will depend upon the potential demand from the selected target markets and the intensity of competitor rivalry.
- The following screening involves looking at political and legal forces. High political stability creates a favourable invest condition. Developed countries in Europe, North America and the Asia Pacific area have stable political systems, hoteliers can choose to purchase freehold properties or negotiate long leasehold agreements in these regions of high political stability. While countries that have considerable political turmoil, like Iraq,

Pakistan, Zimbabwe, East Timor and Myanmar, are more risky and therefore less attractive to international hospitality companies. In countries with high political instability, the preferred entry option is to franchise to a local company or negotiate an equity-free management contract, because local organizations understand how to manage their own political risks better than foreign companies (Bowie and Buttle, 2004).

● One of the primary considerations is the entry barriers that may exist, such as restrictions or limits on local ownership of business operations. It also typically involves consideration of socio-cultural forces, such as language, work habits, customs, religion and values. For example, when hotel groups move to Dubai, it is crucial to build up a series of working relationships with the royal families, government officials and local companies. Hotel groups also need to consider recruiting staff from another country as only a very limited number of local people will apply for jobs in hotel industry.

● The final stage of screening is typically focused on competitive forces. In some examples multinationals decide to enter a competitive market because they believe the potential benefits far outweigh the drawbacks. By going head to head with the competition, the company can force itself to become more efficient and effective and thus improve its own competitiveness. For example, London is a very competitive location for international hoteliers, while the Asian Hotel Group, Shangri-La decided to run the best hotel in London.

Example: The legend of Shangri-La and its unique hospitality is making its way to Europe

In 2009, Shangri-La will reach an even higher level of attainment, when it launches a new luxury hotel inside the spire of London Bridge Tower. It is a new symbol for London. At 1,016 ft. high, London Bridge Tower is regarded as one of the most ambitious architectural endeavours in the United Kingdom. Its height will make it one of the tallest buildings in Europe, while its soaring spire shape will make it one of the most distinctive.

As with every property in the group, the Shangri-La Hotel at London Bridge Tower will operate on a simple yet powerful philosophy of Shangri-La hospitality from warm, caring people. This uniquely Asian view of service embodies the core values of respect, helpfulness, courtesy, sincerity and humility, and has been the cornerstone of the Shangri-La success.

Source: www.shangri-la.com/london/shangri-la/en/

● Before making a final selection, multinationals usually enhance their information by visiting on-site locations and talking to representatives or local officials. Such field trips are very common and can do a great deal to supplement currently available information.

Global market segmentation

Global market segmentation identifies specific segments of potential customers with homogeneous attributes who exhibit similar responses to a marketing mix. Levitt (1960) said that consumers in different countries seek variety and new segments will emerge in multiple national markets. For example, ethnic food, such as pizza and curry is in demand worldwide.

Global market segmentation is based on demographics (including income and population), psychographics (values, attitudes and lifestyles), behavioural characteristics and benefits. Market segmentation assists in corporate-level strategic planning (e.g. Marriot's growth strategy requires identifying country/regional segments for increased sales). In functional or operational level, market segmentation helps decide to pursue a standardized or adapted marketing mix.

Demographic segmentation

Demographic segmentation is based on measurable characteristics of populations: income, population size, age distribution, gender, education and occupation. Several global demographic trends have been identified by sociologists and economists – fewer married couples, smaller family size, longer life expectancy, changing roles of women, higher incomes and living standards. Some key demographic facts and trends could be supported by the following data:

● British consumers over 60 years now are more than consumers aged 16 years and under.
● Asia has more than 600 million consumers of 16 years and under.
● Combined buying power for African-, Hispanic- and Asian-Americans is $1 trillion a year.
● Family size becomes smaller. Average British woman has 1.7 kids in 2004.

Segmenting global markets by income and population

Income is a valuable segmentation variable since a market consists of those willing and able to buy. Customer's purchase ability is essential when hospitality companies consider their target markets. While 70% of world GNP comes from the Triad (the European Union (EU), North America and Japan), only 15% of the world's population lives in the Triad.

GDP and other income measures converted to dollars should be calculated according to purchasing power (i.e. what the currency will buy in

Table 5.1 The top 15 biggest economies in the world, 2006

Rank	Country	GDP (millions of US$)
1	United States	12,485,725
2	Japan	4,571,314
3	Germany	2,797,343
4	People's Republic of China	2,224,811
5	United Kingdom	2,201,473
6	France	2,105,864
7	Italy	1,766,160
8	Canada	1,130,208
9	Spain	1,126,565
10	South Korea	793,070
11	Brazil	792,683
12	India	775,410
13	Mexico	768,437
14	Russia	766,180
15	Australia	707,992

Source: Wikipedia, The free encyclopedia, www.en.wikipedia.org/wiki/List of countries by GDP (nominal).

the country of issue) or through direct comparisons of product prices. For example, while the US ranks eighth in per capita income, its standard of living is second only to Luxembourg's. Another example is the GDP of India is much less than GDP of Italy, while India's GDP in term of purchase power is much bigger than that of Italia (Table 5.1).

Because the US market is enormous (e.g. GDP $12.48 trillion in 2005 national income, a population of 298 million and per capita income of $41,800), non-US companies target American consumers. Despite high per capita incomes, many other industrialized countries are small in terms of total annual income (e.g. Sweden's per capita GNP is $24,487, but its population of 8.9 million makes national income only about $220 billion).

The 10 most populous countries account for more than 60% of the world's population. Concentrated income in the high-income and large-population countries means that a company can target buyers in 10 or fewer countries (Table 5.2).

There are large, fast-growing, high-income segments in countries like China and India (e.g. an estimated 100 million Indians are "upper middle class", with average income of over $1,400). For low-priced products,

Table 5.2 The 10 most populous countries		
Rank	Country	Population
1	China	1,313,973,713
2	India	1,095,351,995
3	United States	298,444,215
4	Indonesia	245,452,739
5	Brazil	188,078,227
6	Pakistan	165,803,560
7	Bangladesh	147,365,352
8	Russia	142,893,540
9	Nigeria	131,859,731
10	Japan	127,463,611

Source: CIA (2006), www.cia.gov/cia/publications/factbook/index.html

population is more important than income for market potential. In hospitality industry, it also make sense, you could find the cheapest Big Mac is in the world in 1990s. McDonald's adjusts its products in different countries considering local customers' purchasing power as well as the company's long-term strategy.

Age segmentation is a useful demographic variable. One global segment is global youth. Shared interest in fashion, music and lifestyle exhibits remarkably consistent consumption behaviour for name brands, novelty, entertainment, trendy and image-oriented products. MTV, Coca-Cola, McDonald's, Starbucks, Swatch and i-Pod pursue the global teenage segment. Another global segment is the global senior or elite: older, affluent, well-travelled consumers with money for high-end, exclusive products, luxury cars, upscale beverages and cruise holidays.

ACTIVITY

Log onto two or three holiday tour operators websites that target different markets, for example Club 18-30 (www.club18-30.co.uk), SAGA (www.sagaholidays.co.uk) and Sandals (www.sandals.com/). What differences can you identify?

Explore the sites and compare the packages they provide: activities, locations, price, accommodation, image, language, etc.

■ Gender segmentation

Gender segmentation is a sensible approach for many hospitality companies. Some hospitality products or services may be specifically designed

Table 5.3 Food preference differences between the genders

Men are	Women are
More taste-driven in their food choices	Highly concerned about nutrition
More in sync with restaurant portions	Likely to eat less
Confirmed meat lovers	Confirmed fruit lovers
Comforted by familiar foods	More adventures in food choices
More likely to crave entrees than desserts	Snackers with a sweet tooth
More frequent restaurant patrons	Apt to eat out less often

Source: Lydecker, T. (1994). Men & women: Two different markets sharing a table. *Restaurant USA*, August, pp. 26–30.

and provided to men or women. Companies that focus on the needs and wants of one gender will find opportunities. Table 5.3 (Lydecker, 1994) shows the differences between the genders according to their food preferences, restaurant can design their products according to increase certain gender customers' consumption. For example, McDonald's provides super size or extra super size meal to target male customers.

There are a number of women only hotels in London, the New York Hotel in Earls Court is a small award-winning hotel that exclusively gay, while Reeves Hotel in Shepherds Bush is a women only hotel and is lesbian-friendly (Bowie and Buttle, 2004). Even a big hotel group, like Hilton London Park Lane, has recently launched a women only floor designed for female business professionals. Through travel-quest (www.travel-quest.co.uk/index.htm), you can find many choices of hotels for women only, gay women only and gay men only hotels.

Some pubs clearly targeted their customers group: men, women or homosexual. The bedroom is also a very popular pub in America!

■ Ethnic origin, religion and nationality

Bowie and Buttle (2004) argue that ethnic origin, religion and nationality are very important variables that are closely linked to each other and to culture. One consequence of these cultural influences is the very different attitude to food. Kosher cuisine is one of the well-known religious foods for Jews, while fasting during Ramadan is equally important for Muslims. The differences between Eastern and Western style cooking are recognized by international hotels, such as the Shangri-La and the InterContinental, who provide both styles of cooking at breakfast, lunch and dinner.

In many countries, the population includes ethnic groups of significant size. The United States has three major ethnic segments: African-Americans, Asian-Americans and Hispanic-Americans. Each segment forms a subset (e.g. Asian-Americans include Thais, Vietnamese, Japanese and Chinese). Hispanic-Americans numbered 35 million in 2000, and have a positive reputation for working hard, with a strong family and religious orientation. Other stereotypes point to a more negative reputation and the dangers of ghetto lifestyles and gang wars. The market appraisal must try to get behind these stereotypes and construct a viable representation of the market segment.

Hotels located in Europe and America are targeting significant sales from other markets like China, Japan and Korea. There has been a large increase in these countries' international outbound travel over the past 10 years and the trend will continue in the future 20 years. Although English is common language in the business world, hoteliers cannot assume that all their potential international customers can speak English. To satisfy customers' needs, they need to provide many new amenities and services:

● multilingual front desk staff who can speak Chinese, Japanese or Korean;
● hotel brochures, information packs and restaurant menus written in Chinese, Japanese and Korean;
● oriental food option (rice is very important for oriental food and therefore for oriental customers' satisfaction);
● other amenities in the room, such as slippers and shampoo;
● Cable TV with Chinese, Japanese and Korean channels.

■ Global targeting

Targeting evaluates and compares identified groups and selects one or more with the highest potential. A marketing mix is created to provide the best return on sales and the maximum value to consumers. After segmenting the market, the marketer creates a product-market profile. To penetrate an existing market, a hospitality company must offer more value than competitors with better benefits, lower prices or both.

The criteria for assessing opportunity in global target markets include: segment size and growth potential; competition; and compatibility and feasibility. We will consider these in turn.

Current segment size and growth potential

Is the market segment currently large enough to make a profit? Does it have high growth potential? China, India, Russia and Brazil represent many people's idea of a market with growth potential in industries, such as hospitality and leisure.

Example: Carlson Hotel Worldwide's ambition in India

Carlson Hotels Worldwide is aiming to launch 40 hotels in India by 2008. The fifth-largest private hospitality group in the world with over US $38 billion turnover, the Carlson group will open a bouquet of its hotel brands like Radisson, Reagent International, Country Inn, Park Plaza and Park Inn in the next 3 years.

Speaking on the launch of Park Plaza in Gurgaon, K B Kachru, Senior Vice President-South Asia of Carlson Hotels said: "We will open 40 more hotels by 2008 and would become the single-largest operator of hotel chains in India".

"The group will target New Delhi, Mumbai and Bangalore for its premium hotel brands like Radisson and Reagent International. Carlson has signed a management and franchise agreement with Bestech Group, the owners of the Park Plaza in Gurgaon".

Source: www.carlsonhotelsmedia.tekgroup.com/

Compatibility and feasibility

Hospitality managers must decide how well a company's product will fit a market. There are several criteria: Does the product create value? How much adaptation, if any, is required? Will restrictions, tariffs or currency exchange rates drive up the price? Is there a segment compatible with the goals and the sources of competitive advantage?

Standardized global marketing resembles mass marketing, creating the same marketing mix for a broad mass market of potential buyers. Standardized global marketing, also known as undifferentiated target marketing, assumes that a mass market exists around the world. Product adaptation is minimized, and exploitation is intensive.

Concentrated global marketing involves devising a marketing mix to reach a specific **niche**, a single segment of the global market. Concentrated targeting is employed by hospitality companies who serve niche markets, striving for global depth and not national breadth.

Example: YHA focuses on first-time travellers in the global market

In February 2006, the Youth Hostel Association has announced its advertising strategy, as part of an £18 million hostels and image overhaul, to target global young people who are travelling independently for the first time.

Source: YHA website at www.yha.com

Differentiated global marketing, also known as multisegment targeting, targets two or more market segments with multiple marketing mix offerings. This strategy allows a company to achieve a wider market coverage, such as Accor has with its super budget hotel chain Motel 6, pricing from $40 per night, its budget hotel chain Ibis from $80 per night, its business hotel chain Novotel from $150 per night and its luxury hotel chain Sofitel from $300 per night.

■ Marketing mix

When a hospitality company has completed the initial screening of the foreign markets and decided to move into the new marketplace, then they need to carefully develop a marketing mix plan. A marketing mix consists of the controllable variables, that is, product and branding, promotion, location, distribution channel, and price designed to create value for customers and achieve competitive advantage for the company. The essence of marketing is to surpass the competition in creating perceived value for customers. The value equation guides this task (Plate 9):

$$value = benefits/price.$$

Plate 9
Value and price –
Casita Los Mangos,
Majahuitas Resort,
Mexico.
Source: Ruth Clarke

Looking at this building, roughly translated into English as the Mango House, what price would you put on it? How does this compare to the modern air-conditioned five-star hotels to be found in the big Mexican resorts of Acapulco and Cancun? In fact this retailed for $375 per night! The value comes from the exclusivity of the resort, the location and the service offer. The resort is only reachable by boat and even at that price is very popular!

The marketing mix is integral to the equation because benefits combine product, promotion, location and distribution. Value as perceived by customers can be increased through an improved bundle of benefits or lower prices (or both). Hospitality marketers can improve the product and service or create better communications strategies. Marketers can increase value by cutting costs and prices. None monetary costs are also a factor, so marketers may find that customers are decreasing their time and effort to learn about or find a product. A hospitality company which offers a combination of superior product, service distribution, or convenient location and lower prices will enjoy an advantageous position.

Products

In global competition, product is the most basic element of marketing mix. Firstly we need to identify the differences between local products and global products.

A local product or brand is one that has achieved success in a single national market, such as Abeku hotels in Japan. Sometimes a global company creates local products and brands to cater to the needs and preferences of particular country markets.

Example: Abeku Hotels in Japan

The Japanese have a concept that combines efficiency and ingenuity into an abeku, also called fashion hotels or love hotels. The abeku often resemble European castles or Alpine chalets and provide garden settings. Nearly all offer 360-channel television, videos, stereo, sauna and in-room refreshments. But what the abeku really offer is a private sanctuary. Japan's high population density and traditional use of lightweight walls (for safety in earthquakes) result in close living arrangements. Privacy in abeku is preserved with a touch-screen reservation system and state-of-the art automation. Guests can check in, out and pay their bills without being seen by anyone else.

Business is booming for these hotels, with Sunday being an especially busy day. Length of stay can range from several hours to several days. Abeku accounts for 20,000 of Japan's lodging facilities.

Source: *Washington Post*, 13 August 1990,

A global product meets the wants and needs of a global market; it is offered in all the regions of the world, including both developed and developing countries. A global brand, such as Coca-Cola or Four Seasons, has the same name, similar image and similar positioning throughout the world. The benefits of global products and global branding include the economies of scale associated with a single global ad campaign and a single brand strategy.

The level of standardization or adaptation is a major product decision in international marketing (Usunier, 2000). Bowie and Buttle (2004: 120) argue that the international hospitality product needs to take into account local country cultural differences and make suitable adaptations to gain local consumer acceptance. Identifying target markets is crucial when developing the international product. If the target market is mainly from the home country, then the product can be standardized using the home country style. For example, if the InterContinental Hotel in Bangkok primarily targets American or British customers, it can legitimately seek to keep American style or British style food or service. If its main customers are local people or South East Asian tourists, it should commit to adjusting the range of services to fit the demands.

The primary reasons behind the tendency of hospitality companies to alter their products or services to meet local conditions are legal, cultural and/or economic in nature.

- **Economic reasons:** Levels of income, differences in income distribution, and the extent and condition of available infrastructure can all affect demand for a particular product. Often, price-reducing alterations are required if a company wishes to participate in developing country markets.
- **Cultural reasons:** Cultural factors affecting product demand may or may not be easily discerned. While religious beliefs may offer clear guidelines regarding product or service acceptability, other factors such as design, number, body language and artistic preferences may be much more subtle. For example, hotel managers should avoid using Room number 514 in Chinese hotels, because it sounds like "I want to die".
- **Legal reasons:** Product-related legal requirements vary widely by country, such as the regulations about casino businesses on hotel premises.

Visit the Disney Hong Kong website www.disney.com.hk/, Disney Paris website www.disneylandparis.com/ and Disney Tokyo website www.tokyodisneyresort.co.jp. Explore which Disney products are global, and which have been adapted to local features.

ACTIVITY

Service quality

This is a global issue as international customers increasingly expect high quality services whatever the differences in environment settings.

The followings are dimensions of service quality, and are the elements that consumers are most likely to perceive when making judgements.

- Tangibility: Service can be associated with physical facilities, equipment, personnel and promotional materials.
- Reliability: The ability to perform the promised service dependably and accurately is critical to service quality.
- Responsiveness: The willingness of providers to be helpful and give prompt service is very important to buyers.
- Assurance: The knowledge and courtesy of employees and their ability to convey trust and competence are essential.
- Empathy: The caring, individualized attention that a firm provides its customers encompasses a number of dimensions.

Service quality is a big challenge for hospitality companies, whilst it also provides plenty of opportunities for the companies that want to excel. The following case shows how Marriott have attempted to provide better service for its customers, as they recognized that many of them take national or international flights frequently.

Case: Check-in Your Flight in Marriott Hotel

Marriott International, Inc. has begun rolling out dedicated lobby computer stations with printers so guests can check in to their airline flights and print out their boarding passes before they leave for the airport. The new service will be available at all Marriott Hotels & Resorts and Renaissance Hotels & Resorts in the United States and Canada. Installation has been completed at 32 hotels already and will be available at nearly 150 more within the next 2 weeks. The company is targeting September for the new check-in service to be offered at every US and Canadian hotel, more than 400 in total.

The conveniently located lobby computer stations will serve one purpose – for guests to check in to their flights and print their boarding passes quickly. This will give guests some peace of mind by reducing their concerns about possible traffic congestion to the airport or long airline check-in lines that might delay their departure.

The process is simple. When guests use the computer stations, they will be able to click on icons of the major airlines appearing on the screen, and then be taken to the airlines' websites to complete the check-in process and the printing of their boarding passes. This new self-service amenity is complimentary to all guests.

Source: 27 June 2006, PRNewswire, Washington, www.prnewswire.com/

Price

Price represents the value asked for a product. Although usually expressed as a monetary value, in the case of barter transactions it may not be. The complexities of pricing are exacerbated in the international arena.

- Every nation has government regulations that influence pricing practices. In some countries, for example, there are minimum and maximum prices that can be charged to customers.
- Consumer tastes and demands vary widely in the international marketplace, and these differences result in hospitality companies having to price some of their products differently. For example, companies may find they can charge more for products or services sold overseas because of the demand. A second factor influencing market diversity is the perceived quality of the product.
- When doing business overseas, hospitality companies often end up assuming the risks associated with currency fluctuations. This risk is particularly important when these hospitality companies have to meet a return on investment target, because this objective can become unattainable if the local currency is devalued.

When pricing a new product or service, a company or business unit can follow a marketing strategy of skim pricing or penetration pricing. For new product pioneers, skim pricing offers the opportunity to skim the cream from the top of the demand curve while the product is novel and competitors are few. Penetration pricing offers the pioneer the opportunity to utilize the experience curve to gain market share and dominate the industry. Normally skim pricing is a short-term phenomenon and is used to gain high profits quickly in order to pay for expensive development and marketing costs before new entrants engage in price competition. It therefore cannot be used to raise long-term operating profits unless the firm also follows a differentiation strategy. A penetration pricing strategy sets an aggressively low price to attract a maximum number of customers (some of whom may switch from other brands) and to discourage competition. We can see this strategy widely used by budget hotels, airlines and fast food chains.

For companies aiming to promote their hospitality products and brands by standardizing the product offer, it is almost impossible to operate a uniform price position. Bowie and Buttle (2004) identify the difficulties in setting a pricing policy for companies operating in international markets:

- the different currency and cost structure between countries;
- global, regional and local competitors' impacts;
- the different stages of product life cycle in each country;
- different inflation rates and fluctuations in the currencies (inflation of UK in 2002 was about 2.5% while it was more than 25% in Argentina);
- the ability to repatriate profits which varies significantly from one country to another.

Pricing decisions are affected by competitive action and the regional economic situation. For example, the price you pay to stay in a five-star luxury hotel in Kuala Lumpur is only enough for you to stay in a three-star hotel in Hong Kong, or the most basic accommodation in Tokyo. If competitors do not adjust prices in response to rising costs, management is constrained in adjusting prices.

> **Example: Hotel price increases in Malaysia**
>
> Several four- and five-star hotels in the Klang Valley have started raising their average room rates (ARRs) by between RM10 and RM100 depending on room category. Other hotels are expected to follow suit.
>
> "Rack rates have been increased up to 16%, while corporate rates for all market segments across the board have been raised by 7–8%", Malaysian Association of Hotels Vice President Ivo Nekvapil said, "even after the increase in room rates, Malaysia would still be the cheapest place in the region to visit, given the strong major currencies against the ringgit".
>
> She added that with more tourists expected this year, hotel occupancy rates will not suffer even with the increase in room charges. "I expect all five-star hotels to increase their rates. Klang Valley hotels are doing so, and so are hotels in Penang. The increase is healthy. It will not take business away".
>
> *Source*: Malaysian Association of Hotels (2005),

■ Location and distribution channel

One major difference between hospitality marketing and consumer goods marketing can be found in the contrasting ways in which they deal with the concept of place. Consumer goods marketing is concerned with "placing" products, or delivering products from manufacturers to the retailers and then customers, while hospitality products or services are consumed in the location where they are provided, in the home country or host countries.

Conrad Hilton, the Founder of Hilton Hotels, and Ellsworth Statler, Founder of the Statler Hotel chain, are both credited with saying that the three most important factors for success in the hotel business are "location, location and location". When the international markets have been identified and the products or services have been agreed, the next crucial marketing decision is to find the appropriate location for the hospitality business. The characteristics of a location extensively influence potential hospitality target markets and determine the demand potential.

Bowie and Burton (2004: 135–6) explore one classification of hospitality locations:

● Capital city: Capital cites, such as London, Paris and Madrid, usually generate strong demand from government, business and tourism markets. They are popular destinations for international and domestic visitors and often hotels can achieve very high room occupancy and yield.
● Gateway locations: Gateway locations are located close to convenient destinations, such as major airport, shipping ports and railway station. Large numbers of travellers stay in gateway locations, such as

Hong Kong, with large numbers of travellers flying between Asia, Europe or America preferring to stay in Hong Kong for a short of time, which in turn generates large demands for hotel and restaurant services.

● Resort or tourism destinations: Major tourism destinations are often described as "honey-pots" because of the large volume of international and domestic tourists. Tenerife in Spain, Luxor in Egypt, Phuket in Thailand and Bali in Indonesia are examples. In high season, the room occupancy is very high while in low season it may suffer in these locations.

Other locations include business city, provincial city, highway locations and rural locations.

Look at the example and explain why Maxim selected Las Vegas, rather than New York or Boston for its first hotel.

Example: The ultimate male fantasy: a Maxim Hotel in Vegas

Maxim, the lads' mag that had its humble beginnings in the UK a decade ago, is about to make it big in Las Vegas, with plans to build a luxury Maxim Hotel and Casino complex at the heart of world's gambling capital. Maxim's parent company, the London-based Dennis Publishing, announced the location of the nine-acre complex, which will have 2,300 hotel rooms and a 60,000 square feet casino. It is promising the biggest and best swimming pools on the strip.

This hotel certainly will be unique compared with other hotels in Las Vegas, which give customers special value.

Source: *The Independent*, 21 July 2006, www.news. independent. co.uk/media/article625628.ece

---

The American Marketing Association defines the channel of distribution as "an organized network of agencies and institutions which, in combination, perform all the activities required to link producers with users to accomplish the marketing task". Distribution here refers to the physical and legal path that products follow from the point of production to the point of consumption.

It is often difficult to standardize the distribution system and use the same approach in every country, because there are many individual differences to be considered. Consumer spending habits can negate attempts to standardize distribution. The location where consumers are used to buying will also influence distribution. The predominant distribution channel for hotels remains direct contact with the property through telephone, fax or e-mail, which, according to Horwath's Worldwide Hotel Industry Study, accounted for 34% of all advance reservations in 2002, but this is down from 38% in 1995. This proportion varies between 27.5% for hotels in Africa and the Middle East and 40.5% for hotels in Europe. Even in the technologically advanced USA, the country's leading franchiser, Cendant, estimates that 70% of its room nights are generated by walk-in customers. Hotels' in-house or outsourced central reservations offices represent approximately 26% of advanced reservations (including call centres and hotel representatives). Travel agents are most important as a distribution channel in Africa/Middle East, Asia and Europe, whereas tour operators take the largest percentage of reservations in Africa/Middle East and Oceania (Table 5.4).

Table 5.4 Composition of advance reservations by percentage, by region.

	World	Africa and Middle East	Asia	Oceania	Europe	North America	South America
Direct enquiry	34.2	27.5	33.0	34.3	40.5	32.2	35.7
Own reservation system	14.4	14.4	12.7	12.3	7.8	21.4	27.6
Independent reservation system	3.1	0.0	3.2	3.4	2.4	4.0	2.5
Travel agents	17.7	20.2	22.4	15.7	22.0	11.4	10.7
Tour operators	11.4	16.9	10.1	13.9	10.6	7.7	4.2
Hotel representatives	8.7	8.8	10.2	6.0	9.7	9.6	8.9
Transportation company	1.1	0.9	1.0	2.1	0.9	0.6	2.7
Website/Internet	3.3	6.1	3.9	4.2	2.3	2.7	3.0
Global distribution systems	6.1	5.2	3.5	8.1	3.8	10.4	4.7
Total	100.0	100.0	100.0	100.0	100.0	100.0	100.0

Source: Worldwide Hotel Industry Study 2003/Horwath.

ACTIVITY   If you need to book a hotel in Turkey for 2 weeks, how many methods can you use?
Compare the advantages and disadvantages of each booking method?

■ Promotion

Promotion is the process of stimulating demand for a company's goods and services. Promotion strategies may be categorized as **push** (personal selling and trade sales promotion) or **pull** (advertising, consumer sales promotion and publicity). Most hospitality companies use a combination of both. Factors that will determine the mix of push and pull strategies include the type of distribution system, the cost and availability of media, customer attitudes towards sources of information and the relative price of the product as compared to disposable income.

Promotion consists of the messages intended to help to sell a product, that is, direct and indirect forms of communication designed to inform, persuade and/or remind a target audience about an organization and its products. The promotion mix consists of personal selling, advertising, sales promotion/support and publicity/public relations activities.

Advertising is a non-personal form of promotion in which a firm attempts to persuade consumers to a particular point of view. In many cases hospitality companies use the same advertising message worldwide. However, there are times when the advertising must be adapted to the local market. Two of the most common reasons include: (a) the advertising message does not make sense if translated directly and (b) the product or service is accepted in different ways compared with that in home country.

Hospitality companies use a number of media to carry their advertising messages. The three most popular are television, newspapers and radio. In particular, the use of television advertising has been increasing in Europe, while in other regions, such as South America and the Middle East newspapers remain the major media for promotion efforts. However, there are restrictions regarding what can be presented. Examples include: some countries prohibit comparative advertising, in which companies compare their products against those of the competition; some countries do not allow certain products to be advertised because they want to discourage their use (e.g. alcoholic beverages, gambling or junk food) or because they want to protect national industries from multinational competition; and some countries, such as most Islamic countries, censor the use of any messages that are regarded as erotic.

■ Standardization of advertising programmes

Advertising consists of any paid form of media (non-personal) presentation. Because advertising adds psychological value to a product or brand, it is more important in consumer than in industrial products. Global advertising is the use of the same advertising appeals, messages, art, copy, photographs, stories and video segments in multiple country markets.

Market segments can be defined globally – for example, youth culture – rather than ethnic or national culture (e.g. athletic shoes targeted to a worldwide segment of 18- to 25-year-old males). This assumes that human wants and desires are similar if presented within recognizable situations; people everywhere want value, quality and technology, as well as love and respect.

When hospitality marketers design advertising messages, they need to recognize the cultural differences between the creators and the recipients of the advertisements. Tamotsu Kishii identified seven characteristics that distinguish the Japanese from Americans when considering what is acceptable in advertising:

1 Indirect rather than direct forms of expression are preferred in the messages.
2 There is often little relationship between ad content and the advertised product.
3 Only brief dialogue or narration is used in television commercials, with minimal explanatory content.

4 Humour is used to create a bond of mutual feelings.
5 Celebrities appear as close acquaintances or everyday people.
6 Priority is placed on company trust rather than product quality.
7 The product name is impressed on the viewer with short, 15-second commercials.

ACTIVITY　Review the advertisement for a hotel in a national newspaper, a local newspaper and a magazine.

● Identify its target audience.
● How effective do you think it will be?
● Are there any other media that could support these advertisements?

■ International branding

A brand is an identifying mark for products or services which helps to give instant recognition and can also help save promotional cost. The American Marketing Association (1960, as quoted in Wood, 2000) proposed the following definition of a brand: "A name, term, sign, symbol or design, or a combination of them, intended to identify the goods or services of one seller or group of sellers and to differentiate them from those of competitors" (Plate 10).

International brands today are acknowledged by marketers as the driver for better, more sustainable results and as an internal as well as an external source of inspiration, which creates both high recognition and relationships in the global market. An international brand can be defined as a mechanism for achieving competitive advantage for firms in the global market, through differentiation; brands are created using the marketing mix in a way that is synergistic. Brands are strategically positioned in different countries' markets by offering benefits that are distinct from local and international competitors and that are desired by consumers, which if achieved also has the benefit of creating brand loyalty. Hence, competitive advantage is achieved.

International branding includes a more complex process compared with branding in domestic market. There are some issues which should be underlined in relation to the international branding process they are as follows.

■ Cultural sensitivity

● Cultural sensitivity is really a matter of understanding the international customers, the context and how the international customers will respond to the context.

Plate 10
Recognizable brands in the Chinese market. *Source*: Author's photograph. Although this focuses on the restaurant in the foreground, if you look carefully you will see further along the street the sign for KFC!

● Hospitality companies need to determine whether to promote a local or foreign image for their products. The products of some countries may be perceived as being particularly desirable and of higher quality than products from other countries. A firm may be able to enhance its competitive advantage by effectively exploiting this perception. This reinforces why the hospitality marketers need to study carefully when they move into different countries. Even a company as well established as Disney has become aware of a totally different response to the opening of its theme parks in Paris compared with the one in Tokyo.

- When a hospitality company acquires a foreign company, it automatically acquires its brands in most situations. In some instances those brands will be maintained; in others they will be folded into a larger brand in order to capture economies of scale and to promote global brand recognition. When you look into the InterContinental's history of hotel acquisition, even on its own website, you can find that sometimes the purchased hotel company retained its original name, rather than changing to the parents' company brand. This is a decision that InterContinental would have made according to their perception of the individual brand values with the targeted customers.

◼ Encoding

- Both the translation and pronunciation of brand names pose potential problems in many markets. Often the problems are obvious, but other times they are quite subtle, yet critical. In addition, brand symbols (shapes and colours) are culturally sensitive in many societies.
- Literal translation is only a limited answer to language differences. Language translation is only a part of the encoding process; the message is also expressed non-verbally.

◼ Selective media transmission

- The type of medium chosen for the message depends on the nature of the information, its level of importance, the context and status of the targeted audience, the timing involved and the need for personal interaction, among other factors.
- In different countries, the types of media have different positions. For example, hospitality companies prefer to use newspapers in the Middle East to attract business people because they are felt to be more trustworthy than other media in that region.

◼ Decoding of feedback

- Checking the decoded message by feedback is essential to ascertain whether the intended message has been successfully put across (Table 5.5).

Business Week (August, 2005) provided the table of the 100 top brands in the world. Coca-Cola is the undisputable top brand, with a brand value almost three-times higher than that of its nearest challengers who are not insignificant in their own right! Disney and McDonald's managed to maintain very good ranking on the table, but the performances of KFC and Pizza Hut are not enough to overcome the low-carb trend. Bulgari has

Table 5.5 The top brands in the world.

Rank 2005	Rank 2003	Company	2005 brand value in $million
1	1	Coca-Cola	67,525
7	7	Disney	26,441
8	8	McDonald's	26,014
61	49	KFC	5,112
63	51	Pizza Hut	4,963
94	NA	Bulgari	2,715
99	93	Starbucks	2,576

Source: Business Week (2005)

sought to use its exclusive image established in the jewellery business to support its move into the development of luxury hotels and resorts, which in turn they hope will enhance their brand.

Aaker and Joachimsthaler (2000) recommend that companies should attempt to create strong brands in all markets through a strategy of global brand leadership, which is using organizational structures, processes and cultures to allocate brand-building resources globally, to create global synergies, and to develop a global brand strategy that coordinates and leverages country brand strategies.

In order to establish global brand leadership, organizations should consider the following guidelines:

- Create a compelling value proposition.
- Think about all the elements of brand identity and select names, marks and symbols that have the potential for global use.
- Research the alternatives of extending the brand rather than adopting a new brand identity globally.
- Develop a company-wide communication system.
- Develop a consistent planning process.
- Assign specific responsibility for managing branding issues.
- Execute brand-building strategies.
- Harmonize, unravel confusion and eliminate complexity.

The real success story of branding in recent years has been the way in which companies have used their brands to turn the satisfaction of complex and even spiritual needs into their commercial transactions (Anholt, 2003). This may best be seen in hospitality with the growing number of brands that have aligned themselves with positive attitudes towards the natural environment.

The "brand value" which marketing adds to products and services is not a tangible value, which means that it cannot be measured very easily. However, it does represent capital to the organizations because it enables producers and sellers to charge more money for their products and services. It effectively becomes a multiplier of value and, as such, represents a substantial competitive advantage.

Multibranding has become one of the most popular brand strategies and is used by many companies in the hospitality industry. It is recognized that multibranding offers a fine opportunity to grow a business, simply because one brand cannot really cover all of the customers' needs in all of the various segments of a market that have been targeted (Van Sister, 2004). Multibranding can, in fact, also be considered as one of the most effective brand strategies, but to deliver such benefits it requires continuous professional skills and ongoing management with a marketing focus from the companies.

Since many markets are strongly fragmented, it makes sense to introduce extra brands in order to compete effectively across a category. The advantages that a multibranding strategy can offer include the enhanced opportunities for customer relationship management, which enables organizations to fulfil consumer needs more precisely. Also it gives the opportunity to position brands more clearly and build strongly identified brand values at the same time. Also it has the ability to handle pricing strategy in segmented markets. Finally if there is a brand problem requiring serious products recalls or challenges to the dominant image, this does not have such a direct impact on the other brands within the organization. It can be said that almost all sectors and most leading companies have active multibranding strategies in place.

One useful example can be found in a consideration of the multibranding strategy in operation at Marriott Hotels. Being a leading worldwide hospitality company, Marriott lodging operates and franchises hotels under 16 different brands. They offer complete family hotels: from luxurious full-service hotels and resorts to all-suites hotels. With those 16 different brands, Marriott feels it is well positioned across all segments of the markets in the hospitality industry. One important advantage is that all those brands are tied together by one reservation system, which helps the company in terms of accuracy and flexibility.

The multibrands of Marriott include:

- TownPlace: A mid-priced, extended-stay brand. Provides all the conveniences of home in a residential atmosphere.
- Springhill suites: Moderately priced, all-suite lodging brand. Guest suites that are up to 25% larger than the standard hotel rooms.
- Marriott Vacation Club International (MVCI): Spacious one, two and three bedroom villas in different resorts.
- Horizons by Marriott Vacation Club: Value orientated vacation ownership resorts communities.
- The Ritz-Carlton Hotel Company, L.L.C: Worldwide symbol for the finest in accommodations, dining and service.
- The Ritz-Carlton Club: A collection of private residences in highly desirable resort destinations.
- Marriott Execustay: Fully furnished corporate housing offering accommodation for more than 1 month.
- Marriott Executive Apartments: Corporate housing brand designed to meet the needs of business executives.

- Marriott Grand Residence Club: Fractional property ownership in second home destinations.
- Residence Inn by Marriott: Designed to be a home away from home.
- Fairfield Inn by Marriott: Consistent quality lodging at an affordable price.
- Marriott Conference Centres: A quality-tier brand specializing in highly effective small- to mid-sized meeting.
- Marriott Hotels & Resorts: Flagship brand of quality-tier, full-service hotels and resorts.
- JW Marriott Hotels & Resorts: The most elegant and luxurious Marriott Brand, providing business and leisure travellers with a deluxe level of comfort.
- Renaissance Hotels & Resorts: Quality-tier full-service brand that provides guests with the ambiance of a boutique.
- Courtyard by Marriott: Moderately priced lodging brand. Designed by business travellers for business travellers.

As we can see from all the different brands that Marriott has worldwide, there are a variety of choices for almost every segment of the market. In doing this, Marriott has effectively increased the diversity in every segment of the industry and attempted to ensure that if there was to be a problem with one brand, they could cover it with the others and allow the company to remain successful.

Marriott believes that they can gain preference from their brand by being where their customers are. These brands can be found in every corner of the world and Marriott's aim is to continue to expand further to other cities, resort destinations and suburban markets. Furthermore Marriott have recognized that their brands comprise only 1% of the lodging market outside the United States and this leads them to believe that there is a tremendous opportunity for growth.

Starwood is a major competitor for Marriott and it has also used a multibrand strategy in its global expansion. Starwood's hotel brands consist of the following six main brands.

1 **W Hotels**: "A fresh alternative combining the personality and style of independent hotels with whatever you want, whenever you want it service". Intriguingly the W brand has such iconic status that Millennium & Copthorne (one of Starwood's competitors) has decided to limit the use of the M brand within its own operations and marketing strategies.
2 **Sheraton**: "The global upscale hotel brand that offers warm and caring service in a traditional, yet stylish environment". As the largest of Starwood's brands, the Sheraton brand was ranked sixth of all worldwide hotel brands in 2003. This was seen as a remarkably good achievement in consideration of the number of rooms it has in comparison to other hotel brands, which reinforces the sense of strength in the brand.
3 **Four Points, Sheraton**: "All the services you'd expect from a full-service hotel, for a moderate price".
4 **St Regis**: "Delivering the most discreet, personalized and anticipatory level of service to each and every guest".

5 **The Luxury Collection**: "From old world grandeur to modern architectural design – an assembly of the world's finest hotels and resorts". Some luxury collection hotels and St Regis hotels are co-branded and these properties often have famous names under their own right .

6 **Westin Hotels & Resorts**: "The 'upper upscale' brand with 109 hotels, including 34 world-class resorts, that is synonymous with The Heavenly Bed".

Not only have Starwoods ensured that each of their brand types are physically different from the others, but they have grounded this by ensuring that every property is also individual to help reinforce the brand differentiation strategy. Starwood Hotel Group as a whole and in particular the Westin brand have utilized innovation within part of the company brand image it presents. It has a long history of being the first hotel company to offer certain facilities (AHMA, 2005), aiding its presentation of itself as being a leader in the industry.

Finally in this chapter we would like you to consider the following account of the Best Western group and their approach to international marketing. As you read through the case think through the factors that have driven Best Western to adopt such an approach.

Chapter Case Study: Best Western and Its International Marketing Strategy

Best Western International Inc. independently owns and operates more than 4,100 hotels in 79 countries, making it the largest hotel chain in the world in 2005. Best Western is an example of an international hotel consortium. It is a non-profit membership organization that consists of members who own and/or operate individually owned properties. Best Western offers members the unique advantage of retaining their independence while providing the benefits of a global reservations system, marketing, advertising, increased bargaining and buying power, training and quality standards. Members pay annual fees based on a percentage of gross rooms revenue. The hotels are predominantly three- and four-star properties. Best Western mainly operates in the mid-scale hotel market, but the company also offers a slightly higher standard of hotel through the brand "Best Western Premier". All Best Western hotels offer BestRequests™, 16 of the most frequently requested guest amenities and services. Best Western Premier hotels offer an enhanced level of service.

Best Western was founded in 1946 by M.K. Guertin and began as an informal referral system among member hotels. By 1963, Best Western was the largest chain in the industry, with 699 member hotels and 35,201 rooms. Best Western began global expansion in 1964 when Canadian hotel owners joined the system. Best Western entered Mexico, Australia and New Zealand in 1976, further establishing its international presence.

Best Western's headquarters are located in Phoenix, Arizona, USA. The company has consolidated reservations offices in USA, Italy, Philippines and England. Best Western is governed by a seven-member board of directors, elected by Best Western member hoteliers in seven geographic regions in North America. Board members must be Best Western member hoteliers, they are elected to a 3-year term and may be re-elected once. Internationally, Best Western operates through different affiliate organizations.

Global Market Development

Best Western first expanded internationally over 40 years ago and is already the largest hotel chain in the world but the company is intent on expanding further. This section will analyse Best Western's global strategy using key strategic issues.

Global strategic ambition refers to the role the company wants to play in the world market-place. Best Western's ambition is to continue in its role as a global player. The company aims to maintain its position as the world's largest hotel chain and be the number one choice for guests and hoteliers in the mid-scale hotel market. The company's mission statement is "to enhance brand equity and increase member value".

Global positioning consists of the choice of countries and segments in which a company wants to compete. Best Western aims to identify regions worldwide where the brand is under-represented and add properties to raise visibility and awareness. The company is already well represented in key areas such as North America and Europe and has identified the emerging Asian market, particularly China, as an area of key growth. Best Western aims to have 100 hotels in China by 2007, reflecting the country's growing customer base and status as a tourist destination. Best Western has identified strategic Asian markets that would benefit from a value-priced global brand. The company has opened an office in Beijing to support its aggressive Asian expansion.

Best Western has previously adopted a focused approach to segmentation, concentrating on the mid-scale global hotel market. The typical guest at a mid-scale hotel is aged 44 years and stays an average of 2.5 days. This shows that the customers are either on business or usually just passing through on their way to another destination. The company has started to broaden its segmentation approach with the addition of the Best Western Premier brand aimed at more upscale target group. This brand may also encourage people to stay longer.

Best Western has chosen to follow a differentiation focus strategy for the mid-scale hotel market. The introduction of the service standard programme (BestRequests™) enables the company to offer customers better service and amenities and therefore serve the target market more effectively than its competitors. While other hotels may have standards programmes in place, none of them are as comprehensive as Best Western's. The company offers free Internet access in all its North American hotels. The majority of other hotels who offer Internet access charge for the service. The company also has the added advantage that all of its hotels are independently owned meaning that they retain their individual character and style, which is something that no other mid-scale hotel can offer. Best Western has hotels that were formerly castles and many of the hotels in Europe are magnificent old buildings.

International Branding

This section will focus on Best Western's policy and implementation of branding. This is a hugely important concept for a company, especially in the increasingly competitive hospitality industry. Best Western currently operates a two-tiered branding structure with the addition of Best Western Premier, a more up-scale sub-brand, alongside the standard Best Western brand.

Best Western hotels are unique in the fact that they all retain their individual character, reflecting their geographical location, as well as harnessing the power of a global brand name.

One of the major advantages for member hotels joining the Best Western organization is the acquisition of the brand name with its strong global presence and consumer recognition. The advantage for the company is that the brand receives more exposure. Former CEO Tom Higgins, speaking in 2003, described the brand as being "a tremendous marketing advantage". The brand has strong global power which equates to more consumers recognizing and remembering the brand and relating this to high quality and value for money. This in turn, gives properties more power to attract customers. The company takes pride in being the largest hotel chain in the world and this is evident in the use of the slogan "The World's Largest Hotel Chain®" which appears alongside the company logo on the website and advertisements. The company logo has been updated through the years to reflect the changing status of the company. The current blue logo was adopted in 1994 and is a modern, colourful logo featuring a strongly symbolized crown. The Best Western logo is now one of the world's best-known hotel trademarks and is instantly recognizable. The international promotion of the company logo is a huge factor in growth and consolidation. Best Western has spent more than €500 million in the last 10 years on international promotion and advertising.

Each affiliate organization is responsible for implementing its own strategic business plan; however, brand strategy and identity management are centralized and the decisions are made at the headquarters in Phoenix. This is to ensure that the standards are the same universally. One of the potential pitfalls of a consortium like Best Western is inconsistency in standards in its hotels worldwide because they are independently operated. The company introduced a strict new global branding identity initiative in 2003 to ensure that all member hotels complied with branding requirements. The new standards provide consistency throughout all the member hotels worldwide, ensuring a better experience for customers and therefore helping to build a respectable global reputation and brand identity.

The addition of the new Best Western Premier brand was seen as an important step in helping the company to continue expansion throughout the world. It is the company's first brand extension and shows the company's intention of breaking into a more upscale hotel market. The Premier brand is aimed at travellers who want the quality of an upscale hotel at the good value prices associated with the Best Western brand. The company has developed a new logo for the brand to distinguish it from standard Best Western hotels. The addition of the Premier brand aims to encourage more hotels to join the Best Western association and more people to stay in Best Western hotels. The brand will also help to enhance the company's reputation for quality service and value. The brand is currently only available in Europe and Asia; this may be an attempt to raise awareness of the overall Best Western corporate brand in these areas. The Best Western brand already has a good reputation in North America so maybe it was thought to be unnecessary to launch the Premier brand there.

Conclusion

Best Western has a good worldwide reputation for providing quality accommodation and service along with good value for money. The company takes pride in being "The World's Largest Hotel Chain®" and continues to look for opportunities to expand worldwide. The uniqueness of the company is a major attribute. Members benefit from the brand name and customers are able to stay in an individualistic environment knowing that the standard will be quality and consistency. The company's expansion into Asia will help to increase exposure and ensure that it remains one of the leading brands in the mid-scale hotel market.

■ Conclusion

Every multinational organization in the hospitality industry will need a marketing strategy designed to help identify business opportunities within the global market and to take advantage of them. It is the hospitality managers' task to consider critical marketing areas, such as market screening and the marketing mix, including reviewing product and service modification, location, pricing and branding. Meeting the needs of different customers in different countries is the key to hospitality companies' success in international marketing.

In this chapter, we have explained:

● marketing and international marketing concepts;
● market potential review;
● global market segmentation;
● international marketing mix (4P);
● products modification;
● international branding.

These discussions should have helped to give you an insight into this element of the manager's role in marketing international hospitality and the complexities facing organizations who want to explore the global market. In Chapter 6 we will consider the strategies available to organizations seeking to enter the competitive world of international hospitality.

■ Review questions

1 Explain the cultural factors which make international hospitality marketing more complex than single market marketing.
2 How can companies use the 4Ps to strengthen their position in an international market?
3 How much localization can you identify in international hospitality marketing.
4 "Globalization will mean that eventually there is only one market". Explore the arguments that support or deny this statement in terms of international hospitality marketing.

CHAPTER 6

International hospitality market entry

■ Introduction

Hotel companies try to achieve competitive advantages through various methods, one of which is their choice of mode of market entry. This chapter will present the rationales behind six popular foreign market entry modes, introducing you to the wholly owned subsidiary, joint venture, strategic alliance, franchising, management contract and consortia approaches. We will then compare their advantages and disadvantages. This chapter will discuss how several leading hospitality companies have chosen their international market entry strategies.

With the increasing competition in the international hospitality industry, large companies are beginning to realize that they have to compete in all the world markets for their products in order to survive and develop. It is therefore important for multinational hospitality companies to reflect upon the benefits of entering foreign markets. We would suggest that usual considerations include:

- Business growth: When growth opportunities become limited in the home market, companies are often driven to seek new international markets. A mature fast food product or standard hotel service with restricted growth in its domestic market often has new life in another country where it will be in an earlier stage of its life cycle.
- International branding and recognition: Loyal customers will use the same brand when they travel around the world.
- Economies of scale: Big companies can achieve these with higher levels of productivity and purchasing power, for example, lower per-unit cost in global advertising campaigns.
- High competitiveness: Multinationals can access more resources when entering foreign markets and attract labour from within the global human resource pool.
- Incentives: Governments in countries seeking new infusions of capital and technological know-how often provide incentives to attract multinational corporations.

■ Types of foreign market entry strategies in the hospitality industry

There are six major foreign market entry methods favoured by hospitality companies. They are:

1 Wholly owned: When a company undertakes the development themselves, including buying land, building the hotel/restaurant and operating it all as part of their company.
2 Joint venture: This refers to the creation of a partnership between a domestic company and a foreign company for the purpose of jointly developing and managing hospitality operations.
3 Strategic alliance: This is when companies are tied together by a common reservation and marketing system.
4 Licensing/franchising: Essentially licensing permits a company in the target country to use the property of the licensor. Franchising is when the franchisor (parent) grants to the franchisees the right to use the parent's name, reputation and business skills at a particular location.
5 Management contracts: A contract is drawn up between a management company with an established reputation and a property owner, who then runs the property for the owner for the return of management fees that have been agreed between both parties.
6 Consortia: Hotel consortia represent affiliations through membership of an association. These organizations primarily offer membership services to hotels for a fee.

We will now consider the implications of the different approaches.

Wholly owned subsidiary (by foreign direct investment)

The desire for partial or full ownership outside the home country drives the decision to invest. Foreign direct investment (FDI) describes the investment flows out of the home country as companies invest in or acquire plants, equipment or other assets in the target country. FDI allows companies to produce, sell and compete locally in key markets.

The main advantage is that they allow tight control for the parent company. The main disadvantage is that they are costly to set up and require detailed knowledge of local conditions. FDI involves the transfer of resources including capital, technology and personnel. It may be made through the acquisition of an existing entity or by the establishment of a new enterprise. The following example shows how the Accor group expect to benefit from the direct investment to build hotels in one foreign market.

Example: Direct investment in Polish hotel market

Poland's largest hotel chain operator Orbis, part of the French Accor group, is complaining that the weak euro and strong competition are biting into the company's profits. The answer lies in the building of a new cheap hotel chain next year. An appropriate investment programme will be started within the next few months. "We want to enter the segment of cheap hotels. We plan to create a chain of about 20 one-star hotels first in the towns where we don't have any other hotels. This concerns, among others, former provincial capitals, such as Gorzow", said Krzysztof Gerula, a member of the company's management board.
Source: Accor (2005), www.accor.com

Some hotel chains that owned their own hotels decided that due to rising costs, it would be better to dispose of their properties and concentrate on the operational side. Such as in February 2006, The Youth Hostel Association (YHA) was to sell 32 of its 227 properties across England and Wales in a bid to reduce its £34 million debt. The disposal followed a 12-month review by the charity's Board of Trustees.

Joint ventures

Joint venture is a direct investment that two or more companies make and share the ownership. The key issues to consider in a joint venture are ownership, length of agreement, pricing, technology transfer, local firm's capabilities and resources, and government intentions.

A typical joint venture is where two partners come together and take 50% responsibility each for running the new venture.

The advantages of joint venture are:

● Easier access to other countries' markets.
● Sharing of risks and costs. A company can limit its financial risk and exposure to political uncertainty.
● Achieve synergy by combining different value chain strengths. One company with in-depth knowledge of a local market might find a foreign partner possessing well-known brands.
● Finally, a joint venture may be the only way to enter a country if governments favour local companies, and impose high tariffs on foreign investment or regulate the level of foreign control that is acceptable.

The disadvantages of joint ventures are:

● Conflicts of interest may occur. The partners may not have the same priorities and the organizational culture may be very different.
● Partners must share risks as well as rewards.

- A company incurs significant costs associated with the control and coordination issues of the joint venture.
- One of the companies may lose control over its know-how and therefore could establish a potential rival.

ACTIVITY

Why did McDonald's choose the business form of joint venture when they first decided to move into Moscow?

Example: Fairmont Hotel and its joint ventures

Fairmont Hotels and Resorts (FHR) is one of North America's leading owner/operators of luxury hotels and resorts. FHR's managed portfolio consists of 83 luxury and first-class properties with more than 32,000 guestrooms in Canada, the United States (including the world famous "Plaza" in New York City), Mexico, Bermuda and Barbados, and in recent years has acquired properties in London, Monte Carlo and Dubai.

FHR was founded in 1907 by sisters Tessie and Virginia Fair, whose first hotel was opened in San Francisco. In 1999 Canadian Pacific Hotels and Resorts acquired Fairmont Hotels and FHR was born. FHR is a growth organization, and uses its brand of luxury and its strong reputation to establish a global presence. The company also has sound financial stability and because of this they are able to extend their brand into expensive sites away from North America.

FHR, in current years, have begun to enter international markets.

- The Fairmont Dubai, United Arab Emirates: The opening of the Fairmont Dubai through the joint venture, in July 2000, was the first investment in the hospitality sector in Dubai, if not the United Arab Emirates, by an international hotel operator. It was also the first investment of the joint venture and the first strategic opportunity to grow the FHR brand name.
- In a recent expansion into Europe, FHR headed into a joint venture with Kingdom Hotels and the Halifax Bank of Scotland. The venture, announced on 22 December 2004, suggested that they were to invest in luxury hotels in key European markets, with a potential buying capacity of £800 million.
- Fairmont Monte Carlo, Monaco: The European joint venture's first investment was the purchase of the Monte Carlo Grand hotel in Monaco, a 619-room landmark property on one of the most coveted stretches of the Côte d'Azur. The property was opened in March 2005. The agreement marked another important milestone in FHR's mission to extend its global market. The position of the hotel, the first in Europe, is well placed; Monte

> Carlo is an expensive, superior and luxurious city, and shares these traits with the Fairmont.
>
> ● The Savoy, London: The acquisition of the Savoy, by FHR was completed in January 2005, again through the joint venture. Although the hotel was bought by Saudi Prince Alwaleed Bin Talal, the acquisition was through the prince's Kingdom Hotels International trust. FHR has the management rights to the hotel, in which the prince has a 5% stake. The acquisition of the Savoy was an important move for FHR, as they are keen to target the British market. The Savoy is one of the most recognized hotels in the world, subsequently FHR have entered the British market with the best.
>
> *Source*: Fairmont Hotels and Resorts, www.fairmont.com

Joint venture partners may come from different industries and the new venture can gain synergies from the agreement. The following case provides an example of this synergy with partners from fashion companies joining with some of the hotel industry's biggest brands.

> **Example: Italian luxury goods producers in the hotel business**
>
> An interesting exercise in cross-branding has occurred with the entry of several Italian jewellery and fashion designers into the boutique hotel business. These ventures generally have taken the form of an alliance with an existing hotel company or a property developer.
>
> One of the most highly publicized of these alliances is the Marriott-Bulgari link-up announced in February 2001. According to the plan, Bulgari, the Rome-based jeweller, and Marriott International have invested $70 million each into a joint venture hotel operation called Bulgari Hotels and Resorts. The hotels will be managed by Marriott's wholly owned luxury brand subsidiary, Ritz-Carlton, but will focus on Bulgari's luxury brand image, featuring Italian cuisine, furnishings and amenities. Although, originally, the initial units were supposed to be opened in London and Southern California, the first hotel is in fact to be inaugurated in Milan during the second half of 2003. The property, which is secured by a 10-year lease, offers 52 rooms and suites and includes a lush 4,000 square metre garden. In the medium term, Bulgari expects to create a portfolio of hotels worth US $800 million, with sales amounting to $300 million by 2008.
>
> Similar news was announced in early 2003 between Rezidor SAS, the licencee of Carlson Companies hotel brands in Europe, the

> Middle East and Africa, and the well-known Italian fashion house, Cerutti. The aim of this joint venture is to develop a new "lifestyle" hotel brand with the goal of capturing the "fast-growing, stylish, mid-market". This plan is to roll out designer rooms, bars and restaurants of an Italian genre, as well as the occasional spa.
> *Source*: www.marriott.com and www.rezidorsas.com

Strategic alliances and global strategic partnerships

A strategic partnership is an agreement between two or more competitive multinational enterprises for the purpose of better serving a global market. In contrast to a joint venture where the partners may be from different businesses, companies in the same line of business almost always form the strategic partnerships. The Hilton Hotel Corporation and Hilton International is a good example. These two companies shared the name Hilton, although each was totally independently owned, they formed a strong strategic alliance from 1997. They join together in:

● worldwide promotion and development of the Hilton brand;
● sharing the same loyalty programme, HHonors;
● participating in each other's hotel projects;
● developing a worldwide mid-category brand name, Hilton Garden Inn.

On the 29th of December 2005, Hilton Hotels Corporation announced an agreement whereby it will acquire the lodging assets of Hilton International for approximately £3.30 billion (or $5.71 billion) in an all-cash transaction.

Strategic alliances exhibit three characteristics:

1 Participants remain independent after the formation of the alliances.
2 Participants share the benefits of the alliance as well as control over the performance of assigned tasks.
3 Participants make ongoing contributions in technology, products and other key strategic areas.

A partnership is a quick way to develop a global strategy without incurring any great costs. Reasons for forming alliances and partnerships include:

● Providing access to national and regional markets.
● Providing learning opportunities.
● Enabling companies to share costs for a project.
● Resolving lack of skills and resources within a company by forming an alliance with a company with those resources.

Despite the positive benefits of these opportunities, strategic partnerships have some disadvantages especially as the partners share control over the tasks, which creates a series of new management challenges. There are also potential risks associated with strengthening a competitor from another country.

Case: Starbucks' Market Entry Choice

In order to enter the international markets, Starbucks used three methods of market entry as part of their global strategy. This was implemented through:

- wholly owned subsidiaries,
- joint ventures,
- licensing.

Wholly owned subsidiaries

The company-owned operations accounted for approximately 85% of net revenues in the fiscal year 2003. This highlights the importance of the company-owned operations and reinforces the need for these subsidiaries to be located were the company is familiar with the market. Consequently, the majority of Starbucks company-owned stores are located in USA, UK and Australia. The cultures are similar within these countries and Starbucks can concentrate on the markets they know, whilst taking part ownership in the markets they are unfamiliar with. In doing this all the net revenues will go directly to the company.

Joint ventures

US companies such as Starbucks have been forming joint ventures with international partners at a growing rate of 27% annually since 1985. This highlights the popularity of this mode of entry into international markets. Joint ventures enable the company to enter another country with fewer assets at stake, thus experiencing lower risk. In addition, the parent company's expertise and local knowledge can be joined together.

Companies having business agreements with Starbucks must be able to contribute to their mission. To ensure correct selection, Starbucks has set standards that potential international partners must comply with. These are the following:

- shared values and corporate culture;
- strong multiunit retail/restaurant experience;
- dedicated human resources
- commitment to customer service
- quality image
- creative ability, local knowledge and brand-building skills;
- strong financial resources.

In the early 1990's Howard Schultz was interested in the Japanese market. However, he was advised that Japanese people would not want to walk around with a paper cup of coffee and would not like the non-smoking environment. Despite a tough economic environment and advice from consultants Mr Schultz and his team went ahead to open up their first store internationally. In 1996 they entered the Japanese market when they formed a joint venture with Sazaby inc. forming "Starbucks coffee Japan limited". A joint venture was an ideal mode of entry for Starbucks, as the potential popularity of their product was unknown. The joint venture allowed Starbucks to be involved in the Japanese market whilst continuing to specialize in the market where they were most competent in the US. The joint venture proved advantageous for both the companies. For Sazaby it gave them the opportunity to generate more sales and greatly increase their customer base. For Starbucks the alliance created lower risks for entering the new country, and insights to local knowledge.

Sazaby inc. is a well-established company in Japan known for creating brands in dining, clothing and households goods for over 30 years. The two companies combined their marketing skills and know-how to develop a new type of coffee store, customizing coffees and offering new lifestyle concepts. The companies also share similar corporate values. The expertise in coffee making and coffee bean sourcing provided by Starbucks, along with the local understanding of the Japanese market and ability to pinpoint locations from Sazaby, has created a clear market leader.

Stores have expanded rapidly since 1996 and now there are over 500 outlets in Japan (Levy, 2005). In July 2003 the new store in the Nagano prefecture broke the worldwide first-day sales record. The products they have created have been received enthusiastically by the Japanese customers, increasing domestic competition and greatly expanding the market for other coffee chains.

Licensing

Starbucks predominately have company-owned stores in the USA, but in certain circumstances Starbucks enter into licensing agreements. This is when companies provide access to real estate which would otherwise not be available, such as airport locations, national grocery chains, major food service corporations, college and university campuses and hospitals. As part of these agreements Starbucks receives licence fees and royalty fees.

International company-owned outlets now account for less than half of establishments overseas in 2003, whilst in 1999 company-owned operations was the most popular choice. This shows that Starbucks have modified their strategy to use the "shared risk" market entry modes, such as licensing agreements and joint venture as they are a safer choice in unknown markets.

Source: Starbucks (2006).

ACTIVITY   When are multinational enterprises, likely to use an international joint venture? When would they opt for a strategic partnership? Defend your answer.

■ Non-investment management arrangements

In recent years, there has been a move away from direct investment and leasing to non-investment management arrangements (NIMA) as the form of enterprise that is preferred by hoteliers and caterers. Franchising (licensing), management contract and consortia are three of the most important choices used by the hospitality industry.

Licensing

Franchising is one kind of licensing; therefore we first have a look of what a licence is. According to Rugman and Rodgetts (2003), a licence may be defined as a contractual arrangement in which one firm (the licensor) provides access to some of its patents, trademarks or technology to another firm in exchange for a fee or royalty. Licensing is an attractive alternative to direct investment when the political stability of a foreign country is in doubt or when resources are unavailable for direct investment.

Franchising

Franchising in the hospitality industry is a concept that allows a company to expand more rapidly by using other people's money than if it had to acquire its own finance (Walker, 2004). The franchisor grants certain rights, for instances, to use its brand, trademark, signs, operating systems and procedures, reservation system, marketing plan, purchasing discounts and so on for a fee. In return, the franchisees agree by signing the franchise contract to operate the hotel, restaurant and so on in accordance with the conditions set by the franchisor. Franchising is a way of doing business that benefits both the franchisor, who wants to expand the business rapidly and the franchisee, who has financial resources but lacks the specific expertise and recognition.

Franchising origins are in Bavaria, but it has been adopted by various types of businesses in many countries. For example, McDonald's generates 47% and Coca-Cola 80% of their income from international franchising operations.

There are currently over 2,500 franchise systems in the United States with more than 534,000 franchise units. This represents 3.2% of all businesses, controlling over 35% of all retail and service revenue in the economy. Two main types of franchise have been identified, they are:

1 Product and trade name franchise: An example of this is where Coca-Cola agrees to sell its syrup and the right to sell its trademark to independent bottlers (Franchisees).
2 Business-format franchise: This involves trademarks and products but marketing strategies, quality control, operating and interchange between the franchiser and the franchisee. This type of franchise is common in the hospitality industry. Examples include McDonald's, Holiday Inn, Subway and KFC.

Franchising in the hospitality industry began from 1907, when the Ritz Development Company franchised the Ritz-Carlton name in New York City. Holiday Inns also used franchising strategy to grow its size and popularity in America in 1950's and 1960's. About the same time, a new group of budget motels emerged. Motel 6 in California slowly spread across the country, as did Days Inn and others. It was not until 1960s that Hilton, Sheraton and other brands began to franchise their names. Franchising was the primary growth and development strategy of hotels and motels during 1960s to the 1990s. However, franchising presents two major challenges for the franchisor: maintenance of quality standards and avoidance of financial failure on the part of the franchisee (Czinkota and Ronkainen, 2002) (Table 6.1).

Table 6.1 Companies that franchised the most hotels, 2002

Hotel company	Hotels franchised	Total hotels	% of hotels franchised
Cendant	6,513	6,513	100.0
Choice Hotels	4,664	4,664	100.0
InterContinental Hotels	2,834	3,333	85.0
Hilton Hotels Corporation	1,721	2,084	82.6
Marriott International	1,612	2,557	63.0
Accor SA	897	3,829	23.4
Carlson Hospitality	813	847	96.0
US Franchise System	494	494	100.0
Société du Louvre	366	900	40.7
CHE Group plc	314	372	84.4

Source: Hotels Magazine.

As we can see from this table, franchising is the most frequently used form of hotel brand development, as it requires little investment on the part of the international hotel chains whose main expenses are for marketing and managing their affiliates. The challenge for a hospitality franchisor is to maintain uniform standards across all franchisee units in the network. If one hotel does not keep the brand's standards, it damages the image of the whole group. Except for the risks cited above, franchising is a low risk endeavour from the point of view of a chain, since the franchisees carry virtually all the investment and business risk. According to Mintel (2005a) International Hotel Industry, Mintel International Group Limited, an average franchise contract has a duration of 10 years, although a few can go to 20 years or even longer. Franchisees pay an initiation fee when they join the brand, which is typically around $35,000 depending on the size of the hotel. Later, on a yearly basis, the franchisee pays royalty and marketing fees to the chain. The royalty fee, which is a payment for the right to use the brand name, varies from 3% to 7% of rooms' revenues, with an average of 4.3% for the American hotel industry. Marketing fees, ranging from 1% to 4.5% of rooms' revenues are calculated separately as they are split from the general revenues of the chain, and should be spent exclusively on the marketing of the hotel brand. Other franchising fees may include a charge for the use of the reservation service, typically amounting to 1.5–2.5% of rooms' rates. Franchisees also need to fund the loyalty programmes by paying into the system a few dollars for each night a programme member stays in their hotel. When customers redeem their loyalty programme points by staying at one of the chain's hotel for free, the fund reimburses the hotel usually at its average rate.

As a method of distribution, franchising provides many opportunities for growth and profitability. However, when considering a franchising relationship, both parties should carefully evaluate the alternative forms of ownership and operation. The individual goals and objectives of each party have to be weighed against the trade-offs of a franchisor–franchisee relationship. In essence, franchising is a strategic alliance between groups of people who have contractual responsibilities and a common goal. By choosing to invest in a franchise operation, an owner is expressing the belief that they will be more successful using someone else's business system rather than investing their own money in an independent operation and developing their own business system.

Case: InterContinental's Market Entry Choices

InterContinental Hotels Group owns, manages, leases or franchises, through various subsidiaries, more than 3,500 hotels and 534,000 guestrooms in nearly 100 countries and territories around the world; 2,983 of their hotels are franchised which contribute to 53% of InterContinental Hotels Group overall profit per year. Therefore the management of the franchising strategy is particularly important for the InterContinental Hotels Group Company, especially in the international hotel market and to achieve their corporate strategies.

InterContinental Hotels Group Finance Director, Richard Solomons, pointed out the main advantages of franchising to the InterContinental Hotels Group: "(a) capital to fund the brands' expansion primarily provided by third parties, (b) faster unit growth to achieve scale, (c) high barrier to entry business, (d) need scale to drive high relative returns for franchisees and (e) spread of ownership brings motivated owners and reduces InterContinental Hotels Group exposure to any one owner".

InterContinental Hotels Group need to make sure that, with the large number of franchised hotels that they own, relationships with the franchisee does not create potential for conflicts and does not lead to the failure of some franchised operations. InterContinental designed-specific policies that would overcome problems associated with management relationships, such as: (a) providing the correct level of training that will ensure the same standard operational procedures are adopted in all the hotels and (b) to ensure that all the hotels receive enough capital so they do not carry too much debt too early.

On 10th March 2005, InterContinental Hotels Group agreed to sell 73 of its UK hotels for £1 billion to consortium LRG Acquisition; however InterContinental would continue to manage the hotels they have sold. This strategic move ties in with InterContinental's strategy of shifting from outright ownership to become, instead, a broadly based hotel management and franchised hotels group. Finance Director Richard Solomons said: "This is a significant step forwards in the execution of our strategy and we have achieved attractive management contracts".

Source: www.ihgplc.com and news.bbc.co.uk

According to Beid and Bojanic (2006) and Nield (2003), franchising has its advantages and disadvantages as a market entry method.

Many companies are choosing to expand their operations using the franchise approach because of its advantages. The advantages for the franchisor include:

- The franchiser can expand internationally, at far greater speed and with much reduced capital investment.
- One impact of this rapid expansion is the realization of cost economies from operating at a higher level of volume. The company will get better prices on supplies and be able to allocate fixed costs over a larger number of units, bringing down the average cost, such as global advertising and purchasing.
- The franchiser does not need to do day-to-day management. Franchising motivates franchisees to work for themselves. The franchisers also save payroll cost.
- The franchiser may not want to take too many risks. The franchisor is able to diversify the risk of doing business.
- The franchiser receives income from initial fees and royalties. They also generate profits from equipments and supplies.
- The franchisees play an important role in the selection and retention of employees. Franchisees are always motivated by the system.
- Franchise owners are very careful to monitor the performance of the franchise because they benefit directly from the profitability of the unit.

There are also a few disadvantages associated with being a franchisor.

- Difficulty of controlling franchisees. This may be easy to control in the home country but may be extremely difficult in other countries. Even though operating standards and procedures are written into the agreement, they are not always followed.
- There is a trade-off between risk and return. The sharing of risk and ownership results in the sharing of profits as well.
- Government or legal restrictions may mean that a franchise cannot operate in the way that it wishes to. Franchisors are also easy targets for legal actions, such as antitrust suits and class action suits. Also, injury claims are prevalent in many service industries. For example, McDonald's has been sued by obese people who accused the fast food restaurant of causing their weight problems.
- Re-developments of products and the franchise package are not easy. Cultural differences make franchisers think about how to adapt their products and services before they move into other countries.
- There are difficulties in the coordination of the global and the regional management. Franchising offers less flexibility to managers.
- Protection of trademarks and copyright in foreign market is another contentious issue.
- Finally, recruitment of suitably qualified franchisees may be a problem in some countries. Franchisees may not have the necessary qualifications or attitudes to run a successful franchise unit in the product or service category.

Because of the problems outlined in the above discussion, it has been suggested that franchising may become more common in the slightly later stages of new market development, especially in developing countries.

There are many advantages to joining an existing operation rather than starting from the beginning. The benefits for franchisees include:

- First, there is an established product or service with a brand name and an identity in the marketplace. Franchisees get a proven business system and avoid having to learn by trial-and-error.
- It is normally very costly and time-consuming to build a brand image in the hospitality industry, while the importance of the brand name appeal is enormous. KFC franchisees have many more opportunities than other fried chicken shops to survive in a new foreign market.
- Franchisees benefit from the franchiser's experience and they also receive technical and managerial assistance from the franchisor. Franchisors transfer the knowledge they have accumulated as they progressed through the learning curve, thereby accelerating the process for franchisees.
- Franchisees benefit from the quality standard that is already in place for the franchise. There is a system of controls that guide the operations and provide for a certain level of quality and consistency.
- There is often less of a capital requirement for opening a franchise unit relative to the start up costs for an independent operation. Franchises have a track record that can be used to estimate demand, design the facility, schedule employees and order inventory. Franchisees also save cost because of franchise's centralized buying power.
- There are opportunities to expand the business within the region. Franchisees are usually given guidance of site selection and some form of territorial rights to add units based on demand. Franchisees also have better access to financial assistance compared with independent business.
- Franchisees can benefit from the franchisor's national or international advertising programme. An independent restaurant would not be able to afford to place advertisements in major magazines or during prime time TV shows.
- Finally franchisees have been proven to have a much greater chance to survive compared with independent business.

There are also some disadvantages to becoming a franchisee.

- First, there are franchise fees and royalties that must be paid in return for the benefits just described. These expenses are normally a percentage of sales and result in a decrease in the profit margin.
- Franchisee must follow the standards and procedures in the agreement. This restricts the franchisee's ability to control the whole operation in that certain requirements regarding products, service, price ranges and expansion are imposed by the franchisor.
- Some franchisors provide unsatisfactory training programmes and other supports.

- The problem of market saturation. There are more than 600 McDonald's in London.
- It is very complicate to terminate the agreement if the franchisee would like to change brands or sell the business.
- Finally, the franchise's reputation and image can be negatively affected by the performance of individual units.

Case: Franchising In Fast Food Industry – Subway

Description of operation: Subway, the world's largest submarine sandwich franchise offers a reasonable well-structured franchise programme. Our concept is low investment, simple operation and delicious healthful fast food. Number of franchised units: over 20,000 restaurants in 73 countries.

Number of company-owned units: 1
In business since: 1965
Franchising since: 1974
Franchise fee: $12,500
Capital requirements: $86,300–$213,500
Financing options: Third party

Training and support provided: Two-weeks training with 50% hands-on and 50% classroom. Continued support from headquarters and development agents.

Subway was once again named the top franchise opportunity by entrepreneur, a US-based business magazine. By the year 2010, Subway continues to grow globally and intends to have opened a further 7,500 Subway restaurants opened outside Canada and the USA. To do this Subway has thought up a well-structured franchise programme. This involves keeping the start-up costs low and the operation efficient and uncomplicated.

There is a simple three-step process to opening up a franchised property of Subway. There are opportunities to open franchises up all over the world. The first step is to research into the company and decide if it is the right company or not. Subway has put together a whole range of resources like a brochures and online seminars to work through the opportunities available. The next step is to apply and fill the application in, this is also available online. The last step is to look into applying for investment to fund the operation.

Franchisee is responsible for including, finding the location, funding, hiring and operating of the restaurant, etc.

Subway's franchise fee is $12,500, while Burger Kings fee is $18,000 and McDonald's is $45,000.

Source: Subway, www.subway.com/StudentGuide/, www.franchises-4u.com/ restaurant.asp and www.totalbusiness.org.uk/adetail.aspx?codeP=1542

Management contracts

The use of business management contracts dates back to the time of the British Empire and its colonies in 19th century. The concept was later developed in the United States and then re-exported to the rest of the world. This type of contract emerged due to an absence of professional training in many sectors (Cunill, 2006). A business management contract can be defined as a contract under the terms of which a company agrees to manage another one, on behalf of and at the risk of the latter, in exchange for financial remuneration (Sharma, 1984). Other authors, such as Pérez Moriones (1998), define hotel management contracts as an agreement between a hotel management company and the company owning the hotel, under the terms of which the management company runs the hotel. The owner normally does not make any operational decisions but is responsible for providing the necessary capital and for meeting the payment of construction expenses and debts. The management company receives a fee for its services and the owner receives the remaining profits after all costs have been deducted.

The hotel industry is where management contracts are most widely used. InterContinental Hotel, which was set up in 1946 as a subsidiary of Pan American World Airways, began to run some of its Latin American hotels under management contracts in the 1950s. With the increasing cost of land, construction costs and mortgage interest rates from the 1970s, investment on the large properties became very expensive and risky. The management contract was becoming popular because of the way it transfers the investment risk from the hoteliers to the property owners. This type of management contract also allowed hotel chains to expand rapidly in domestic and international markets, achieving greater economies of scale and global branding impacts.

Property investors now have accepted the fact that management skills and brands are some of the main ingredients needed for successful hotel operations. Therefore it is better for them to turn to a hotel management company to run the property instead of attempting to do this themselves. In many situations, even before a new hotel is built, an agreement is made for the management contract. This enables the hotel management company to give advice and consultancy on important issues, such as location, room design, leisure facilities and decoration. The management company also need to start parts of their activities well before the hotels' inauguration, such as recruitment, training and marketing.

Nield (2003) argues that management contracts are the best method of market entry when the contractor possesses management know-how and the owner of the hotel wants no part in the day-to-day operation of the business. He defines the management contract as an agreement where one company (A) runs a hotel or other enterprise for another company (B). Therefore, management companies (A) offer:

● brand image for example, Hyatt Hotel;
● operating standards;
● management systems for consistency;
● staff recruitment, training and management;
● reservations and referral capabilities.

The other company (B) receives:

● profit;
● new markets;
● financial safety.

	Management companies	Investment companies
Advantages	Fast chaining: Hotel management companies can develop much faster using this method with very limited risks.	Reduced risks in running the hotel business.
	Financing the property: The management companies need a little or no initial investment.	Generally, minimum profit is guaranteed and the capital investment will be paid back
	The reduced risk: The risks for management companies running the hotel deriving from excess building costs, market recessions or changing markets are all significantly reduced.	With the recognition of a prestigious hotel brand name, the value of the property may increase
	High return on investment (ROI). Due to the low amount of investment required from hotel management companies, very high financial and economic earning can be achieved.	
Disadvantages	Obtaining only part of the profits.	Lost control of daily operations of the property.
	Loss of the propertys potential appreciation. In the past 5 years, in many parts of America and Britain, property prices have more than doubled.	The management company may not have the necessary experience, knowledge or resources in managing overseas' business.
	The owners may interfere despite the contract in some of the management issues, limiting the management companies' operational potentials.	
	Management companies may lose the contract in certain stage.	

Figure 6.1
Advantages and
Disadvantages for
management
companies and for
investment
companies

At first most companies operating in this area were sought after as they offered the hotel owner a form of "insurance" based on their expertise or "know-how". This allowed the management contractors to dictate the terms of the contract, so that they might charge:

● a percentage of revenue;
● a percentage of profit;

- fees for group services for example, marketing;
- additional fees for reservations system.

There are some advantages and disadvantages for both the management companies and property owners (Nield, 2003; Bowie and Buttle, 2004; Cunill, 2006) (Figure 6.1):

Early stage management contracts were completely one-sided, benefiting only the management company. The management company's business profits were implicitly guaranteed via a fixed basic fee that was paid regardless of the real profits, meaning that management companies did not need to worry about the costs of the business (Cunill, 2006). However, the 1980s brought about an end to this, as the number of companies operating in this field brought about competition, which in turn changed the nature of the contracts. This situation has now changed so that the client can decide many terms of the contract. Typically, a management contract may contain guaranteed profit, penalties for underperformance, profit sharing, a fee and a share of profit. Property owners can even ask the management company to contribute a certain amount of capital, for example, towards the pre-opening costs and the initial working capital required for the development. Some financial contributions to the business can involve a strategic alliance between the owners and the management company.

At the moment, competition between hotel chains means that owners can be more selective. Cunill (2006) pointed out, that generally speaking, large international hotel chains have more specialist management skills and better reputation in the field, while many new small- or medium-sized specialist management companies have also been formed without huge overhead. They also provide more flexibility in contracts and operations. These small- or medium-sized management companies tend to have a short-term contract from 1 to 10 years.

Case: A Small Industry Example

Marshall Management, Inc. a leading, mid-sized hotel management company, today announced that it has signed seven new management contracts with two separate ownership groups. The new contracts raise to 15 the total number of hotels Marshall Management has been selected to manage this year to date in 2004.

Six of the seven hotels are owned by Independent Property Operators of America, LLC (IPOA), a real estate investment group. The seventh property – a Holiday Inn Express currently under construction in Kent, Ohio – is owned by a private investment group and is expected to open in April 2005.

The six-hotel IPOA portfolio includes four Comfort Suites and a Hampton Inn & Suites, all located in Northern Indiana and a Comfort Inn in North Carolina.

"We have a long history and proven track record of operating hotels in the Midwest", said Michael Marshall, President of Marshall Management. "These hotels are well located, and we intend to immediately install our proprietary marketing and management programmes to further enhance their profit potential".

Marshall Management, founded in 1980, has special expertise in operating three- and four-star branded hotels and resorts, averaging 100 to 400 rooms, in urban and central business districts, suburban/drive-to and resort locations. In addition, the company has a proven track record managing independent resort properties. Located in Salisbury, Md., the company has managed a wide array of leading hotel brands, including Hilton, Sheraton, InterContinental Hotel Group, Choice and Cendant. Additional information about Marshall Management may be found at the company's website: www.marshallhotels.com

Source: 7 October 2004, Magna Hospitality Group, Business Wire.

International consortia

This far we have considered the big players and their international presence but what about the independent hotels? How can they compete in international markets against the multinationals? The answer is that there is a way and that is to join an international hotel consortium. Nield (2003) explained that an international hotel consortium is a collection of independent hotels in many countries that come together to combine their resources. These hotels cooperate to gain specific corporate benefits through economies of scale from purchasing, trading and marketing activities (Roper, 1997). The well-known hotel consortia include Best Western, Golden Tulip, Logis de France and leading hotels of the world.

Case: Distinguished Hotels International To Launch

Distinguished Hotels International (DHI), a new marketing and management consortium of more than 150 independent hotels around the world, will officially launch in London November 8–11 during World Travel Market 2004. The company will be headquartered in New York and will operate sales offices in New York and London. The creation of DHI represents the merger of UK-based Grand Heritage Hotels International with DHI in the United States, which features seven hotels managed by the Magna Hospitality Group LLC. The new company will offer corporate and leisure travellers a prestigious collection of luxury properties in the UK, Ireland, mainland Europe, Africa, the West Indies and North America. Each hotel is described as "uniquely different" with exceptional amenities and significant architectural and/or historical features. DHI's formation reunites William F. Burruss, who founded and served as President of Grand Heritage Hotels International until the company was sold in 1997, with Timothy Hadcock-Mackay, the current owner and CEO of Grand Heritage Hotels International in Europe. As President, Burruss will handle the day-to-day operations for DHI, and Hadcock-Mackay will serve as Chairman, focusing on new hotel membership. "We will offer leisure and business travellers a 'one-of-a-kind' travel experience with very high standards", said Burruss, who also serves as Chairman of Magna Hospitality. "They will be able to choose from a list of more than 150 independent, luxury hotels, castles, chateaux, stately homes, resorts, and health spas and inns located around the world. Unlike chain hotels, each DHI property – whether city centre or resort hotels – will be unforgettably unique, offering the top-quality guest amenities and architectural elegance for which Grand Heritage has always been known". Although DHI will manage some of the properties, its central role out of the New York sales office will be to market its hotel affiliates to potential visitors, including leisure travellers, business travellers, company executives, government dignitaries, celebrities, and meeting and trade show planners.

Source: www.distinguishedhotels.com

In the hospitality industry, consortia are typically found in the hotel sector but there is also some evidence of their activities in the restaurant market. Hotel Consortia represent affiliation through membership. These organizations primarily offer membership services to hotels for a fee. Nield (2003) explained that the consortia offer:

- Reservations systems, for example every Best Western hotel immediately link to their centralized reservations system.
- Referrals systems: Note how on KLM flights you are offered accommodation with Golden Tulip.
- Purchasing: The power of the consortium may equal the power of the chain. The consortium may negotiate discounts for its members because of large purchasing power.
- A full marketing package: Including brochures and full travel arrangements. Best Western has packages with the travel agency Going Places.
- Sales offices in major cities worldwide.

Example: Best Western BestRequests™ standards

Best Western is the biggest hotel brand in the world and it is a hotel consortia. Best Western hotels are independent, but they all keep the same BestRequests™ standards:

- dataports in all rooms;
- free high-speed Internet access[e];
- free local calls under 30 minutes[a];
- free long distance access[a];
- complimentary in-room coffee/tea makers[b];
- 50% non-smoking rooms[c];
- hairdryers in every room;
- iron and ironing board in every room[b];
- complimentary toiletries available upon request – that is razors, shaving cream, sewing kits, toothpaste;
- guestroom TVs offering at least one English language channel with international news;
- bottled or canned water available on-site, 24-hours-a-day;

- photocopy facilities available on-site for hotel business travel needs during normal business hours;
- king-size beds available in a minimum of 10% of rooms[d];
- clocks in all guestrooms;
- music provided in all guestrooms (e.g. clock radio);
- bottled shampoo.

Implementation of BestRequests® October 2001 in US, Canada and Caribbean; January 2002 in all other countries.
[a]US and Canada only due to telecom services and tariffs
[b]In-room or on request outside of the US, Canada and Caribbean
[c]20% outside US, Canada and Caribbean
[d]Queen-size bed outside US, Canada and Caribbean
[e]North America only

Source: www.bestwestern.com

■ Which method of entry should you use?

Douglas and Craig (1997), suggest that the way in which a company enters a market acts as a signal of the organization's behaviour and defines how the organization will do battle with its competitors in the future. While Doole and Lowe (2001) note that the way in which a company enters an international market depends upon several factors, for example, their organizational objectives; the financial resources available; the competition within the market; the nature of the product or service being offered; and the host country's resources, staff and political and legal systems. Nield (2003) argues that it depends on the distinctive competency of the company that is, what is it that the company is good at that gives it its competitive advantage. If a company has a distinctive competency that is easily copied it will require control and would therefore need a method of market entry where the competency is not given away. On the other hand, if the company's distinctive competency cannot be copied it could utilize a "looser" method of market entry. In general, top companies whose distinctive competency is technological knowledge should think about the benefits of entering the market as a wholly owned subsidiary. Specifically, companies whose distinctive competency is specialized management should consider the benefits of entering the market with a combination of franchises and subsidiary operations.

Example: Cendant signs franchise deal for Russia

Cendant Corp.'s Hotel Group today announced the signing of a deal with Hermitage Hospitality Ltd. to franchise Days Inn®

hotels in Russia and the other 14 countries of the former Soviet Union. The lodging franchise agreement covers the nations of Estonia, Latvia and Lithuania as well as all 12 countries that make up the Commonwealth of Independent States: Armenia, Azerbaijan, Belarus, Georgia, Kazakhstan, Kyrgyzstan, Moldova, Russia, Tajikistan, Turkmenistan, Ukraine and Uzbekistan.

Finally, the choice of one or more entry strategies will depend on the following:

1   the critical evaluation of the company's resources and capabilities;
2   the critical business environmental factors in host country;
3   the advantages and disadvantages that each choice would make to the overall vision and objectives of the company.

When it comes down to a choice of entry method for a particular hospitality company, there are more specific factors relating to that company's situation that must be taken into account. These include:

✓ capital,
✓ company size,
✓ branding,
✓ management skills,
✓ local knowledge,
✓ human resources,
✓ costs.
● After the full consideration of these factors, some entry strategies will be seen to be no longer appropriate. Managers will then decide between equity (wholly owned or joint venture) and non-equity-based alternatives (NIMA) recognizing that both present different risks and returns.
● Entry strategies need to be conceived as part of a well-designed business strategy. International strategic formulation requires a long-term perspective and it needs to match other functional strategies within the organization as well.

Which market entry method should Subway use if they want to entry Vietnam market? Why?   **ACTIVITY**

Chapter case study: Marriott International

The first Marriott Hotel was opened in 1957 in Virginia, USA. Previous to this Marriott had evolved from a root beer stand opened in 1927. After continued expansion the company name changed to Marriott Corporation in 1967. This accelerated growth strategy continued into the

1990s with the acquisition of the Ritz-Carlton Hotel Company, Renaissance Hotel Group and ExecuStay corporate housing company. The acquisitions allowed Marriott to enter new markets with an immediately strong position and now Marriott International operates and franchises more than 2,600 hotels and resorts around the world. They operate in North America and in Asian countries, such as China, Japan and South Korea. In Europe, France, Germany, UK, and Latin America and Caribbean.

Their long-term goal is to have a presence in every gateway city, major resort destination and high-demand suburban market around the world. In the USA, they manage or franchise approximately 8% of the total lodging market; outside the USA, they represent only 1%.

Marriott Hotels are operated using a variety of different types of ownership. Many are owned and operated by Marriott International. For example in 2003 they added 185 new hotels and timeshare units with over 31,000 new rooms. Approximately one-third of this room expansion was from conversions to Marriott brands by owners and franchisees of competitor brands.

Also in their plan to reduce the capital intensity of the business, Marriott is planning to increase the number of joint venture partners for new resort developments and by broadening their marketing and sales agreements to include resorts developed by others.

Joint venture has also been a successful market entry mode for Marriott International. At the end of March 2005, they completed a 75% investment with their joint venture partners courtyard. This investment is said to be accelerating pace of renovations and upgrades in the joint venture hotels. Thus also helping to further expand the Courtyard brand's industry-leading preference and generate even higher returns on investment, as stated by Arne Sorenson, Marriott's Executive Vice President.

Another way of strategy that Marriott uses is to buy and build properties and then sell them with an operating agreement, doing this they make money from the property and also from the right to use their brand.

In addition to the market entry modes mentioned above Marriott operates wholly owned hotels and strategic alliances. The global strategic alliances offering promotional and database marketing programmes which have been of no or little cost to Marriott. The partnerships are with:

- 23 airlines;
- financial services companies, such as Amex and VISA;
- consumer brands including AT&T and Hertz.

Within the UK, until recently, Marriott Hotels were operated as franchises by Whitbread PLC. This method of ownership is used all over the world as it allows Marriott to enter new markets with reduced risk, even within the USA Marriott Hotels are operated as franchises by third parties, such as White Lodgings. Further to this a 50:50 joint venture has been set up with Whitbread to run the Marriott properties within the UK, however this is a temporary measure whilst the hotel stock is sold on. After this the hotels will be operated under long-term management contracts. Marriott relies on the prominence of their brand to sustain this growth and support the methods of entry they use.

Despite their size they are still looking for new markets to move into. At the beginning of 2005 it was revealed that Marriott are "looking for a second partner with which to expand its Courtyard by Marriott chain in the UK". Whilst it was also revealed that "buying a budget hotel franchise – to compete against competitors, such as Accor's Ibis – remained an option". This shows that their motivation is often to be more competitive.

Overall Marriott International has successfully used many of the market modes of entry to attract and retain customers internationally.

Source: Caterer-Online (2005) and www.marriott.com

■ Conclusion

We have seen how in the real world, the international hospitality market situation is always complex and decisions can become complicated. We have studied the following market entry methods:

- whole-owned subsidiary,
- joint venture,
- strategic alliance,
- licensing or franchising,
- management contracts,
- consortia.

Our review of the activities of most of the significant players in the international hospitality industry has demonstrated that they fall into one or more of these categories. For instance, an owner may manage some of their own hotels, manage others which do not belong to them, or have varying amounts of majority or minority shareholdings in properties which they manage. To make the final decision about international entry, hospitality enterprises need to review their competences and the host countries' facilities and resources. This will be undertaken using analytical techniques, such as those elaborated in earlier chapters and set within an understanding of the cultural dynamics of those markets. The final decision will be part of the organizations strategic review and we will address this process Chapter 7.

■ Review questions

1 Why do companies choose to invest in an international market?
2 What factors lead them to select between the various options outlined in this chapter?
3 How would you justify advising a company in terms of the levels of risk involved in the various options?
4 If you enter a market without local knowledge what could the consequences be?

CHAPTER 7

Strategic planning and international hospitality enterprises

Chapter objectives

After working through this chapter, you should be able to:

- To define both strategic management in global business environment
- To gain knowledge of the impact of global environmental factors on strategy formulation
- To understand the strategic management process
- To use Porter's five forces model with SWOT and PEST analyses to formulate strategy
- To identify organizations' and countries' competitive advantages
- To understand how to use develop hospitality companies business and corporate strategy
- To consider global strategies when multinational enterprises (MNEs) expand their business overseas

■ Introduction

Strategic management is a capstone subject for management courses and it has been used by all kinds of enterprises and non-profit organizations. It applies knowledge and skills gained from functional subjects such as marketing, human resource management, accounting and finance. This chapter provides an outline of the strategic planning process and analytical frameworks in international hospitality industry. It enables students to gain an appreciation of the fast changing environment in which hospitality organizations operate, to identify the resources and competences in the organizations, and to evaluate different level strategic options and managerial issues in global environment.

■ Strategic planning and global strategy

Strategy is a broad and general plan developed to reach long-term organisational objectives. Strategic planning is a long-term planning that focuses on the organisation as a whole. Wheelen and Hunger (2004: 6) define strategic management as "a set of managerial decisions and actions that determines the long-run performance of a corporation". Strategic management has been recognized by managements and economic academics as the most important activity in business management and it is key to modern enterprises' survival and development.

Research indicates that organizations that engage in strategic management generally outperform those that do not. The attainment of an appropriate match between an organization's environment and its strategy, structure, resources and operations has positive effects on the organization's performance. According to Bruce Henderson, founder of the Boston Consulting Group, a company cannot afford to follow intuitive strategies once it becomes large, has layers of management, or its environment changes substantially. Not too long ago, a company could be successful by focusing only on making or providing services within its national boundaries. International considerations were minimal. As the world's environment becomes increasingly dynamic and complex, strategic management has been used by most hospitality enterprises as one way to make the environment more manageable and maintain competitive advantages. Traditionally hospitality industry is a fragmented industry dominated by thousands of independent small firms serving local or national customers, while now the industry is getting consolidated through external chaining and internal growth in order to gain economies of scale and sustainable competitiveness. Strategic management plays an important role when multinational hospitality enterprises expand their business across national borders.

Steps in developing international strategies management are similar to normal strategic management, but need more consideration of global business issues and international competition. Figure 7.1 outlines the elements in the basic strategic planning process that underpins the discussion in this chapter.

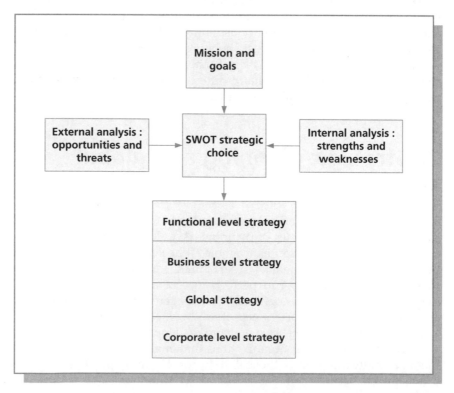

Figure 7.1
The strategic
planning process

■ Mission and objectives

Organizational mission is the purpose for which or the reason why an organization exists. A mission statement is a written document developed by management that describes and explains what the mission of an organisation actually is. The importance of organisational mission is obvious. It addresses that critical question all the businesses need to ask themselves: Where are we going? Mission statement will point out organizational direction in a relative long term. It helps increase probability of an organization's success for several reasons. It helps management to focus employees' effort in a common direction; serves as a sound rationale for allocating resources; it pinpoints broad but important areas within an organization. A company may also design a values code into its mission statement.

John Keane said a strategist need to see the company not as it is … but as it can become. A company's mission statement can focus, direct, motivate, unify and even excite a business into superior performance. The first job of a strategist is to identify and project a clear vision. From the following mission statement examples, stakeholders of these companies will know what they want to become in the international hospitality industry. It is clear that Subway and Marriott want to be undisputable global leaders in their sectors, while Tussauds Group target European market.

- Subway: To provide the tools and knowledge to allow entrepreneurs to successfully compete in the QSR (quick service restaurant) industry worldwide by consistently offering value to consumers through providing great-tasting food that is good for them and made the way they like it.
- Marriott: To be the worlds leading provider of hospitality services.
- Tussauds Group: To deliver real growth in profit to take Europe's leading entertainment worldwide.

Example: Starbucks' principles and mission statement

- Mission statement: Establish Starbucks as the premier purveyor of the finest coffee in the world while maintaining our uncompromising principles while we grow.

The following six guiding principles will help us measure the appropriateness of our decisions:

1 Provide a great work environment and treat each other with respect and dignity.
2 Embrace diversity as an essential component in the way we do business.
3 Apply the highest standards of excellence to the purchasing, roasting and fresh delivery of our coffee.
4 Develop enthusiastically satisfied customers all of the time.
5 Contribute positively to our communities and our environment.
6 Recognize that profitability is essential to our future success.

ACTIVITY   A Mission statements vary widely from one company to another. Why is one mission statement better than another? Develop criteria for evaluating hospitality organizations' mission statements.

B Using the Internet, find the mission statements of three multinational companies in one hospitality sector. Which mission statement is best? Why?

International hospitality companies need to develop organizational objectives, which reflect and flow naturally from an organizational mission. According to Hill and Jones (2004), well-constructed goals have some main characteristics: they are precise and measurable; they address crucial issues; they are challenging but realistic and they specify a time period in which they should be achieved.

A company's global objectives usually fall into the areas of marketing, finance, profitability, performance and development. Goals for market volume and profitability are usually set higher for international company than for domestic operations because of the allowance for greater risk involved. In addition, financial objectives must consider different tax regulations in other countries and exchange rate fluctuations.

■ Environmental analysis

After recognizing the corporate' mission statement, the next thing you need to do is environmental scanning. According to Wheelen and Hunger (2006), environment scanning is the monitoring, evaluating, and disseminating of information from the external and internal environments to key people within the corporation to avoid strategic surprise and ensure the long-term health of the firm. In this unit, we mainly discuss external analysis.

Why we need to do the external scanning, one reason is environmental uncertainty, which is the degree of complexity plus the degree of change existing in an organisation's external environment. It can be argued that without environmental uncertainty, there would be no need for strategic management. The Arab oil embargo in 1970s is the single most influential event causing the formation of strategy departments in many US corporations. The embargo showed managers just how vulnerable their companies were to environmental change. September 11th, followed by Iraq War, are the most significant events that reshape global business environment in recent years. As a key part of strategic management, environmental scanning is a tool used to help avoid strategic surprise and cope with an uncertain environment. In the new century, the global environments become more and more complex and unpredictable. However, those companies which engage in environmental scanning and strategic planning tend to be more successful than their non-planning competitors.

Environmental scanning is the process of information gathering, analysing and forecasting relevant trends in terms of business opportunities and threats. It pinpoints environmental factors that will affect operations in geographic areas of existing home marketing and potential foreign markets.

According to Wheelen and Hunger (2006), there are two layers in external environment: societal environment and task/industrial environment, as shown in Figure 2.1.

Societal environment

General forces that do not directly touch on the short-run activities but often influence its long-run decisions.

Task/industrial environment

This consists of those elements or groups that directly affect the corporation and, in turn, are affected by it. The task environment is the industry within which that firm operates.

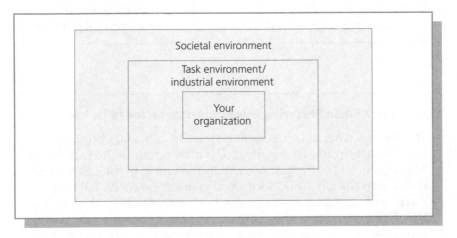

Figure 7.2
External
environment

As an international organization, the company should choose varying levels of scanning in societal environment: multinational, regional and national. The multinational level of analysis provides a broad assessment of business environment through monitoring, identification and forecasting significant worldwide trends global activities, such as the consequence of rapid growth oil price in 2006. At the regional level, the analysis focuses in detail on critical environmental factors to identify opportunities and risks for international companies in a region where a group of countries share seminar culture, history and geographical features, such as the devastating impacts of 2005 Boxing Day Tsunami and the conflicts between Israel and Lebanon. The national level of analysis focuses on the size and nature of the market, along with any possible operational problems, for example the competition between British cities to host the first Mega Casino.

Example: Tsunami aftermath

Occupancy of hotels in Phuket, Krabi and Phangnga has plunged to 10% in the aftermath of the tsunami and is expected to decline further to single digits, according to the Thai Hotels Association (THA). THA President Chanin Donavanik said the hotels in the six tsunami-hit provinces, particularly in the three major tourist destinations, were facing more cancellations without any new reservations in the first month of 2005.

If the situation does not improve in the next 2 to 3 weeks, some 500,000 people in the hotel and tourism-related industries were expected to lose their jobs, he said yesterday.

Most of the hotels could not afford to pay salaries to their staff and have yet to receive supporting funds from the government due to red tape, as there are nine agencies involved in the tsunami-relief campaign. The THA plans to ask Prime Minister Thaksin Shinawatra to order all of the relevant agencies to speed up the fund disbursement process. The Association of Thai Travel Agents (ATTA), meanwhile, plans to set up a crisis management centre to handle problems affecting the tourism and hospitality industry.

Source: Bangkok Post, January 2005, www.bangkokpost.com

Example: Middle East crisis brings tourism sector to its knees

The serious crisis in Lebanon and Israel in July 2006 bringing the Middle Eastern tourist industry to its knees despite the fact that it has registered the biggest growth in the world in the last decade, the United Nation World Tourism Organization (UNWTO) said in a statement issued by the organization's secretariat in Madrid. The UNWTO recalled that the tourist sector has become a vital part of the social and economic fabric of the region and it is an important component for the livelihoods of its people. While international tourist arrivals worldwide grew at an annual average of 4%, the average growth rate of arrivals in the Middle East during this period was 11%, and the number of arrivals to the region almost tripled, leaping from 13.7 million in 1995 to 39.7 million in 2005.

During the first month of 2006, the key destinations in the region started posting outstanding double digit results. Lebanon posted a 37% growth in the first quarter of the year. Israel too was experiencing similar levels of growth (25%) while Egypt, Jordan and other major destinations in the gulf also showed positive results. The overall problem for tourism in the area given, the current situation is compounded by the destruction of basic infrastructure and the absence of normal transport and communication facilities. As yet no foreseeable time frame for a return to normalcy can be outlined, the UNWTO said. At this point the primary issue for the sector is the safety of tourists and their rapid repatriation from risk zones. "This is yet another example of where tourists and the tourism industry are hostage to global events beyond their control," UNWTO Secretary-General Francesco Frangialli said. "We will work closely with our members to help those who are suffering and to rebuild the tourism economy."

Source: UNWTO 27/07/2006 www.world-tourism.org

There are so many things happening everyday in the world. For hospitality companies, they can choose 5 to 20 issues and assess them by the following steps:

● Identify likely trends and pick up strategic environmental issues from external environments which are closely relevant to hospitality industry.
● Assess probability of trends occurring and list all the probabilities form low to high.
● Ascertain likely impact of trends on your company and make the list from low to high.

Normally societal environmental scanning should cover the topics we considered in the discussion in Chapter 3 about the PEST analysis, with such topics as the political, economic, social and technological areas.

■ Industry analysis: forces influencing competition

An industry is a group of firms that produces products that are close substitutes for each other. Industry analysis is an in-depth examination of key factors within a corporation's task environment. In an industry, competition drives down the rate of return on invested capital towards the rate earned in a "perfectly competitive" industry. Rates of return greater than the "competitive" rate stimulate an inflow of capital, while those below the "competitive" rate force a withdrawal from the industry and a decline in competition.

Michael E. Porter identifies five forces that influence industry competition: the threat of new entrants, the threat of substitute products or services, the bargaining power of buyers, the bargaining power of suppliers and competitive rivalry. The stronger each force is, the more competitive the industry and the lower the rate of return that can be earned. This five-force model was developed in 1980. Until now, it is one of most important tool used in industry analysis.

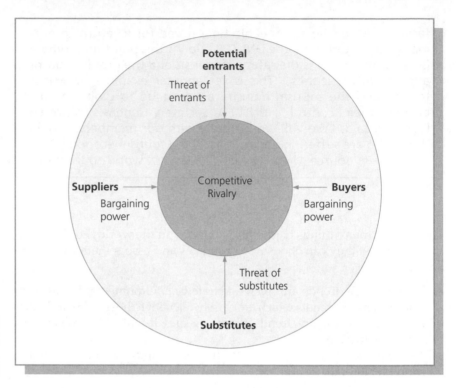

Figure 7.3
Five-force model
Source: Porter, M.
(1980)

Threat of new entrants

New international entrants bring new capacity, a desire to gain market share and position, and new approaches to customer service. New entrants mean prices pushed downward and margins squeezed, resulting in reduced long-term profitability. Whilst hotel chains have been busy spreading their brands over a wide variety of lodging products, some companies in the entertainment, restaurant or luxury product segment have made way into the hotel business attempting to capitalize on an already well-established brand image. For example, Italian jewellery and fashion designers move into the boutique hotel business in 2001, the Palazzo Versace opened its doors on Australia's Gold Coast not far from the renowned "Surfer's Paradise" beach. Built at a cost of US $108 million the luxury resort includes 146 rooms, 59 suites and 72 condominiums. Guests are surrounded at every moment by reminders of the late designer, as they drink from Versace glasses, sit on Versace chairs and dry themselves with Versace towels. Future plans include the development of six more Versace-designed luxury hotels in the Middle East, Asia and North America.

To discourage potential competitors moving into the market, established hospitality companies tend to set Entry Barriers through:

● brand loyalty,
● absolute cost advantages,
● economies of scale,

- customer switching costs,
- government regulation.

Bargaining power of buyers

Buyers are most powerful when a company depends on them for business, but they themselves are not dependent on the company. Because of its huge purchasing power, tour operators like Thomson can decide contract terms when they talk with small and middle size hotels in Greek or Turkish resorts.

Bargaining power of suppliers

Suppliers are most powerful when a company depends on them for business, but they themselves are not dependent on the company. Utility companies have much bargaining power over hotels and restaurants in United Kingdom. From 2005 to 2006, the whole hospitality industry in Britain experiences massive increase of gas and electricity bill.

Threat of substitute products

The availability of substitute products places limits on the prices market leaders can charge. High prices may induce buyers to switch to the substitute.

The modern transportation era means that tourists can have a wide choice of holiday destinations and accommodations. It could be cheaper for a British couple to have 2 weeks holidays in Thailand or Turkey instead of Britain and they can stay in much better hotels and enjoy different food, better weather and personal services.

Rivalry among competitors

Rivalry refers to actions taken by firms in an industry to improve their positions and gain advantages over each other. It is the major force which influences hospitality organization in industry environment. Strong demand conditions moderate the competition among established companies and create opportunities for expansion. When demand is weak, intensive competition can develop, particularly in consolidated industries with high exit barriers.

International market rivalry analysis is one of the most important areas for environmental analysis and strategy formulation. For example, will the infrastructure support new companies in hospitality industry? Is there room for additional competition? What is the relative supply and demand for the proposed product or service? The ultimate profit potential in an industry in a given location will be determined by industry rivalry. Rivalry manifests itself in price competition, advertising battles, product positioning and attempts at differentiation.

Plate 11
Identifying the offer
and the rivals
Source: Author's
photograph

This is the entrance to Chinatown in Liverpool. It has both a symbolic and a marketing function. It highlights the offer of the area dramatically and marks it off from the rest of the city. Something similar, but interestingly visually different is achieved in Manchester. There is a pattern of identification, of branding, but also a creation of difference.

Case: Five Forces Analysis of Starbucks

Starbucks is now the largest US coffee chain. According to the company fact sheet, as of February 2006, Starbucks had 6,216 company-operated outlets worldwide: 5,028 of them in the United States and 1,188 in other countries and US territories. In addition, the company has 4,585 joint venture and licenced outlets, 2,633 of them in the United States and 1,952 in other countries and US territories. The company is committed to offering the highest quality coffee and the Starbucks experience. Let's have a look of Starbucks' industry environments.

What is the threat of new entrants?
Newly established coffee shops and cafes in host countries could be found in many countries everyday. The new entrants may be retailers, banks, hotels or restaurants.

Starbucks production process is relatively transparent, and potential entrants could easily replicate some of their resources and operation process. Therefore entry barriers into the coffee bar market are not high for both large multinationals or small independent companies.

What is rivalry among existing companies?
Existing international coffee shops in other countries are major competition for Starbucks international, such as Costa or Café Republic. Players in the foodservice industry are increasingly offering more competition, such as McDonald's McCafé.

What is the threat of substitute products or services?

The threat of substitute products is high. Coffee is Starbucks focused product, and there are so many other drinks, especially in countries where tea may be the popular beverage. However, Starbuck's range of teas, different strengths of coffees and iced beverages reduce the risk of substitutes in international markets. In Westernized countries increased health awareness may possibly reduce coffee intake.

What is the bargaining power of buyers?

Buyers bargaining power is moderate. Starbucks does not depend their business on small group of buyers, although ice creams and canned drinks are distributed through supermarkets and cafés are everywhere in major cities.

What is the bargaining power of suppliers?

Starbucks has control over the suppliers. Starbucks good reputation depends on a consistent connection with premium suppliers. As the coffee beans are produced by farmers in less-developed countries they have little power. This explains why the company has given immense support to the farmers. Starbucks is fair-trade certified, which means they encourage farmers to sell their beans at premium price. This not only achieves higher quality coffee but assures that coffee consumed in Starbucks has been ethically produced.

■ Internal analysis

After the environmental assessment, the second major step in weighing international strategic options is the internal analysis. Internal analysis is extremely important for resource-based approach. Resource-based approach is one of the major approaches used by most companies when they design strategies. This analysis determines which areas of the company's operations represent strengths or weaknesses (currently or potentially) compared to competitors, so that the company may use that information to its strategic advantage. The internal analysis focuses on company's resources and operations, and global synergies. The strengths and weaknesses of the firm's managerial expertise and functional capabilities are evaluated to determine what core competences the company has and how well they can help the company exploit foreign opportunities.

What is resource? There are many definitions. Generally speaking, it is an asset, competency, process, skill or knowledge controlled by the corporation. Wheelen and Hunger (2006) suggest evaluating key resources by VRIO framework:

- Value: Does it provide competitive advantage?
- Rareness: Do other competitors possess it?
- Imitability: Is it costly for others to imitate?
- Organization: Is the firm organized to exploit the resource?

Strategic managers assess its resources, capabilities and key success factors compared to those of its competitors. They must judge the relative current and potential competitive position of firms in that market and location – whether that is a global position or that for a specific country or region. Lasting key resources and competences have high durability and low imitability. Wheelen and Hunger (2006) define durability as "rate at which a company's underlying resources and capabilities (core competencies) depreciate or become obsolete" and imitability as "rate at which a company's underlying resources and capabilities (core competencies) can be duplicated by others".

Most companies develop their strategy around key strengths, or core competencies. Core competencies represent important corporate resources because, as Prahalad and Hamel explain, they are the collective learning in the organization, especially how to coordinate diverse production skills and to integrate multiple streams of technologies. Managers must also assess their firm's weaknesses. Of course, the subjective perceptions, motivations, capabilities and goals of the managers involved in such diagnoses frequently cloud the decision-making process.

■ The Four Building Blocks of competitive advantage

Competitive advantage exists when there is a match between a firm's distinctive competencies and the factors critical for success within its industry. Hill and Jones' (2004) Four Building Blocks of competitive advantage provides a good model for hospitality companies to identify their distinctive competencies from following Four Building Blocks and then develop matched strategies.

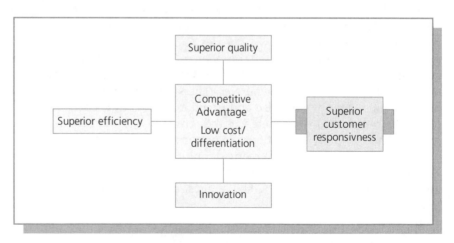

Figure 7.4
Four Building Blocks of competitive advantages
Source: (adapted from Hill and Jones, 2004)

Superior efficiency

This may be in terms of worker output, average cost per unit. Efficiency is an input/output measure, and does not measure effectiveness or goal-seeking behaviour.

To reduce cost, many companies choose to externalize costs by:

- subcontracting (e.g. companies who contract-out their cleaning and catering).

or reduce costs by:

- Locating work in low-cost areas (e.g. moving hotel group call centre from UK to India).

"Economies of scale" is another key area for superior efficiency in hospitality industries.

Innovation

Innovation refers to the act of creating new products/services or processes.

- Develop new products/services, which have superior attributes to existing products/services, therefore attractive new customers.
- Create new process to produce products/services, which will reduce cost or improve product/service quality. The following case shows that even the most sophisticated technologies can be used by hospitality industry.

Example: Hotel tycoon to test space station technology

A hotel tycoon's dream of building an inflatable commercial space station is taking a step towards reality – with the launch of a satellite to test the technology behind the planned orbital outpost. The fact-finding mission scheduled for this week will explore the feasibility of Robert Bigelow's plan to build a working commercial space complex by 2015. When finished, it will consist of balloon-like modules strung together like sausage links and serve as an orbiting space hotel, college or entertainment venue.

The planned lift off from Russia of Bigelow Aerospace's privately funded Genesis I spacecraft will mark the beginning of the start-up's attempt to break into the commercial spaceflight business. Bigelow, who made his fortune with the Las Vegas-based Budget Suites of America hotel chain, has remained tight-lipped about the exact launch date of its prototype.

Source: AFX International Focus, 12th July 2006.

Superior quality

A product or service is said to have superior quality when customers regard it has greater value compared to the rival products/services.

Superior quality may be an absolute measure, such as the highest specification aircraft/food/hotel, etc. or perceived quality, viewed by customers.

Customer responsiveness

To achieve superior responsiveness to customers, a company should be able to do a better job than competitors of identifying and satisfying customers' needs. Achieving superior quality is integral to achieving superior responsiveness to customers. Another area is to customize goods and services for individual customers, which is especially important in hospitality industry.

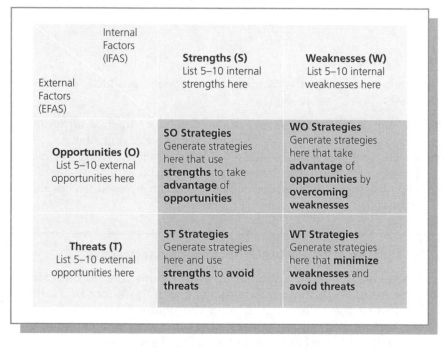

Figure 7.5
The strategic
application of the
SWOT matrix
Source: Weihrich
(1982: 60)

Organizations are only successful if they are well-suited to their environment. It is critical for managers to understand the significant forces in the environment which may provide threats or opportunities for their organization. They can then be prepared to cope with the significant environmental influences.

The SWOT matrix illustrates how management can match the external opportunities and threats facing a particular corporation with its internal strengths and weaknesses to yield four sets of strategic alternatives. The real value of this technique is not to suggest a particular strategy the firm should follow, but to act as a brainstorming tool to help create a series of alternative strategies management might not otherwise consider. It forces strategic managers to develop both growth and retrenchment strategies, even though they might not believe that both sets of strategies are applicable to their corporation's situation. The matrix is a logical extension of SWOT analysis and helps keep strategic managers flexible in terms of possible options. The strength and weakness portion of SWOT allows the manager to look at the strengths and weaknesses of the firm – they determine what the organization can do. An analysis of external opportunities and threats tells managers what the company might do. Matching the two segments should provide a reasonable direction for what the firm should do given its particular situation. SWOT analysis allows the manager to match the external environment of the firm with the internal environment. A proper match will allow the firm to be more effective and efficient.

■ Corporate value chain analysis

Value chain analysis, as proposed by Porter, is a way of examining the nature and extent of the synergies that do or do not exist between the internal activities of a corporation. It was first designed for manufacturing industry, while now service industry also uses it as a tool in internal analysis. The systematic examination of individual value activities can lead to a better understanding of a corporation's strengths and weaknesses. Its advantage over other methods of analysing a company's internal environment is its ability to visualize a company in terms of strings of product value chains which can be tied together in places to achieve economies of scope.

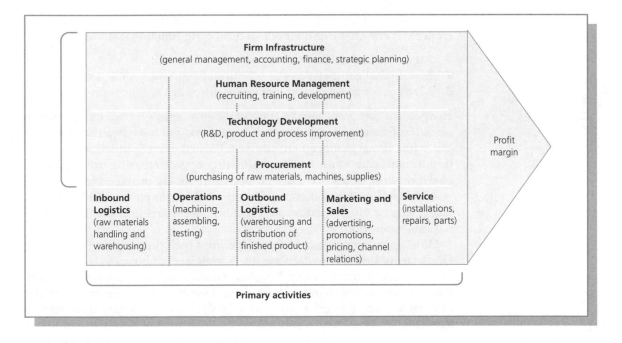

Figure 7.6   The corporate value chain model
Source: Porter, M. (1985, 1988) and Wheelen and Hunger (2004: 86)

Analysis process

- Examine each product/service line's value chain. Core competencies and core deficiencies.
- Examine the "linkages" within each product/service line's value chain. Connections between the way one value activity is performed and the cost of performance of another activity.
- Examine the synergies among the value chains of different product lines or business units.
  Economies of scope.

Strategy options and decisions

After external and internal environment analysis, managers need to make strategic decision at different level. Functional strategy is the lowest level and corporate is the highest level strategy.

Functional level strategy

Michael Porter has developed a framework of generic business strategies based on the two sources of competitive advantage: low cost and differentiation. These sources, combined with the scope of the target market (narrow or broad) or product mix width (narrow or wide), yields four generic strategies: cost leadership, product differentiation, cost focus and focused differentiation.

Achieving competitive advantage demands that the company make choices. There are three methods determining functional strategy:

1 Identify business unit's core competencies.
2 Ensure that competencies are continually strengthened.
3 Manage competencies so that competitive advantage is preserved.

Hospitality companies make functional strategies on marketing, human resource, finance, operations, etc. These strategies have been discussed in other functional management courses. We just want to mention one functional level issue – outsourcing. Outsourcing is purchasing from someone else a product or service that had been previously provided internally. It is important decision no matter the hospitality company want to use cost leadership or differentiation strategy; no matter it is in domestic or international operation.

Hotel operations are notorious for having a high proportion of fixed costs. One way for hoteliers to decrease the overall level of business risk is to render their cost structure more flexible. Outsourcing can often be a solution. For instance, instead of retaining a full-time staff, hotels have the possibility of ordering up staff, on a day-to-day basis, from temporary employment agencies, who maintain a specialized division for the hospitality industry. Another area that is being increasingly outsourced is laundry services, both for the clients and the hotel itself (sheets, towels, curtains, etc.) Many hotels simply rent their linen from a supplier who takes care of washing it.

Food and beverage services are activities that cost hotel managements a lot of time and headaches, but are usually not very profitable (in Europe and North America, not in Asia). Hotel restaurants have a reputation for being stuffy, unexciting and mediocre. For example, in the United Kingdom the value of the hotel catering market increased by only 12% between 1998 and 2002, as compared with a 22% increase of the total eating out market in real terms. Now increasingly, hoteliers from the high end to the low end are engaging in some form of outsourcing of their food and beverage operations. There are several possible structures that can be put in place. Budget hotels simply make it a point to be located near restaurants. An example is the roadside Travelodges in the United Kingdom, which are often situated close to Little Chef.

Strategically, outsourcing value-creation activities to subcontractors is opposite of vertical integration. Any function can be outsourced, if it is not critical to a firm's success (is not one of its distinctive competencies). Outsourcing should begin with an identification of a firm's distinctive competencies (which will continuously be performed within the company). All other activities are then reviewed to see whether they can be performed more effectively and efficiently by independent suppliers.

Advantages of outsourcing

- More efficient at performing (the company may reduce its own cost).
- By outsourcing a non-core value-creation activity to a supplier that has a distinctive competency, the company may better differentiate its final product/service.
- Remove distractions and focus resources on strengthening its distinctive competencies.

Risks linked with outsourcing

- Too dependent on an outsourced activity.
- Loss of control of scheduling.
- Loss of important competitive information.

Choose an international hospitality company; explain what kind of activities it can outsource and what cannot outsource. Why?   **ACTIVITY**

Business level strategy

Michael Porter has pointed out the generic business strategies. "Generic" refers to the fact that these strategies could be pursued by any company, operating in any industry. Business level strategy refers to the plan of action that strategic managers adopt for using a company's resources and distinctive competencies to gain a competitive advantage over its rivals in a market or industry, such as hotel, restaurant or cruise industry, while corporate strategy can be used among different industries.

The three business strategies are cost leadership, differentiation and focus strategy.

Cost leadership strategy

- A company's goal in pursuing a cost leadership is to outperform competitors by producing goods and services at a lower cost.
- This strategy can lead to above-average profits, especially in competitive market.
- To become the cost leader a company must make choices about its product, market and distinctive competencies. easyJet is an excellent example.
- Competitor's ability to imitate the cost leader's methods easily is a threat to this strategy. Customer satisfaction is another concern, especially in the global market.

Case: Only One Pound from Luton to Nice – Why Not Book easyJet?

easyJet was founded in 1995 when the Greek entrepreneur Stelios Haji-Ioannou leased two aircrafts and introduced scheduled routes from London Luton to Edinburgh and Glasgow. The following year easyJet received its first wholly owned aircraft and introduced new routes including international services to Nice and Barcelona. In 1997 easyJet launched its website, easyjet.com and the first Internet booking was taken 1 year later, in April 1998. As a result of a rapid expansion easyJet acquired 40% of the Swiss carrier TEA Basel AG in March 1998. The growth continued and by the year 1999 easyJet had three base airports; London Luton, Liverpool and Geneva. In the same year easyJet also introduced its first services wholly outside the United Kingdom. The company had now grown significantly and in November 2000 easyJet was listed on the London Stock Exchange. The development continued and in 2001 easyJet introduced a massive route expansion. The following year easyJet acquired British Airways low-cost brand "Go" and became Europe's number one low-cost airline. As a result of the merger easyJet continued on the chosen path and introduced a number of new routes in 2003. In 2004 easyJet launched the accommodation service, easyJetHotels. Today easyJet has a huge presence in Europe with 212 routes across 64 airports. easyJet's head office is located at London Luton airport. In 2005 easyJet had approximately 4,152 employees.

From a strategic point of view easyJet's history can be summarized in one word, expansion. From the beginning easyJet has expanded its operations aggressively by introducing new routes every year and they have recently launched new products and services such as accommodation, travel insurance and car rental. Passenger statistics indicate that in its first full year, 1996 easyJet carried 420,000 passengers and in 2005 this figure rose to 29,558 million passengers.

From the beginning easyJet has adopted cost leadership as their business level strategy and outperformed competitors by providing services at a lower cost. easyJet achieves cost leadership trough eliminating unnecessary costs. This is carried out in a number of ways:

- Using the Internet to reduce distribution costs.
- Maximizing the utilization of each aircraft.

- Ticketless travel.
- No free meals or drinks on board.
- Efficient use of airports.
- Paperless operations.
- Point-to-point short-haul flights.
- No seat assignment on board.
- Outsourcing certain operations such as luggage handling and fleet maintenance.

Even though the use of secondary airports is an important part of easyJet's cost management they still use major airports on some routes. Ryanair on the other hand uses only secondary airports which gives them advantage in terms of keeping the costs to a minimum.

In the beginning easyJet used a single aircraft fleet (Boeing 737) that could be utilized throughout the network, but in 2005 their fleet consisted of 54 Boeing 737 and 55 Airbus A319. Despite two different types of aircrafts easyJet aims to benefit from the "any aircraft, any route" model. This model will reduce the cost of maintenance and spare parts together with enabling the use of an interchangeable crew.

Passenger statistics

Year	Annual total ('000)
1995	30
1996	420
1997	1,140
1998	1,880
1999	3,670
2000	5,996
2001	7,604
2002	11,400
2003	20,300
2004	24,300
2005	29,558

This cost leadership enables easyJet to minimize costs but it also has a few downsides. Such a cost structure reduces easyJet's flexibility (e.g. seat assignment and luggage allowance) which in turn might affect the value perceived by customers. Business travellers are usually ready to pay more for more legroom but easyJet's highly standardized product does not allow this. easyJet mainly uses secondary airports which might significantly increase the travel times and the total travel cost.

This business model has been and still is the backbone of easyJet's success. easyJet and other low-cost carriers realized the dissatisfaction about the high fares charged by mainstream airlines and chose their strategy accordingly. However, cost-cutting has not been the only thing contributing to easyJet's success. The above-mentioned concepts have not only enabled easyJet to radically cut costs, they have also been innovative products and services in the airline industry.

Source: www.easyJet.com, 2006.

Differentiation strategy

- The objective of differentiation is to achieve a competitive advantage by creating a product or service that is perceived to be unique in some way.
- The differentiated company's ability to satisfy customers' needs in a way that its competitors cannot means it can charge a premium price.
- This strategy can lead to above-average profits because a differentiator can charge a premium price rather than by reducing cost.
- Generally, differentiator segments its market into many niches, offering products for many market niches.
- Differentiation can be achieved through quality, innovation responsiveness to customers.

The risks for a differentiator

- The differentiator must maintain its perceived uniqueness in customers' eyes against agile imitation.
- A source of uniqueness may be overridden by changes in consumer tastes and demands.
- A differentiator must be cautious in setting prices.

Case: Differentiation Strategy in Hard Rock Café

The Hard Rock Café (HRC) was the first themed restaurant on a major scale to be established in the UK and proved to be an instant classic, attracting droves of customers with its first rate, but moderately priced casual American fare, warm service and ever present rock 'n' roll music and sensibility. Since the establishment of the Hard Rock organization, the brand has developed a global profile with outlets in many major cities and HRC T-shirts worn all over the world.

The first HRC opened its doors to the public on June 14, 1971, in London, Founded by Isaac Tigrett and Peter Morton, two enterprising and music-loving Americans. The HRC is currently a wholly owned subsidiary of The Rank group which is one of the United Kingdom's leading gaming and entertainment companies. In the past 30 years, The HRC has grown from a modest London pub to a global power consisting of cafes, hotels, casinos, live music venues, a rock museum, an annual 'Rockfest' concert and is one of the most universally recognized trademarks. There are currently 111 HRCs worldwide in 42 countries, of which half are owned and the rest franchised out (Mintel, 2003), this has put the chain firmly in the service industry making it a truly global phenomenon. The HRC offers a special experience to its devoted, ever-expanding clientele and remains conscious to its founding objectives: delicious food, good music and a high-energy atmosphere their guests will never forget.

The Hard Rock's total revenues for 2004 were $426 million versus $382 million for 2003; this shows a growth of 11.5% (Hard Rock International, 2004). Operating profit showed a 35.3% increase with $51.0 million for 2004 versus $37.7 million for the same period in 2003 (Hard Rock International, 2004).

At the Hard Rock, the experience concept is to provide not only a custom meal from the menu, but a dining event that includes a unique visual and sound experience not duplicated anywhere in the world. It is felt that this differentiation strategy has proved a big success due to the fact that the organization is clearly aware who their customer is and what the customers needs and values are.

Source: Hard Rock Café, www.hardrockcafe.com

Focus strategy

- The focus strategy positions a company to compete for customers in particular market segment, based on geography, customer type or market segment.
- Selecting a niche by type of customer might mean serving only the rich, the very adventurous, very young or very romantic customers.
- A focus strategy can be pursued using either a differentiation or a low-cost approach. In essence, a focused company is a specialized differentiator or a cost leader. The following example of the Four Seasons Hotel is about the differentiation focus.

Case: Four Seasons Focuses on Luxury Travellers

Four Seasons is one of the world's leading managers of luxury hotels and resorts. The core goal for Four Seasons Hotel is to be recognized as the undisputed global leader in luxury lodging.

Four Seasons endeavour to offer business and leisure travellers the finest accommodations and experiences beyond compare in each destination in which they operate. Four Seasons has a portfolio of 70 luxury hotel and resort properties (containing approximately 17,300 guest-rooms) several of which include a residential component. These properties are operated primarily under the Four Seasons brand name in principal cities and resort destinations in 31 countries in North America, the Caribbean, Europe, Asia, Australia, the Middle East and South America.

Four Seasons developed a substantial base of knowledge and understanding regarding its customers, who they are, how they live, work and spend their money. More importantly, the company knew how to translate the refinements and desired atmosphere of its customer base to its hotels and resorts. Moreover, it successfully conveyed this translation and concept in its marketing messages from the very beginning. For example, the first advertisement campaign created awareness among its target market and helped define its position in the hotel sector. Further, in order to identify potential customers, Four Seasons identified those companies among the top 1,000 that generated significant amounts of business travel to existing or scheduled locations. The list developed was highly select and the emphasis was on persuading prospects from that list that Four Seasons offered a distinctive product they should try.

Pricing strategies and status management: The pricing strategy, often is one of the highest priced in the market, reinforces its image and positioning. Even in down periods it will offer attractive packages instead of reduced price promotions, which hurt the image. Four Seasons consists of not associating its name with any lower-rated or lower-priced brands to protect the image and preserve the status.

Four Seasons Hotel is the innovator in the industry. Many common practice today has been Four Seasons; innovations. The innovations include: European-style concierge service, private concierge service, home-cooking programme, exceptional restaurants, vegetarian dining, private reserve, executive suites, complimentary newspapers, 24-hour business services, 24-hour room service, digital display for the hearing impaired, complimentary early arrival, bathrooms with phones and high-speed Internet access.

"Create guest experiences beyond compare so that their first choice for luxury travellers" is one of the company's key objective, and clearly you can see it from Four Season's business strategy.

Source: Four Seasons Hotel, 2006 www.fourseasons.com

The risks for a focuser
- high costs,
- the focuser's niche may disappear,
- large differentiators may compete for the focuser's niche if it becomes very profitable.

Strategic failure: stuck in the middle

Michael Porter argues that a business unit which is unable to achieve one of the competitive strategies is likely to be "stuck in the middle" of the competitive marketplace with no competitive advantage. That unit, according to Porter, is doomed to below-average performance. Cost leader or differentiator could be stuck in the middle when business environment changes.

■ Sustainable competitive advantage in hypercompetitive industry

According to D'Aveni (1994), companies in a hypercompetitive industry learn to quickly imitate the successful strategies of market leaders – making it increasingly difficult to sustain any competitive advantage. As the entry barrier to hospitality industry is fairly low, in certain circumstances, the industry will become hypercompetitive industry. Competitive advantage in a hypercompetitive industry comes from an up-to-date knowledge of environmental trends and competitive activity coupled with a willingness to risk a current advantage for a possible new advantage. Companies must thus be willing to upgrade their own successful products or services in order to sustain their competitive advantage. Since hypercompetitive industries go through escalating stages of competition, the only real sustainable competitive advantage lies not in a company's products or services available now, but in its ability to learn and to adapt to constantly changing conditions.

■ Global competition and national competitive advantage

The strategic choice as to where a company should position itself along the globalization–regionalization continuum is contingent upon the nature of hospitality industry, the type of company and its goals and strengths, and the nature of its subsidiaries. In addition, each company's strategic approach should be unique in adapting to its own environment. Many companies may try to "Go Global, Act Local" to trade off the best advantages of each strategy.

As Yoshino and Rangan explained, global competition occurs when a firm takes a global view of competition and sets about maximizing profits worldwide, rather than on a country-by-country basis. If a company encounters the same rival in market after market, it is engaged in global competition. Global competition is beneficial to consumers around the world (e.g. in the US, foreign companies offered better automobile products, performance and prices). Global competition expands the range of products and services, and increases the likelihood that consumers will get what they want. The downside of global competition is the potential to destroy local brands and some of jobs.

Strategic orientations

When multinationals carry out their global strategic planning, most of them have specific predispositions. According to Chakravarthy and Perlmutter (1985), and Rugman and Collinson (2006), there are four pre-dispositions – ethnocentric, polycentric, regiocentric and geocentric:

1   A multinational with an ethnocentric predisposition relies on the val-ues and interests of the parent company in formulating and imple-menting the strategic plan. Primary emphasis is given to profitability and the company tries to run operations abroad the way they are run at home. This predisposition is used most commonly by companies trying to sell the same service or product abroad that they sell at home.
2   A multinational with a polycentric predisposition tailors its strategic plan to meet the needs of a local culture. If the company is doing busi-ness in more than one culture, the overall plan is adapted to reflect these individual local needs. The basic mission of a polycentric multi-national is to be accepted by the local culture, and to merge into the country.
3   A multinational with a regiocentric predisposition is interested in both profit and public acceptance (combining the ethnocentric and polycen-tric approaches), and uses a strategy that allows it to address both local

and regional needs. The company is less focused on a particular country than on a geographic region, such as South America or East Europe.

4   A multinational with a geocentric predisposition views operations on a global basis. The largest international corporations often use this approach. They produce global products with local variations, and staff their offices with the best people they can find, regardless of country of origin. Multinationals, in the true meaning of the word, have a geocentric predisposition. However, it is possible for a multinational to have a polycentric or regiocentric predisposition if the company is moderately small or limits operations to specific cultures or geographic regions.

Global strategy

Companies that compete in the global marketplace face competitive pressures for cost reductions and pressures to be locally responsive. How to keep multinationals' competitive advantages in foreign markets? According to Hill and Jones (2004), these companies have four choices: international strategies; multidomestic strategies; global strategies and transnational strategies.

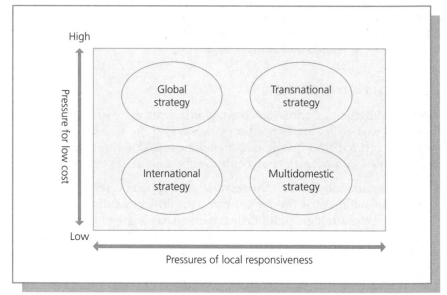

Figure 7.7
Global strategy
options
Source: Adapted from
Hill and Jones (2004)

International strategy

● Companies pursuing an international strategy transfer the skills and products derived from distinctive competencies to foreign markets, while undertaking some limited local customization.
  Examples: McDonald's, Wal-Mart.

Multidomestic strategy

● Companies pursuing a multidomestic strategy customize their product offering, marketing strategy and business strategy to national conditions.
  Examples: AOL, OK magazine.

Global strategy

● Companies pursuing a global strategy focus on reaping the cost reductions that come from experience curve effects and location economies.
  Examples: Dell computer, Motorola.

Transnational strategy

● Transnational strategy involves a simultaneous focus on reducing costs, transferring skills and products, and local responsiveness.
  Examples: Coca Cola, Sony (try to achieve).

According to Porter (1998) particular attributes in individual countries influences industry development: factor conditions, demand conditions, related and supporting industries, and firm strategy, structure and rivalry. This is often presented as a diamond shape which delimits the environment in which firms compete.

● Factor conditions

Factor conditions refer to a country's endowment with resources and may be divided into five categories – human, physical, knowledge, capital and infrastructure:

1 Human resources: The quantity of workers, their skills, wage levels and the work ethic constitute the human resource factor. Countries with a supply of low-wage workers have an advantage for labour-intensive production. Such countries are at a disadvantage for producing sophisticated products with skilled labour.

2 Physical resources: The availability, quantity, quality, and cost of land, water, minerals, and other natural resources determine a country's physical resources. Size and location fall in this category, since proximity to markets and sources of supply, as well as transportation costs, are strategic considerations.

3 Knowledge resources: The availability of scientific, technical and market-related knowledge endows a nation with knowledge resources. This factor is a function of research facilities and universities. This factor is important for sophisticated products and services and for doing business in sophisticated markets.

4 Capital resources: Countries vary in the availability, amount, cost and types of capital available. The nation's savings rate, interest rates, tax laws and government deficit affect this factor. Firms paying high capital costs are unable to stay in a market faced with competition from a

nation with low capital costs. Firms with the low capital costs keep prices low and force firms paying high costs to accept low returns or leave the industry.

5 Infrastructure resources: Infrastructure includes a nation's banking system, healthcare system, transportation system, communications system and the availability and cost of using them.

Demand conditions

The demand conditions for products and services determine the rate and nature of improvement and innovation. Several characteristics of home demand are important to create competitive advantage.

Composition of home demand determines how firms perceive, interpret and respond to buyer needs. Competitive advantage occurs when home demand sets the quality standard and defines buyer needs. This information is not available to foreign rivals and this advantage is enhanced when home buyers pressure firms to innovate quickly and frequently.

Size and pattern of growth of home demand is important only if home demand is sophisticated and anticipates foreign demand. Large home markets offer economies of scale and learning while dealing with familiar, comfortable markets. America and the United Kingdom are the examples. If home demand reflects or anticipates foreign demand, large-scale facilities and programmes will be an advantage in global competition. Rapid home market growth is another incentive to invest in and adopt new technologies faster, and to build large, efficient facilities.

Case: Starbucks' Global Strategy

'We are building the Starbucks brand and developing the global infrastructure to create a valuable growth vehicle well into the future' (www.starbucks.com).

Companies such as Starbucks Coffee Japan Ltd create new products for their specific market but still provide the standardized products set by the parent company. Products such as a "Jelly Frappuccino" were produced specifically for Japan. In addition some of the countries need different layouts than the standardized designs in USA. Starbucks Coffee Japan have altered counter heights, packaging and merchandise to suit Japanese customers. Starbucks global strategy has enabled reduction in major development and manufacturing costs and other value chain activities, and helps achieve economies of scale as fixed costs are spread over more units of production.

The company has in a sense developed its own language, Mr Schultz comments:

"When we first opened the Starbucks in Japan, the first customer could barely speak English, but without doubt he spoke clearly and said 'Tall caramel Frappuccino' ".

This shows that the products are highly standardized and well-known around the world. Therefore, Starbucks well-designed global strategy has been successful and gained competitive advantage. Starbucks are still certain that their business model works in other business environments around the world.

Source: Griffin and Pustay (2005) and Kotler *et al.* (2003).

Visit the Disney website www.disney.com. Explore the international sites related to the company. Think what is the scope of the company? How is Disney positioned internationally? Write a summary that explains how Disney is positioned strategically in its international operations.

ACTIVITY

Corporate level strategies

The principal concern of corporate strategy is identifying the **business areas** in which a company should participate, the value-creation activities it should perform, and the **best means** for expanding or contracting business, in order to maximize its long-run profitability. We discuss two key issues related to corporate strategy: (1) the firm's overall orientation towards growth (directional strategy) and (2) the industries or markets in which the firm competes through its products and business units (portfolio strategy). Directional strategy is composed of growth, stability and retrenchment. Vertical and horizontal integration as well as concentric and conglomerate diversification are discussed as examples of corporate growth strategies. International entry strategies are also listed as growth strategies. Portfolio analysis is explained as a technique for managing various product lines and business units for their maximum cash flow.

Growth strategies

It is most widely pursued strategies by hospitality companies. Internal mechanism of growth strategy is to grow naturally by the organization itself, while external mechanisms include the following:

- Mergers: Transaction involving two or more companies in which stock is exchanged but only one company survives.
- Acquisition: Purchase of a company that is absorbed as an operating subsidiary of the acquiring company.
- Strategic alliance: Partnership of two or more companies to achieve strategically significant objectives that are mutually beneficial.

Example: Acquisition of First Choice

- In 1998, First Choice acquired two key UK tour operators: The Unijet Travel Group and Hayes & Jarvis. Other acquisitions included Bakers Dolphin and Intatravel.
- In 1999, it acquired premium niche market operators Meon (Meon Villas and Longshot Golf Holidays), Flexigroup (ski holidays and conferences) and Sunsail (leading yacht charter and watersports club operator), and within retail, Ferrychoice.
- In 2000, First Choice announced the acquisition of Holiday Hypermarkets, which now has 36 sites across the United Kingdom.

> • In 2001, it acquired the Ten Tour Group's European Tour Operating Businesses and Barceló Travel Division. Following recent acquisitions, First Choice now has a European presence in France, Spain, Portugal, Belgium, Germany, Holland, Austria, Switzerland and Southern Ireland.
>
> *Source*: First Choice Website www.firstchoice.co.uk/

If companies plan to keep developing their future business in their own products or services in hospitality industry, they can use horizontal or vertical integration. Horizontal growth is the expanding of a company's activities into other geographic regions or by increasing the range of products and services offered to current markets. It often involves the acquisition of another company in the same industry (an example of external growth), but it could also be through the expansion of a company's products in its current markets (e.g. through line extensions) or expansion into another geographic region (an example of internal growth).

The benefits of horizontal integration

- Realize economies of scale.
- Reduce duplication between the two companies.
- Offer a wider range of products for customers.
- Manage industry rivalry by reducing excess capacity in the industry.
- Reduce the number of players in an industry.

Limitation of horizontal integration

- May destroy value rather than create it.
- Protection against the horizontal integration.

Vertical growth, in contrast, involves a company's taking over a function previously performed by a supplier or a distributor. This would typically involve the addition of activities in other industries either forward (downstream) or backward (upstream) on the industry value chain of current products or services. The additions are primary justified in terms of support of the current product lines regardless of their being in other industries (and thus can be argued to be diversification).

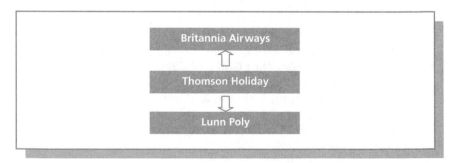

Figure 7.8
An example of
vertical integration
of Thomson Holiday

Benefits of vertical integration

- Build barriers to new entry, limiting competition.
- Keep the product quality and differentiate the core business.
- Better planning, coordination and scheduling.

Disadvantages of vertical integration

- It may raise costs.
- It may inhibit a company changing its suppliers.
- It may not balance the supplies and demands.
- Bureaucratic costs may be high. (Bureaucratic costs: the costs of running an organization.)

Entering the lodging business was a logical step in Disney's vertical integration, as it enabled the company to earn extra revenues and profits through providing accommodation for its theme park attendees. The first luxury resort complexes were opened in 1971. Since then, Disney has developed individually themed hotels which are segmented into economy, moderate, premium, first class and deluxe price categories. While it owns the hotels at Disneyland and Walt Disney World (apart from two), in Paris, its hotels are operated under management contract, and in Tokyo, they are merely licensed. In all, the company currently owns 15 hotels with a capacity of 19,569 rooms, and manages seven others under contract.

Strategic alliances

Under certain conditions, companies can realize the gains associated with vertical integration without having to bear the associated bureaucratic costs. For example, First Choice announced in 2000 a strategic alliance with Royal Caribbean Cruises Limited. Long-term contracts are useful, but short-term contracts are seen as having very limited value for companies.

How does horizontal growth differ from vertical growth as a corporate strategy? Please use hospitality companies as examples.   **ACTIVITY**

Diversification

When MNEs grow, they also can use diversification strategies. The businesses grow into related industry or unrelated industry. Financial consideration is one reason and companies also search for synergies between individual businesses. easyGroup is a good case of diversification growth strategy successfully developed by easyJet.

Case: easyGroup: Conglomerate Strategy

Besides budget airline, easyGroup has expanded its brands into the following business areas.

easyHotel

With a market strategy directed towards short-stay consumers who are looking to stay in an international city centre on a budget, the brand has a motto of "the earlier you book, the less you pay" (www.easyHotel.com, 2006).

easyInternetcafe

With the easyInternetcafe's come easy.com manned centres. With a uniformed staff member always available to answer any questions or enquires about any easyGroup companies, staff members are available at hand to also direct consumers to the relevant easyGroup website so that they may purchase the goods or services of their choice.

easyCar

Offering "outstanding value for money [and a] reliable service at a low price" (www.easyCar.com, 2006). The brand implement this strategy by carrying out various techniques that comply with simplifying the product they offer whilst using their purchasing power to benefit the customer. This comes in the form of low-cost support and putting the consumer first.

easyValue

The easyValue website primes itself on online shopping comparisons. In eliminating time, its competitive edge is its ease and convenience in that everything is available in one place. It gives the consumer the top five products within a range of shopping categories that includes appliances, clothing, computers, electronics, home and garden products, and jewellery. Also available is a rating of the product an approximate price range and reviews of the product.

easyMoney

Offers the first online credit cards

easyCinema

Whilst providing knowledge of all UK cinema's, the latest movie news, UK Box Office Rankings, and reviews of latest releases, easyCinema's main aim is to provide a low-cost product to the consumer. In doing so, the brand provide both an online cinema seat booking service along with pay-as-you-go online DVD rental.

easyBus

Focuses on offering a cost effective express minibus service linking London Central and Luton Airport providing high frequency and low-cost services to meet the demand for affordable public transport within this area. This is illustrated through the regularly used principle of "the earlier you book, the less you pay" (www.easyBus.com, 2006).

easy4men

Producing a wide range of toiletries, the easy4men range are aimed at the "no-nonsense man who does not care about expensive advertising featuring professional footballers or other models" (www.easy4men.com, 2006). easy4men also state that their products satisfy the basic grooming of a man "who is happy with who he is".

easyJobs
"A business [that is] easier and cheaper to consumers", easyJobs state that those looking for jobs can browse through a large selection of offers all in one place, whilst simultaneously benefiting employers by reducing recruitment costs.

easyPizza
States that they have "re-engineered the pizza preparation and delivery industry in order to reduce the price of pizzas to consumers" (www.easyPizza.com, 2006). Adding that ultimate quality is also guaranteed, as are consistently high standards.

easyMusic
States that they give the "best value music downloads" (www.easyMusic.com, 2006), adding that they offer a wide selection of current hits and back catalogues that start at 25p a track, the best value in the market according to the easyMusic brand.

easyCruise
easyCruise's main aim is to "offer a unique holiday experience to independently minded travellers in their 20s, 30s and 40s'. Itineraries for travel are flexible over a period of 1 week.

easyMobile
Intends to "bring mobile telephony services to our customers that offer the best mix of quality, service and attractive prices" (www.easymobile.com, 2006).

easyWatch
With a range of 16 watches to choose from the ranges cater for men, women and children and come in various colours (as well as the trademark orange). The brand states that their target market is "today's consumers who travel and enjoy life whilst being smart about the use of the Internet to cut out the expensive margin of the high street watch retailers ..." (www.easywatch.com, 2006).

Source: easyGroup, www.easy.com/

Marriott and Howard Johnson are two well-known hotel chains whose origins are in the food and beverage sector. Marriott, a Washington, DC based restaurant chain, whose original brand was called "Hot Shoppes", virtually invented airline catering in the 1950s. The group opened its first hotel near the Washington National Airport in 1957, some 30 years after the company had been founded as a root beer stand franchise. Likewise, Howard Johnson, which was founded as an ice cream stand on the beach in Massachusetts in 1925, opened its first hotel in Savannah Georgia in 1954. Kempinski, the German luxury hotel chain, too, has its origins as a caterer in pre-war Berlin. For the German speakers, the name of the Swiss hotel chain Mövenpick betrays its origin as a restaurant operator in Zurich in the late 1940s. The group only got into the hotel business in the early 1970s when it opened its first two properties. Even today, the name Mövenpick is more widely associated with the group's ice cream business (which has now been sold to Nestlé) and restaurants than with hotels.

■ Portfolio analysis

Business portfolio analysis is a strategy development tool which utilizes two factors to indicate potential business strategies. The two factors are: (1) relative market share and (2) market growth rate. The appropriate strategy is determined by the organization's position in a four-cell matrix.

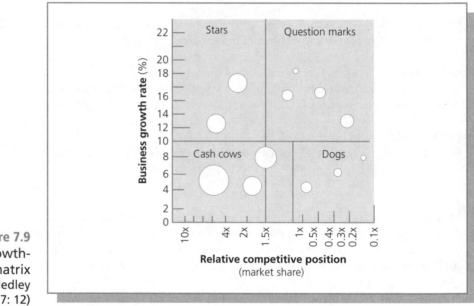

Figure 7.9
The BCG growth-share matrix
Source: Hedley
(1977: 12)

The Boston Consulting Group Growth-Share Matrix includes the following quadrants:

1 Stars are strategic business units (SBUs) having a high share of the high-growth market and typically need large amounts of cash to support their rapid and significant growth. These will someday become the "cash cows."

2 "Cash cows" are units that have a slow market growth rate, but the organization controls a large portion of the market. These units generate large positive cash flows which may be used in other units.

3 "Question marks" are high-growth industries in which the firm is a minor competitor. If the firm can become a major competitor, these units will become "stars."

4 "Dogs" are units which are characterized by slow or no market growth, and the firm is a small competitor relative to the market leader. These units are a drain on organizational resources.

The concepts or assumptions underlie the BCG growth-share matrix

The product life cycle and the experience curve underlie the Boston Consulting Group (BCG) growth-share matrix. The development of question marks into stars and then into cash cows suggests the introduction, growth and maturity stages of the product life cycle. Dogs appear to be those products or units on the decline stage of the product life cycle. The experience curve discussed in unit 4 is certainly key to understanding the implications of the BCG matrix.

BCG matrix is a useful tool, while different products have different product life cycles. What applies to one product probably will not apply to another. Examples can be shown of companies which have supported their products to extend their lives by "putting a tail" on the maturity part of the curve. The experience curve of the industry as a whole or of one company might not hold true for a particular company. The experience curve does not "just happen"; a company has to invest a lot of time and money into getting that experience. You can find many examples of this kind in hospitality industry.

Portfolio analysis has its advantages:

- Top management evaluates each of firm's businesses individually.
- Use of externally oriented data to supplement management judgement.
- Raises issue of cash flow availability.
- Facilitates communication.

The disadvantages are:

- Difficult to define product/market segments.
- Standard strategies can miss opportunities.
- Illusion of scientific rigour.
- Value-laden terms.

The basic theme of portfolio analysis is its emphasis on cash flow. Portfolio analysis puts corporate headquarters into the role of an internal banker. In portfolio analysis, top management views its product lines and business units as a series of investments from which it expects to get a profitable return. The product lines/business units form a portfolio of investments which top management must constantly juggle to ensure the best return on the corporation's invested money.

Portfolio analysis is a popular approach to aid the integration and evaluation of environmental data. It is just as useful for a single business corporation with a number of separate products as it is for a large corporation with autonomous operating divisions. By carefully examining both market or industry factors and business strengths or market share, it is possible to pinpoint factors of strategic importance to corporate or divisional success. Portfolio analysis thus serves as a convenient technique for comparing external opportunities and threats with internal strengths and weaknesses.

■ Conclusion

This chapter provides an overview of the strategic planning process in the international hospitality industry and should have allowed you to gain an appreciation of the changing strategic directions in which international hospitality enterprises operate. In this chapter, we have explained:

- The definition of strategic management and the general processes of strategic planning.
- The impact of key strategic issues on the management of organizations in the international hospitality industry.
- The strategic role of the analysis of international hospitality enterprises' external and internal environments.
- Functional level strategies and outsourcing.
- Generic business strategies.
- Global strategic orientations and strategic options.
- Corporate level strategy including directional and portfolio strategy.

We have considered how strategic options are formulated and how the range of managerial issues concerned with implementing strategic options are considered. We also introduced some appropriate concepts and frameworks for analysing the case study material drawn from the actual experiences in the industry. This has served as a review of the previous chapters and consolidated the accounts we have given from Chapter 3 onwards.

■ Review questions

1 How can an international hospitality organization add value to its operations?
2 What are the benefits of using the SWOT matrix?
3 How does cultural understanding impact on the international strategy process?
4 Do Porter's five forces operate the same way in hospitality as they were seen to in other, more traditional industries?
5 Review the factors which make the different growth strategies appropriate at different times for different companies.

CHAPTER 8

International human resources management: managing diversity

After working through this chapter, you should be able to:

- ■ Understand the background to different approaches to international management
- ■ Define key management concerns for the hospitality industry
- ■ Evaluate the actions taken to manage diversity in the hospitality industry both internally and externally

■ Introduction

The employment issues involved in international hospitality are considerable. There are a huge number of multinational enterprises within the hospitality industry around the world and the hospitality industry has been increasingly subjected to and contributed to the process of globalization in the last two decades. As Yu (1999) notes the big brand names of Hilton, Sheraton, Hyatt, Holiday Inn, McDonald's, KFC and Pizza Hut figure prominently in the landscapes of many countries. Due to this massive growth, there has been a greater demand for managers to take into consideration strategies that need to be appropriate within different countries. In many countries a business which is developed domestically will differ significantly from businesses in other countries as they strive to take into account the varying business and cultural environments from one country to another.

We have witnessed increased demands for standardized, globalized products and services within the worldwide market. With large corporations expanding throughout the world, they have had to respond to a challenge to ensure that they adapt to the requirements of international business and to a lesser extent local customs and practices. There are a variety of issues that international companies should be aware of, including the way global issues are presented within the specific countries they operate in, and the companies in the international hospitality industry need to adopt strategies that will meet the social, environmental and economical needs of the countries and locations.

Managers perform various roles depending on the circumstances, which can include:

- leading,
- acting as a figurehead,
- communicating information,
- negotiating,
- allocating resources,
- handling disturbances,
- planning,
- overseeing implementation of plans,
- evaluating.

There are many factors that influence the role played by managers and it must be remembered that national culture is one of those factors. National culture within the working environment influences people and their responses to systems and management. Therefore, a workforce within one culture may respond differently to a workforce within another. Hence it is important for international managers to respond differently and adapt themselves in different circumstances in order to achieve the same outcome.

We have already established that we believe international businesses are heavily influenced by the cultural values of different societies. As Yu (1999) observed international hospitality managers operate in an international context and have to perform their functions of managing, interacting, negotiating and compromising with people of different cultural backgrounds. How a company reacts to changes in culture will contribute to the success or failure of that business. A company that wishes to do business abroad should firstly determine how practices vary in different countries and then decide if any adjustments need to be made, to ensure their business operates in an efficient manner. International human resource management is the process of selecting, training, developing and compensating personnel in overseas positions and here we want to focus on the challenge of managing diversity.

It is of vital importance that companies within the hospitality industry can do this effectively to ensure that they succeed as a profitable company. According to Lockwood *et al.* Teare and Olsen (1992: 319) "Human Resource strategies need to be developed that will reinforce the drive toward quality. These strategies will start with recruitment and selection, but must also include conditions of service, communication, training and reward strategies". As this statement suggests, companies must not only select an excellent workforce, but also be able to retain it. One of the weaknesses the hospitality industry has is its reliance on an unskilled workforce as it is well known that this industry does not pay well, leading to high staff turnover.

Within international human resource management there are four different processes that a company could choose to adopt. These are as follows.

Ethnocentric

This is where management positions are filled entirely by people from the company's country of origin. For example, managers would be appointed from the domestic market. It is often felt that they understand the company better and are more familiar with their goals, policies and procedures. There are disadvantages, managers may not fully understand the country that they are operating in and the culture and language will be different to what they are used to. This could cause some problems as managers try to adapt their ways to fit in with the local culture.

Polycentric

Here the company hires local managers from the host country. They would know the area and understand the culture and therefore would be able to manage their staff more effectively. However one problem with this approach is the fact that they may have difficulty dealing with the international company and may find it difficult to handle some of the company's core values.

Geocentric

Here the best managers are recruited within or outside the company, regardless of their nationality. For example, if the company feel that the best managers for their business are people from China then they will recruit them, however if they feel that managers from America will do a better job then they will recruit staff from America.

One big advantage with this approach is the fact that the company will get the best staff, having hired them based on their experience and knowledge.

Regiocentric

This is for regional businesses and would involve recruiting managers from within the wider geographic region of operation. This has benefits of transferability but may also gloss over the needs for local knowledge in particular areas.

Approaches to internationalization

ACTIVITY

Think back to the ideas about market entry we introduced in Chapter 6 and try to work through the implications for the different entry modes with these different approaches to international HRM. Do different entry modes require a particular strategy? For instance how would the policies that a joint venture might pursue compare to those of a sole investor?

The selection of any one of these approaches creates the context in which the managers must operate and communicate within the organization. Managers communicate both through action and inaction. To keep open lines of communication, managers must follow through with action on what has been discussed and then agreed upon, such as a contract. The management of cross-cultural communication depends largely on a manager's personal abilities and behaviours. The behaviours associated through research with cross-cultural communication effectiveness are: respect, empathy, tolerance for ambiguity, orientation to knowledge, interaction posture and other oriented role behaviours.

■ The formal and the informal organization

Defining the organization can only be undertaken when there are clearly stated objectives. According to the classical schools of management thinking, there is a clear need to establish a framework of order and command by which the activities of the organization can be achieved. The centrality of the objective to the organization means that the structure will be defined to effectively deliver that objective. We believe that this is what we have seen in the examples from the industry where there has been a clear attempt to clarify and structure the companies' positions in relation to diversity. This has many advantages and often simplifies the complexity of international management.

Coherence, coordination and clarity are the guiding principles of formal organizational design. The structure has to be designed irrespective of the people of the organization, as the people may change but the organization will still seek to achieve its objectives. This allows us to utilize some of the principles from the classical approach and also to look at the way this would be interpreted by systems theory, where structure must be designed to maintain the socio-technical system, holding both the structural and technological requirements in balance (Schaffer, 1990).

Woodward (1980) identified that alongside task functions (the things that organizations must do to ensure their continuation), there were also element functions (these are functions that are not directly related to task but facilitate the achievement of the task such as planning). Woodward suggested that there should be a clear definition between the two types of task and element function, otherwise she argued that managers would begin to take responsibility for things that should have been dealt with by directly task-related personnel.

■ Centralization and decentralization

We can also see that the division of work arises at two levels within the organization:

1 The authority of individual managers within a chain or group.
2 Specific delegation.

There are seen to be advantages and disadvantages to both. The advocates of centralization argue for better decision-making, easier implementation, shared policy, improved coordination, economies of scale and lower over-heads. It may also further specialization within the organization.

However, it may also create a more bureaucratic organization, creating a longer chain of command. Decision-making may be cumbersome if everything needs to be referred to the top. Too much centralization can be seen to stifle creativity and innovation.

Decentralization allows decisions to be made closer to the operational level. It also offers opportunities for empowerment and more effective support of staff.

Formal structures have clearly defined spans of control. In practice organizations need to look at how many vertical levels of control are intro-duced as well as looking at the horizontal span of control of individual managers. This is true within local operations as well as looking at the relations between the head office structures and those operating in the field.

Managers in formal organizations should have clearly defined authority for certain tasks and responsibility for results. These line relationships can be presented in schematic form to draw a picture of the organization – we have all seen examples of these organizational charts in hotels.

In complex organizations line relationships are matched by staff relationships where staff with similar interests from different lines or functional areas come together (for instance maintenance staff, accounting, etc.). These cross-cutting interests will complicate the lines of definition, communication and decision-making.

One of the most active companies internationally has been McDonald's and they have adopted a formal approach towards their operations that believes that centralized control and training is the best way forward.

Example: McDonald's are structured along functional lines. Their chief executive oversees five major areas of activity:

1 Operations (equipment and franchising).
2 Development (property and construction).
3 Finance (supply chain and new product development).
4 Marketing (sales marketing).
5 Human resources (customer services, personnel, hygiene and safety).
   www.bized.ac.uk/compfact/mcdonalds/mc7.htm

■ The informal organization

The position we have outlined above has taken the principles from the classical approach to management but we would stress that these guidelines may not fully describe the organization, nor capture its true sense of cultural dynamic. The formally defined organization has to operate in the real world with real people in the positions in the hierarchy and thus will also function as a social organization. Within the social organization, there is less – sometimes almost no – definition of the relationships involved and the informal organization will develop spontaneously. People will be involved to greater or lesser extents at different periods in the history of the company and of their involvement with the company (Gray and Starke, 1988). The informal organization is another aspect of management thinking which is often presented as an iceberg, where the visible top of the iceberg is the officially recognized part of the system and the unseen, majority of the iceberg represents the informal system. For adherents to the classical school, such informal complications should have been addressed, controlled, policed and effectively managed.

However, it is now widely recognized that the informal organization can serve a number of important functions:

● Satisfying social needs at work, creating avenues for the expression of personal identity and generating a focus for a sense of belonging.

- Motivation: Status (earned rather than prescribed), social interaction with colleagues who might even become friends, variety and informal methods of work.
- Extra communication: The importance of informal communications, gossip even, should not be underestimated as it carries great weight in organizations. I heard it through the grapevine messages may have greater significance attached to them than formal messages from the management.
- Stability and security through informal network and norms: The informal groups reinforce and support themselves, helping to develop and nurture the individuals in the group.
- Criticizing the formal structure: The informal networks can operate as a safety valve for the formal organization, perhaps also serving as early warning systems of potential problems and unrest.

Example: The smokers' ghetto

With the introduction of smoking bans in more and more places, it has become common for people to meet in the car parks, outside the main entrance and anywhere else that seems convenient to top up their nicotine levels. The traditional workplace boundaries, for instance between management and staff, between accommodation and catering, between marketing and finance, do not appear in these new spaces.

Plate 12 The nicotine gathering. *Source*: Vonzerö 2005 bt.

> The people gathered together have a common interest in smoking and this is what brings them together. We can perhaps see the possibilities of a democratization of the workspace here as the highest and the lowest employees come together to smoke. It has created a new informal space which has led to new unpredictable patterns of communications in organizations.

Mullins (2001) takes the informal structure as a way for managers to influence the workforce, but what is missing from his account is the way that the informal system can actually undermine the formal one. The informal system can be a source of dissent and resistance to the official management, especially in centralized organizations.

Human resource strategy

McDonald's human resource strategy emphasize the training and development of its employees. They claim to provide career opportunities for people to achieve their potential. The firm offers both full- and part-time career opportunities, which can help staff to combine work with family or educational commitments. Job progression is used to encourage employees who got their first job in the company to progress to management positions. This is based on the performance of the staff member, but they can demonstrate that over 40% of McDonald's managers started as hourly paid staff members in the restaurants. They also claim that over half of the company's middle and senior managers have moved up from restaurant-based positions. All employees receive a structured development programme as well as externally recognized qualifications in health and safety, food safety and first aid. Moreover, the company's hourly paid staff receive benefits such as: free life assurance (value dependent on service), private health care (for employees aged 19+ with 3 years of service), sponsorship programme, as well as service awards (at 3, 5, 10, 15, 20 and 25 years service).

McDonald's have a promise to their customers and employees which is that "we aspire to Be the Best Employer in Each Community Around the World". They are highly focused on their staff and also try to ensure that constant communication is available from the management to the employees, using tools such as McNews, a franchisee newsletter and their "bright idea's" employee suggestion scheme. They claim that these all contribute to treating their staff as equals and allowing their staff to contribute their views, ideas and opinions to the overall running of the company. McDonald's and its franchisees are among the nation's largest employers of working parents, older workers, individuals with disabilities and teenagers – many of whom are women and from minorities.

Job satisfaction, turnover and absenteeism

The issues of turnover and absenteeism in the tourism industry often mean that studies begin from the point of alienation and frustration at work. Blauner (1964) suggested that there were four dimensions along which alienation could be expressed. These were:

1 Powerlessness: The experience of a lack of control.
2 Meaninglessness: Standardization and division of labour produce a situation where workers cannot see where they fit into the whole operation.
3 Isolation: A feeling of not belonging to or being involved with the integral work group or important people.
4 Self-estrangement: Especially where work is seen solely as a means to an end.

Management responses must seek to develop a sense of attachment to both the work situation and the organization. This can be affected by the formal structure, managerial style, technology and the organization of the work itself. Within hospitality, many opportunities can be created for joining in with the delivery of the offer.

The HCITB 40 (the Hotel and Catering Industry Training Board) report recorded the negative perceptions of employees feeling that jobs in the industry were low status, low paid, servile, had little variety and lacked job satisfaction. A later report by the HCTC 41 (the Hotel and Catering Training Council replaced the HCITB) found that there were many opportunities for satisfaction through customer contact, frequent contact with the management that could offset the negative feelings. Attempts to retain staff and minimize turnover have addressed these issues (Table 8.1).

Table 8.1 Likes and dislikes in hospitality jobs

Likes

1. Challenge, direct involvement, autonomy, independence and rewarding work.
2. People, the public and professional contacts.
3. Working environment and opportunity for growth and development.
4. Fast pace, change.
5. Benefits and prestige.

Dislikes

1. Long hours, nights and weekend schedules.
2. Low pay.
3. Stress, demanding supervisors and duties, no personal time, quality of life.
4. Routine, no advancement or growth, no importance or recognition.
5. Company politics, management.
6. Labour shortages, poor staff, lack of employee motivation, employees' and co-workers attitudes.

Source: Pavesic and Brymer (1990).

Motivations and attitudes to work become a core concern here and we must recognize that these are constructed differently in different places at different times. Individuals are working for a variety of reasons and respond to incentives in different ways. Their circumstances outside work may change and impact on their attitudes to work. These must also be understood in the context of the local cultural attitudes. The areas of resistance and support can be underpinned by elements of the local cultures. It is not clear that all workforces respond the same way to management initiatives irrespective of where they are or where they come from.

Case: An Overview of the Hilton

Human resource strategy

Despite the recessions following the terrorist attacks of September 11th, where most hotel companies started retrenching staff to keep labour costs under control, Hilton has maintained its staff base over the last couple of years. Most notable is the fact that despite the increase in the number of hotels over the last few years, their total staff count remains the same if not lower than the previous years. This is primarily though substantial investments in developing self-check in kiosks at large hotels like Hilton New York, Chicago (with over 1,500 rooms each) attributing to overall reduction in manpower between the years 2002 and 2003. Therefore an investment in technology as an alternate to manpower seems to be their strategy for profit maximization. However, their hotels run the risk of becoming too "impersonal" lacking any human touch due to the widespread usage of technology. Also a closer look at the 2001 and 2002 annual reports indicate the company's commitment to its people welfare through benefits (medical insurance, stock options plans, etc.). However, the 2003 report does not indicate such interests. This may be a result of the company tightening their belts for overall profit maximization.

In addition to the awareness and demand for diversity in the workforce, Hilton hotels have been trying to maintain a delicate balance with its manpower resources. As per their 2003 annual report, they have been named as "50 Best Companies for Minorities" by the Fortune magazine. Hence, it seems that with the recent expansion plans in emerging markets within the European Union and South Asia, the company has adopted a focused approach towards quality in terms of human resource.

Source: From the Hilton website.

The idea of technologizing the solution works in specific areas but there are a large number of touch points in hotels, where human interaction is necessary or desirable, and these cannot easily be replaced by technology. Hilton's recognition that despite its investment in technology it will also have to invest in people is a proper recognition of the dynamics of the industry, where people remain central both as customers and hosts.

The incessant high staff turnover within the hospitality industry means that the human resources department is central to the success of any business. McDonald's in particular have recognized this as being crucial in maintaining both customer and staff loyalty.

McDonald's pride themselves on providing fast food with a smile, but, in order for them to carry this out effectively, McDonald's have to ensure their staff experience a high level of job satisfaction. They believe this will help to prevent high staff turnover, which is beneficial to the company as high turnover in any company always results in high recruitment and training costs. McDonald's employ over 1.5 million people in over 119 countries around the world, providing many job opportunities to local residents in many under-developed countries who may otherwise not had the opportunity to work. Many of these are younger people, with 64.55% of the company's employees being aged between 16 and 20 years old. In addition McDonald's have an equal opportunities employer with a crew ratio between male and female of 52:48 (www.mcspotlight. org/issues/intro.html).

So, with these generous conditions, why was it that in the Spring of 2007, the company found itself battling with the compilers of the Oxford English Dictionary to have the term 'Mcjob' removed because of its negative and perjorative definition as a boring and meaningless job? (HVG 2007).

"The basis for our entire business is that we are ethical, truthful and dependable. It takes time to build a reputation. We are not promoters. We are business people with a solid, permanent, constructive ethical programme that will be in style years from now even more than it is today." (Ray Kroc, 1958 from www.mcdonalds.com/corp/invest/gov.html).

McDonald's International and United Kingdom offer a wide range of training programmes and incentives to ensure a low staff turnover. Benefits for hourly employees include free meals, paid holidays, free life insurance, education programmes (Hamburger University) and the stock purchase scheme. They also offer competitive salaries for management positions, including intensive training, which all assist in maintaining staff. Some salaries are given in Table 8.2.

Table 8.2 McDonald's pay structures	
Operations Manager	**£30,000–40,000**
Supervisor	£20,000–28,000
Restaurant Manager	£15,000–23,000
First Assistant Manager	£13,000–18,000
Second Assistant. Manager	£11,500–14,000
Trainee manager	£11,000
Junior Business Manager	£9,000

Source: www.mcspotlight.org/company/publications/mcfact_section3.html#S3e.

These rates have varying attraction. In low wage economies they become very attractive, whereas in other high wage economies they may be perceived as low wage rates and therefore deter entrants to the labour market.

There are various other ways, apart from the salaries, in which jobs can be made to appear more rewarding. These include:

● Job rotations: Changing roles within the organization to gain greater experience of the operation and finding a different routine.
● Job enrichment: Adding elements to the responsibilities within the post that enhance its character and status.
● Job enlargement: Finding additional elements that can be added to the existing portfolio to give greater interest.

Analysis of workplaces has identified five core job dimensions, which can be adjusted to find a more satisfying work balance. They are:

1   Skill variety
2   Task identity
3   Task significance
4   Autonomy
5   Feedback.

These core job dimensions contribute to three psychological states:

1   Experienced meaningfulness of the work.
2   Experienced responsibility for outcomes of work.
3   Knowledge of the actual results of the work activities.

It was observed that the higher the employee's perception of belonging in any of these three categories, then the greater the likelihood was that they will experience job satisfaction. However when you are analysing work perceptions, it is worth noting that it is possible to be dissatisfied with a low score on only one dimension. These indices have to be interpreted locally to ensure that local cultural differences are taken into consideration.

Managing change

Many cultural differences if not managed appropriately will lead to mis-understandings and can hinder a manager's effective operation. Mullins (2001) observes that change is a pervasive influence on organizations but as we observed with Hofstede's work different countries demonstrate different willingness to accept change. When you are studying the international hospitality industry you have to consider both the product and service issues which are identified in the management literature, as both can impact on the total offer. Hellriegel *et al.* (1992) suggest five factors that influence the direction and the rate of change:

1   Changing technology
2   Knowledge explosion
3   Rapid product obsolescence
4   Changing nature of the workforce
5   Quality of working life.

We have seen these before as factors in the operational environment. Management responses will differ depending on whether the change is foreseen by management. In these circumstances, strategic responses can be organized and prioritized. Other changes are unforeseen and have to be dealt with reactively rather than proactively. Stasis in the hospitality industry may be impossible given the number of elements involved in the operation and the pace of change which the industry has consistently demonstrated. This means that change will be an ongoing and an inherent part of the management of hospitality organizations.

Change management has to operate at a number of levels within the organization to be successful (although you should remember that all these levels operate at the same time in the real world) (Figure 8.1).

- Symbolic: This refers to both the tangible and intangible symbols of an organization.
- Peripheral: Minor amendments that do not seem to effect the strategy of objectives of the organization.
- Core: Major changes to objectives and/or structures that significantly alter the direction of the organization.

Figure 8.1
Managing levels of change.

The workforce sometimes has a strong attachment to the symbolic which is not always recognized by the management, but again underlines the need to understand the cultural dynamics in the organization.

There are a number of factors that inhibits change, both from the management and the employee perspective (Figure 8.2).

Managerial resistance to change	Individual resistance to change
• Necessity of large resources • Disturbance to stability and predictability • Comfort zone lost • Threat to power or influence	• Fear of the unknown • Habit • Inconvenience or loss of freedom • Economic implications • Security in the past • Threat to status or symbols • Selective perception

Figure 8.2
Resistances to change.

Successful change management seems to involve the recognition of a wide range of human and social factors, especially where we are concerned with change in an international context. Where these can be addressed within the organization within an acceptable framework for the organization and for the employees, the proposed changes are likely to be embraced positively. It is worth noting that every one of these factors is subject to local interpretation and therefore constitutes a double challenge for an international business which must carry the change both within the domestic operation and also the international parts of the organization.

Human and social factors of change underpin any attempt to successfully manage change. We would suggest that change is most likely to be implemented effectively where the following conditions exist:

- An environment of trust and shared commitment.
- Full and open communications.
- Benefits of change and potential opportunities.
- Encourage team management and cooperative spirit.
- Work on job design, methods of work organization and creating cohesive groups.
- Suitable economic incentives schemes.
- Review of recruitment and selection, training and re-training.

Hotel management in Cuba and the transfer of best practices   ACTIVITY

We would stress that these conditions are culturally defined and interpreted. Cerviño and Bonache (2005) analysed the management challenges faced by international hotel operators when applying universally accepted management principles within the Cuban hospitality market. The article presented a scenario where the state's role in the protection of the socialist revolutionary principles, combined with the need to adopt some market-based management practices, constitutes a singular case in the world of hotel management. In the current Cuban institutional context, the implementation of some western best management practices can produce significant results, while others produce negative outcomes, and therefore should be held back until the institutional context is changed. The argument has implications for managers in suggesting that from a hotel perspective, the application of universally accepted best management practices must be carried out practice by practice and country by country.

This should make you think about the dilemmas of managing hotels in a still highly centralized socialist country but with an increasingly market-based economy. Review the arguments in this chapter and think through the principles which would be difficult to fit into a highly centralized state system.

Managing cultural diversity: 1

This demonstrates once again how important culture is within any global industry as it needs to be understood before a company can adopt changes in other markets (Alvesson, 2002). McDonald's offer an interesting example. The more diverse their customers have become, the more McDonald's have placed a greater importance on the diversity of their suppliers and believe that this more diverse supply chain helps them to meet the needs of their target markets. This can actually help to put wealth back into countries as McDonald's use locally supplied ingredients to support their operations. After McDonald's had expanded to other countries, they were aware they had to change their products to suit the culture they were going into, for example the offer and sourcing of Halal chicken nuggets in Sri Lanka.

"McDonald's have been featured in 'The Best Companies for Minorities', and was honoured with the Catalyst Award for its commitment to women's progress, and was recognized by Black Enterprise and Hispanic magazines as one of the 100 best employers for African Americans and Hispanics" (www.media.mcdonalds.com/secured/company/diversity/).

McDonald's also claim to employ a greater proportion of women and minorities than any other company in the world, representing over 50% of its total workforce. Additionally in the United States, McDonald's hold diversity appreciation education seminars for managers and executives, with over 14,000 managers participating in these culturally informative sessions. These seminar groups encourage the employment of a various selection of staff members, allowing McDonald's to diversify into other countries and cultures and give the best service possible in those new markets. The programmes are:

- MCW – (managing the changing workforce). All managers attend these sessions to help explore attitudes and the impact of cultural assumptions and gender.
- WCD – (women's career development). Allowing women at corporate and regional levels to be more assertive, building professional relationships, helping them to grow within the company.
- BCD – (black career development). This is for entry level managers helping participants understand and manage professional relationships of various backgrounds. Also helping with career development, understanding the dynamics of leadership.
- MCD – (managing cultural differences). All franchisees and employees at restaurant level attend these sessions to avoid stereotyping, preventing cultural and gender assumptions.

McDonald's real influence have been in establishing organizational systems of complete control at every stage from raw product to process factory, from worker to consumer. Although they did not invent such processes, McDonald's have probably been the most successful transnational food corporation at refining, coordinating, standardizing and developing them into a total system. They have established these pioneering practices and diversified in every country they have moved into (www.aworldconnected.org/article.php/486.html).

Diversity therefore has to be seen as a multifaceted concept, applying to the working conditions within the company and without. An organization can claim to be diversified if it recruits staff with different demographic profiles (age, gender, ethnicity) but it should also look to its supply chain to ensure that diversity is found there. The operations may be in a single country or international and the diversity questions would still need to be answered. Local sourcing becomes even more important in international hospitality. Finally there is a question of diversity in demand: Does the organization cater for a diversity of customers or does it provide a standardized offer to a single group? Diversity within the organization is likely to translate into a diversity externally, with suppliers and customers recognizing the opportunities that such diversity may offer them to develop a satisfying relationship with the company. This echoes a point we made in Chapter 2 about the way the touristic culture was developing, as we suggested there that was a greater sense of value being given to the different and authentic. This is the expectation that organizations can match with a highly developed diversity policy.

Marriott have recognized that culture characterizes national groups and influences the behaviour of individual members. They have also noted that it is not the only influence on individuals' values. Other factors that they have identified as being able to shape an individual's reaction to the organization include:

- Genetic transmission
- Family

- Gender stereotypes
- Age.

The application of this in Marriott means that within the working environment it is important to understand individuals and where they are coming from, as it helps to resolve problems or realize opportunities for growth and development. Managers on most occasions, however, make decisions and direct through judgements of groups, units, departments or the entire company as it is more practical to do so but even these need to be informed by a cultural understanding of the conditions of the decision.

When dealing with cross-cultural management, communication skills are of the utmost importance, as managers need to adapt to other cultures to lead their members. However the diversity in culture can provide both opportunities and difficulties. Competitive advantage can be gained through the ability to attract, retain and motivate people from different cultures thus helping in cost reduction, maximizing creativity and problem solving.

Marriott International have engaged in cultural diversity successfully by working under strict central control with local flexibility in different cities all round the world. Managing the cultural diversity of all of their staff has been given a top priority within the organization as the senior management believes their employees are the company's greatest assets. In the words of J.W. Marriott Jr., "Culture is the life-thread and glue that links our past, present and future" (Source: www.marriott.com).

Marriott International developed the policy of treating all of their employees fairly and provides training and advancement opportunities to all their members of staff. They feel it is the best and possibly the only way to attract, develop and retain the very best of their talent. Thus adaptation has allowed business relations to develop and continued growth has been achieved.

With Marriott seeking to retain their position as a leading player in the hospitality industry, they have adopted strategies to try to ensure that their commitment to the benefits of diversity is encompassed in every one of their hotel locations in the world, as they believe this helps growth and profit opportunities within the ever-changing markets. Marriott's commitment is business focused as the diversity of the global workforce is seen as helping to create greater opportunities for the business through an increasingly diverse group of suppliers, customers, owners and franchisees.

The dedication shown by Marriott International and their workforce has been a highlighted success. This year according to DiversityInc magazine, Marriott have been ranked 12th out of 50 companies for their handling of a diverse workforce. The survey is the only national ranking of its kind in America and is the most in-depth empirical analysis of corporate diversity management. J.W. Marriott Jr., Chairman and CEO, proudly added: "Our determination to provide opportunities for our associates and customers is one of the main reasons people want to work and do business with us. It gives our company strength and a competitive edge. We're proud that we've set the standard for the entire hospitality industry" (Source: marriott.com/news/detail.mi?marrArticle=89393).

Due to the organization's commitment to global cultural diversity, Marriott point to a dedicated workforce in many countries and in many cultures, which in turn have enabled them to become a successful international organization.

McDonald's real influence have been in establishing organizational systems of complete control at every stage from raw product to process factory, from worker to consumer. Although they did not invent such processes, McDonald's have probably been the most successful transnational food corporation at refining, coordinating, standardizing and developing them into a total system. They have set up these pioneering practices and diversified in every country they've moved into (www.aworldconnected.org/article.php/486.html).

However despite these strict internal controls, McDonald's may not be viable in every country as there may be resistance from external cultural forces. France, for example, is widely recognized as the gastronomic capital of the world, and McDonald's attempt to promote the most commercialized, standardized type of food did not go as planned in that country. Kincheloe (2002) demonstrates the way that McDonald's are perceived differently in different countries, being seen in many places as a sign of affluence, whereas in many developed countries such as United States and United Kingdom the perception has shifted. The French, in particular, did not take well to the proposal of the commercialized restaurants being built in traditional villages such as the Roquefort cheese village in which protestors actually knocked down the half built McDonald's which they thought had ruined their village.

Managing cultural diversity: 2

Another example of a formal approach to managing cultural diversity comes from the Hyatt Corporation. The Hyatt Corporation has hotels and resorts located across the world and Mintel (October, 2003) noted that 27% of the hotels were located outside of their main markets in North America, Europe and the Middle East (Figure 8.3).

Hyatt's cultural detail

Hyatt recognizes the importance of the symbolic level of change and development and as a result pays close attention to the smallest detail in every hotel they operate worldwide. Each hotel is distinct to the country it is situated in. They take artwork from the specific country to accentuate design and interior of the hotel. They aim to follow local tradition when it comes to decor around hotels. They offer local cuisine style restaurants as well as international style restaurants. They do this not only to create a sense of atmosphere, but also to blend in with the location and the local culture by showing the depth of the appreciation they have for these issues. After considering the Hyatt operations and their websites, it is clear that they see themselves as a culturally diverse company.

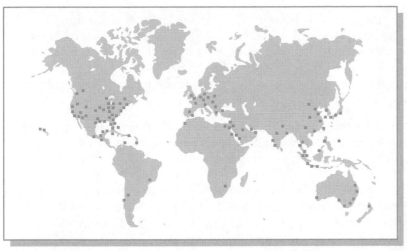

Figure 8.3
Hyatt hotel locations
across the world

Managing Cultural Diversity, Hyatt

The central concern of the Hyatt human resource strategy is the successful attempt to "assemble a workforce of happy, loyal employees whose diverse perspectives combine to spark innovation and who can market to the spectrum of customer niches from which they hail" (www.chiefexecutive.net, 2005).

The majority of multinational companies, including Hyatt, tend to use their own individual "best practice" methods to successfully implement measurable goals for their strategies, most of which involve incentives of some form. Serious commitment and clear objectives for policies are required for any form of strategy to be successful. Managing diversity in a multinational organization is an incredibly difficult task, but needs to be defined in an achievable way and have strong policies to support it. The framework will need to be used in each and every country but with the sensitivity to recognize that differing cultures need to be understood locally and this means that each property has to adapt to the environment in which it is set.

Hyatt and diversity

Diversity is one of Hyatt's greatest values and is a company core value. Hyatt's goal for diversity is "To lead our industry by being an employer and hospitality company of choice for an increasingly diverse population" (www.hyatt.com/corporate/hyatt/diversity/index.jhtml).

One of the most intriguing aspects of Hyatt's approach is the way it has sought to formalize the importance that the company gives to diversity. Hyatt has instituted a "Diversity Council" consisting of 24 employees/managers representing various sections of the company. They meet three times a year to discuss issues related to diversity to establish how well the company is recognizing the subject along with an assessment of the strategies that are set out to assist in the full inclusion of all minorities. The council aims to increase awareness of diversity issues including such issues as respect to women and minorities. Due to the success of the council Hyatt plan to create a larger external board consisting of national minority representatives, meeting planners and convention bureau representatives from within the Hyatt Corporation. They claim that expense is no object for the diversity strategies pointing out that

"Hyatt's vice president of diversity for example has a $400,000 annual budget ..." (www.chiefexecutive.net, 2005) but they also note that this is "... just a piece of Hyatt's multimillion-dollar commitment to diversity. And that's even in bad times. It's the one area we have constantly underwritten" (www.chiefexecutive.net, 2005).

By looking into issues around cultural diversity, Hyatt has devised a number of ways to implement awareness through its staff:

● Hyatt uses mandatory diversity training for all members of staff. Training covers aware-ness of valuing differences, by treating others with respect regardless of race or gender.
● They also implement training, which helps to emphasize the special needs of peers or Hyatt customers.
● "Spanish – Hyatt Style, Management is cross-cultural communications training to improve communications and relationships among employees and guests" (www. hyatt.com/corporate/hyatt/diversity/diversity_employer_of_choice_training.jhtml?ssnav=3).
● Hyatt also has communication training for non-English-speaking employees, which is called "**English as a second language**" **(ESL)**, aiming to improve communication relation-ships among Hyatt employees and their guests.

Hyatt has been recognized by a number of magazines and diversity related businesses for their efforts in creating and effectively managing diversity throughout the company. The company has strived to ensure that they can do whatever they can to introduce diversity knowledge to all employees in their organization around the world.

It is a core value within Hyatt culture to implement a diverse workforce no matter where in the world a hotel is. This shows that they value employee's and customer beliefs, cultures and needs. In America they can claim that "(Hyatt) has a diverse workforce but, unlike some others in its industry, has a good representation of African Americans, Latinos and Asian Americans in its management and among its highest-paid employees" (Hyatt Corporation, 2004: 1).

It is Hyatt's belief that if cultural diversity management is implemented and its staff at all lev-els educated to appreciate the benefits, then they will use this to the company's advantage and this will lead to greater levels of customer service and benefit to their customers. This demon-strates that within cultural diversity, Hyatt takes into account and appreciates their customers.

The website offers an example of where the good intentions are compromised by practical-ities. The website hotel pages are standardized in English, but they also offer the page in the local language for people. Hyatt could consider encouraging greater diversity by adding a selection of languages to every hotel page they have, rather than just the home language of that hotel and English. This would recognize the true diversity of their guests but would gen-erate an enormous amount of work!

Importance of diversity management

To Hyatt, diversity is a "serious business". Specific programmes have been incorporated and 15% of potential employee bonuses depend on the achievement of diversity goals set by these programmes. They state unequivocally that "Establishing diversity as one of Hyatt's core goals is a primary and an integral part of our corporate culture" (www.hyatt.com, 2004).

Hyatt has sponsored many students with a variety of backgrounds and cultures, all of whom have studied within the hospitality sector. The students become interns for Hyatt, which the company use to help assess the ever-changing levels of diversity and to assist with the understanding and teaching of different cultures.

Multinational organizations are ranked throughout the world for their practice of diversity management and the level of diversity they have within their company overall. Marriott International are thought to have the most diverse workforce worldwide, however they rank only 41st with regards to the ranking of the best company for diversity management. Hyatt have ranked far better than this. "Hyatt, ranked 18th was cited as the second most diverse workforce ..." (www.hotelexecutive.com, date unknown).

Types of diversity management

Hyatt, as a large international corporation, can be seen as demonstrating an extremely high level of cultural awareness and as a rule has diversity management at the forefront of each decision and strategy they implement. The management of diversity can be looked at in two main ways that parallel our thinking about the development of globalization:

- Convergent: The thought that every individual will one day be exactly the same in relation to thinking, ideas and culture with society.
- Divergent: The thought that every individual is becoming more and more different in every sense.

From our research it could be assumed that Hyatt International are very "divergent" in their approach to diversity. They tailor each property to suit its surrounding and encourage their employees to use the differing cultures and forms of diversity to aid the corporation in expanding their knowledge and understanding. This will inform both current practice and the company's plans for expansion.

Knowledge and understanding of different cultures and values is of major importance when recruiting and employing staff for an international corporation. The process involves selecting, training and developing employees for a vast variety of jobs not only in the home country, but also overseas.

Chapter Case Study: Starbucks: Managing Cultural Diversity

The management of food and beverage operations must be especially aware of the changing trends, as the industry is facing a chronic skills shortage and an ever-increasing number of foreign workers are being used to fill these gaps, thereby increasing the diversity in the workplace. The organizations working towards the globalization of many food and beverage operations must also be aware of the diversity of the different countries in which they operate.

Diversity management must become a part of company policy, however in order for it to be effective it must be embedded within the culture of the company, from senior management through to front-line staff.

Effective diversity management can have numerous positive effects on business performance, such as greater understanding of customer needs, higher employee retention rate and increased sales. Ineffective diversity management however can bring added problems to the workplace such as demoralization of employees, reverse discrimination, hostility and high staff turnover.

Part of Starbucks' mission statement is to embrace diversity as an essential component in the way they do business. (The full mission statement was discussed in the previous chapter.)

Starbucks believe that to operate successfully in the global marketplace diversity needs to be embraced within every aspect of the business. This includes:

- the Workplace,
- training,
- suppliers,
- communities in which they operate.

The workplace

Starbucks commitment to diversity begins with attracting and retaining a dynamic and diverse work team. They try to mirror the customers and communities they serve, which creates an environment where all of the customers and partners feel comfortable and welcome. To attract a diverse representation of qualified candidates, Starbucks link with a number of local and national community-based organizations. For example in America they make links with the National Black MBA and the National Hispanic MBA and the women in foodservice forum.

On a quarterly basis, Starbucks monitor the demographics of their workforce to determine whether they reflect the communities in which they operate. They also look at representation within specific positions and evaluate whether there are pathways to higher-level positions. Based on available data they have from partners who voluntarily disclose their race and gender, at the end of fiscal 2003:

- Starbucks US workforce is comprised of 63% women and 24% people of colour.
- Of Starbucks executive team – vice presidents and above – 32% are women and 9% are people of colour.

Figures taken from Fiscal annual report (2003).

Training

Diversity content is woven through Starbucks general training and development modules, as well as management training courses.

Diversity courses are also offered at Starbucks to address partners' relevant business needs. These include:

- Diversity Learning Journey.
- Bias-free Interviewing Workshops, which prepare managers and recruiters for the hiring process.

Starbucks take the hiring and recruiting process very seriously they are very careful whom they employ as it costs £2,300–3,000 to recruit and train each employee

- Within 2 weeks of commencing employment all employees will have undergone training that includes diversity training, learning about the diversity amongst the employees and also amongst the customer base (DDA training also provided).
- Training is ongoing throughout employment.

- The company claims to spend so much time and money on training in order to retain its staff and as a result has a very low staff turnover rate.
- Training is consistent throughout Starbucks, therefore once an employee has been trained they can work in any store and the company is happy to transfer staff between stores.
- Terms and conditions are discussed and agreed before employment commences.
- Starbucks partners are also informed about their anti-discrimination policies and anti-harassment policies, which are put in place to protect employees against gender, ethnicity, religion, age, sexual orientation and other forms of discrimination.

Suppliers

Starbucks have developed a supplier diversity initiative, which ensures that each supplier selected shares the company's core values to meet key requirements, which include:

- Quality
- Service
- Value
- Stability and sound business practices.

A diverse supplier must meet certain criteria for example, the company must be 51% owned, operated and managed by women, minorities or socially disadvantaged individuals.

Diversity in communities in which Starbucks operate

In 1998, Starbucks formed a joint venture with Johnson Development Corporation (JDC), which is owned by Earvin "Magic" Johnson. They created Urban Coffee Opportunities, LLC (UCO), bringing Starbucks stores to diverse communities. At the end of fiscal 2003, there were 52 UCO locations in the United States. Starbucks UCO stores offer communities an inviting, comfortable place for neighbours to gather.

While customers are assured a consistent *Starbucks Experience* at the stores, they may find the music is tailored to local tastes, subtle differences in the food offerings and mural art that is unique to the stores. A UCO store can be a catalyst for creating jobs and encouraging business development in the communities where the stores are located. At the end of fiscal 2003, the locations employed 971 Starbucks partners.

The Starbucks Foundation and Starbucks community and giving programmes provide support to non-profit organizations that serve diverse communities. They also partner with various community organizations to provide employment opportunities to their constituents.

Developments in diversity

During 2003 diversity included the hiring of a vice president of global diversity. Starbucks spent more with diverse suppliers compared to last year. And UCO opened 17 stores in diverse communities.

Here are some of their plans for 2004:

- Implement a global strategic diversity plan that will effectively increase diversity at all levels within the company, including an emphasis on succession planning.
- Increase the number of UCO stores in diverse neighbourhoods.

- Create a stronger business and communications strategy for Supplier Diversity to increase the amount of business Starbucks do with diverse suppliers.
- Increase the amount we spend with diverse suppliers to $95 million by identifying new certified diverse suppliers for future business with Starbucks, as well as encourage more of our existing diverse suppliers to become certified.
- Create a new position at Starbucks to oversee the Supplier Diversity Program.
- Develop strategic alliances with national organizations that serve diverse constituents, such as the National Association for the Advancement of Coloured People (NAACP) and the National Council of La Raza.

■ The management challenge

Mullins (2001) draws attention to the complexity of managing in the hospitality industry and we have noted that the international field is even more complex. The challenges facing the managers have been highlighted through the chapter, firstly by locating the theoretical traditions which have been developed to explore management and then by examining various themes which can be found in the operation of management within the international hospitality industry.

We have questioned our understanding of the purpose of management but in this review we will focus on the issue of quality within international hospitality organizations. We need to differentiate between the challenge of ensuring quality – defining our standards, moving beyond fitness for purpose and finding ways of assuring that quality – and of seeking continuous quality improvement or heading for excellence.

The seminal management book, *In Search of Excellence* (Peters and Waterman, 1982), remains one of the biggest selling business books ever. The platform for Peters and Waterman's work was the McKinsey 7-S model (Figure 8.4).

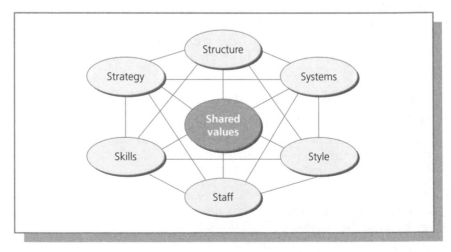

Figure 8.4
McKinsey 7-S model elements.

The essential message of *In Search of Excellence* became the recognition of:

- People
- Customers
- Action.

These "soft" factors were treated in the same way as hard ones, when previously the only "hard factors" were considered to be the "numbers". Peters and Waterman found eight common themes which they argued were responsible for the success of the corporations, which have become pointers for managers ever since. Here is a summary of the eight themes (Figure 8.5).

1. **A bias for action**, active decision-making – "getting on with it".
2. **Close to the customer** – learning from the people served by the business.
3. **Autonomy and entrepreneurship** – fostering innovation and nurturing "champions".
4. **Productivity through people** – treating rank and file employees as a source of quality.
5. **Hands-on, value-driven** – management philosophy that guides everyday practice – management showing its commitment.
6. **Stick to the knitting** – stay with the business that you know.
7. **Simple form, lean staff** – some of the best companies have minimal HQ staff.
8. **Simultaneous loose–tight properties** – autonomy in shop-floor activities plus centralized values.

Figure 8.5
In Search of
Excellence – the
eight themes.

However the authors have subsequently argued that the book's central flaw was in suggesting that these points would apply for ever, when they most certainly have not. If they were to rewrite now, they would not tamper with any of the eight themes, but add to them: capabilities concerning ideas, liberation and speed.

This rehearses and represents many of the principles we have covered in the chapter where we have looked at the differences between the classical approaches and more human focused approaches. The contextual understanding of the situations and the ability to develop appropriate managerial responses are crucial to the effective management of any hospitality or tourism organization. As we have shown the cultural diversity issues involved in international hospitality only serve to reinforce the need for sound human resource strategies. We would also argue that the cultural contexts of operations require adjustments to many conventional management approaches and that such solutions cannot be adopted without careful adaptation to the local cultures of everyday life and work.

■ Review questions

1 Do organizations need to manage cultural difference both within and without the business?
2 What are the factors that shape the way that resistance will be constructed in different locations within an international market?
3 Does internationalization argue against corporate systems?
4 Can local conditions affect the motivations of employees?

CHAPTER 9

Entrepreneurship and SMEs in the global market

■ Introduction

This chapter provides a wide-ranging review of small- and medium-size enterprises (SMEs) business in the international hospitality industry, with particular reference to entrepreneurship. Firstly, it explains the basic concepts of entrepreneurship and SMEs, then these concepts will be linked with the international hospitality industry. Many start-up companies are now beginning with a global focus because of the availability of international knowledge, experience and expertise of their founders. More demands from customers, more niche markets and technological advances make it possible that these small or medium size hospitality companies can access both worldwide markets and resources.

Chapter case study: Gordon Ramsay International

Gordon Ramsay, the celebrity chef who is almost as renowned for his colourful language and fiery temper as he is for the award-winning dishes he creates, is to receive an OBE in the New Year Honours list. The Glasgow-born former footballer said he was "humbled and delighted" to receive the honour, which is in recognition of his services to the hospitality industry.

He spoke of his delight that his efforts had been recognized by the Queen – but also paid tribute to those who work alongside him. "I feel that this recognition is as much for my team as it is for me. I'm lucky enough to work with the most amazing people whose hard work and dedication is an endless source of inspiration to me."

Ramsay has risen to national prominence thanks to hit television shows such as Hell's Kitchen, Ramsay's Kitchen Nightmares and The F-Word. But it was thanks to his success as a restaurateur that he first made a name for himself.

Released by Rangers after failing to make it into the first team, he turned to cooking and after catering college worked under the likes of Marco Pierre White and Albert Roux. By 1993, Ramsay was head chef of the newly opened Aubergine restaurant in London and within

3 years he had been awarded two Michelin stars. After an argument with the restaurant's backers, he opened his own restaurant in Chelsea, called Gordon Ramsay. The establishment was a huge success and became London's only three-starred Michelin restaurant.

His restaurants today include Petrus, Gordon Ramsay at Claridge's, The Berkeley and The Connaught, while his media career continues to go from success to success. His first international restaurant opened in Dubai in 2001, Tokyo in 2005, New York and Florida in 2006. Gordon oversees every detailed aspect, with his international teams dedicated to the highest standards.

How does he manage all these? Gordon has been working hard at it all day – meeting partners in the Victoria headquarters of his company, Gordon Ramsay Holdings (GRH), before finalizing plans for new ventures in New York, Florida and Los Angeles. He may be best known as the Michelin star who has become a small-screen star in The F-Word – a show in which he spends most of his time lampooning other TV chefs. But new figures confirm that he is as fiercely successful in the boardroom as he is in the kitchen. The latest returns from Ramsay restaurants show that profits were up by about 10% last year. In spite of two high-profile setbacks – the closure of Pengelley's restaurant in Sloane Street and a costly dispute with M1NT private members' club in Knightsbridge – GRH is on course to report operating profits of around £7.5 million when the group publishes its full accounts in a few weeks.

Business analysts believe that GRH's restaurants – Restaurant Gordon Ramsay in Royal Hospital Road, Claridges Hotel, the Connaught Hotel, the Savoy Grill and Banquette at the Savoy Hotel, the Boxwood Cafe and Petrus in the Berkeley Hotel, Maze, a modern Asian tapas-style restaurant/bar in Grosvenor Square, La Noisette in Sloane Street, the Conrad Tokyo in Tokyo and Verre in Dubai – are now worth £80 million. That puts Ramsay's 69% stake at £55 million – a threefold increase in as many years. A recent £8.5 million golden-handcuffs deal to stay at Channel 4 – both BBC1 and ITV failed to lure the host of Ramsay's Kitchen Nightmares and The F-Word – takes his net worth to more than £60 million, more than double that of his nearest rival, Jamie Oliver.

Admire or despise his bullying, despotic style, Ramsay is undoubtedly at the top of his game. Not that he considers what he does as playing. Now, ever anxious for more Michelin stars and more headlines, he is taking on a supersized challenge to match his supersized ego. "Far be it from me to be arrogant," he says with a knowing smile, "but I think the time is right to go global;" 2006 autumn he opens his first restaurant in the toughest food market: New York. Days after he launches Gordon Ramsay at the London (NYC) Hotel on West 54th Street, Ramsay will head south to open Cielo, another restaurant, in Boca Ratan, Florida. The east coast openings will be followed by a restaurant at the London (LA) Hotel on Sunset Boulevard in Los Angeles in 2007. Ramsay estimates that his combined US turnover will be £30 million a year for the next 10 years.

Ramsay's flagship three-Michelin-star Royal Hospital Road restaurant has just closed so technicians can install a £100,000 webcam system to enable him to see what's going on in New York and all his restaurants around the world. "We'll have clocks up for the different time zones, too. It will look like a f****** multinational corporation in there," he jokes.

Gordon is 39 years old. How did he grow his business empire so fast and big? By learning from the mistakes of others. During the 1990s' restaurant boom, he landed his first jobs in Michelin-starred outfits in London and watched his mentors open dozens of restaurants across the capital – only to close them again when the market went flat. "I wanted to learn from their mistakes," he says. "I realized that they had all gone into competition against each other. They opened very similar restaurants, all bearing their name, all serving similar food, with no infrastructure to back them up." Ramsay took a different tack. He decided to work with the competition, not against it. He persuaded banks and other backers to lend him the money to set up GRHs in the late 1990s. He ran just two eponymous restaurants – in Chelsea and, from 2001, Claridges – but set up eight run by talented chefs he had worked with on the way up.

"I'd met all these great young chefs. I wasn't going to be so stupid as to let them go and set up in competition with me as my predecessors had done, so I made them partners." He persuaded Marcus Wareing to take charge at the Savoy Grill, Angela Hartnett to run the Connaught and Stuart Gillies to operate Boxwood Cafe. Jason Atherton set up Verre in the Hilton Hotel on Dubai Creek, before returning to London to open Maze.

GRH supports all its restaurants with its own cash, from £1 million in the case of Maze to £3 million in New York. It's London-based staff of 60 handles bookings and logistics but each head chef chooses the menus. "That way all the food is distinctive and we all support each other." Except for Tokyo and Dubai, where Ramsay acts as a consultant and appoints key staff, GRH rents the space, deals with the costs and takes home the revenues.

It is high risk, high return and not every venture works out. Pengelley's restaurant collapsed spectacularly last year after only 7 months with losses of £850,000. "When things are not working, we get out fast," says Ramsay. Explaining the closure, he says Pengelley "was the first chef not to come through our ranks and therefore was not up to speed with our disciplines and systems".

In spite of these high-profile setbacks, Ramsay's diversification strategy seems to be working. Business at the Savoy Grill alone is up threefold on last year, and Maze's Atherton has just won a Michelin star, taking the group's tally to eight.

It is hard to believe that a man with Ramsay's talents and drive would not have succeeded in life, but this particular route might never have happened if Ramsay hadn't fallen for his mate's girlfriend 10 years ago.

When he was working in London in the early 1990s, a friend was dating Tana Hutcheson, a Montessori teacher and former manager of Terence Conran's Pont de la Tour restaurant. Ramsay wooed her, the couple married and had four children. It was Tana's father, Chris, a self-made businessman who ran a successful printing firm in south London, who backed Ramsay's early investments with £500,000. Today, Hutcheson is the business power behind the Ramsay empire.

After Ramsay finishes cooking in Claridges or Gordon Ramsay at 2 AM each morning, Hutcheson arrives at the firm's offices in Victoria by 6 AM – GRH is effectively a 24-hour operation. He is on the board of the company with Ramsay and the pair talk dozens of times a day. Ramsay is quick to acknowledge Hutcheson's importance. "He has taught me business. He has shown me more in the past 5 years than my real father did in 30 years."

Lately, Ramsay's 24/7 schedule and raft of new openings have sparked criticism that he has "spread himself too thin".

But can Ramsay really provide exactly the same experience across the globe in London, New York, Tokyo, Los Angeles and Florida?

"If you buy an Armani suit in Tokyo, instead of London, you don't ask the assistant if Giorgio stitched it himself. What you are paying for is the level of perfection, the level of quality. That's what I guarantee."

The Armani of food? It has a certain ring to it – one that appeals to City investors. Recent reports have suggested that Ramsay is planning to cash in and sell out to one of the City's burgeoning private-equity firms. His response is another verbal hotplate. F****** bollocks. This business is what I do. It's my passion. Every day that I go into the kitchen I want to elbow the cook out of the way. I've got the hunger and the fear.

"I've only just got to the summit and I intend staying here longer than many chefs in this country think is possible. We're opening at the new Heathrow Terminal Five. We're looking at Amsterdam and Prague. There's no limit."

Brief information of Gordon's international restaurants

Verre, Dubai

The Hilton Dubai Creek's signature restaurant *Verre* by Gordon Ramsay is a lesson in understated elegance. The 70-seat restaurant is dominated by a glass panel around the room, lit with tiny-coloured uplights, to counter the minimalism of the white linen, white china and simple silver cutlery creating a truly fine-dining experience.

Verre by Gordon Ramsay, the epitomy of fine dining, won the What's On magazine Awards 2005 award for the "Chefs' Choice 2005" voted for by all the Executive Chefs of five star hotels in Dubai, as their favourite restaurant outside that of their own.

Verre's cuisine has a lightness of touch that has become Gordon's hallmark, using a mix of the finest produce available in Dubai – particularly the fish – as well as flying in fresh ingredients from around the world. Executive Chef Jason Whitelock works with a dedicated team including members of the London brigade, who in turn oversee every aspect of catering in the lifestyle property, from the signature restaurant, through the other outlets including the Glasshouse Mediterranean Brasserie and Issimo Martini Bar. Just as in Gordon's restaurants in London, the cuisine will be complemented by the finest cellar, with well-informed sommeliers on hand to deliver the perfect addition to every dish.

"*Verre* was my first restaurant outside the United Kingdom and represents a huge challenge – but a thoroughly enjoyable one. There is a real buzz about Dubai and I am proud to be a part of it. In my mind, Dubai is one of the most vibrant cities around." (Gordon Ramsay)

The Hotel is located in the Dubai Creek business district and consists of 154 rooms and suites, each combining contemporary design with the highest levels of comfort and offering dramatic Creek views.

Conrad, Tokyo

In July 2005 Gordon Ramsay opened his first restaurant in the Shiodome district of Tokyo, Japan at the world-class modern luxury hotel, the opening marked an exciting and much anticipated new development in Gordon Ramsay's career.

"It has always been an ambition of mine: Tokyo is such a cosmopolitan city with the most vibrant people and high level of produce. We have enjoyed wonderful custom from Japanese diners over the years in Britain so it is a privilege to give something back and I am very much looking forward to offering the same standard a little closer to home!" (Gordon Ramsay)

The modern French restaurant, located on the 28th floor looking out on the dynamic Tokyo skyline, features two sections with a choice of fine dining and casual all-day dining. The restaurant is open for lunch and dinner, and offers a special Sunday brunch. The restaurant also features Gordon Ramsay's trademark Chef's table: an exclusive seating arrangement placing diners within the exciting confines of the kitchen, featured in the fine dining section, offering a glimpse of Ramsay's lightness of cuisine that has made him one of the world's leading restaurateurs.

Both dining concepts: *Gordon Ramsay at Conrad Tokyo* and *Cerise by Gordon Ramsay* will be overseen by Head Chef Andy Cook. Prior to heading the kitchen at the Conrad, Andy worked at the two-Michelin-starred restaurant Marchesi near Milan. In 2000 he joined Gordon's eponymous restaurant in Chelsea as Commis Chef before taking over as Chef de Partie at the three-Michelin-starred restaurant. In 2001, Andy moved to *Gordon Ramsay at Claridge's* as Sous Chef, where he assisted in the opening of this prestigious restaurant. At the Conrad, Andy and his team bring Gordon's world-renowned cuisine and distinguished service to a new, international audience.

Blackstone, New York

In Autumn 2006 Gordon Ramsay will continue his very successful partnership with Blackstone through their latest collaboration into New York. This latest opening will be located on the site of the former Rihga Royal Hotel and boasts over 520 suites. Currently undergoing a $50 million refurbishment under the direction of designer David Collins, the hotel will reopen as The London (NY).

The fine dining restaurant, seating around 50 guests, will be based upon *Restaurant Gordon Ramsay* at 68 Royal Hospital Road, Chelsea, London. This eponymous restaurant holds three Michelin stars and is the jewel in the crown of the Gordon Ramsay restaurant portfolio. The service and the wine list of the New York restaurant will be pitched at the level of its London counterpart.

Gordon's Head Chef will be Neil Ferguson, who has been part of Gordon's stable of talented chefs for several years. His experience includes; *La Tante Claire, The Square, Aubergine, Restaurant Gordon Ramsay* and *Angela Hartnett at The Connaught* in London and *L'Esperance* and *L'Arpège* in France. The Restaurant Manager will be Jean-Baptiste Requien from *Gordon Ramsay at Claridge's*.

The dining room and kitchen will both be stunning, offering all day dining for up to 80 guests. A traditional afternoon tea menu will be served alongside more relaxed orders through the room service menu. The fantastic bar will be the true heart and soul of the hotel creating a vibrant area for guests to enjoy exciting cocktails. There will even be a Chef's Table in the kitchen overlooking the central pass, something Gordon is famed for in London. Here guests can enjoy the atmosphere and excitement of the kitchen whilst dining in luxury.

Source: Schofield (2005), Adridge (2006) and Gordon Ramsay (www.gordonramsay.com)

Entrepreneurship

Although there is no accepted generic definition of the term "entrepreneurship" (Ucbasaran *et al.*, 2001), essentially the term refers to individual opportunistic activity that creates value and bears risk, and is strongly associated with innovation: it is a process of opportunity recognition and pursuit that leads to growth (Sexton and Kasarda, 1992). Inc. magazine claims, "Entrepreneurship is more mundane than it's sometimes portrayed ... you don't need to be a person of mythical proportions to be very,

very successful in building a company." In general, an entrepreneur is the one who creates a new business, facing risk and uncertainty for the purpose of achieving profit and growth by identifying opportunities and assembling the necessary resources to reach the goal.

Record numbers of people have launched companies over the past decade. A recent report from the National Panel Study of US Business Start-Ups found that eight million people, or one in 25 adults, were actively engaged in trying to launch a new business. In a recent survey of college seniors, 49% of the men and 31% of the women said they were interested in pursuing entrepreneurship when they graduate. This resurgence of the entrepreneurial spirit is the most significant economic development in recent business history.

The boom in entrepreneurship is not limited solely to the United States; many nations across the globe are seeing similar growth in the small-business sector. Entrepreneurs have introduced innovative products and services, pushed back technological frontiers, created new jobs, opened foreign markets. A variety of competitive, economic and demographic shifts have created a world in which "small is beautiful." Society depends on entrepreneurs to provide the drive and risk-taking necessary for the business system to supply people with the goods and services they need.

Why do so many people want to be entrepreneurs? There are potential major benefits of being an entrepreneur, such as the opportunity to gain control over your destiny, the opportunity to make a difference, opportunity to reach your full potential, opportunity to reap unlimited profits, opportunity to make a contribution to society and receive recognition for your efforts. While at the same time, you have to realize the potential drawbacks of being an entrepreneur, such as the uncertainty of income, the risk of losing invested capital, long hours and hard work, lower quality of life until the business gets established and huge responsibility. It has been shown that the five most frequently cited reasons to undertake a start up or work for entrepreneurial businesses are: joining the family business; wanting more control over future; tired of working for someone else; wanting to fulfil lifelong goal; having been downsized or laid off.

Internationalization and entrepreneurship

Internationalization has been shown to have many of the characteristics associated with entrepreneurship (Wright and Ricks, 1994), such as risk-taking in uncertain environments, the adoption of innovative behaviours, new market entry arising from the awareness of unexploited opportunities and the involvement of entrepreneurial managers (Pavord and Bogart, 1975; Ellis and Pecotich, 2001).

Exploring the genesis of the international entrepreneurial perspective, Oviatt and McDougall (1994: 47) defined International New Ventures as "a business organization that, from inception, seeks to derive significant competitive advantage from the use of resources and the sale of outputs in multiple countries."

Oviatt and McDougall (1994: 60) identified and described the emerging phenomenon of international new ventures that had "integrated the traditional multinational enterprises (MNE) concepts of internationalization and location advantage with recent entrepreneurship research on alternative governance structures and with developments in strategic management on the requirements for sustainable competitive advantage". These international new ventures had their origins in significant and observable commitments of resources in more than one country. This theory can be contrasted with the staged development of firm internationalization that had traditionally been applied by researchers, which categorized firms as risk-averse and reluctant internationalizers.

Over the past decade the links between entrepreneurship and international business (Knight, 2001) have been explored. There are a number of aspects of entrepreneurship that invite exploration of international and global markets. This is particularly so in knowledge-based sectors that have considerably higher export growth than the average in many developed nations (Austrade, 2002), and where business models are often designed around global niches on a global scale (Styles and Seymour, 2006).

As with domestic studies of entrepreneurship, there is no agreement as to what the field of international entrepreneurship should encompass. The term has evolved over the past two decades as interest in the topic has grown. The definitions of international entrepreneurship are various. Many of the definitions show their true field of interest by their definitions. For example:

- Wright and Ricks (1994) define international entrepreneurship as company-level business activity crossing national borders, with the research focus being on the relation between businesses and the international environments in which they operate – arguably more a strategic management viewpoint.
- While McDougall and Oviatt (2000, p. 903) suggest "a combination of innovative, proactive and risk-seeking behaviour that crosses national borders and is intended to create value in organizations." The study of international entrepreneurship includes research on such behaviour and research comparing domestic entrepreneurial behaviour in multiple countries. Firm size and age are not defining characteristics here. Thus, international entrepreneurship behaviour in large, established companies, often referred to as "corporate entrepreneurship," is included. Further, international entrepreneurial behaviour may occur at the individual, group or organizational levels.
- Oviatt and McDougall (2005: 7) regard international entrepreneurship as "the discovery, enactment, evaluation and exploitation of opportunities" – across national borders – to create future goods and services. It follows, therefore, that the scholarly field of international entrepreneurship examines and compares – across national borders – by whom, and with what effects those opportunities are acted upon.
- Dimitratos and Plakoyiannaki (2003: 189) define international entrepreneurship as "an organization-wide process which is embedded in

the organizational culture of the firm and which seeks through the exploitation of opportunities in the international marketplace to generate value".

Styles and Seymour (2006: 134) summarize all the key concepts from the above definitions of international entrepreneurship as: behaviour that crosses national borders; discovery, enactment, evaluation and exploitation of opportunities; creation of value; with unique combinations of resources. Styles and Seymour (2006: 134) finally arrive at the definition: "International entrepreneurship is the behavioural processes associated with the creation and exchange of value through the identification and exploitation of opportunities that cross national borders."

SMEs and Entrepreneurship

SMEs have a close relationship with entrepreneurship, especially in the hospitality industry. There are 48,730 hotels, 44,420 restaurants, and 87,435 pubs and bars in Britain and most of them are small businesses (Jones, 2002). Jones (2002: 1) explained, "Non-professionals come into the industry for a whole range of reasons … and think of the hospitality sector, whether it's a small restaurant, a guest house, a small hotel or even a pub, they think they bring their life skills to that particular job and can run it successfully, while nobody goes into an airport and says 'I can fly this'." Many people choose to start their small-business in the hospitality industry because of the relatively low entrance barriers, but it is often not as easy as they expected.

In America, the Small Business Administration (SBA) defines a small business as a firm that (a) is independently owned and operated, (b) is not dominant in its field, (c) is relatively small in terms of annual sales and (d) has fewer than 500 employees. According to SBA figures, 80% of all US companies have annual sales of less than $1 million and belong to this small-business category. The growth in the number of small-business start-ups is fuelling global economy in the 21st century. SMEs account for over 95% of businesses, create roughly 50% of total value added worldwide and, depending on the country, generate between 60% and 90% of all new jobs (OECD, 1997). Some of the data about contributions of the small businesses to the American national economy are presented below:

- There are 25.5 million businesses, 98.5% of all businesses in the United States would qualify as small businesses.
- Small-business employs more than 52% of the private sector workforce.
- Small businesses also create about 70% of new jobs.
- Small companies bear the heaviest load of training new workers.
- They also generate 20% more innovations per employee than large companies (Plate 13).

Plate 13
Another SME, another entrepreneur
Source: Vonzerö 2005 bt.

This is a good example of entrepreneurial opportunism. This was a traditional Hungarian restaurant which has been transformed into the El Paso steakhouse by dynamic new owners. The restaurants in Csopak on Lake Balaton normally only open for the short summer season, but they have decided to keep El Paso open all year round to build a new clientele amongst the locals.

Characteristics of entrepreneurs in SMEs

SMEs are of two distinct types: lifestyle businesses and high-growth ventures (Coulter, 2003). More than 80% are modest operations with little growth potential (although some have attractive income potential for the solo businessperson). A family run B&B, the corner florist, local pub and the neighbourhood pizza parlour fall into the category of lifestyle businesses – businesses built around the personal and financial needs of an individual or a family. Lifestyle businesses are not designed to grow into large enterprises. In contrast to lifestyle businesses, some businesses are small simply because they are new. Many companies – such as Easy Jet, GRH or E-Bay – started out as small entrepreneurial companies but quickly outgrow their small-business status. These high-growth ventures are usually run by a team rather than by one individual, and they expand rapidly by obtaining a sizable supply of investment capital and by introducing new products or services to a large market.

Entrepreneurs are high achievers and they have some common characteristics, including:

- Confidence in their ability to succeed: They need to be optimistic about the chances for success and this is the basic quality.
- Desire for responsibility: They prefer to be in control of their resources and to use those resources to achieve their goals.
- High degree of commitment: An entrepreneur's commitment to their goals and the business determines how successful their company ultimately becomes.
- Preference for reasonable risk: Entrepreneurs are not high–risk takers, but are instead calculating risk-takers.
- Flexibility: Entrepreneurs must be willing to adapt their businesses and themselves to meet changes.
- Skilled organizers: Entrepreneurs know how to put the right people and resources together to accomplish a task.
- Persistence: Successful entrepreneurs have the willpower to conquer the barriers that stand in the way of their success.
- High levels of energy. Entrepreneurs are more energetic than the average person. Typically, they work long hours, for example 70 hours a week.
- Future orientation. Entrepreneurs tend to dream big and then formulate plans to transfer those dreams into reality.

Another study of business owners by Yankelovich Partners for Pitney Bowes Inc. identified five different entrepreneurial personalities:

1 Idealists: Idealists started their businesses because they had a great idea or wanted to work on something special. Idealists enjoy creative work but are impatient with performing administrative tasks such as financial analysis or legal matters.
2 Optimizers: Optimizers are the second largest category. They enjoy the freedom and flexibility of owning a business and would not be willing to work for someone else. They want their companies to grow, but their focus is on profits rather than on revenues. These business owners are highly knowledgeable about financial issues and use technology to keep costs down and productivity up. They worry less than other business owners because they see themselves as maintaining control over their businesses. They also have learned balancing their home and business lives.
3 Hard Workers: Hard workers love their work and are more likely than any other group to put in extra hours to achieve the targets. They tend to be detail-oriented and are the most growth-oriented entrepreneurial group. They are financially aggressive and exercise broad control over the details of running their businesses. Hard workers typically have long-term business plans and stick to them.
4 Jugglers: Jugglers have a difficult time delegating authority and responsibility. They prefer to do things themselves to make sure everything meets their high standards. They are highly energetic people who are good at handling multiple tasks simultaneously. Jugglers feel pressure

to maintain positive cash flow in their companies and are always looking for ways to improve their businesses.

5 Sustainers: Sustainers are more likely to have inherited or bought their companies. They are the least comfortable with technology and prefer to put in more time than to figure out how to apply technology to solve a particular problem. Sustainers are the most conservative group and do not strive to achieve significant levels of growth. Maintaining a good balance between business and home life is important to them.

Female small-business owners

The number of women-owned small businesses has increased sharply over the past three decades – from 5% to 38% of all businesses. These companies generate approximately $3.7 trillion in sales each year. The 9.1 million women-owned companies across the United States employ 27.5 million workers, about 20% of all company workers in the country.

Small business has been a leader in offering women opportunities for economic expression through employment and entrepreneurship. More than half of all women business owners started their own businesses because they had an entrepreneurial idea or wished to further advance their careers. Increasing numbers of women are discovering that the best way to break the "glass ceiling" that prevents them from rising to the top of many organizations is to start their own companies. In the following case, Julia Hands, one of thousand women entrepreneurs in the hospitality industry, has shown her talents and management skills in a short period of time.

Case: Julia Hands is Chosen As One of the UK's Top 10 Entrepreneurs

Julia Hands, chief executive of Hand Picked Hotels, a collection of exquisite country house hotels, has been chosen as one of the top 10 entrepreneurs in the United Kingdom in the National Business Awards – known as the Oscars of the business world.

This latest accolade for Julia Hands and Sevenoaks-based Hand Picked Hotels was announced at a glittering ceremony at Grosvenor House last night (8 November) where Julia was named as one of the 10 finalists in the Credit Suisse Entrepreneur of the Year category in the National Business Awards.

Julia Hands, a former City lawyer, said: "I am delighted to be chosen as one of the UK's top 10 entrepreneurs. It is a tremendous compliment, not only for me but for the enormously loyal, talented and enthusiastic team at Hand Picked Hotels. This award is as much for them as for me."

Hand Picked Hotels has won four other major accolades in the past year, including the top award in the Tourism and Leisure business sector for the First Women Awards, organized by the CBI in conjunction with Real Business Magazine, plus AA Hotel Group of the Year 2004–2005, the Business Excellence Award and being selected as one of the top 50 companies to watch in 2005 by Real Business Magazine.

In creating Hand Picked Hotels 4 years ago, Julia Hands set out to "cast off the chain" mentality and encourage the renaissance of highly individual, luxurious country house hotels. All of the Hand Picked Hotels collection are former country houses with a long historical lineage and were "built for pleasure" – a tradition Julia is eager to maintain. Her vision for Hand Picked Hotels was to "create a unique collection of architecturally stunning and exquisitely refurbished country house hotels set in beautifully maintained grounds, offering the highest standards of cuisine and service, which will make each guest's stay a memorable one."

The AA Hotel Group of the Year 2004–2005 award was made in recognition of Hand Picked Hotels' commitment to perfecting their collection of 14 hotels. More than £35 million has been invested so far to refurbish and update the hotels, with the creation of fabulous interiors and state-of-the-art spas at several of the hotels.

In addition to working on restoring the hotels to their former glory, Hand Picked Hotels has focused on the quality of its service and its cuisine, focusing on exquisite food and fine wines. In the last 3 years all 14 hotels have achieved two AA rosette status, with Norton House in Edinburgh winning three AA rosettes. Four hotels have achieved recognition as being amongst the AA's top 200 hotels in the country.

Ethnic minority small-business owners

Similar advances are also showing up in ethnic minority segments of the population. Data from the US SBA show that between 1987 and 1997, the number of minority-owned firms grew by 168% — more than triple the 47% rate of US businesses overall. Minority-owned firms now employ an estimated 3.9 million people. Asians, Hispanics and African Americans, respectively, are most likely to become entrepreneurs in the United States. Like women, minorities cite discrimination as a principal reason for their limited access to the world of top level and hence the impetus towards entrepreneurship. A similar situation can be found in Britain. For example, Chinese restaurants in the United Kingdom have been established since 1908 and today the Chinese takeaway represents the second largest takeaway sector in the United Kingdom, valued at an estimated £827 million in 2002. The Indian curry is among the British favourite dishes and as such is increasingly available in a wide range of outlets from general restaurants as well as the specialist market. The value of the Indian takeaway market was estimated at around £674 million in 2002 according to Mintel report (2002).

Furama is a family owned small hotel management company in Singapore, now they plan to move into the global market.

Case: Furama Eyes Global Hotel Management Deals

Homegrown hotel management company Furama Hotels International (FHI) is eyeing a stronger regional footing and hopes to corner a market catering to niche hotel owners.

The low-profile firm has taken over the management of the previous Novotel Apollo hotel at Havelock Road, now renamed Furama Riverfront. Novotel, the brand managed by French giants Accor, ended its 5-year management leasing arrangement earlier this year. The hotel, along with another named Furama City Centre in the Chinatown area, is majority owned by listed Apollo Enterprises. FHI is linked to Apollo's controlling Ng family, though it is not part of the public entity. Both the four-star-rated hotels in Singapore are operating at healthy occupancy levels of about 90% each and rates are set to return to pre-SARS levels next year.

FHI business development manager Kevin Ng, who is a member of Apollo's Ng family, said in an interview that the company hopes to clinch 5–10 sales contracts first next year, before trying to convert them into management deals after reaching a certain comfort zone with the hotel owners.

The company is talking to an Australian hotel chain and is also looking at the Indochina and South-east Asian markets, he added. FHI is aiming for 20–30 sales or management contracts in 3–5 years' time. "There are a lot of regional hotel owners out there who do not have the connections to global sales nor can they afford, or have the desire, to let international hotel brands manage their assets," Mr Ng said. "We are well-positioned to help them get into the global sales arena and will seek to work with these owners on how to manage their properties. We would also cost much less than an international brand." Such names typically attract management fees of US $1 million a year at the low-end, with contracts lasting at least 20 years.

Doing global sales for hotel owners would mean helping them market their assets to major travel wholesalers like UK's Kuoni or Germany's TUI, as well as gain entry to major trade events like the Asian Travel Fair (ATF). FHI corporate sales director Jason Peck said, "A smaller hotel set-up may not have the resources to, say, have someone based in Japan to sell to the market there or get into the ATF, which costs about US $10,000 per entry."

Source: www.furama.com

Young entrepreneurs

Recent surveys have found that 60% of 18 to 29-year-olds say they hope to launch their own businesses. There are many examples of young entrepreneurs in hospitality industry.

Example: Papa John

As a high-school student working at a local pizza pub in Jeffersonville, Indiana, John Schnatter realized that there was something missing from national pizza chains: a superior-quality traditional pizza delivered to the customer's door. His dream was to one day open a pizza restaurant that would fill that void.

In 1984, "Papa" John Schnatter knocked out a broom closet located in the back of his father's tavern, sold his prized 1972 Z28 Camera, purchased $1,600 worth of used restaurant equipment, and began selling his pizzas to the tavern's customers. The customers loved the pizza so much that John was able to expand by moving into adjoining space, eventually leading to the opening of the first Papa John's restaurant in 1985.

> Today, Papa John's boasts nearly 3000 restaurants in 49 states and 20 international markets. Papa John's also owns or franchises more than 100 Perfect Pizza restaurants in the United Kingdom.
>
> *Source*: www.papajohns.com

Entrepreneurial enterprises go global

SMEs historically have not been associated with international business, As international business has long been regarded as the domain of large, resource-rich companies. Evidence from Asia, Europe and North America indicates that increasing numbers of SMEs are involved in international business (e.g. Economist, 1993; Rennie, 1993). This recent evidence suggests that internationally active SMEs are becoming more frequent. Based on an empirical study of trends in 18 industrialized countries, the Organisation for Economic Cooperation and Development (OECD) notes that SMEs now account for about a quarter of international business in most industrialized nations. Internationally active SMEs are emerging in notably large numbers throughout the world, and they tend to be more dynamic and grow faster than strictly domestic enterprises (Bell, 1995).

Widespread usage of fax, e-mail, the Internet and other such communications technologies is making internationalization a more viable and cost-effective option than just a few years ago. Such technologies are providing important competitive advantages to SMEs, allowing them to efficiently transact business throughout the world (Oviatt and McDougall, 1995). SMEs are also affected by the forces of globalization, including falling trade and investment barriers and the far-reaching activities of large MNEs. Increasing cross-national competition is pressuring SMEs to internationalize. This, combined with increasing opportunities to pursue foreign markets and the ability to profit from expanded scale and scope in their operations, has created many incentives for smaller companies to internationalize (Oviatt and McDougall, 1995).

Compared to MNEs, smaller companies do not have bureaucracy and expensive existing information systems. They are often more innovative, more adaptable and have quicker response times when it comes to implementing new tactics and meeting specific customers needs (Verity, 1994). With the growing role of direct marketing and buyers with specialized needs, SMEs can increasingly serve niche market segments that span the world (Oviatt and McDougall, 1995).

The entrepreneur needs to prepare by asking and answering the following questions:

- Is there a profitable foreign market in which the company has the potential to be successful for an extended period of time?
- Does the company have the right resources, skills and commitment to succeed in this foreign market?

- Are there pressures domestically that are forcing the company to seek global opportunities?
- How well do you know the culture, history, economics, legal system, etc. of the country which you are considering?
- Is there a feasible exit strategy if the business environments change or the new venture is not successful?

Some strategies for hospitality SMEs to go global

Innovation

An important characteristic of small businesses is that they tend to be more innovative than larger companies. *Innovation and creativity* are key factors for hospitality entrepreneurial success. Morrison and Thomas (1999) point out that renewal of products or services by adding value through the application of expertise and imagination can help hospitality enterprises keep competitive edge.

In the following case studies, Bob Burn demonstrates the qualities needed for hospitality entrepreneurship in the global arena.

Chapter case study: The Return of a Genuine Hotel Entrepreneur

Bob Burns, the Hong Kong hotelier who built the Regent name into one of the most recognizable hotel brands worldwide, is back in business. The American-born entrepreneur is negotiating with Japanese financiers to form a company to operate ultra-luxury hotels. The first properties are likely to be in Shanghai and Hanoi.

Mr Burns says, "I'm going to draw a map with Hong Kong in the middle and keep operations confined to Asia." The circle around Hong Kong is 10,000-km wide, embracing China, Japan, all of Southeast Asia and India.

The amiable American cannot hide the disappointment he still feels about having to sell his 65% stake in Regent International Hotels in 1992.

In a complex business deal, Mr Burns had made provisional agreement with Wharf Holdings to sell his interest in the company, and later it was required by Canada-based Four Seasons chain, Regent's rival in the luxury bracket. Mr Burns walked away with more than US $100 million. But his love for the hotel business never diminished. His pride peaked in 1980, when the landmark Regent Hong Kong opened. The 514-room property became an icon of the industry and was flagship of the group. That hotel was sold in 2001 to the US-based InterContinental Hotels Group and the Regent name disappeared from Hong Kong. But it had left a lasting mark; the innovation of combining Asian service excellence with western concepts of efficiency and luxurious space has since been widely copied.

Now, Mr Burns says, it is time for another sea change. At 75, he has been in the hotel business since he started his working life as a teenage bus boy at the Waldorf Astoria and in the kitchens and laundries of New Jersey resorts as a teenager during the Second World War.

He founded the Regent hotel management company in 1969, after coming to Hong Kong to work with Hilton. The flagship in Tsim Sha Tsui won plaudits after it opened in 1981 and was voted best hotel in the world by several polls.

When Mr Burns reluctantly was forced to sell the Regent chain in 1992, it totalled 20 prestigious hotels in four continents. Under the terms of the sale, he agreed not to go into competition with the company for 4 years. By the time that had lapsed in 1996, he was 67 years. "I was rich but unemployed," he says.

But he hasn't been idle. "Friends kept asking me to help them with new hotels," he says. They still do: at present he's involved in Singapore, where two old British military clubhouses on Sentosa form the hub of an imaginative new property; and in Tuscany, Italy, he is advising on the transformation of an old convent winery into a deluxe property. He also purchased the historic Villa Felttrinelli and devotes his energy to the 21 room ultra service-oriented boutique hotel built by a renowned Milanese architect in 1892.

Just as the Regent brand created a new benchmark for hotels three decades ago, Mr Burns hopes the new brand – the name has yet to be finalized – will set fresh standards for the hospitality industry. "There have been significant changes in the past few years in the design of hotels and the philosophy of running hotels," he says. But now it's time for another change. We can be different, innovative.

"There are all kinds of things you can now do in a hotel – designers are so much better." He says he wants 10 of the new style, freshly branded hotels, up and running in a decade, with Hong Kong as the corporate headquarters. Finance for the new venture will come from the same partners he worked with in the pioneering era of the Regent brand.

Bob Burns wants 10 of his new hotels operating within a decade. The reason he is so confident about his company is because of his key resources – hotel management skills and concepts, which are tacit knowledge.

Source: Sinclair, K., 2005, South China Morning Post and www.ehotelier.com/browse/news_more.php?id = A3754_0_11_0_M; www.usatoday.com/travel/destinations/www.villafeltrinelli.com

Change initiation

The capability of identifying an opportunity for creation or innovation, and ability to turn it into a reality is a key element for hospitality entrepreneurship. Morrison and Thomas (1999: 151) illustrated this concept with Holiday's development. Kemmons Wilson founded what is now called Holiday Inn Worldwide in 1952. In 1951 he and his family of five children decided to visit Washington on holiday. Everywhere they went they found that while a room cost $6 to $8 each child was to be charged $2 extra. This annoyed Wilson and he vowed to develop a chain of hotels where children could stay free as long as they slept in the same room as their parents. Wilson's hotels would also feature free parking, air-conditioning, free in-room TV and swimming pool. By the late 1970s Wilson and his associates ran a hotel chain of more than 400,000 rooms. Wilson changed the rules of the "hotel game", innovating in the development of a radically new concept.

There are lots of opportunities available in hospitality industry. According to a survey of 1,600 people by pollster YouGov, a lack of home comforts is hotel guests' number one complaint; 27% of the people interviewed put this at the top of their list, although a quarter said that loneliness was the worst aspect of staying in a hotel. To make hotel rooms more comfortable and to consider customers' special requirement will be a lasting challenge for international hoteliers. If any hospitality entrepreneur can make his or her hotel more like home, it will certainly win the customer's trust.

Niche marketing

Hospitality companies can concentrate their efforts on a single market segment and because of this it enables hospitality operators to really understand the needs and wants of their customers in that market segment.

With more than 36 million households travelling with their pets in the United States, taking at least two vacations per year, and spending an average of $1,000 or more per trip, this translates into a huge sum of money spent in an exceptionally niche market. Unfortunately, fears of damages, barks, bites and allergies keep many hoteliers safely on the sidelines away from the action. Due to the demand for accurate, actionable information about becoming a pet friendly hotel, BringYourPet.com recently released the book, *Making Your Property Pet friendly: A How-To Guide*. Small hotels can be more flexible compared with large hotel chains in serving the needs of customers travelling with pets and become pet friendly hotels relatively easily.

Competing with large companies, the SMEs can have advantages if they remain in close contact with their markets and remain more open-minded and willing to try new things. The feeling still exists that big companies tend to say no more often than they say yes. For example, all the large hotel groups compete with each other for the luxury customers segment in Dubai, while small- or medium-size hotel companies actually can find the budget accommodation market will offer a very promising opportunity in the future.

Example: Cost-conscious travellers will soon have more choice

The increasing importance of Dubai as a business hub for the Middle East has led to a reappraisal of hotel demands in the country. The trend has been to build five-star luxury resorts and business hotels, but the lack of more affordable hotels for business travellers is now being addressed.

A new chain, Refad Hotels and Resorts, was launched at 2004s Arabian Travel Market, and Express by Holiday Inn, from the InterContinental Group, is moving into the emirate. Up to 20 economy-branded hotels will be introduced in the Middle East by 2009, appealing to cost-conscious business travellers. Meridien plans three properties in Dubai, as well as the 422-room Grosvenor

House under construction in Dubai Marina. Hilton is also looking at another "four, possibly more" properties in Dubai.

Yet, despite all the huge plans on the drawing board, Dubai is struggling to match bed space to existing demand. Beds are likely to remain at a premium in the next 2 years – only two opened in Dubai this year, the 330-room Al Qasr at the Madinat Jumeirah and the 250-room Traders Dubai, part of the Shangri-La group. The desire for more choice by business travellers is perhaps reflected in the fact that Traders, which opened only in May, was last month named Best New Business Hotel in the World by Business Traveller magazine.

Dubai's long-term challenge is to ensure that demand keeps up with capacity. Dubai still grabs the headlines, but investment and development plans are mushrooming across the UAE and beyond.

Source: Dominic Ellis. October 2004, Business Wireless.

International branding

It takes a long time to develop a positive brand image in the minds of consumers. Many of the top hospitality brands have been around since the 1950s or even longer. Brands provide consumers with quality assurance, and this is especially the case in an industry like hospitality, where consumers are primarily looking for comfortable accommodation, and good food and drink efficiently served by friendly staff (Bowie and Buttle, 2004: 109). Therefore it is well worth SMEs developing their brands and images in their targeted market segments. Once consumers have experienced and liked a hospitality brand they will be more likely to use it again, since the brand promises to reduce the risks for the customer when travelling away from home.

Case: Branding Vital for Survival: Banyan Tree Chairman

For home-grown resort group Banyan Tree Holdings, branding is viewed as an imperative for survival, not a reward for success. "To us, from the very beginning, it's not something that it'll be nice to have in order to succeed," said executive chairman Ho Kwon Ping in a recent interview. "It's something that if we did not have, we would not be able to survive. It's really a necessity – not a luxury, not a result of success. It's a cause for success."

It is no wonder then that Banyan Tree takes its branding very seriously. The company, which runs hotels and resorts in Bangkok, Phuket, Bintan, Seychelles and Maldives, has been used by academics as a case study – even appearing in management books as an example of a successful Asian brand. Mr Ho reckons it's because the history and development of Banyan Tree is possibly of some use to other companies. In the case of Banyan Tree, the group identified a target niche market within a certain price segment, and then differentiated itself from the rest of boutique hotel/resorts with a pool-villa concept. As a result of its focused brand building, Banyan Tree has been able to be a price maker, even commanding higher room rates during the Asian financial crisis while other players were cutting theirs.

"People associate Banyan Tree with spas, with pool villas, not with a 600-room city hotel," said Mr Ho. "And one of the reasons why I think our brand is strong is because we design every single Banyan Tree Hotel. We never bought any hotel, we never converted any hotel. So when you design from scratch, you are able to create that product identity which then associates with the brand." It is not cheap owning the whole process from feasibility studies to construction to furniture purchase, Mr Ho admits. But it's the best way to protect the brand.

That said, brand consistency does not mean every Banyan Tree resort looks the same, regardless of geographical location. The idea is to be consistently focused on the type of market with different products. "When people come to Banyan Tree, they do not want Banyan Tree Mexico to look and feel like Banyan Tree Phuket or Banyan Tree Seychelles. So the difficulty for us here is that we have to have uniqueness within an overall framework of consistency – and that's a challenge all the time."

Source: www.iesingapore.com/ief05 23 January 2005.

Technology and the Internet

The Internet together with e-commerce has opened up the international markets for SMEs in the hospitality industry. Not only does the Internet make it easier to start a business, but it allows small companies to compete on a level playing field with larger ones. Small businesses can use the Internet to communicate with customers and suppliers all over the world, any time of the day, and to access the types of resources and information that were previously available only to larger companies (Coulter, 2003). Most small companies follow a four-step evolutionary process before conducting global business on the Web: connecting to e-mail; using the Web to conduct international market research; building a functional website and finally receive order/reservation and provide service on the Internet. Clearly, hoteliers have an interest in promoting the Internet channel, as it is far cheaper, especially direct booking on the hotel's own site. A WTO report on e-commerce estimated that the cost of direct reservations by traditional means (such as a travel agency means paying 10% commission) could be as much as 300–500% higher than processing the same reservation through the Internet (less than £1 per booking).

Strategic alliance or joint venture

Strategic alliance or joint ventures lower the risk of entering global markets for small businesses. They also give small companies more clout in foreign lands.

The international joint venture (IJV), a form of strategic alliance, is an important means of international expansion as we saw in Chapter 5.

A growing number of SMEs have employed this mode in their expansion. Despite the increasing popularity of international joint venturing as an internationalization strategy for SMEs, the effectiveness of this strategy has been underexplored in the entrepreneurship literature. While researchers in the areas of strategy and international business have explored the performance of IJVs, they tend to focus on ventures established by large firms. Their findings may not be generalizable to SMEs' IJVs, given the significant differences between smaller and larger firms.

Case: Joint Together Managing Hotels in China

TEDA Travel Group is the only full service Chinese travel and real estate service company publicly traded on the US markets. Currently, TEDA Travel Group is providing management services to hotels and resorts throughout China. In addition to its property management division, TEDA Travel Group also owns the largest timeshare operation in China, as well as a portfolio of real estate investments. Leveraged on its existing core businesses and the brand name "TEDA," one of most recognized names in China, TEDA Travel Group intends to become a market leader in the fast growing Chinese travel and real estate services industry.

TEDA signed a definitive agreement to purchase a majority interest of Shanghai Bowking Hotel Management Co. Limited, a leading boutique hotel management company in China.

Mr Godfrey Hui, CEO of TEDA Travel Group stated, "This acquisition will strengthen the Group's position as a leading hotel management group in China. It also allows us to expand into Shanghai, China's largest and most comprehensive industrial and commercial city. In recent years, occupancy rates for the better and more desirable hotels in Shanghai run very near 100% year round. This was a primary reason for seeking acquisition properties in Shanghai."

Started in 2000, Bowking is a leading boutique hotel management company in China. Based in the vibrant city of Shanghai, Bowking is led by a hotel veteran-cum-professor Mr Nan Zhang. Bowking will orchestrate the opening of no fewer than five four-and five-star hotels in China this year.

Mr Nan Zhang, CEO of Bowking, comments, "We are delighted to join TEDA Travel Group. The management and business expertise provided by Teda Travel Group is crucial for a fast growing company like Bowking. We'll benefit dramatically by becoming a part of the prestigious Teda brand."

"We will continue to balance our growth prospect against what we pay. This is the second of a series of similar acquisition which is part of our current strategy and we are seeing the positive effects to the Group already," concluded Mr Hui.

Source: TEDA Travel Group, Inc. www.prnewswire.com

ACTIVITY Understanding the challenges of implementing best practices in hospitality and tourism SMEs.

We want you to consider the barriers to the application of best practices in hospitality and tourism SMEs. The arguments are developed on an article about SMEs in the United Kingdom (Hwang and Lockwood, 2006). Think through the issues involved in operating an SME and list the possible barriers that may make adopting best practice difficult for you as you strive to develop your business.

Hwang and Lockwood (2006) conducted in-depth interviews with owners, managers and staff in 89 award-winning businesses in the hospitality and tourism industries. Their results suggest a model identifying seven key capabilities that underlie the adoption of best practices and six barriers to their implementation. The seven key capabilities for hospitality and tourism SMEs were said to be:

1 customer-focused goals,
2 planning and control,
3 partnering and networking,
4 internal and external communication,
5 achieving consistent standards,
6 strategic workforce management,
7 cash flow and performance management.

They identified six barriers to implementing best practices. These were:

1 changing demand,
2 limited resources,
3 lack of skilled labour,
4 lifestyle,
5 lack of competitive benchmarking,
6 location.

They argued that all of these could create turbulence in the operational environment.

The deadly mistakes of entrepreneurs going international

Small businesses have a much higher failure rate than larger businesses; 60% will fail within 6 years and this rate will be even high in international markets. The main causes of small business failure in international markets are:

- Managerial incompetence: Management inexperience or poor decision-making ability is the chief problem of the failing enterprise. The owner-leader lacks the knowledge or international experiences needed.
- Lack of strategic management: Too many small business managers neglect the process of strategic management. If you fail to plan, you plan to fail. Clearly defined strategy is necessary for creating and maintaining a competitive edge in international market.
- Ineffective marketing and branding: Sometimes entrepreneurs believe that if they provide good service, food and beverage, customers automatically "will come." This is not true in the modern marketplace,

especially if you want to appeal to international customers. Marketing Communication is a key element of SMEs' success.

- Undercapitalization: Any successful business venture requires proper financial control. Entrepreneurs tend to be overly optimistic and often underestimate the financial requirements of launching a business or the amount of time required for the company to become self-sustaining.
- Uncontrolled growth could be another deadly mistake.
- Poor location: Always ask "location, location, location" when you do hospitality business, no matter whether it is in the home country or foreign countries. Entrepreneurs need to investigate before they locate and find answers to some key issues like: What it costs and what it generates in sales volume?

Becoming a global entrepreneur does require a modification in the mind-set of the company. To achieve success in the global market, entrepreneurs in the hospitality industry require to:

- Know their business in depth – What is their unique selling point in the international market.
- Learn to understand their customers from the perspective of the customer's own culture, not their own.
- Adopt a more respectful attitude toward culture and customs in foreign market.
- Work with motivated, multilingual employees.
- Retain a desire to learn constantly about global markets.
- Keep a high level of service quality and constantly improve it.
- Innovate at all times.
- Be alert and respond quickly.
- Train employees to think globally.

■ Conclusion

The chapter started with the clarification of concepts of SMEs and entrepreneurship in the global environment. It has explained why "going global" has become an integral part of many small companies' or entrepreneurs' strategies. Companies that move into international business can reap many benefits, including offsetting the declines in the domestic market; increasing sales and profits; extending their products' life cycles; lowering costs; improving their competitive position; raising their quality levels and becoming more customer-oriented. This chapter also has described the main strategies small businesses have for going global, such as e-commerce, Innovation, joint venture and franchising.

We have also considered:

- The potential benefits and drawbacks of owning a small business.
- The forces that are driving the growth in entrepreneurship.
- The development of international entrepreneurship.
- The SMEs and its economic impact.

- The characteristics of SMEs and its trends.
- The strategies for SMEs go international.

This review has attempted to locate the entrepreneur within the overall context of the international hospitality industry. They will also be subject to the pressures to act responsibly which we will address in the next chapter.

■ Review questions

1 Why is international hospitality seen as such a positive locations for SMEs?
2 Do the characteristics of successful entrepreneurs also explain some of their failures?
3 Are there advantages to being an SME in the international market?
4 Do entrepreneurs need help? If so what sort of support would you suggest?

CHAPTER 10

Managing social responsibility in international hospitality

After working through this chapter, you should be able to:

- Define ethical and social responsibility concepts in the global environment
- Examine the approaches used in defining international social responsibility
- Understand which aspects of social responsibility must be applied to international hospitality service operations
- Critically determine the role of values in hospitality cultures for both the suppliers and customers

■ Introduction

In this chapter we will consider the demands from within the hospitality industry and from outside it for companies to operate in a socially responsible way. We will introduce you to a number of approaches to the definition of ethics and apply them to a range of situations currently facing hospitality businesses, including green issues and sustainability. From the 1990s, the notion of business ethics has re-invented itself moving from a quiet corner of the academic discussions about business strategy onto the centre of the stage in the guise of corporate responsibility. It has not been an easy journey as it is based upon a series of headline business disasters that exposed the poverty of ethical behaviour in some very major players in the world market. This is not the place to tell a history of corporate malpractice, but it is worth noting that the growing sense of responsibility and a corporate duty to a wider social grouping than the shareholders has emerged within a particular conjuncture. We observed the trend towards environmental awareness amongst consumers in our discussion of the operating environment and this has certainly made it easier for companies to adopt a new agenda.

We want to begin our account with a look at the founding principles of ethics and then look at how these are translated into business ethics. This will give us a platform to evaluate the emergence of the notions of corporate and social responsibility. We will also consider how these corporate agendas have been informed by the beliefs of the groups who opposed the rise of the large corporations. It is reassuring to see how an idea that belonged in the ivory tower of the academic world in the 1980s is now seen as central to the business agenda, and companies have finally realized that sustainable policies can not only make them more attractive to the more aware consumers but also contribute to better business performance.

■ Right and wrong

It is often said that we all know the difference between right and wrong and that we have all been brought up to recognize the distinction.

The study of ethics makes it seem more difficult, as different positions within ethics construct different categories of right and wrong. There are schools of thought that want to see the imposition of universal codes of behaviour that would brand behaviour as good or bad no matter what the circumstance be. Others are more contextual and are more open to competing justifications of what motivated the behaviour or what the outcomes of the behaviour were. For instance, a universalist position, such as duty theorists or deontologists, would argue that it is always wrong to lie but a consequentialist or utilitarian view may argue that a small lie, that makes people feel happier can be morally justified. The distinction between rules, guidelines, morals or principles of living ("morality") that exist in time and space and the systematic reflection upon them ("ethics") is still worth observing. The idea that morality refers to what all reasonable persons will conform to in all situations at all times requires much more careful attention, especially given the culturalist position we have developed throughout the book so far. As in previous discussions, we would reject simplistic claims for universal application, but we would recognize that some behaviours are always going to be condemned no matter what the cultural setting is.

That would be wrong then?

Example: Woman gets jail for mouse-in-soup scam at restaurant

Associated Press 6 July 2006, 08:30 AM

NEWPORT NEWS, VA.: A woman who tried to extort money from the Cracker Barrel restaurant chain by putting a dead mouse in a bowl of soup was sentenced to a year in jail.

Carla Patterson, 38, and her 22-year-old son, Ricky Patterson, sought $500,000 from the chain after claiming they found the rodent in the vegetable soup the woman ordered at a Newport News restaurant on Mother's Day weekend in 2004.

A jury convicted the Pattersons of conspiracy to commit extortion in April. The Pattersons maintained their innocence, but evidence included tests showed the mouse had not been cooked and had not drowned but instead died of a fractured skull.

Carla Patterson wept Wednesday as a judge imposed the jail sentence and a $2,500 fine. Defence lawyer Michael Woods said Patterson plans to appeal.

Ricky Patterson's sentencing, which had been scheduled for Wednesday, was postponed until September 14. He is at Virginia Peninsula Regional Jail in Williamsburg after pleading guilty to forgery in an unrelated check-fraud case (Figure 10.1).

Universal	Right	Wrong
Contextual	Reasonable	Concerning

Figure 10.1 Approaches to morality

Both approaches would have little problem in interpreting the above example as wrong! Gambling is a more problematic with as many opposed to the idea as there are committed to it. We have been following the developments in China with great interest, where gambling is illegal except in Hong Kong, with horse racing, and Macau with the casinos. The ethical questions are difficult. If gambling is acceptable, then why hold it to a very small country? But if it is not, why encourage the huge growth that we are seeing in Macau. The following case study will introduce you to the background to Macau.

Chapter case study

In September 2005 the Asia Times carried an article about the investment in gambling in Macau that coincided with one of us visiting there. They argued that Macau was not Las Vegas, adding the caveat that at least it was not yet. However, at least one report suggested otherwise. Macau was indeed becoming the Las Vegas of Asia, with an estimated US $7.4–12 billion worth of new development, centred on entertainment and casinos. It was seen that China's strategy was to turn Macau into the Las Vegas of Asia, according to a report by Hong Kong-based UBS Investment Research, "Macau Gaming – Let the Games Begin". It argued that the political incentive is driven by the upcoming 10th anniversary of Macau's handover to China in 2009. UBS says a common language, proximity (with a billion people within 3 hours' flight time), and the limited variety of entertainment venues in China, give Macau a competitive advantage. The report also notes that China's economic growth provides a sustainable base for gaming enterprises in Macau. Last year, Macau earned US $5.4 billion from gaming – narrowly beating the Las Vegas Strip (US $5.3 billion) as the world's largest gaming centre.

The former Portuguese colony, a peninsula and two islands about 60 kilometres (and at least 60 decibels) away from Hong Kong, first legalized gambling in 1847. When Macau returned to Chinese sovereignty in 1999, the authorities immediately cracked down on triads whose open warfare had downgraded Macau's reputation from seedy to unsafe. A pivotal decision by the Macau Government in 2002 ended the 40-year gambling monopoly of Stanley Ho's Sociedade do Jogos de Macau (SJM or "Macau Gaming Society" in English). The government granted three new gaming licenses, with 1.7 million square feet under construction at more than 500 sites. Investment came from Las Vegas itself, with Steve Wynn of the eponymous chain Wynn Resorts, and Sheldon Adelson of the Las Vegas Sands empire coming to Macau to bankroll the billions.

Two of the new licenses went to new players – Wynn's Resorts from Las Vegas and Galaxy Consortium, controlled by Hong Kong group K-Wah. Several sub-concessions were also issued, including one to Las Vegas Sands, whose Chairman, Sheldon Adelson, last month unveiled plans to build a $15-billion replica of the Las Vegas Strip on the Cotai Strip in Macau (Cotai is the reclaimed land between two islands – Taipa and Coloane). Sheldon told Hong Kong reporters the strip could have as many as 60,000 rooms. The strip has been carved into seven parcels of land. At this stage, six hotels, each supported by a casino, are planned, with leading hotel groups, including Starwood, Marriott, InterContinental, Regal and Four Seasons committed to plans collectively worth $2.5 billion. Adelson saw an eastern version of the Las Vegas Strip on landfill between Macau's outer islands of Coloane and Taipa, anchored by his $2 billion Venetian Macao. Ahead of the Venetian's 2007 debut, the Sands opened a $240 million downtown casino in May 2004, giving Macau its initial look at the Las Vegas way of doing things. From the pure gold glass exterior to shiny black 15,300 square meter open plan interior with a 50 tonne chandelier and 20 meter high ceiling, the Sands sets a different tone to the gambling dens of the Ho's flagship Hotel Lisboa. It is also significantly different from Las Vegas: this Sands has no hotel (just 51 suites for invited high rollers; do not try to book, if they have not contacted you then you are not invited!) and no retailing. In Vegas, hotels obtain around 50% of their revenue from outside the casino, from restaurants, retail, rooms and related attractions; in Macau, the take beyond the tables re-presents just 3% of the gross.

Today, most people come to Macau for one reason: to gamble. Asia Today suggested that the top five reasons included: romantic weekending from Hong Kong; commercial sex, ranging from Russian streetwalkers to massage parlours; eating Macanese, the original fusion cuisine; and seeing the legacies of Chinese culture and Portuguese rule dating to 1557 that won Macau a place on the United Nations World Heritage List.

Tourist numbers are skyrocketing, from 7.5 million in 1999 to 16.7 million last year and are expected to reach 20 million this year. Current figures show 55.8% of visitors come from mainland China, many taking advantage of the liberalized rules that allow travel to Macau by individuals, rather than only as part of those flag-waving, bus-riding, restaurant-jamming tour groups. Another 30% come from Hong Kong, 1 hour away on Ho's jetfoil ferries making 80 trips a day, and 8.3% from Taiwan.

The average stay of Chinese visitors is only 1.25 days. The strategy of the Macau Government is to double that stay by providing more attractions, but currently there are not enough hotel rooms. Despite the rapid rate of development it will probably take 5 years before Macau has enough rooms to meet the anticipated increase in tourist arrivals. As the new hotels get up and running, a major concern will be the supply of fresh produce – including seafood, vegetables and fruit and wines.

As well as casinos and hotels, a wide range of entertainment facilities will be built in Macau in the coming years to liven up tourist attractions in the former Portuguese enclave. Aside from construction of the casinos, hotels and entertainment complexes, Macau will need additional housing, hospitals, schools and other facilities to house its growing population. Macau has a population of 500,000 and will have to rely on migrant workers to fill the newly created jobs. There will be a need for both education offshore and new joint ventures with vocational schools in Macau to train new workers. Macau has already started to import workers from the Philippines and India, according to some sources.

The second area is the civil service. The government has had to adjust its civil service infrastructure to deal with the huge volume of work coming from the waves of investment activity. It will have to issue work permits for the thousands of workers who will arrive to work in Macau's casinos and construction sector, deal with new licenses and monitor the industry.

House winnings at Macau's 19 casinos are poised to exceed $6 billion this year, overtaking Las Vegas and its more than 200 casinos as the world's top gambling earner. Macau's average daily take per table is around $18,000 (slot machines account for less than 2% of Macau's gambling take); better than five times the average for Las Vegas. Macau has a simple formula for its big money action: higher stakes. In Vegas, you'll find $1 tables, but in Macau the betting starts at HK $100 (US $12.85; Macau's official currency is the pataca with a fixed exchange rate of 8 to $1, but Hong Kong dollars are so common that casino limits are denominated in them, and they circulate on par with the slightly less valuable pataca), and those tables are hard to find. The real action, however, is not in the HK $300 blackjack or the Chinese big–small dice game, but VIP baccarat in plush, private rooms. High rollers, known as whales, account for about 80% of Macau's gambling revenue. The government takes a 35% tax on casino profits, comprising three quarters of its revenue.

Adding millions of visitors and Las Vegas developers to Macau's 465,000 residents and 450-year East-meets-West tradition has had a dramatic impact. GDP growth last year ran 28%, including an insane 49.4% in the second quarter, distorted by the impact of severe acute respiratory syndrome (SARS), which had misleadingly depressed the numbers for previous years. But Macau's 2003 GDP growth was 14.2%, so SARS didn't bring things to a complete halt. This year's growth will come in just under 10%. Unemployment has fallen from 7.1% in 2002 to 4.1% today, and it's still dropping, as construction continues and more hotels and casinos come on-line and start hiring.

Thousands of expatriates will come because Macau's labour pool does not have the skills needed for all the new resorts. That's most evident in the dearth of hotel and casino personnel comfortable with English. A pit boss who explained Caribbean Stud Poker to me turned out to be from Malaysia, a veteran of the Genting gambling resort outside Kuala Lumpur, lured to Macau on a lucrative contract.

There's also concern that the economy remains largely in overseas hands. Casino tycoon Ho is a Hong Kong resident and the other gambling licensees are also from outside Macau. Hong Kong firms dominate construction (and, increasingly, property sales) with some specialists imported from as far as Australia. It may be possible to take advantage of these international firms by enlisting them in local training programmes, including mentoring by executives for government and private sector and making their professional development programmes available to all locals – or at least showing Macau the training models to follow.

The government should be applauded for recently establishing a quality of life task force to step back and look at the big picture. There are also efforts to preserve Macau's unique legacy. The World Heritage List was a good first step, but the surrounding areas need protection, not just the monument. The Chinese Government in Beijing recognize the value in emphasizing and promoting the idea that Macau is different. Preservation is a challenge because space is at a premium. Macau measured 17.7 square kilometres in the 1980s and has added nearly 10 square kilometres since then. Reclamation is nearing its practical limit, and there's even talk of expanding to the mainland's Hangqin Island if demand for resort sites continues to grow.

Residential real estate prices have broken out of a decade-long slump, rising nearly 50% since 2003. Macau's income is about 57% of those in Hong Kong, but property prices are roughly 27%. Developers are hoping for an influx of expatriates as Cotai opens.

Other players in the gaming boom

Gaming in Asia is not only booming in Macau. Singapore approved two integrated resorts with casinos, to be built on Sentosa Island and a newly reclaimed area known as Marina Bayfront in 2005. Not to be outdone, the Philippines Amusement and Gaming Corporation (PAGCOR) has plans for a $15-billion project on reclaimed land in Manila Bay to rival Macau. Rafael Francisco, President of PAGCOR, said last year that he would like to speed up the project to catch up with Singapore and Thailand, which is planning an integrated resort at Khao Lak, near Phuket.

A major problem for the Philippines is the expiration of PAGCOR's charter in 2008. Investors would like to be assured that the government will extend PAGCOR's charter beyond 2008. Negotiations are on hold until the Congress of the Philippines passes a bill extending PAGCOR's charter, probably for another 2 years. PAGCOR is mindful that neighbouring countries like Singapore have already announced their plans for casinos. They argue that if the bill is not acted on quickly by Congress, the government's master plan for developing gaming may not proceed as envisaged – especially if potential investors continue to look at neighbouring countries as an option.

There is no doubt that the economic miracle in Macau is predicated upon the presence and extension of gambling and it seems that the ethical arguments are being submerged under the economic priorities. There is certainly no attempt to transfer the universalist perspective from the mainland to the island (Plate 14).

Plate 14
Casinos and target
markets
Source: Author's
photograph

This casino is specifically targeting the Chinese community in Manchester, relying on the great interest amongst many Chinese people to gamble to make this business a success in the middle of a large English city.

Discussions of ethics began to appear in business literature as the nature of the business relationship was questioned. In a simple model of capitalist business relations, the company owes a responsibility to its backers, those with equity in the company in a financial sense and business performance will be judged by the rate of return on these investments. This narrow relationship was questioned when businesses were thought of in a wider setting, with responsibilities to their workers, the local communities and the environment. These discussions introduced a new term into the discussions with the emergence of the term stakeholder. The term was originally defined in Freeman's discussion of business ethics as "Any group or individual who can affect or is affected by the achievement of an organisation's objectives" (Freeman, 1984: 46). This means that the traditional business relationship with the shareholders had to be questioned as many of the people covered by this definition had no financial stake in the company. It means that the management have to prepare an account of the organization that does not just satisfy the financial demands of the shareholders but also the social demands of the stakeholders. The literature further makes a distinction between the strategic stakeholder – those concerned with realizing objectives inside the organization – and the moral stakeholder – where the emphasis is on balancing stakeholder interests often outside the organization (Frooman, 1999) (Figure 10.2).

Shareholders	Local residents	Governments and NGOs
Customers	Suppliers	Businesses (involved)
Employees	Competitors	Services

Figure 10.2
Stakeholder groups

Communication with shareholders was already well established and most organizations have channels to get feedback from customers and staff through surveys, focus groups and appraisals. We would argue that that the better-managed companies would be involved in a dialogue with most of these groups already.

It becomes clear whenever we list stakeholders that we cannot elaborate the full complexity of stakeholder claims in the international hospitality industry. However, rather than saying the term effectively includes everyone – as we are all affected by developments in hospitality and tourism – and reduce the concept's usefulness, we believe it is better to look at how we might approach the stakeholder. Mitchell et al. (1997) suggested three dimensions of stakeholder salience:

1 the power that a stakeholder group is perceived to hold;
2 the legitimacy that the stakeholder group is thought to have;
3 the perceived urgency of the stakeholders' demands.

We would also highlight the activities of the non-governmental organizations (NGOs), where perhaps special attention needs to be focused on their role not only as stakeholders in their own right but also as organizers of stakeholders. Residents groups may be able to promote effective opposition to companies at a local level, but it is the rise of importance in NGOs that is most challenging as they can articulate these challenges at a higher level. As governments scale back activity in market economies, the NGOs are becoming the well-organized, effective and vociferous conscience of society, representing those least able to represent themselves. Many NGOs have adopted a posture of constructive engagement and dialogue with companies. True dialogue can often lead to creative and effective solutions that a company may not otherwise have seen.

■ Sense of place

We believe that for hospitality the stakeholders should include the local residents, the communities in which the business operates. Again most enlightened companies will have strong connections with the local community, corporately and individually through its employees. This is difficult to achieve when you are entering a new international market. A new hotel development may have the greatest direct impact by employing as many local people as possible, but through adopting a policy of local sourcing it may have a more far-reaching influence. Commissioning local artists and artisan products in the hotel, combined with offering local food and drink products, and promoting local musical and dance performances can all help to develop a stronger sense of local identification. This is a bonus for the local people but it may also benefit the traveller, as the visitors seem to increasingly welcome a "sense of place", something that the large brands will be challenged to offer but will increasingly have to accommodate.

■ Shades of green

We have followed the sustainability debates with great interest and some participation since the publication of the Bruntland Report, Our Common Future in 1987 which placed a sense of sustainability at the centre of discussions about development. Our work was largely tourism based at the time and many people seemed surprised that the question asked was not whether there should be sustainable tourism but whether there should be tourism at all – or where there more sustainable opportunities in different sectors. In practice tourism had a great deal to offer to all sorts of communities and the conversations could quickly move on to what sustainable tourism would mean for a particular region or destination. Sustainable tourism development was taken to be development that sensitively developed tourism in a region that would protect the social and environmental context for the next generation whilst making a viable return on the investment in tourism in the long term. The World Tourism Organization (1998) defined it as development that "meets the needs of present tourists and host regions while protecting and enhancing opportunities for the future. It is envisaged as leading to management of all resources in such a way that economic, social and aesthetic needs can be fulfilled while maintaining cultural integrity, essential ecological processes, biological diversity and life support systems".

Some definitions included the dimension of subsidiarity – moving decisions to the most local level possible and developing community participation. However, what usually happened was that the discussions focused almost exclusively on the environment and the economic, relegating the social and cultural to a minor role. Economic considerations were at the forefront as these were days when the economic power of tourism was first being acted upon. However, the environment gradually gained more recognition and concerns were expressed for the green environment and eventually it became possible to talk about the greening of the industry. Many questioned whether the concern was real or rhetorical and there were many shades of green in evidence in the industry. Murphy and Price (2005) summarize the history of the movement quite beautifully in their article, which includes this illustration (Figure 10.3).

Light green tendencies	Dark green tendencies
Advocate and strongly pro-adaptancy	Cautionary and knowledge based
Benefits of tourism assumed	Benefits of tourism must be demonstrated
Precious view of tourism as a sector and sectoral self-interest dominates	Tourism need not necessarily be a component of sustainable development in an area and sectoral integration required
Maintain tourism activity in existing destinations and expand into new ones	Widen economic base if high dependency on tourism and engage in full proactive assessment of new tourism development
Tourism products must be maintained and evolve according to market need (nature is a commodity)	Natural resources must be maintained and impacts reduced (preferably minimized) where possible with products tailored accordingly (nature has existence value)
Environmental action only when required and beneficial (i.e. legal obligation, to tackle specific problem, marketing benefit and cost saving)	Considered as a matter of routine
Narrow scope and geographical scale of environmental concern	Wide range of potential and actual impacts considered beyond immediate geographical setting (hotel, complex, destination area)
Disperse and dilute activity (spread)	Focus and concentrate activity (confine)
Industry self-regulation as the dominant management approach	Wide range of management approaches and instruments required
Introspective focus on tourism research and management literature	More likely to re-invent the wheel
Most likely to have a direct involvement in the industry	Most likely to have a training in an environment-type academic discipline

Figure 10.3
A continuum of commitments to sustainability
Source: Murphy and Price (2005: 177)

The debates have moved on with significant contributions from both the governments and the industry. It is now recognized that the hospitality industry has played a part in promoting the recognition of the environmental aspects of sustainability but is lagging behind in thinking through and operationalizing the economic and socio-cultural aspects.

■ Sustainable development

We normally work with the theoretical model of sustainable tourism which we now depict as a three-legged stool (Figure 10.4).

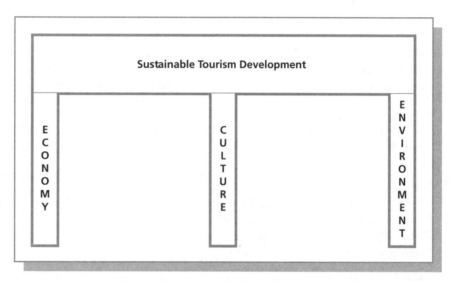

Figure 10.4
The interconnections of sustainable tourism development

The sustainability depends upon the equivalence in the three aspects being maintained, any distortion leads to the stool tipping over. This creates a metaphor that works for us!

Other industries have been quick to address such issues. Leading firms such as Shell and BP have adopted management system approaches to tackle the difficulties of being a sustainability friendly operator. In the hotel industry, it seems that we are lagging behind best practice in other sectors. The leading brands have begun to embrace a more sustainable approach, but for the vast majority of the hospitality industry there is still much work to be done about basic environmental management issues let alone the intangible issues associated with sustainability.

Sound environmental policies are intimately linked with operational quality in order for a business to be sustainable economically as well as environmentally and socially. Emerging integrated management system methodology enables hotel operators to address quality, environmental and all management issues under one management framework. The model has been constantly redrawn and re-specified, but the one offered by the TTI combines our essential elements with the business lessons to be drawn from them (Figure 10.5).

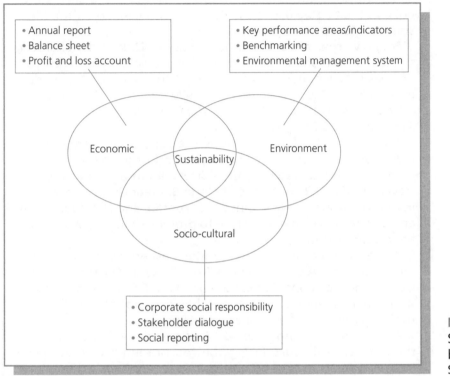

Figure 10.5
Sustainability in business terms
Source: TTI

■ Social and cultural issues and stakeholder dialogue

Addressing social and cultural issues has always proved less easy to capture in a traditional management system approach than the other elements. How operators deal with these factors should vary with the constituency or stakeholder group in the locations. Handling all people with respect and dignity is a prerequisite, but allowing time for inviting and sharing opinions may have to be built into management thinking, organizational structures and operating budgets.

Example: The good, bad and ugly of responsible tourism

04 August 2006, 1:59 AM
   Yeoh Siew Hoon sat in a cold, brightly lit conference room in Singapore this week and was made to feel a little uncomfortable with the experience.

In the movie "Thank You For Smoking", there's a scene where three spin-doctors discuss how difficult their respective jobs are.

Nick Naylor represents the tobacco industry, Polly Bailey alcohol and Bobby Day Bliss guns. Together, they make up the MOD Squad – Merchants of Death.

Polly is worried about being kidnapped but Nick scoffs at her fear, saying if anyone should be kidnapped, it should be him. "Tobacco", he boasts, "generates a little more heat than alcohol. My product puts away 475,000 people a year, 435,000 tops, that's 1,200 a day".

He mocks his friends. Alcohol? 100,000 a year tops, 270 a day. And guns? 11,000 a year, 30 a day.

"Excuse me if I don't exactly see terrorists get excited about kidnapping someone from the alcohol industry", he says.

So there I was, watching the CSR Squad in action at the first travel-specific CSR conference held in Singapore this week. CSR, in case you don't know, stands for Corporate Social Responsibility and it's the new spin being given to promote a company's corporate profile as good citizens.

It's becoming a headline issue of late, especially in the spate of movies such as "An Inconvenient Truth", "Who Killed The Electric Car", "The Constant Gardener" or "Fast Food Nation", all of which take on, in one form or another, corporations profiteering to the detriment of the planet and its people.

According to the organizers, CSR Asia, and speakers, it is one of the most critical issues facing the tourism industry – the need for travel companies to become more responsible citizens and to be accountable to the triple bottom line, financial, social and environmental.

Yet, as Dr Harold Goodwin of the International Centre for Responsible Tourism observed, no one is responsible because tourism involves too many "freeloaders" and too many stakeholders.

Quoting Sir Colin Marshall, who said that tourism was essentially the renting out of other people's environments, Dr Goodwin asked, "What do you do about the freeloaders? We have 1% to 3% who deal with the issues, the rest get away with it".

"Whose responsibility is it? Everybody's and nobody's".

The irony of sitting in a brightly lit, freezing air-conditioned meeting room with no natural daylight coming in was also not lost on the outspoken doctor. "Who's going to take responsibility? For example, does it have to be so bright and does it have to be so cold in here? We need to ask these questions – especially by people talking about CSR".

The speakers gathered for the conference meanwhile all shared what each was doing in the field of CSR. Lyndall De Marco, Executive Director of IBLF – The Tourism Partnership, called it a "quiet revolution".

"Guests are making it an issue as well as shareholders. Banks are asking, where is my money going? Is it being used to do good or bad?"

CSR, she said, can be a point of difference for companies. "Who are the good guys? Who are the bad guys?"

Well, at this conference, it was obvious that everyone who was there was good. In the session I attended, Cathay Pacific shared its commitment to protecting the environment, saying it recognized the issue of fuel emissions as a political hot potato and Intrepid Travel talked about its Responsible Tourism philosophy.

Michael Ma of Indochine Winebar and Restaurants, said his outlets did not serve shark's fin soup, blue and yellow fin tuna, and caviar and sturgeon from Iran and Russia. "Don't eat shark's fin soup", he urged his audience.

So where were the bad guys? Out there, I suppose. And the freeloaders? Also out there. And oh yes, China, the biggest market yet to come to a travel cinema near you? What are the good guys doing to engage China's travel industry on CSR?

De Marco confessed, "Very little, I am afraid, at the moment although we are trying. We are only three or four people and we have to cover the world".

See, it's just like in the movies. The bad guys always outnumber the good guys. Except in the movies, one good guy can kill hundreds of bad guys at the same time.

In real life, yes, the CSR Travel conference is a great start for all companies, big and small, to take heed. There are however no quick, happy endings in sight.

■ Corporate sustainability

Moon and Bonny (2001) highlight a number of changes within the world economy that are leading many major international organizations to adopt more ethical practices. Specifically, they suggest that technological innovation, globalization, the importance of intangible assets, the competition for talent and the growing use of economic networks are leading to changes towards more ethical practices. In these circumstances, they advocate an approach to business management which depends on forging business relationships with key stakeholder groups. Increasingly, business organizations are suggesting that a more stakeholder model of the firm, and ethical practice in relationships with customers, employees and suppliers, is a more sustainable approach to business management (Trevino and Nelson, 1999; Moon and Bonny, 2001). Ethical business practice is now seen as an essential element in building strong competitive advantage, because it reinforces loyalties that are difficult to copy. The values that were developed by the sustainable development campaigners have now found a home in the board rooms. As a service industry, the hospitality industry can be said to be relatively clean compared to other sectors. Hence there has been little specific government legislation enacted to stimulate action or enforce standards onto the industry, so most of the programmes put in place have been voluntary. Not all aspects of the hospitality industry are in the same position as this example from the fast food debate makes clear.

ACTIVITY **Accepting or understanding social responsibility**

Elkington (2001) was the first to use the phrase "triple bottom line" in exploring how the environmental agenda has evolved into a broader sustainable development programme, which takes the social impact of businesses into account. In other words, businesses are increasingly judged against the "triple bottom line" – that is their ability to deliver profit, to contribute to environmental preservation, and to act in accordance with social justice. Accounting for one's impact on the environment and on society is more than being accountable to shareholders, but to a broader constituency of stakeholders. He identifies the core issue as the need "to turn conventional business thinking" on its head and to change "attitudes, values and approach".

Do you think this is what has happened or do you believe organizations are accepting the triple bottom line because it is simply an extension of the single bottom line they know and understand?

■ A question of responsibility

Eat This, Don't Eat That: Who Controls What We Consume?

Example: A lawsuit against KFC raises issues about foods that aren't good for us

By Bharathi Radhakrishnan, ABC News Medical Unit

14 June 2006: The news that KFC is being sued for the fat levels in its fried chicken raises an important question: Should legal and government entities try to limit what Americans eat?

A non-scientific ballot on ABCNEWS.com suggests most Americans have a free-will mind-set. Asked if KFC should offer more healthy options by changing its menu items, 2,652 readers voted that KFC should be left alone while 951 voted that the menu needs to be changed. The results are current as of 3 PM. Wednesday. **Vote** in our new poll here: **Trans Fats Regulations?**

Yet trans fat – found in high quantities in KFC's chicken – is linked to a lot of dangerous health problems, argues the Center for Science in the Public Interest, which sued the fast food chain. People need to know this, the Center says.

But many people disagree, saying legal procedures do little to truly educate the public, not to mention that singling out fat content does little to help people understand what makes food healthy or unhealthy.

"I don't think you can legislate these kinds of things, because this is an issue of choice", said Madelyn Fernstrom, Director of the Weight Management Center at the University of Pittsburgh Medical Center. "You need to label foods' content so people can limit their quantity of it. Labelling food as 'bad' is not as important as paying attention to portion control".

She and others support educating the public about healthy food choices, such as using food-warning labels.

"The consumer has a right to know what is in the food they choose to buy", said Conrad Earnest, director of the Center for Human Performance and Nutrition Research at the Cooper Institute. "That said [I am] strongly in favour of having KFC products and others like it labelled accordingly". Earnest suggests labelling fast food items that contain trans fatty acids with a certain symbol next to it on the menu. He stated that ultimately such labelling would fall within the hands of the federal Food and Drug Administration.

While this may help to educate consumers, singling out trans fats could gloss over other important health issues when it comes to eating.

The fast food sector is a good example of how companies will have to work hard not simply to develop products and services but also to present them within an acceptable social climate.

Moon and Bonny say (2001: 17), "In the new economy the ability to forge relationships with diverse stakeholders, including employees, customers, suppliers, pressure groups and opinion setters is crucial. How they perceive a business and what they say about it has a direct impact on its reputation, success and, ultimately, its share price". They argue that positive reputation is best understood as the goodwill of all stakeholders, and the process of understanding stakeholder perspectives and views is fundamental to being able to manage reputation in a way that minimizes the risk of damage (Moon and Bonny, 2002).

■ Definition

It is important to understand the meaning of corporate sustainability, as defined by the Dow Jones Sustainability Group Index, because it is this that is being developed in the organizations. It is a business approach to create long-term shareholder value by embracing opportunities and managing risks deriving from economic, environmental and social developments. You will recognize the basic elements of the definition but the focus has been shifted from communities to shareholders. However, this creates the so-called "triple bottom line" approach that businesses across all sectors are now exploring and claiming to be enlightened. As a result, sustainability can be analysed from the point of view of its three inter-related component parts – economic, environmental and social but in the terms of a business analysis rather than an ethical one.

■ Economic

The economic perspective is the one that businesses are most familiar with. Over the years, companies have developed a whole range of tools to measure and report on their activities. Definitions can still vary (profits, for instance), but globalization has applied pressures on businesses to agree an accepted body of rules and the production of comparable figures. For example, accounting standards have been developed to bring a uniform approach to reporting through the balance sheet and profit and loss account. The financial tools are now being applied to wider aspects of business performance as ways are sought to cost the environmental and social impacts of the businesses.

■ Environmental

Environmental factors were identified by Agenda 21 as some of the "key performance areas" and having identified the aspects that need to be managed, they can be made more real, especially for those only used to thinking in economic terms, by assigning monetary values to each area. These highlight the specific impacts that should be taken into account by companies. The concerns are no longer abstract but become closely linked to issues that have a bearing on the businesses' profit and loss accounts, for instance water consumption and energy usage. Methods have now been sufficiently developed over the years to analyse associated costs by breaking them down into a series of "key performance indicators". Thus instead of looking at the energy bill in total, it is more meaningful to assess energy consumption by department or guest night.

The results can then be compared to previous periods, or against other properties in a "benchmarking" exercise, to indicate how the company is performing. In this way, the management of energy is aided by tracking usage against key denominators, and by comparing and contrasting experience in different locations or at different times. Once a way to start measuring something has been developed, it usually becomes more possible to have control over the area. Benchmarking tools have been developed for hotels by Green Globe and the International Hotels Environmental Initiative (IHEI).

Case: The Benefits of Sustainability ... Well the Environment At least!

Environmental performance will increasingly affect hotel competitiveness becoming a core component of corporate reputation. A good image will go beyond public relations and branding and have to be supported by solid evidence of good practice. In the case of the environment, good practice is aligned with good housekeeping and operating efficiencies, which can lead to significant cost savings, customer loyalty, investor interest, and contented and motivated employees.

Scandic, now part of the Hilton Group, has reported that its environmental programme has generated cost savings of more than US $2 million since its inception in the mid-1990s. The Marriott Manchester Hotel, Golf & Country Club completely turned around local opposition to its planning application and now enjoys a highly motivated and loyal staff as a result of pursuing its environmental management activities with Green Globe. It subsequently generated savings of over £60,000 in utilities between 1999 and 2000.

There is a growing case history of financial savings enjoyed by operators as a result of environmental initiatives and the message is starting to spread. Payback times are often under 1 year for specific initiatives, but many of the benefits cannot be quantified so easily although clearly there are intangible and non-financial benefits to be captured.

If the impact of positive action is advantageous on the cost side, there are also benefits to be gained on the revenue side, by attracting the growing number of concerned travellers who take the environment into account when making their travel purchases. Studies such as those by MORI (UK, 1998) and the Tear Fund (UK, 2000) indicate that for at least 55% of travellers it is one of the factors they take into account and rising in importance.

Having taken the trouble to implement an environmental management system and move towards a sustainable business, there is a wide range of voluntary certification schemes to give independent verification and recognition of your achievements, which can be used to signal your environmental credentials to all stakeholders especially consumers. Generic schemes, such as ISO14000 are being pursued within the industry, but more importantly, industry-specific schemes are also growing in popularity. Green Globe, for instance, offers a sustainable travel and tourism system enabling companies and destinations to progress from initial awareness and learning through benchmarking and systems implementation to full certification.

Social

Where there has been great progress in breaking down the environmental into manageable pieces for organizations to handle, the third element of sustainability, the social and cultural issues, has not been so fortunate. It has proved more difficult to develop an easily adopted approach to measure business impacts. It has been recognized that the social and cultural issues are important as they cover the wide range of actual and potential impacts upon the organization's stakeholders. The rise in attention given to "CSR" reflects the importance given to the need for this wider perspective, but there has been no general agreement on a costing that could be applied.

We considered the challenges to the fast food sector in Chapter 9 on the hospitality environment but we did not directly address the sector's response. Here we would ask you to consider the ethical stance being developed.

Example: McDonald's CEO decries fast food "fiction"

By Dave Carpenter, AP Business Writer 25 May 2006

Chicago: McDonald's Corp. CEO Jim Skinner told shareholders Thursday not to believe the recent surge of "fiction" maligning fast food and pledged that the company will be more aggressive and creative in setting the record straight.

Skinner's comments at the fast food chain's annual meeting were the strongest evidence yet of its initiative to counter negative publicity from a new children's book and soon-to-be-released movie, both associated with the 2001 book *Fast Food Nation*.

"These days, big equals bad", he said at the meeting at McDonald's headquarters in Oak Brook, IL. "And fiction some-how has become more compelling than fact. You have every rea-son to be proud of your company, our values and our social responsibility record".

Skinner said McDonald's is a leader in food safety and quality, toy safety, employment opportunity, training and development, charitable giving, animal welfare and the environment.

"Fictitious information irresponsibly published and reported in the media has people questioning the quality and safety of fast food in general", he said. "But at McDonald's, we work closely with our suppliers to develop and implement the highest stand-ards, and have for over 50 years".

Concerns about the nutritional content of fast food have risen in recent years along with obesity rates among both children and adults. McDonald's has responded to complaints by consumer advocates to make its food healthier by offering more salads and fruit items and other menu options.

But that pressure has stepped up in 2006 with the publication of *Chew On This*, co-written by *Fast Food Nation* author Eric Schlosser, and publicity about the upcoming film version of *Fast Food Nation*. The book adds to criticism of the fast food industry for its perceived role in increased obesity and views McDonald's and the industry harshly on the issues of food safety and employ-ment security, among others.

The company said last month it would "ramp up" promotion of its healthier menu choices in response to the new book, taking a more active tack than it did following the 2004 documentary, "Super Size Me", which skewered the fast food business.

"We are committed to taking action that will most impact con-sumer perception and trust. And we will be more aggressive and cre-ative in setting the record straight", said Skinner, who then showed a company podcast touting it as a leader in food quality safety.

A farm worker and a human rights activist assailed the com-pany at the meeting for running a public relations campaign instead of addressing what they called a human rights crisis in the tomato fields of Florida.

"The workers who pick the tomatoes that go on McDonald's sandwiches and salads work under conditions that can only be described as sweatshops – poverty wages, no overtime pay, no right to organize and no benefits", said Lucas Benitez, co-founder of the Coalition of Immokalee Workers in Southwest Florida.

Skinner responded that McDonald's has worked closely with its suppliers to maintain the highest standards for its workers and will continue to do so.

Shareholders voted in favour of a resolution urging the McDonald's board of directors to seek shareholder approval of any severance agreements with senior executives that would reward them with sums triple or more the combined size of their base pay plus bonus – payments widely known as "golden parachutes". Chairman Andrew McKenna said the board would consider the recommendation.

The shareholders rejected a resolution asking McDonald's to identify and label all genetically engineered ingredients in its products.

McDonald's shares rose 31 cents to close at $33.26 on the New York Stock Exchange. They are down 1.4% in 2006.

■ What's happening in the hotel industry?

In travel and tourism, there have been many excellent initiatives and some considerable progress made, but we cannot say that environmental, let alone sustainable friendly practices are widespread in any sort of comprehensive or systematic way in the hospitality industry. Recent research undertaken by Agenda 21 and Green Globe with ISHC, the International Society of Hospitality Consultants, revealed that the main motivations to move towards sustainability were finely balanced between proactive and defensive measures – concern for the environment being matched by fear of regulatory compliance (Table 10.1).

Table 10.1 Main motivations for action with regard to sustainability

	Yes	No
Regulatory compliance	72%	28%
Concern for the environment	71%	29%
Good public relations	71%	2%
Cost containment	58%	42%
Risk management	46%	54%

Source: International Society of Hospitality Consultants (2005)

The top three issues addressed were:

1 energy management;
2 social and cultural issues;
3 land use planning.

As we have seen above energy is no surprise, being one of the largest non-staff cost items on a hotel's profit and loss account, but we would have expected water and waste to feature more highly. Given the heavy focus on hotel development of many of the respondents, the presence of land use planning is not really a surprise, but the import-ance of social and cultural issues was an unexpected bonus. In the last decade, the impact of activities on the local population has, quite rightly, risen greatly in importance, with a strong linkage to the growing awareness of this cornerstone of sustainability and CSR and the concern to find solutions to the measurement issues.

The PricewaterhouseCoopers research into the leading hotel brands established that nine of the ten leading hotel companies had an environmental policy, but only one was externally verified. Only four had a formal environmental management system, with another one planned. All 10 companies were recorded as engaging in stakeholder dialogue, in the sense of communicating their environmental activities. Almost all published their activities on their websites, in annual reports or separate environmental reports. They also engage with their customers through posters in their rooms and with staff through bulletins. Four published separate environmental reports, with two others planning to do so. We would question how far this was a dialogue as the examples cited demonstrate only a one-way communications model.

■ The drivers for positive action

The research by PricewaterhouseCoopers identified a series of drivers for improved environmental and social management in the hotel sector. These were categorized as internal and external drivers (Figure 10.6).

Figure 10.6
Drivers for improved environmental and social management
Source: Adapted from a table in Pricewaterhouse Coopers, Hospitality Directions – Europe Edition, July, 2001a

Internal drivers	External drivers
Maximization of shareholder value	Investor requirement
Minimizing risk and liability	Regulation
Direct cost savings	Industry bodies promoting best practice
Enhancing brand and customer loyalty	Consumer and employee expectations

■ The future of sustainability

We can see a concern emerging that complicates the positive examples we have been reviewing. Many companies have already committed to a quality management system, or a health and safety management system, and we fear that the additional burden of implementing an environmental management system could then be seen as a luxury that may be postponed to an unspecified future date. This is especially true if the business case for sound environmental management has not been effectively communicated throughout all the levels of the industry. The same fear is compounded in looking at the social and cultural issues which are less well developed.

However, we can see that one of the latest developments in the industry is the integration of management systems, which offers the ability to capture and manage all the key issues that management wishes to address in one system, be it compliance with legislation or external standards, or internal factors, such as quality. The methodology is now becoming available in the hotel sector and is applicable to any size of business. It allows good environmental practices and social policies to be linked with quality and business improvement, thus addressing the core issues of a company's operations within the operation of one system.

■ Social reporting

It has become popular for companies to issue environmental reports as part of their annual summaries and these are seen to be an excellent means for self-appraisal and measuring results (not to mention self-promotion!). Environmental reporting has been joined by social reporting, in an attempt to address the needs of a sound stakeholder dialogue. The danger, though, is that they become a public relations event, creating a one-way monologue. Where what would really be needed is an effective and systematic way for organizations to listen to views from other stakeholders – this could be simply put in business terms as the creation of an enhanced corporate research function to gauge views from the broader society or adopting the language of sustainability organizations could seek to involve their stakeholders in an open dialogue.

We are convinced that considerable improvements in organizational performance are possible, but it requires a high level of commitment from the senior management commitment within the organization and a consistency of approach that demonstrates that this is a core value of the organization's culture. We can demonstrate that environmental management has often driven by junior employees, but the way in which a company interfaces with the society in which it operates has to be set by the senior management, who must lead by example. In the final analysis, sustainability is affected by and impacts all areas of the operation and so should be addressed at the most senior level with a commitment from all top management that can filter down through the organization with the concomitant allocation of the appropriate resources. We believe that sustainability demands a holistic and integrated approach to business, with anything less all the efforts would appear shallow and insincere and may even have a negative impact on the company's reputation and brand loyalty of the organization.

■ Sustainable business value

We would support those who have looked to ground the concept of sustainability within the language and frameworks of business cultures. As we have argued the concept of sustainability involves taking a long-term holistic view of business decisions, in which the impacts on all stakeholders are taken into account so as to build sustainable business value (i.e. maximizing profits and shareholder value in the long term). This can be visualized in the diagram developed by PricewaterhouseCoopers, which highlights the range of areas with which management has to be concerned (Figure 10.7).

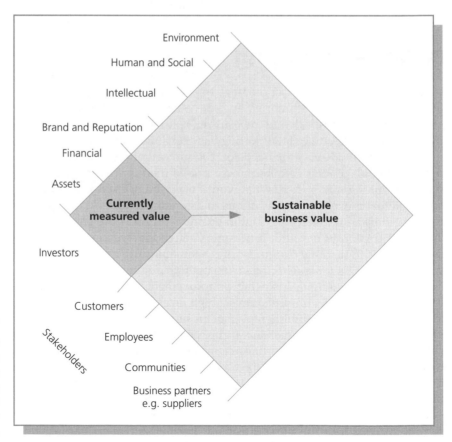

Figure 10.7
Building sustainable business value
Source:
Pricewaterhouse Coopers, New Europe and the Hospitality Industry (2001b).

These arguments can be taken further as the value models become more sophisticated and refined. Moon and Bonny advocated a model which they called "Value Dynamics" as a means of representing the holistic nature of business comprising an assortment of tangible and intangible assets. Most organizations, in line with traditional business reporting techniques tend to include only physical assets and financial resources in their balance sheets. The Value Dynamics model suggests that intangible assets are important aspects of total company value, and that these should be used to calculate worth. Traditional indicators of company assets are listed on the left hand side of the diagram whilst intangible assets measuring the value of the organizations business relationships are listed on the left (Figure 10.8).

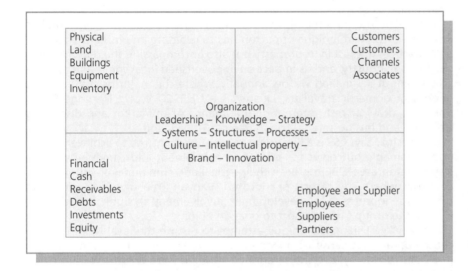

Figure 10.8
Value Dynamics: asset relationships. Source: Moon and Bonny (2001: 18)

Value Dynamics provides a model that could be used to build a business case for stakeholder evaluation of hospitality organizations. It shows how stakeholders link with both tangible and intangible assets and suggests that successful organizations are likely to be the ones that manage the relationships between the range of assets most effectively. Clearly shareholders and other equity stakeholders invest money expecting a level of return on their investment in the form of dividends and asset growth. The value of the shareholder investment will in part be enhanced by levels of customer satisfaction which result in improved reputation, willingness to return and recommendations to other potential customers. Shareholder value will also improve if the relationship with employees results in increased satisfaction and reduced staff turnover. This latter cost can be quite considerable, though rarely accounted for in hospitality organizations. Improved retention of staff also improves the human capital that individuals accrue through increased knowledge of their jobs and customers. Improved links with suppliers can further add to business value as process are more robust, and the reputation of the organization is enhanced as a fair business partner, and prompt payer for good supplied.

An addition to this model has been suggested, with the inclusion of the concern for the value of good community relationships that also add to the value of the business, through an improved public relations profile.

ACTIVITY Read through the following case study and attempt to apply the value dynamics model to the example. This will require you to think about what the aims of the Banyan Tree were and how they can claim the value of their actions.

Banyan Tree Lijiang Promotes CSR

2 November 2006

As the first international resort to operate in Lijiang, Banyan Tree Hotels & Resorts is faced with unique opportunities to promote and integrate sustainable practices not just in its property but also encompassing the region's thriving tourism industry, and its impact on impoverished local communities.

With about 3.5 million visitors annually, where the majority of visitors are budget or domestic travellers, Lijiang as a UNESCO World Heritage Site is poised to draw a fresh international audience of upmarket and discerning travellers and businessmen through Banyan Tree Lijiang.

Banyan Tree says CSR is a key brand value of Banyan Tree to achieve positive and sustainable outcomes for business, environment and community issues. Having integrated CSR into both the physical and communal environment in countries where the resorts are located, Banyan Tree says it continues to reflect its rigorous social development involvement through Banyan Tree Lijiang, the group's latest resort to open in China.

Banyan Tree Lijiang is a unique attempt to restate the local Naxi style in a contemporary, yet sensitive, manner. Working closely with Urban Planning and Construction bylaws, the exterior of the villas were constructed with local materials, such as exotic pink stone and grey Naxi bricks that proved weather-resistant and energy efficient. All natural materials including pine, teak and traditional red clay roof tiles sourced from local kilns lend authenticity to the recreation of a Naxi village in a resort setting.

Banyan Tree Lijiang has also implemented human resource policies to reinforce its cultural and social commitments. Of the more than 200 full-time associates that are employed by Banyan Tree Lijiang, 67% are local residents from Yunnan, where 28% are from the local minority communities. Associates enjoy worker-welfare programmes, such as English improvement courses, dedicated transportation and suitable accommodation options.

In nearby villages, Banyan Tree has implemented community projects, providing infrastructure, including electrical wiring and water piping to families of Geino Village and Xiya Village, students at the Lanbao Primary School, residents of the Tibet Hospital of Diqing Prefecture and monks at Da Bao Si Monastery. Another beneficiary is Lijiang Ethnic Orphanage, which received upgraded facilities, such as beds, water tanks, solar water heaters and safety features, in addition to 500 books donated by Banyan Tree guests.

Banyan Tree Lijiang was also instrumental in a charity fundraising event, the Walk For Chalk Shangri-La 2006, a project organized by the Chi Heng Foundation in support of AIDS orphans in rural China. Banyan Tree's sponsorship of accommodation and meal package valued at US$35,000 enabled the

Chi Heng Foundation to raise over US $250,000 for the children's schooling and welfare needs.

To encourage more qualified tourism professionals from the local communities, Banyan Tree has launched a new scholarship programme at the Lijiang Cultural & Tourism University. Five scholarships will be awarded to promising students from Lijiang annually.

Some of the positive initiatives that are being taken operate out with the traditional boundaries of the companies themselves, but are looking to deliver social benefit to local communities. Prêt a Manger distribute their unsold sandwiches to homeless communities and this example demonstrates the work of a hotel group.

Chapter case study: The Best Western for a Better World

The Best Western for a Better World (BWBW) initiative is a multifaceted community service programme which was introduced in 1992 and was founded by members Richard Watson and former Director Calvin Howe together with the executive team in Phoenix. In 2001 the project helped with the clean-up project after the atrocity of September 11th, Best Western staff joined others in Boston to clean up the Long Island area and re-decorate a homeless shelter.

After the Tsunami struck last winter Best Western committed funds to help the region recover, the company pledged $1 million with an instant contribution of $100,000 given to Habitat for Humanity International – a Christian ministry committed to eradicate poor quality housing. Since then the company has enabled its guests to donate money via their website and encouraged its member hotels to give $3.00 per room sold to the appeal. Twenty per cent of the funds raised are to be used for Best Western employees and their families who were affected by the tsunami, the remaining 80% to go towards rebuilding the area. Two Best Western hotels were directly affected by the disaster, the Best Western Premier Bangkok Hotel & Spa in Phuket and the Best Western Palm Galleria in Phang Nga. Kong gave his condolences for the people affected by the Tsunami, he states "Best Western has a growing presence in Indonesia, Thailand and India, and we see it as our responsibility to help the local communities in times of need" (www.bestwestern.com/newsroom, 2005).

Since the programme started the company has brought aid to areas of the former Soviet republics of Armenia, Belarus and Russia. Best Western is committed to helping communities around the globe when disaster strikes and it can be said that they are a socially responsible organization and they do take humanitarian efforts seriously. It is important for large firms today to be seen as supporting local communities and to dissuade their guests from thinking they are a large corporate hardhearted multinational company.

■ Conclusion

We have demonstrated how the concept of ethics has come into the corporate world of international hospitality management, by looking at how social and corporate responsibilities link to the basic ethical frameworks. There are deontologists and consequentialists debating the future of the industry, without, for the most part, recognizing the ethical underpinning of their arguments.

The popularity of social responsibility has taken a very long time to establish and the development of a positive climate for the adoption of sustainable policies took a great deal of effort. The virtues of such claims were not obvious to the businesses in the industry and the concepts did not appear to translate into the financial account. However, with better management systems and more transparent costing systems, it is possible to demonstrate that there are financial as well as social benefits to companies in operating sustainably. It has become an important part of the recognition given to social responsibility that the intangible costs and benefits surrounding people, local cultures and communities have also been fully recognized even where they cannot be fully measured.

■ Review questions

1 Are business ethics universal or contextual in international hospitality management?
2 Can you apply the same ethical code in China, Cuba, the Maldives, the USA and the Yemen? Explain your thinking.
3 Has sustainability sold out? Has it lost credibility by adapting to business thinking or gained greater currency?
4 How far is CSR a motivator for positive actions in local communities?

CHAPTER 11

The analysis of international hospitality management

After working through this chapter, you should be able to:

- Understand the concept of international hospitality management
- Recognize the analytical elements of international management and how they are applied in international hospitality management
- Critically analyse international hospitality organizations and their developments

■ Introduction

This chapter has been designed to be an integrative and reflective rehearsal of what we said in this book. We want to take one major case and demonstrate how the concepts we have introduced in the previous 10 chapters come together to produce a critical analysis of developments in international hospitality. It has been the most challenging for us as we have had to ensure that we have addressed the key issues we developed in the previous 120,000 words! However, if we return to our model we can see a framework for the analysis in Figure 11.1.

Our analysis will utilize this structure by examining the analytical position and the functional approaches to the core management areas as we outlined them in this book. We have selected the Disney Company as our case for two very good reasons. Firstly there is a great deal of relevant material about the company readily available in published and web-based formats. This means it is possible to read into the official version of the company with the insights gained from our consideration of the theoretical frameworks of international management. Secondly, there could not be a better example for our final analysis. The whole multinational enterprise started with the entrepreneurial flair of one ambitious man and a series of ideas for cartoons. Despite the disappointment of losing the rights to his first major character – Oswald the Lucky rabbit, Disney went on to take over the world with Mickey Mouse and his friends. So great was the success that some of the writings on globalization refer not to McDonald's but to the Disneyfication effect on world culture.

We will present some of the material available to you in this chapter but will refer you to our website and Disney's own if you are seeking further information or more details. You will be led through the areas we have developed in this book, but we are not going to do all of the work for you. As you read through the sections, you can also construct a more complex narrative as you draw out the interconnections between the different facets of management and the operating environment. We have left it to you to make those connections as the argument would become very repetitive if we reiterated the same points over and over again. We are conscious that the idea of reinforcing and resisting forces is implicit in the account we offer but believe that in your reading you can place the factors into the correct

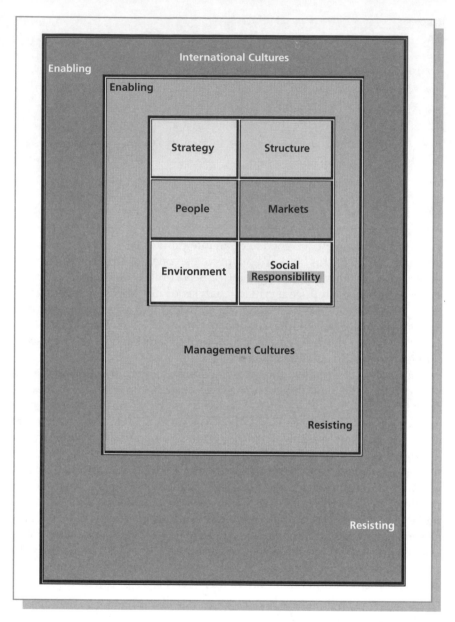

Enabling

Figure 11.1
The cultural
contexts of
International
Hospitality
Management

position analytically, even where we have not presented the full thought
through examination in the text.

Throughout this chapter we want to give you an insight into international hospitality management and how companies come to understand
their position within the industry. We will consider the reasons for Disney
seeking to expand their market, exploring the reasons behind the entrance
into the international market. You will recognize that this deals with both
internal and external factors. The Walt Disney Company and the various

operating companies it trades as, such as Euro Disney S.C.A, are used to demonstrate how a multinational company acts within the international market, as they give a concrete example of an American company entering the European and Asian markets on a large scale but in very different ways.

There were many factors that had to be considered when a company like Walt Disney wanted to enter into the international market and we will focus on Human Resources, showing how Disney uses Human Resource Management to overcome the problems of entering a new cultural environment; Corporate Social Responsibility (CSR) and how Disney managed cultural diversity and overcame what looked like cultural difference. Entering a new cultural environment is something Disney had to look at closely when moving their product into Europe, as it was not the same environment as they had experienced in North America. This report shows how Disney coped with moving their product successfully eventually, using types of diversity management.

■ Company overview

The Walt Disney Company and Euro Disney S.C.A

The Walt Disney Company was founded in 1923, by Walt Disney himself, and was based on story telling and entertainment experiences.

■ Company highlights on the theme parks

- The opening and success of the first theme park– *Disneyland*:
  Walt Disney Company had firm footing in movie-making. Trying to branch out, Walt Disney was intrigued by the idea of a new kind of park where parents and children could enjoy amusement together. In 1954 work began on the first Disneyland Theme Park in America, and 1 year later it opened its doors to the public in California on July 17th, 1955. By 1965, 10 years after the park opened 50 million people had visited Disneyland. Audio-Animatronics was introduced at Disneyland in the 1960s. Disneyland has set the standard for every major amusement park built since then (corporate.disney.go.com).
- The second Theme Park in Florida first with Resorts opened in 1971.
- Other Key Theme Parks opened continually after the first two's success, with EPCOT Center, on 1st October 1982, Tokyo Disneyland on 15 April 1983, Disney Paris in 1992 and the largest one – Animal Kingdom in 1998.
- Merchandising was introduced in park attractions in 1987.
- Disney's membership time-share ownerships were offered in park resorts since 1991, named the Vacation Club.

- Walt Disney World broadened its business; first Education in 1996, then Sports Training and Events, and fitness in 1997.
- Today, Walt Disney Parks and Resorts operates or licenses 11 theme parks on three continents (corporate.disney.go.com).

Disney's business has stretched from filming, theme park and resorts to merchandising, recording, network, broadcasting, education, sport and cruising, etc.

Today Disney is divided into four major international business segments: Studio Entertainment, Parks and Resorts, Consumer Products and Media Networks (Disney-online, 2005). Each area of the company works very closely together and they are all involved in the international market to some extent.

For 75 years Disney's goal has been to: "provide quality entertainment and a world of magic for the whole family." (www.godisney.com last accessed 3rd April 2005).

The Studio Entertainment is what Walt Disney created first back in 1923, and is based on animated features and live action motion pictures. Disney is involved with lots of other large international companies at this level:

- Miramax Films
- Touchstone Pictures
- Buena Vista Home Entertainment
- Hollywood Records

Source: Disney-Online (2005).

Disney Parks and Resorts is what the company is all about now, with eleven theme parks on three continents and a twelfth proposed for Shanghai. Disney also has thirty five hotels, mostly located on site at the theme parks around the world, two major large operating cruise ships and a host of other entertainment offerings. According to a poll in 2003, seven of Disney's Parks ranked inside the top ten most visited worldwide. (Disney-online, 2005).

Disney's consumer products began merchandising in 1929; they are now one of the largest licensers in the world (Disney-online, 2005), and Disney's publishing outfit is the world's number one children's publisher.

Disney media networks encompass a vast array of properties on television, cable, radio and the Internet. The American television station ABC is very closely linked to Disney, and of course they have their own selection of channels which can be viewed worldwide by millions of people (Plate 15).

Euro Disney S.C.A. operates Disneyland Resort Paris, which has become Europe's number one tourist destination. It all started in 1987 when a partnership between the French authorities and Disney was formed to bring a Disney Theme Park and Resort to the heart of Europe for the first time. Paris was chosen not only for its beauty and history, but also for its central location in Europe and ease of access by train, plane and cars. There were also helpful financial incentives available from regional and national governments who were keen to see the project as urban regeneration. Since the Paris Park opened in 1992, the Resort has welcomed

Plate 15
Disneyland Paris
Source: Author's
photograph

more than 140 million guests through the gates. (Euro Disney S.C.A online, 2005) The original deal to bring the multinational company Disney to France was drawn up between The French Government, The Walt Disney Company, The Seine et Marne Departmental Council, The Suburban Paris Transportation Authority (RATP) and the Public Planning Board for the new town Marne la Vallée. In April 1992 the new park opened its doors for the first time, and since then has continued under its owning and operating brand Euro Disney S.C.A even though it has changed its public name several times. Euro Disney was replaced on the 1st of October 1994 by Disneyland Paris, which in turn became the Disneyland Resort Paris on the 16th of March 2003. In 2002 the new extension to Disneyland Paris opened and was called the Walt Disney Studios, so with two theme parks, seven themed hotels and a 28-hole golf course, Disneyland Resort Paris officially became Europe's premier resort. To distinguish the developments Disneyland is now officially known as Disneyland Park Paris. The visitor figures go along way to proving that Disney is, in one sense, a true international company with the ability to bring its American product into Europe and succeed.

The international market

"Businesses today are competing in a world economy for survival, growth and profitability." (Jin-Lin Zhao and Katherine M. Merna, 1992) With this statement in mind it would be safe to assume that there is a great risk involved for any company/organization expanding into the international market. There have been many reasons for companies to expand into the international market, which have sprung both from one's that are internal to the company, or from external factors in the business environment. The figure based on Hamill (1997) and Otto (1993) shows internal and external factors that could be considered alongside proactive and reactive factors for the company when expanding into the international market (Figure 11.2).

	Proactive	Reactive
Internal	Managerial urge Growth and profit goals Economies of scale Offer a unique product Extension of service	Risk diversification
External	Foreign market opportunities Encouragement through change agents Shaping the competition	Small or declining home market Following the competition

Figure 11.2 International market expansion matrix

Using this type of analysis you can see why a company would want to enter the international market, even when there are high risks involved for the company.

■ The operating environment

Internal analysis

A competitive advantage of a company typically refers to their profitability above average. In Chapter 5 we introduced the Four Building Blocks of competitive advantage and here we would like to consider them in the context of Disney (Figure 11.3).

Source: Adapted from Hill and Jones (2004).

Strength

Disney achieved all the requirements outlined. As an established company, it accumulated over 50 years' experience of delivering excellent customer service as well as handling all the sudden changes that come from forces both outside and inside the organization. It also has numerous talented people loyal to it. You can see this from the Disney Legends (A special "Oscar" or "Nobel" Prize in Disney). The Disney organization itself is a tightly structured kingdom. Disney's cartoons exert great influence upon

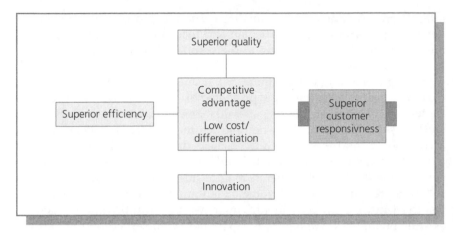

Figure 11.3
The Four Building Blocks of competitive advantage

the older generations, and its movies are well known for today's young-sters. Their TV and films are still acting upon today's children. Disney has become the synonym for magic and dreams which no one can resist. That, according to Disney, is the secret as to how Disney's Theme Parks can cater for both grandparents and grandchildren while hardly anyone else can do it.

Weakness

Disney's huge scale brings it disadvantages as well as benefits. Where the rights are too centralized, conflicts will occur between the board/president and the functional departments. However, if all rights are given to functional departments, there may be conflicts between departments and it is no good for strategic decision-making for the whole company. One part of the Disney empire: the Strategic Planning Department was broken down into the four business segments – Studio Entertainment, Parks and Resorts, Consumer Products and Media Networks in March 2005. The unified department had made many important decisions in the past to help the company conquer difficulties and bring it success. How this separation will affect Disney's future remains to be seen, but it may cause some disputes and communication problems.

25 March 2005 : The Walt Disney Company to reorganize strategic planning division

Burbank, CA, 25 March 2005 – To address today's rapidly evolving global business landscape, Michael D. Eisner, chief executive officer of The Walt Disney Company, and Robert A. Iger, President and Chief Operating Officer and CEO-elect, today announced a restructuring of the company's Corporate Strategic Planning Division. The division will be restructured to more closely align with the company's growth priorities, including creativity and innovation, new technologies and international expansion.

Many of Strategic Planning's activities will be incorporated into the company's four business segments – Studio Entertainment, Parks and Resorts, Consumer Products and Media Networks, as well as Disney's international organization. A smaller corporate group will continue to develop the corporate five-year plan and focus on acquisition opportunities, emerging businesses new to the company's existing portfolio and new technologies.

"Strategic planning will continue to play an important role in identifying the opportunities and challenges presented to our company as we grow our leadership position as the most valuable entertainment brand in the world," said Mr Iger. "This new structure will create efficiency with accountability and empower our business unit leaders in their ongoing efforts to create new, differentiated and compelling entertainment experiences that will ultimately generate long-term shareholder value."

"For more than 15 years, Strategic Planning has been an essential catalyst to Disney's growth by identifying new opportunities and expanding existing businesses. We have been extremely well-served by their efforts and now, the size, scope and dynamic nature of our individual businesses allow for this evolution," said Mr Eisner.

Peter E. Murphy will step down from his current role as senior executive vice president and chief strategic officer and will serve as a senior adviser to Mr Iger. Mr Murphy will advise the company on long-term strategic and technological trends affecting Disney and identify major growth opportunities.

"Peter's vast contributions during his tenure at Disney, particularly his leadership role in the acquisition of Capital Cities/ABC, helped transform Disney into a market-leading global media company," said Mr Iger. "His extensive experience and knowledge of our businesses, technology and strategy will continue to benefit The Walt Disney Company."

"Over the last 17 years, Peter's foresight and talent have played a major role in making Disney what it is today, from his role in transforming strategic acquisitions to the development of new technologies and franchise opportunities, these efforts will continue to benefit Disney shareholders well into the future," said Mr Eisner

Mr Murphy joined Disney's Corporate Strategic Planning Division in 1988, served as the Chief Financial Officer of ABC, Inc. after the Capital Cities acquisition, and was promoted to his current role in 1998. In addition to leading the acquisition of Capital Cities/ABC, Inc., Mr Murphy played an instrumental role in several company acquisitions, including Miramax Film Corporation, Disney's stakes in E! Entertainment Television and US Weekly Magazine, Fox Family Worldwide, Baby Einstein Corporation and the Muppets franchise.

Mr Murphy also aided in the expansion of Disney's cable television presence worldwide, as well as its broadband and wireless services. While in his current position, Mr Murphy also has overseen corporate brand management and new technology development.

Mr Murphy, 42, is a Phi Beta Kappa and honours graduate of Dartmouth College and the Wharton Graduate School of Business.

Contacts: Zenia Mucha 818-560-5300 Michelle Bergman 818-560-8231

www.corporate.disney.go.com/news/corporate/2005/2005_0325_reorg_stratplann.html

External analysis

Sector background

Since Disney opened the world's first theme park in the United States in 1955, its great success has attracted people to invest on theme parks around the world. As statistics showed, there had been 18 theme parks in the United States till 1980 and they had around 60,000,000 visitors annually. In China, over 60 theme park projects were proposed in Shenzhen city in the late 1980s. Although the number of theme parks is growing, Disney's numbers are still growing as seldom can others complete with Disney.

Main competitors

Universal Studios Theme Parks is the biggest competitor with Walt Disney's Theme Parks. The parks and resorts include Universal Studios Hollywood, Universal Orlando,

Universal Studios Florida, Islands of Adventure, the world's most technologically advanced theme park – as well as three luxury Loews Hotels Universal in Orlando. Nearby, Universal acquired Wet 'n Wild, a water park adjacent to the Universal Orlando property. Internationally, Universal Studios Japan in Osaka opened officially on 31 March 2001 and has become the most successful new theme park in history, breaking all-time attendance records by welcoming 11 million visitors in its first year. In December 2002 Universal announced plans to develop Universal Shanghai, a world-class theme park targeted for a 2006 grand opening in mainland China, aiming to compete with Disney's New Theme Park in Hong Kong (corpinfo.universalstudios.com).

PEST analysis

According to the "PEST" theory, the four factors that influence Disney's Theme Parks' external environment are shown in Figure 11.4.

The influences that the four factors may bring to Disney's Theme Parks are:

1 **Political**: 9/11 Issue has influenced the number of tourists coming into the USA. Surely it affected Disney's Theme Parks' business in the USA. After 9/11, the relationship between China and the United States begin to ease, which is a very good opportunity for enter into Chinese market, as it has been a huge interest for the company for long. Disney's decision to build its new theme park in Hong Kong has considered the accessibility and convenience to Hong Kong for Chinese mainland customers after Hong Kong's return to China.
2 **Economic**: Globalization and Merger and Acquisition trends enable Disney's Theme Parks to expand and combine various services together and accumulate all the best things into one theme park. The changes in the service sector and consumer's purchasing ability bring more potential customers to Disney's Theme Parks.

Political factors	Economic factors
9/11 Issue affected tourism. The relationship between the United States and China began to ease after 9/11 issue. Now (2004) it is the best period in the history of the relationship between the two nations. It gives great opportunity for business and for American Company to develop in China. (news.xinhuanet.com). Hong Kong's return to China promotes tourism and business between Hong Kong and mainland China.	Globalization is the most important trend of modern world. It accelerates the opportunities for international business. The percentage that service sectors have in the total economic activities continues to grow. By 2001, it was 52% in developing countries and 72% in developed countries. The competition in service sectors continues to be fierce. However, it reflects a further economic factor that people have more extra money to spend on leisure activities. Merger and Acquisition have become popular means for enterprises, especially international entities.
Social/demographic factors	**Technology factors**
Traditional moral values are awakened and stressed again by people in the United States. In China, people try to balance open culture which has been brought in with traditional worthwhile values. Aging populations with greater disposable income and higher levels of tourist literacy People care more about social responsibility. Green projects are popularized in all developed and many developing countries. Japanese are influenced heavily by American culture. French are sensitive of its own culture protection.	The fast development of Internet technology and telecommunication technology accelerate the growth of every industry, especially within the service sector (gsociology.icaap.org/reports). The innovation and vast use of computer science bring efficiency to every industry; especially give great convenience to customer service. The innovations of media means and multimedia skills contribute to the media industry's development.

Figure 11.4
PEST analysis of
Disney Theme Park

3 **Social**: The way that traditional values are being rediscovered fits neatly with Disney's belief and organizational culture. However, given the culturalist perspective taken in this book, we must recognize that Chinese traditional values are still different from American ones and this creates some sense of resistance. If Disney wants to be successful in China, it will be looking for ways to adapt itself to the culture in some degree. There are lessons to be learned from the experience in Paris,

where Disney was initially hindered because of the cultural rejection from many of the French. Unbelievably, Disney's great success in Tokyo Disneyland was also due to culture, but in Japan they were hosted by a form of cultural adoration for all things American and Disney especially.

In response to the requirements for social responsibility, especially environmental protection, Disney has established the environment as one of its key business objectives. The company has adopted proactive leadership in the management of energy and water resources, air quality, waste minimization, the development of educational programmes and has introduced results-oriented actions and strategic plans for the future.

4   **Technology**: The modern multimedia skills and digital technologies are really magic tools for Disney to build its modern magic World. However, these merits and advantages are available to others to copy. Whoever can handle them can benefit from the technology. However Disney argue that their success does not rely simply on the use of the technology alone, but on how the technology can be used to bring their imagination to life.

■ Global environment impacts

The terrorist attacks of September the 11th had a major impact on the Disney resorts in America. After the attacks the parks suffered a tourism slump, tourists felt uneasy about travelling. Fewer people from America and overseas wanted to travel to an area that was considered to be of high risk from terrorism.

Mintel stated that: *"Global events such as terrorist attacks ... have weakened consumer confidence in travelling abroad"* (Mintel, 2003b). This statement is true especially in relation to the Disney parks as crowds suffered for the remainder of 2001 and throughout 2002.

On the day of the attacks both the American resorts reacted positively. They:

● Evacuated all parks.
● Disneyland resort offered a special reduced room rate.
● Visitors were given an extra day on their admission passports.
● Disneyland hotel and AMC theatre set up a free movie screen.
● Resort swimming pools remained open.
● Video games were set to "free play".
● ESPN Zone opened to hotel guests for free game and non-alcoholic drinks.
● Resort hotel restaurants remained open.

Disney chose to reopen its parks the following day but before they did so, heightened security measures were put into place including:

● Bomb squads searched the parks.
● Security guards were placed at every entrance.
● All bags and packages were inspected.

Disney reacted quickly to the threat of terrorism and immediately put into place several measures to ensure the safety and comfort of their guests. These measures were internal but importantly were also visible to the customers.

As a result of the attacks, Disney have changed several aspects of how their American parks are run to ensure continuous safety of staff and guests. These measures include:

- All bags are now checked on entry.
- Backstage areas are more secure with new inspection procedures and improved security forces in place.
- People entering the backstage areas have to have their cars checked and go through additional safety procedures.
- More officials are out monitoring the parks.
- Sleeping Beauty Castle attraction remained closed for longer. It was seen as being a symbolic target for terrorists and at one stage it was unclear if it would reopen.

Visitor levels to the resort in California have returned to the levels that they were at before the attacks. However the Disneyland resort still experienced low visitor rates in subsequent years. Officials have said that this could have been due to the 50th birthday celebrations in 2005, with people deferring their visit until they could participate in the celebrations.

The continuing focus for the parks is to keep them safe from terror and to hope that there will not be a terror incident at any of the Disney resorts worldwide.

■ Strategy

Five forces analysis

A theme park is based on a particular theme and any park that developed an idea with some culture can be a theme park. They can be adjacent to some natural or historic scenes. This market is not hard to enter, although barriers to entry may be experienced in connection with the scale of investment needed to compete effectively in the market. However, it is quite difficult to become one like Disney's Theme Parks which have worldwide influence, as seldom does some cultural or historical theme have this level of appeal. Disney's Theme Parks are based on the images from its media and film business, which advertise for the parks even when running their own business.

The Supplier power is strong if a company uses only a horizontal growth strategy and seriously depends on outsourcing (Figure 11.5). Disney combined the horizontal growth with vertical growth. It also uses management contracts to appoint designated suppliers, who are allowed to use the Disney brand. These tactics help restrain supplier power.

Buyer power is relatively much stronger now than in the previous decade. However, customers care more about quality rather then price, especially in this industry. Customers who come to the Disney Theme Parks

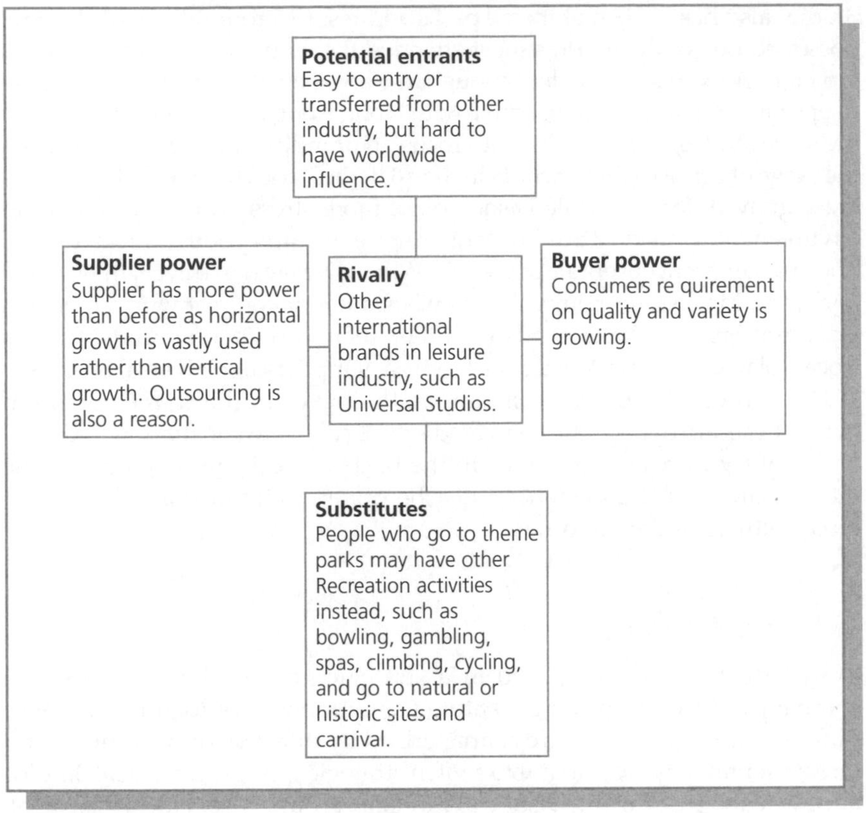

Potential entrants
Easy to entry or transferred from other industry, but hard to have worldwide influence.

Supplier power
Supplier has more power than before as horizontal growth is vastly used rather than vertical growth. Outsourcing is also a reason.

Rivalry
Other international brands in leisure industry, such as Universal Studios.

Buyer power
Consumers re quirement on quality and variety is growing.

Substitutes
People who go to theme parks may have other Recreation activities instead, such as bowling, gambling, spas, climbing, cycling, and go to natural or historic sites and carnival.

Figure 11.5
The five forces of Disney's Theme Parks

are seldom bargain buyers. Disney's Theme Parks are dedicated to its promise of excellent performance, by setting, training and conforming to the various business conduct standards they have developed. This includes ethical and legal standards that have been extended to all of their theme parks around the world. It also continually adds more services and new activities into its theme parks, involving education, sport and vacation opportunities (Walt Disney 2006 Annual Report).

Substitutes can be anything that people do for recreation, for people who go to theme parks all have explicit recreation purposes. Though people may have unique needs to enjoy themselves, a theme park mostly includes a variety of activity to fit different demands. However, a branded Theme Park like Disney's costs much more than a single recreation activity. For this reason, middle-income customers may prefer simpler options, specializing in a favourite activity for regular relaxation rather than going to theme parks. This would leave theme parks as an exceptional purchase and arguably makes the customer less price sensitive.

Disney's Theme Parks' biggest competitor is Universal Studios. Though there are other theme parks having similar attendance rates as a single theme park as Disney's, such as Lotte World and Everland in South Korea, they cannot compete with Disney's Theme Park portfolio as a whole. Universal

Studios also has a chain of theme parks and resorts around the world, and it possessed one of the world's most attended theme parks: Universal Studios Japan. They even felt confident enough to plan a new theme park in Shanghai to open in 2006, to directly compete with Hong Kong Disneyland. They are in the same strategic group who both focus on branding and all try to broaden the range of services they include in their Theme Parks, but the niche markets are slightly different. While Disney place more stress on family and warm environment, Universal Studios targets more towards youth and adventure. They use different corporate strategies. Where Disney make everything in the parks and in its stores named "Disney" (acquire or contract with suppliers), Universal Studios shake hands with the other world's top brands, such as Coca-Cola, Kodak and MasterCard (official suppliers to Universal Studios).

These forces can push a company to the top or pull it to the bottom. If not analysed properly and managed effectively, market share will be lost and profit will decrease. They are the basis of decision-making and the interpretation of the evidence must be done in circumstances that promote cultural understandings.

Strategic groups

Most industries are composed of a strategic group. The members of a company's strategic group constitute its immediate competitors. Because different strategic groups are characterized by different opportunities and threats, it may pay a company to switch strategic groups. Universal Studios is obviously playing in Disney's strategic group. The World Carnival, although it does not define itself as a theme park, can be seen as a very strong competitor of Hong Kong Disneyland, because it is already very popular in Asia. However, the only company that has competitive power and scale to match Disney worldwide at the moment is Universal Studios.

Company mission and goals

One of the most famous sayings of Walt Disney came when he observed that Disneyland would never be completed as long as there was imagination left in the world. That statement still holds true. Disney have striven to find ways of stimulating, motivating and fulfilling imagination in all its theme parks. The mission and goals can be described as "commitment to producing unparalleled entertainment experiences based on its rich legacy of quality creative content and exceptional storytelling" (corporate.disney.go.com).

Strategies

Functional strategies

Functional level strategies are those directed at improving the basic operation. For example: operation management, marketing, human resource management and finance, etc. From within these functions operations managers should help the organization to achieve competitive advantages.

Branding strategy is one of the most important marketing strategies used in Disney. Disney gives all of its products and services the name Disney. In this way, normal things become mysterious and are sold out quickly at a much higher price than its costs and more than the goods of similar quality without the brand. However, more risks occur if one of the good's reputation is ruined, the whole brand may be affected.

Another marketing strategy that Disney preferred is relationship marketing. Disney has founded many clubs to build the sense of a special relationship with their customers. Examples include the Mickey Mouse Club and the Angel Kids Club. One of the most promoted clubs is the Disney Vacation Club, giving customers the opportunity to purchase affordable time-share accommodation if they have spent holidays annually in Disney's Theme Parks and resorts. This also combines with Price strategy and Promotion strategy.

- The human resource strategy of Disney is distinct from Recruitment Strategy and Organization Culture. The theme park and resorts recruits college students every year. There are four main programmes for students based on innovation and imagination, ranging from management performance, to design, art and music producing. They are to be found in the extensive internal training network established within the company:
  - Disney College
  - Walt Disney World College Programme
  - Disney Collegiate Entertainment Programme
  - Disney Imagi-Nations.

This allows the organization to be able to claim, with some confidence, that Disney's staff can be youngest and most active, passionate and imaginative in the industry. The bottom line for the company' recruitment is to identify imagination, and although they often require previous work experience, they will also ask about the applicant's childhood dreams. The company addresses its own culture as magic and wonder; and this is a concern everywhere. Staff are taught that the company culture values them as high-quality elements in their products, and stress that they should share the organization's optimism for the future. They emphasize great storytelling, an emphasis on family entertainment and great talent, passion and dedication from all Cast Members (corporate.disney.go.com/careers/culture).

For many years, growth has been a key financial objective at The Walt Disney Company and it remains so today. About 5 years ago, however, a programme was initiated, designed to balance earnings growth goals by increasing focus on two other financial objectives, cash flow and returns on capital. In short, when the company was able to grow operating income, improve returns on capital and deliver strong cash flow at the same time (as in the fiscal year 2004) the financial results reflect fundamentally sound corporate strategies that are driving growth and increasing the value of the Company for the shareholders (Financial review of Annual Report, 2004).

The Research and Development Strategy is crucial for the Disney Company. As a leading company in leisure industry, it chooses and is pushed to be technological leader. Without creation, the recreation will lose fun. If the company acts as a technological follower, it will lose market share and profitability. Since its foundation, new attractions have been added to each of its Theme Park regularly.

Business strategy

Disney pursued a differentiation strategy. The objective of differentiation is to achieve a competitive advantage by creating a product or service that is perceived to be unique in some way. Disney's Theme Parks are perceived to be magic land and dream land. Because its culture has been delivered to the customers, it is hard to copy for other companies. It is an example of live assets which has an overwhelming power and a long-lasting lifespan. Disney's differentiation strategy also showed through its segmented market. All its theme parks stress the commitment to the family. The EPCOT Center and Captain EO, Star Tours and Splash Mountain in Disneyland and Walt Disney World are ideal for children and teenagers. However, the resorts also intend to produce a fantastic romantic atmosphere for young couples having honeymoons.

A differentiator must be cautious in setting price. Disney's Theme Park in Florida once faced serious performance flaws and management obstacles because of the company's cost cutting policy. To ensure the profitability, the price should not be brought down heavily. This was one of the concerns that led to Disney's decision to build their 11th theme park in Hong Kong, rather than Shanghai. It was thought that Hong Kong would offer better profit margins because the people in Hong Kong, and those with easy access to Hong Kong, had stronger purchasing ability and the economy there was seen to be better.

Disney are proud and careful of their position as a leader in the field. Because of this, they feel ever more investment should be put into innovation to maintain the position as a technological leader than a follower. The quality of their performance and the visitor experience are assured through high-cost training, and it is clear that quality is considered more important than price. It has never been a preferred option for Disney to use Cost leadership strategy, although management is constantly aware of cost and maintain strict controls (Plate 16).

Corporate strategy

The principal concern of corporate strategy is identifying the business areas in which a company should participate, the value creation activities it should perform, and the best means for expanding or contracting business, in order to maximize its long-run profitability and brand value. There are key corporate strategies. One is directional strategy by clarifying the

Plate 16
Scene from
Disneyland
Hongkong
Source: Author Photo

company's status in the market and lifespan and set directions. The other is portfolio strategy by exploring the best combination.

Disney's Theme Park has over 50 years history, but it is still young because it still grows. As early as 1971, 16 years after the first theme park was built, Walt Disney World had added resorts and relevant services to the park to expand the meaning of theme park. It is a new life for theme parks. A few years ago, Disney set new goals to all of its parks and resorts to be tourism destinations. To add attractions to the Parks, Disney undertook a lot of acquisitions, such as ABC broadcasting, Baby Einstein, NBA Games, Avalanche Software, etc. The net figures of cash acquired in acquisition are $2845million in 2002 with $480million in 2001 and $130million in 2003.

In order to consider the best combination of business, Disney defined the core for itself. Those are the four departments as we know:

1 Studio Entertainment
2 Parks and Resorts
3 Consumer Products
4 Media Networks.

To be more focused and have better performance, Disney recently sold its National Hockey League Club based in Orange County – the Mighty Ducks of Anaheim.

Global strategy

International expansion represents a way of earning greater returns by transferring the skills and products derived from their distinctive competencies to international markets. Engaging in international business can expand sales and acquire resources, such as better components, services and products. For example, Tokyo Disneyland is regarded as the world's best Disney Park because the Japanese are very critical of service delivery and they demand the best levels of service. Also, international expansion allows the company to gain foreign capital, technologies and information. It can minimize risk by diversifying the offer throughout the international markets. When Disney's American Theme Parks were suffering from the economic downturn and terrorist attacks in the USA, Disneyland Paris and Disneyland Tokyo were still able to earn profit.

In additional to domestic business management skills, international business management requires cultural understanding. Disney's initial failure in Disneyland Paris is now recognized as being because they were not sufficiently aware of the local cultures (Forman, 1998). Disney's choice to build Disneyland in Hong Kong instead of Shanghai was mainly based on the economic strength of the region, but also because Disney perceived Hong Kong as being regarded as more of a tourism destination in Asia than Shanghai. Shanghai was seen more like a conference and business centre than a recreational or tourist destination. As average purchase ability in mainland China is lower than in Hong Kong, to settle the Theme Park in Hong Kong can avoid the need to consider price reductions. However, Disney has not given up entering into mainland China but they mainly provide media services in Shanghai at the moment.

Four international strategies are mainly used in running international business: International strategy, Multidomestic strategy, Global strategy and Transnational strategy. Disney adopted an International Strategy. They transfer the skills and products derived from distinctive competencies to the foreign markets, while undertaking some limited local customization. Apart from the changes that Lenox China and Mister Donut made to adapt to Japanese sizes and tastes, Disneyland Tokyo is nearly a replica of Magic Kingdom in the United States, including the written signs in English! Disneyland Paris changed eventually to accommodate French as the first language. The future Disneyland Hong Kong will keep the taste the same as in the United States, except that Chinese cuisine will be introduced into the park and Chinese style will be added to the resorts design.

International marketing

It would appear that Disney follows its own clearly defined marketing strategy. It markets its products and services in a variety of ways to ensure that it is attracting the right clientele. This section reviews the different ways.

Video

Disney offer prospective visitors a free video. People see the Disney resorts advertised on TV and they are invited to call and request a free video which shows more of what Disney has to offer. Disney ensures that the video they send out is tailor made for the individual that has requested it. For example, when calling to order, a few questions are asked so that Disney can establish the kind of person it is that is requesting the video, for example, whether the request comes from a family or a young couple.

By taking the time to ensure that the videos fit the profile of each person, Disney is increasing the chance that they will book their Disney holiday. By showing a family what Disney offers them specifically they are selling this aspect of Disney to them and increasing the likelihood that they will visit the resorts at some point.

Haunted mansion ride

This ride is used frequently in marketing. The ride has been the focus of a TV special and a recent film and it has its own merchandise including games, toys, albums and books.

Cross-promotion marketing

Disney regularly promotes several aspects of their businesses together. This can be referred to as a "cross-promotion" marketing technique and is frequently used to promote a successful aspect of the business alongside a not so successful one. In 2003, Disney used its park in California to hold auditions for the struggling ABC network's reality TV shows – "The Bachelor and Bachelorette". This increased publicity and business for the resort and for the ABC network.

Guestology

A popular method of marketing that Disney uses is guestology (internal market research), which allows them to research their clients directly by looking at their needs and wants. Guestology is used at Disney resorts worldwide with one on one interviews with park guests, comment cards issued at restaurants, usage and visitation studies (monitoring movement patterns), mystery shopping and phone surveys. This allows Disney to learn who their guests are, their basic demographics, the number of people in a party, what their expectations are and what their opinions are of the Disney experience.

This is extremely useful for Disney. Disney believe that if they understand their guests and their patterns, they can find ways to please them. For example, knowing that guests may be older and that there may be fewer children around Thanksgiving may be the best time for Disney to hold a food and wine festival for adults.

Guestology can also be developed by listening directly to guests. For example, cast members may overhear guests commenting on issues like the temperature at a ride queue. If a cast member hears several guests comment on the same fact they can act by adjusting the temperature. This is a good example of "cast members" listening to guests and acting on what they hear.

Film promotion

To promote the sequel to the Pirates of the Caribbean, Disney is taking a different approach and sponsored a sleek, 70-foot yacht in an around the world regatta. Disney feels that this will be a different way to catch people's eyes.

Marketing conclusion

Disney is always looking for new and interesting ways to advertise its products and services. Disney believe that it is important to aim their products and services to the correct consumers and this is where the choice of marketing technique comes in. Disney is a global company as it *"integrates operations located in different countries"* (Daniels *et al.*, 2004: 671). Disney have adopted a global marketing technique where they ensure that all their products and services can be marketed similarly across the world. Although there is a recognition that some things need to be changed, for example, with the use of the local language, Disney want to get the same message across. An example of Disney's global marketing technique is the way it celebrated its 50th birthday, consisting of an 18-month campaign dubbed: *"The Happiest Celebration on Earth"* (Maddaus, 2005). The aim of the promotion was to let people know worldwide that the company was approaching this landmark. The campaign was global, featuring all the Disney parks including the new park in Hong Kong. Disney hope to ensure that the marketing is similar worldwide; it wants everybody to recognize the same Disney message.

■ Market entry

The optimal choice among entry modes depends on the company's strategy and practice situation in the foreign country. Disneyland Tokyo uses Licensing. The Oriental Land Company owns the park. Disney provided the master planning, design, manufacturing and training services during construction as well as consulting services after the completion of the facility. Disney received fees for its efforts during the construction phase, and it now receives royalties from the admissions and from merchandise and food sale (Daniels, 2004: 25). For Disneyland Paris, Disney invested only $140 million to take 49% ownership. In addition, it contracted to receive a management fee and a royalty payment on admissions and food sales. However, the Disneyland Hong Kong was not that easy. Disney and Hong Kong government negotiated for nearly a year. The final agreement resulted in a joint venture: Hong Kong International Theme Parks, owned 57% by the government of Hong Kong and 43% by Disney. Disney had to invest $300 million in addition to contributing expertise and the aura of its attractions and cartoon characters.

International human resource management

As we saw within international human resource management there are four different processes that a company could choose to adopt. These were outlined as: **ethnocentric, polycentric, geocentric and regiocentric approaches**. It would seem that Disney uses a polycentric approach. It is important that Disney fits in with the local country and culture that it is operating in. In order to do this managers need to learn about the local culture and how best to interact this with the Disney culture. Disney incorporates two different types of managers – managers from America who can implement and teach the Disney way of doing things and managers from the country where the park will be operating, who can teach the country's culture and how best to implement this culture into the Disney environment. By working together the two types of managers can find a sensible mix between both cultures.

For example, when Disneyland opened in Paris the park took on the American no-alcohol policy to maintain its family image. In France wine is regarded as being an important part of the culture and of everyday life, so the French managers opted for the no-alcohol policy to be abolished. Alcohol is now sold at the park.

Disney's international human resource approach

Human resource management is vitally important to Disney. As well as employing the right managers, it is important that Disney hires the right "cast members."

Disney uses the same hiring procedures throughout the company. This is to ensure the regularity and standards of staff and that all "cast members" can provide each guest with the same quality of service. Disney do make certain adjustments to their hiring and training procedures dependent on the country that they are operating in but the basic policies remain the same.

For "cast members" Disney ensure that they:

- Recognize cast member excellence.
- Provide consistent feedback.
- Hold daily staff meetings.
- Reward cast members for guest service, performance, behaviour and longevity.
- Believe that all cast members have valuable information to share.
- Make all employees feel welcome, valued and important.

In 1995 the Orlando resort celebrated its 25th anniversary. Even though the resort experienced a 15% increase in guest attendance human resources decided not to hire any additional staff. The year's guest satisfaction surveys remained high even though there were fewer staff to cope with the increased demand.

Human resources taught "cast members" how to recognize each other, a half-day training course was introduced to implement this scheme. This method proved extremely successful and has been used in many other areas since.

Diversity management and Disney

- Diversity focuses on differences between individuals.
- Diversity management looks at how best to manage a workforce, managers need to understand the term diversity and adapt their management skills/styles in order to successfully manage a diverse workforce.
- Diversity management reduces resistance to working with members of another ethnic, racial or cultural group.
- Decreases risk of miscommunication and discourages ethnic/racial slurs or jokes.

With the Walt Disney Company having theme parks and resorts on three continents it is very important that they understand the process of diversity management, and how it can affect them as an international business. There are many variables of diversity management including:

- Age
- Gender
- Ethnicity/race
- Physical ability/characteristics
- Sexual orientation
- Income
- Education
- Marital status
- Religious beliefs
- Geographical location
- Parental status
- Personality type.

Not all these variables will affect Disney in the way they would affect other international organizations. For example Disney has resorts in three continents across the world including: Europe, North America and Asia, this means they have to be internationally aware of how different cultures behave, and their cultural beliefs and habits. Culture can often be perceived as differences in human behaviour which are related to; communication, beliefs, religion, social grouping, customs, actions, language, values and ethnic backgrounds. Cultural diversity can result in conflict when there are differences between a person's individual beliefs, values or customs and those of other people or even the organization. These issues arise frequently within working environments. Additionally, managers must ensure that they themselves are aware of and educated about different religions, and that they conduct themselves accordingly to ensure that all members of the work-team are made to feel accepted.

When you start to work for an international company such as Disney, becoming accustomed to the culture of the environment is important, and every new member of staff is required to participate in a 3-day course at the Disney University. This is based on site and offers additional courses such as languages and communication, so every member of staff can become more aware of the culture around them. So when you look back at the definition given at the start of this section you can see how Disney use the University to offer the chance for people to break down the cultural barriers of language and beliefs, and therefore be able to work as a more productive team where all members of staff are able to communicate, and create a better working environment.

There is also an explicit attempt to introduce the values of the organization to all its new employees, as you can see in the "welcome letter" we reprint below. The tone is both morally uplifting but also prescriptive in establishing the expectations that the company have. As a new employee, you are being asked to take on the burden of protecting and enhancing the reputation of an institution, not just a company but Disney!

Example: Dear fellow Disney team member

Throughout the years, our guests, audiences, consumers and shareholders have come to depend on us for quality, creativity, innovation and integrity.

People trust us because of our commitment to them and to the standards to which we hold ourselves. We alone are responsible for upholding our excellence and our integrity. This means acting responsibly in all our professional relationships, in a manner consistent with the high standards we set for our business conduct.

Upholding legal standards of conduct, while mandatory for every Cast Member and employee, is not enough. We are also responsible for maintaining ethical standards. These standards govern how we treat everyone with whom we have contact. These are standards of integrity … honesty … trust … respect … fair play … and teamwork. In short, these are the standards we want Disney to continue to uphold in the years to come. Your company believes that its behaviour as a business should reflect the commitment to the values set forth in these "Standards of Business Conduct."

The Standards in this booklet explain both our legal and ethical standards. Please read them. Be familiar with them. Act on them. And don't be afraid to speak up when you have a concern or a question. Talk to your supervisor, your respective Human Resources representative, or the Corporate Legal Department.

Our Standards of Business Conduct are here to guide our behaviour and to help us live up to the highest expectations of excellence that are "Disney." As we continue to create Disney magic, I hope your actions show your pride in yourself, those you work with, and the Company.

Source: Michael Eisner Bob Iger
Chief Executive Officer President and Chief Operating Officer
www.corporate.disney.go.com/corporate/conduct_standards.html

International human resources and Disney

Disney describes itself as a multicultural company, with employees from all over the world working together for one international company. Disney employees are referred to as "Cast Members" and are given the chance to partake in a wide range of jobs: performer, marketing manager, hotel receptionist and fire-fighter are just a small selection of the jobs available at the Paris resort. The Paris resort currently employs the following:

● 12,200 employees (annual average)
● 500 different professions
● 100 different nationalities
● 19 different languages

Source: Euro Disney S.C.A. (2005).

The Disney University that was mentioned in the previous section is where the employees are trained, and are given the opportunity to acquire new skills and develop skills they already posses. According to the Euro Disney S.C.A. website an average of 50,000 training days are undertaken by employees each year. Disneyland Paris also offers a unique training programme, Hote d'Accueil Touristique, which gives the staff that complete the course a diploma that is recognized by the French Ministry of Employment. The course itself lasts for 15–18 months depending on the area of specialization, and prepares the participant to work in a variety of fields related to the tourism industry, moving between the hotels and the park.

CSR and Disney

The hospitality industry has not enjoyed the best reputation as a great industry to work in over recent years, but now things are set to change with the increased publicity over CSR (Merrett and Hill, 2005). The base level of responsible behaviour for any organization is good legal compliance to standards in such areas as environmental policies, health and safety and employee rights. For hospitality companies pursuing CSR there are ways in which they can demonstrate this including:

● Supporting local communities
● Environment
● Safety and security
● Media relations

Source: Based on Disney Online (2005).

The Disney's company's board, management and employees all over the world are committed to high levels of CSR; they use the following six components, to achieve high levels of CSR throughout their company:

1 Business Standards and Ethics
2 Corporate Governance
3 Community

4 "Environmentality"
5 International Labour Standards
6 Safety and Security.

One of Disney's main concerns is with the environment, and they design their help within the environment to blend the company's needs with the conservation of natural resources. One of the innovations Disney has used worldwide is a water design called "closed-loop waterways", which provide a means of saving natural resources. It traps rainwater and recycles storm and waste water, then after treatment in a small on site wet land and sand filter, this is then used for day-to-day water requirements (Australian Government, 2005).

Disney have practiced waste minimization in all their theme parks since 1991, and has helped recycle more than 650,000 tons of materials. The Disney waste minimization scheme has led to many other things, such as:

- In 2002 alone, Disney donated materials such as electronics, furniture and office equipment to 50 non-profit organizations around the world.
- Disney believes recycling relies on supply and demand, so they buy in bulk and purchase recycled products. For example the deck of a bridge at the Magic Kingdom in Orlando is made from a recycled material composed of wood and plastic.
- There are more than 1,400 products made from that same material at Disney Resorts around the world.

Source: Disney Online (2005).

Both these ideas are important components of resource conservation, but can also lead to significant financial savings for the Walt Disney Company, which in turn can help to maximize profits.

■ Disney's future

Disney's main focus had been on the opening of Hong Kong Disneyland on 12th September 2005. With a successful venture, both Disney and Hong Kong will benefit. Disney hopes to increase Hong Kong's tourism industry, which at present is fairly modest. It hopes to attract 1.4 million outside visitors in its first year of operation and 2.9 million visitors within 15 years. Disney also hope to attract more families to Hong Kong and for the company to improve its relationship and business opportunities with China.

In the first year 18,400 direct and indirect jobs will be created and increasing to 35,800 in later years.

There are some problems associated with the opening of the park. The cost of air transport to the city and the cost of hotel rooms may deter visitors. Disney is counting on Chinese visitors; however mainland Chinese must get exit visas from China and entry visas from Hong Kong before they can travel. The Chinese government gives these out sparingly and the process can take some time.

Disney also needs to take into consideration the popularity of amusement parks in the area. Between 1994 and 1999 more then 2,000 amusement parks were built in China, most of which performed badly. It could be that the area does not have a market that is interested in theme parks or that the market is saturated – as Disney clearly believe it could be that those theme parks were not Disney. In keeping with culture and country traditions Disney have stated that although the park will keep much of the American feel the hotels and restaurants will get a strong Chinese flavour.

This report echoes many of the themes we raised in the discussion of entrepreneurship, but remember the setting is a large company.

Example: Disney's Theme Park try to penetrate Chinese market

Title: *MICKEY MAO*, By: Chandler, Clay, Levinstein, Joan, Ting, Wang, Fortune (Europe), 07385587, 4/18/2005, Vol. 151, Issue 7 **Database:** *Business Source Premier*

The Magic Kingdom meets the Middle Kingdom, as Disney sets its sights on China. But for new chief Robert Iger, who has been leading the charge, wishing on a red star could be a risky strategy.

Last October, on the eve of the National Basketball Association's first exhibition game in China, Walt Disney president Robert Iger stepped before a battery of television cameras flanked by NBA commissioner David Stern, Houston Rockets centre Yao Ming and a cadre of other NBA stars. A press conference to announce some blockbuster marketing deals between the NBA and China? Not quite. The venue for the high-profile gathering was a cramped classroom at Yao's alma mater, Gaoan Road Primary School in Shanghai. As cameras whirred and flashbulbs popped, Iger, Yao and the other NBA luminaries joined a chorus of Chinese children in red neckerchiefs reciting from the pages of a Yao-sized book at the front of the room: "It's a grey, grey rainy day, but Piglet and Roo are ready to play."

Piglet and Roo are characters from A.A. Milne's popular children's stories about a stuffed bear named Winnie-the-Pooh, and Disney billed the storytelling session as part of a worldwide public-service initiative to encourage kids to read. But to properly connect the dots between the beloved bear, the world's second-largest media and entertainment conglomerate, the NBA's tallest player, and the world's fastest-growing economy, it helps to know that Disney owns the rights to Milne's characters; that Disney is the parent company of ESPN sports network; that ESPN secured rights to broadcast the Shanghai exhibition game; and that Iger wants a piece of the China market as badly as Pooh craves honey.

That last also explains why Iger, just anointed successor to CEO Michael Eisner, visited China four times last year. In October, while Eisner was slugging it out with former president Michael Ovitz in a Delaware courtroom, Iger was in Hong Kong inspecting progress on the theme park Disney is building there, in Shanghai catching the NBA game, and in Beijing chatting with China's vice president. Get Disney's new chief talking about China's potential, and he'll rattle off a list of statistics: income levels, Internet pene-tration figures, mobile-phone and cable-television subscription rates. The way Iger sees it, China, with 290 million people under the age of 14 – more potential Mouseketeers than the entire US population – isn't just a growth opportunity, "it's a needle mover."

Iger has taken to goading executives at Disney's Burbank, CA, head-quarters to prove their China savvy: "If I come back from a China trip and I know more than the guy running the business back in Burbank, he's got a problem." Indeed, so keen is Disney's new chief to bring the Magic Kingdom to the Middle Kingdom that he describes himself as the com-pany's China country manager. "On any given day, I may talk to the per-son who's running Baby Einstein to see what he's up to [in China] or call the head of television there. It's constant, constant attention."

That's the sort of relentless focus championed by management experts as the secret to cracking the Chinese market. But with apologies to the Disney song, when you wish upon a red star, it makes a big difference who you are. If you're a large foreign multinational selling autos, mobile phones or fried chicken, have at it: China waits with open arms to take in every dollar you care to invest. But if you happen to be a giant media and entertainment con-glomerate – a Disney, say – be prepared for China's mandarins to wrap you in red tape.

Governments the world over restrict foreign media ownership, but China has raised regulation of the industry to a fine and excruciating art. In the developed world and in many other fast-growing economies in Asia, foreign content providers are at least allowed to purchase airtime for their programming over domestically owned networks. Not in China, where regulators limit the ability of non-Chinese companies to sell, distrib-ute, market and identify the programmes they produce. Even cartoons are tightly controlled. Disney's most significant encroachment into China's air-waves is a half-hour kids' show that mixes Disney programming with short segments produced in China. Yet Disney can't call it Mickey Mouse Club lest its signature rodent get too well known, so the programme airs as Dragon Club. The myriad prohibitions are meant to prevent criticism of China's communist rulers and to shield the Chinese from the evils of Western cultural imperialism. They're also driven, says Lehman Brothers Asia media analyst Stephen McKeever, by "good old-fashioned mercantil-ism" to make sure Chinese players get their share of a burgeoning market.

That's bad news for Iger, who has identified international expansion as a cornerstone of Disney strategy. Though Disney's animated menagerie includes some of the most widely recognized characters on the planet, the financial statements of the company that spawned them remain surprisingly provincial. Last year overseas revenue accounted for $6.7 billion, or 22%, of Disney's $30.7 billion in sales, and generated $1.5 billion, or 35%, of operat-ing profit. Sure, that's enough to keep Dumbo in peanuts. But Iger has long argued that given the brand's global reach, the composition of Disney's revenue should look more like that of Coca-Cola or McDonald's, truly multinational giants that count on non-US markets for more than 65% of sales. Iger is pushing for double-digit growth in foreign sales and a more diversified revenue stream. Foreign markets, he vows, must generate at least half of Disney's profits "within the next 5 years."

Iger's goal implies a radical redeployment of Disney's resources. Last year 70% of the company's overseas sales came from markets in slow-growing Europe; Asia contributed only $566 million, much of that from Japan, where Disney made more than $160 million in royalties from the consortium that runs Tokyo Disneyland. Iger stands little chance of hitting his foreign-profit mark without substantial gains in Asia's emerging dynamos, China and India. Disney won't say how much it earns in either market – like many multinationals, it doesn't disclose financial results by country. But the consensus among analysts and competitors is that Disney earns considerably less in the two countries combined than the $140 million that Ovitz's severance package was worth. That could change quickly as components of Iger's battle plan fall into place. In India, where broadcast regulations allow more leeway, Disney has made inroads with a sports television joint venture and the launch last year of two animation channels. But the big bet is China, where the company has identified theme parks and consumer products as its dominant profit engines.

On its face, counting on those businesses seems ... well, goofy. Movies and media networks, not parks and plush toys, are Disney's mainstay, accounting for more than two-thirds of worldwide revenues last year. In the United States, Disney has sold off its stores, unable to make a go of hawking mouse ears and Piglet pencil boxes on its own. Why should it fare any better in a country famed for plunging prices, razor-thin margins and rampant piracy? And while Disney's flagship US parks are reliable cash cows, the company's record in operating theme parks overseas is spottier than 101 Dalmatians. Burbank balked in the 1980s when Japanese developers pitched the idea of bringing Disneyland to Tokyo, judging the Disneyland experience too American to export. Instead of investing, Disney opted to license rights in Japan in exchange for 10% of ticket sales and 5% of receipts on food and concessions. Big mistake: Japanese families can't get enough of Tokyo Disneyland. "The failure to take an ownership position in Tokyo Disneyland was exceptionally costly," Eisner wrote in his 1998 autobiography, Work in Progress. But his decision to retain a stake in Euro Disney, a theme park outside Paris, proved an even bigger error. The French venture, of which Disney now owns 40%, has been a financial sinkhole. In 12 years of operation, it has never come close to meeting its original target of 17 million visitors a year, despite generous capital infusions from Disney and Saudi Arabia's Prince al-Waleed.

Determined to finally get it right, Disney drove a hard bargain in Hong Kong, demanding a fat stake for a next-to-nothing investment. Desperate to bring jobs and tourists to their then-beleaguered economy, Hong Kong officials capitulated, agreeing to put up $2.9 billion in taxpayer money, donate land and build a network of access roads and railways in exchange for a 57% share. Disney got its 43% for just $314 million, a sum it will recoup almost immediately because it also insisted on a 5% royalty fee for management and operation.

Nestled in a cove on Lantau Island, with views of the downtown skyline six miles away, Hong Kong Disneyland, which is scheduled to open 12th September, will look and feel like the original Disneyland, complete with Main Street, Sleeping Beauty's Castle and Tomorrowland. But there are some modifications. Architects went to great lengths to heed instructions of a feng shui master who, among other things, ordered the entire layout rotated several degrees to foster harmony with the elements. Staff will accommodate guests in English, Mandarin and Cantonese, and food will cater to Chinese palates. Disney projects that the park will receive about six million visitors the first year, about 40% of them from China's mainland.

Hong Kong Disneyland is mostly a dress rehearsal for the main event – a theme park in Shanghai. Iger says Disney has been engaged for some time in "a cordial discussion, if not actual negotiations," with Shanghai officials about opening a park within the next 6 years. There, too, he is playing hard-ball, rebuffing demands to move faster. But the long-term success of Disney's Chinese parks will require more than good feng shui and hard bargaining. In other markets, Disney's film, TV and publishing operations smoothed the way for new parks, ensuring that from the moment they set foot on Main Street, visitors felt at home. In China, says Jay Rasulo, President of Walt Disney Parks and Resorts, "for the first time, we'll be opening in a market where not all of our guests will know us well. The brand recognition is high, but the depth of the storytelling isn't there." That matters, executives say, because guests stay longer, spend more and return more often when they invest emotionally in the characters.

To fill the void, Disney is mounting a grass-roots brand-building campaign – and experimenting with novel marketing techniques. In perhaps the most unlikely union of Mickey and Mao, Disney last year teamed up with the 70 million – member Communist Youth League to host a series of sessions billed as aiding reading skills and creativity. Disney performers toured half a dozen "children's palaces" in Guangdong province, telling stories using the Disney characters and encouraging children to draw pictures of Mickey Mouse. More sessions are planned this spring. Disney's alliance with the youth league doesn't raise eyebrows in a nation where few distinguish between advertising and propaganda. Sometimes it's unclear who's propagandizing whom. At Yao Ming's elementary school, a zealous 12-year-old scolded NBA veteran Bob Lanier for mispronouncing the word "ooze" while reading a Winnie-the-Pooh story. Afterward the boy explained that he knew the proper English pronunciation because his class had spent weeks practising for the event.

Disney's bid for China's hearts and minds reaches back to the 1930s, when its first animated features played at cinemas in Beijing and Shanghai. Disney films, along with most other forms of foreign entertainment, were banned after Mao swept to power in 1949. During the Cultural Revolution, the mere possession of a Mickey Mouse watch would have constituted a serious cultural crime. Mickey had to wait until 1986, a decade after Mao's death, for rehabilitation. In that year Disney signed a licensing agreement with China's national network to supply cartoons for broadcast on Sunday evenings. That remained the extent of Disney's presence in China until well into the 1990s, when ESPN struck a deal to syndicate international sports programming and Disney won permission to publish a weekly comics magazine for children. In 1994, Disney forged the partnership with Beijing TV that created Dragon Club. Now in its 10th year, Dragon Club airs on more than 40 stations across China, reaching an estimated 60 million households. Winnie-the-Pooh figures prominently in CCTV's flagship kids' show, The Big Windmill, and on CCTV's new children's channel. All told, Disney-branded segments reach more than 380 million households, making the company "the No. 1 provider of Western programming to China," according to Andy Bird, President of Disney International.

Iger's own interest in China goes back to his first Beijing visit in 1979, when he was with ABC Sports. "I stayed in a hotel – I swear, this is the complete truth – my mattress was filled with straw," he recalls. "No one spoke English. I spoke no Chinese. It was almost a joke, but a great adventure." He returned in 1994, as the president of ABC-TV, to inaugurate Dragon Club.

But Disney is hardly the only belle at the ball. In programming of all forms, Disney lags behind News Corp., whose China ambitions are no less grand. The centrepiece of News Corp.'s China strategy is its 38% stake in Phoenix Satellite, a Chinese-language network based in Hong Kong. Operated in partnership with a former People's Liberation Army officer, Phoenix owns five channels and boasts that its shows reach 200 million mainland viewers. The company's biggest success is news and current-affairs programming, which offers a livelier alternative to the official fare on state-run channels. Last year Phoenix, listed in Hong Kong, reported a profit of $21 million on ad sales of $100 million. Beijing has also allowed News Corp.'s Star TV to broadcast Chinese-language entertainment programmes via cable networks in Guangdong province.

Viacom, which owns Nickelodeon, announced an agreement with Shanghai Media Group in November to produce children's TV programming. The deal was the first to follow a declaration by China's State Administration of Radio, Film and Television that foreigners are permitted to own up to 49% of Chinese television production companies. Time Warner, the largest of the global media giants (and parent of FORTUNE's publisher), has been least active in pressing for entry into the China market. Its affiliate, Chinese Entertainment Television, has also been granted permission to broadcast in Guangdong, but Time Warner ceded majority interest in 2003 to Tom Group, a media company controlled by Hong Kong billionaire Li Ka-shing.

Each year titles from Disney and Warner dominate the list of films cleared for distribution in Chinese cinemas. Disney's The Lion King was the first foreign film released in China, and the company has distributed more than a dozen others, including Toy Story, Tarzan, Finding Nemo and Pirates of the Caribbean. The terms of China's 2001 admission to the World Trade Organization require Beijing to allow the release of 50 foreign films this year, up from 10 before accession. But those films do limited box office despite China's vast population and the popularity of Hollywood fare. Consumers would just as soon pay $1 for a counterfeit DVD than two or three times that to see a movie on a large screen in a dilapidated theatre.

The breadth of Disney's offerings gives it a distinct advantage in China. Disney on Ice gave 30 performances in three Chinese cities last year and is preparing to expand the tour to 40 cities. Disney is also pushing content over the web in a partnership with Sohu.com, a Chinese Internet portal. Rasulo says, "No company in the world is better than Disney at marshalling all its business lines for brand building."

But how to make that brand building pay? Piracy has crippled Disney's efforts to profit from DVD sales in China. Since entering the market in 1997, Disney has released nearly 500 VCR and DVD titles, more than any other foreign studio. Still, in 2003 it sold just 3.4 million disks. Finding Nemo, which Disney touts as the bestselling animated feature in China, had legal sales of only 284,000 copies. Legitimate discs sell for as much as ten times the price of a knockoff, and most Chinese consumers wouldn't know where to buy them even if they were willing to pay the difference. At the Xiangyang market in Shanghai, vendors tout pirated Disney titles alongside phony handbags. At one table a woman shows shoppers a trash bag stuffed with Disney knockoffs, including: The Incredibles, Aladdin and The Little Mermaid. Nine dollars buys an eight-disc set of Mickey Mouse in Living Colour, with the forged signature of Roy E. Disney on the box. "This Disney stuff sells like crazy, 'she says.' I usually have 100 titles, but I can't keep them in stock."

It says a lot about Iger's battle plan that in December, when he finally hired a full-time China country manager, he picked Stanley Cheung, former head of Johnson & Johnson's consumer products business in China. Cheung's first task will be to expand Disney's retail and distribution network. Disney reported that China consumer products sales topped $128 million in 2003 and that the segment's contribution to overall sales in China is double Disney's global average of 8%. Cheung wants to double the number of Disney Corners, upscale retail outlets selling toys and branded kids' wear, to 2,200 shops by the end of the year. He also sees improved opportunities for Disney products as foreign retailers such as Wal-Mart and Carrefour expand in China. "Regulations are loosening," says Cheung. "We have the right legal structure. Suddenly everything's coming together."

That would no doubt gratify Iger, who joked before getting the nod to succeed Eisner that he could be the subject of his own reality TV show. His suggested title: The Apprentice Survivor Millionaire. Just don't look for it to be broadcast on Chinese airwaves anytime soon?

By Clay Chandler; Joan Levinstein, Reporter Associate and Wang Ting, Reporter Associate

Disney is relying heavily on the success of the new park especially after the criticisms and problems associated with Disneyland Paris. However many of the problems were related to the French culture and the fact that the majority of the French people seemed to be against the idea of the park. Hong Kong is different, the government wants Disney and wants it to be successful. Also Disney have learnt from the Paris opening, they now understand the importance of implementing certain aspects of the host country's culture into the Disney experience.

Disney's main competitor Universal Studios has taken every step to fight for market share with Disney. Disney's new theme park in Hong Kong has cost Disney a lot but there are still hidden obstacles that may affect its profitability. Disney's ambition in China may face several problems, such as low purchase ability; Chinese people's realism in spending money; government restriction and the coordination with Disneyland Hong Kong. That the Strategic Planning Department was taken away may not benefit the company. Challenges may exist in making corporate level strategy decisions, also in coordination with other departments and settling down the staff and managers in the Strategic Planning Department. The change of Disney's president and CEO also brings in a challenge of internal coordination.

However, Disney's rich enterprise culture background and abundant experience in customer service as well as strong power in innovating and investing should be able to sustain itself in the leading place for a relative long time. Most importantly, going to Disney's Theme Parks has become a dream for many people in the younger generations. Its strong customer loyalty base will support it at least for another 30 years.

■ Summary

Disney is a very strong and influential company throughout the world. We have highlighted several areas of importance to the company:

- International Human Resource Management: a polycentric approach is used and the company understands the importance of all its employees.
- Global Environment Impacts: since 9/11 Disney has heightened its security measures which have helped visitor levels return to normal as visitors feel more at ease.
- International Marketing: a variety of methods are used to market Disney's products and services.
- International market entry: the lessons of Paris and the opportunities of Hong Kong.
- Strategic choice.
- CSR.

To ensure Disney is successful throughout its business operations, with regular and consistent results Disney should ensure that it is constantly listening to their consumers and working to meet and exceed their needs, wants and expectations.

There are still problems that can arise in the international management of the company:

- The challenge of entering a new market, and the different cultures that will be viewed in this new market.
- The everlasting problem of staffing, with the expansion of the park in Paris already complete and now incorporating a second park which is

also growing, will Disney be able to keep staffing at the level needed to be at to deliver the high standard the guests expect.

● With the ever increasing threat of terrorism high across the world, how will Disney meet the challenge of security to maintain the safety of their guests in all their resorts?

It is clear that a lot of planning and research needs to be done to make sure the future endeavours of the company match the high standards of their customers. When looking at the future problems, a number of solutions could arise, and in the case of security have already been put into the scenarios. To maintain the trust of the customer, it was felt necessary to provide an extra security presence, because if the guests can see the security then it puts them more at ease in relation to the threat of terrorism.

Staffing will always be a problem for any company involved in the hospitality industry, the ever increasing use of the Internet will be a major factor when they are advertising for positions in the parks. Offering the chance for current employees to transfer over to Hong Kong to be involved with the new operation was a good way of catering for the staffing of the new park in the initial opening period.

Overall Disney is in a good position internationally and makes good use of planning and international operations when looking at all the problems that are faced by an international company both in its home and host country.

We began this book by using Disney as a symbol of cultural change within the concerns about the globalization process and although we have enquired into the operations of the organization, we now want to return to the symbolic. What actually happens at Disney and the operational details are very important as we have outlined in the preceding discussions but they do not tell the whole story or explain Disney's significance for international hospitality management. That impact lies in what Disney is seen to do and the way people see them as doing it. Some of these reactions are based on little or no knowledge of what Disney is really doing or thinking but the perceptions are still very powerful.

We have written a book which we believe stresses the need for managers in international hospitality to be aware of and appreciate the implications of the cultures of their organizations, their managers, their workforce, their customers and the contexts in which they are working. This culturalist perspective poses a challenge to all companies, large or small, that want to work internationally. We are placing a cultural appreciation as high on the management agenda as the financial appraisals that are undertaken before investments are finalized have always been. Disney have come to stand for the worst elements of globalization as critics have seen their expansion as nothing more than American cultural imperialism. We have gone to some lengths to demonstrate that Disney are working in more complex ways than this would suggest but nevertheless the arguments still dog the company. The problems in Paris were not just about the way Disney worked, but about how what they planned and performed was not a comfortable fit with the French and European ways of doing things. The attacks on the theme park were partly motivated by a desire to protect the history and culture of a centre of civilization. One French critic argued that the demands Disney were making on the imaginations of French children would not leave space for the traditional stories of their own childhoods. This would lead to the demise of French culture, arts and music and even philosophy – the nation of famous philosophers was seen to be replacing these rich traditions with the thinking of Mickey Mouse. This is an extreme example but it reinforces our plea that culture has to be taken seriously and sets the context in which all decisions are made.

We also looked at the nature of hospitality in the first chapter and we hope that our focus on the industrial structures and functional aspects of management have not blinded you to that part of our culture. What we see as the heart of management in international hospitality is the sharing of opportunities and the creation of meaningful experiences. The context of the host–guest relationship may have become commoditized and institutionalized but the spirit of the visit remains central to the exchanges that we are concerned with managing.

This is why we would close this book with an argument for our title. We have styled the book *International Hospitality Management*, not managing hospitality in a globalized context. We believe that the cultural perspective entails a commitment to appreciating, valuing and promoting local distinctiveness. Globalization may introduce international standards and opportunities that may benefit all of us in some ways, but it is also in danger of denying the differences that underpin the value of host–guest relationships. If we do all become the same in a standardized, commoditized and homogeneous future, we may as well all stay at home. Only by emphasizing our differences and ensuring that we present them in ways that communicates that difference as a positive to our guests can we encourage the development of a truly international but not globalized hospitality industry. We can work with standards as long as they allow us to implement them within a respectful awareness of our local conditions. As a consequence, we could be seen as advocates of glocalization, taking the best from both the global initiatives and celebrating the contribution of the local. We should search for excellence in our work, whatever we do and whereever we do it, and we should definitely address the questions of quality but we do not all need to produce the same answer.

We believe that the combination of theory and practical case studies demonstrates that diversity is a positive feature of our lives and our work. We hope we have avoided simple solutions in favour of creating a deeper understanding of the processes that underpin the development of international hospitality. Our concern has been to focus on clarifying the ways in which we see the issues that will help and hinder those developments. If we have raised the awareness of the cultural understanding of those processes, we will have at least given you better questions to ask even if we have given you no generalizable answers. We would strongly advocate that the richness that exists in international hospitality must be championed and taken forward with a sense of joy in that diversity.

Bibliography
and references

A

Aaker, D.A. and Joachimsthaler, E. (2000). The brand relationship spectrum: the key to the brand architecture challenge. *California Management Review*, 42(4), 1–17.

Adair, J. (1986). *Effective Teambuilding*. Pan Books.

Adams, J.S. (1979). Injustice in social exchange. In Steers, R.M. and Porter, L.W. (eds.) *Motivation and Work Behaviour*. McGraw-Hill, pp. 124–46.

Adridge J. (2006). Ramsay means business. *The Scotsman*, 27 July, 24.

Agenda and Green Globe with ISHC (1987). *The International Society of Hospitality Consultants Bruntland Report, Our Common Future in 1987*. International Society of Hospitality Consultants (ISHC).

Aguas, P., Costa, J. and Rita, P. (2000). A tourist market portfolio for Portugal. *International Journal of Contemporary Hospitality Management* 12(7), 394–400.

AHMA (2005). History of Lodging [online]. Last accessed 8th February 2007 at URL: http://www.ahma.com/products_lodging_history.asp

Alvesson, M. (2002). *Understanding Organizational Culture*. Sage Publications.

Anholt, S. (2003). *Brand New Justice: The Upside of Global Branding*. Butterworth-Heinemann.

Anon (2003) *McDonalds Fact File 2003 (Student information booklet)*. The Corporate affairs Department. McDonalds Restaurants Ltd.

Aramberri, J. (2001). The hosts should get lost. *Annals of Tourism Research*, 28(3), 738–61.

Austrade (2002). *Knowing and Growing the Exporter Community*. Australian Trade Commission.

Australian Government (2005). Closed Loop Waterways [online]. Last accessed 2nd February 2007 at URL: http://www.deh.gov.au/coasts/pollution/cowipp/nursery.html.

B

Barsky, J. and Nash, L. (2002). *Comfort, Security Give Midscale Hotels Loyal Guests*. [Online] Accessed on 19 April 2005 at www.hotelmotel.com

BBC News – UK Edition (2005). *Intercontinental seals hotel sale*. 10 March 2005.

Beid, R.D. and Bojanic, D.C. (2006). *Hospitality Marketing Management*. John Wiley & Sons.

Bell, J. (1995). The internationalization of small computer software firms. *European Journal of Marketing*, 29(8), 60–75.

Blassingame, K.M. (2003). *Working Their Magic: Disney Culture Moulds Happy Employees*. [Online] Last accessed on 23 March 2005 at www.benefitnews.com/career

Blauner, R. (1964). *Alienation and Freedom*. University of Chicago Press.

Boella, M.J. (1996). *Human Resource Management in the Hospitality Industry*. Stanley Thornes.

Bowie, D. and Buttle, F. (2004). *Hospitality Marketing*. Butterworth-Heinemann.

Brassington, F. and Pettitt, S. (2003). *Principles of Marketing*, 3rd edn. Prentice Hall.

Brotherton, B. (ed.) (2003). *The International Hospitality Industry: Structure, Characteristics and Issues*. Butterworth-Heinemann.

Brown, A. (1995). *Organisational Culture*. Pitman Publishing.

Buhalis, D. (2003). *eTourism: Information Technology for Strategic Tourism Management*. FT Prentice Hall.

Burke, R.J. and Cooper, L.G. (2000). *The Organization in Crises: Downsizing, Restructuring, and Privatization*. Blackwell Publishers Ltd.

Burns, T. and Stalker, G.M. (1966). *The Management of Innovation*, 2nd edn. Tavistock Publications Ltd.
Business Week (2005). *The 100 Top Brands*, 1 August.

C

Calatone, R. and Manzanec, J. (1991). Marketing management and tourism. *Annals of Tourism Research*, 18(1), 101–19.

Cervino, J. and Bonache, J. (2005). Hotel Management in Cuba and the transfer of best practices. *International Journal of Contemporary Hospitality Management* 17(6), 455–468.

Chacko, H.E. (1998). Designing a seamless hotel organisation. *International Journal of Contemporary Hospitality Management*, 10(4), 133–38.

Chakravarthy, B.S. and Perlmutter, H.V. (1985). Strategic planning for a global business. *Columbia Journal of World Business*, Summer, 5–6.

Chandler, C., Levinstein, J. and Wang, T. (2005). Mickey Mao. *Fortune (Europe)*, 151(7).

Chang, Y., Chen, F. and Shon, Z. (2003). Airline e-commerce: the revolution of ticketing channels. *Journal of air transportation*, 9, 325.

Chen, W., Hirst, C., Long, P., Lyons, H. and Whitaker, V. (2006). *Strategic Management*. Pearson Custom Publishing.

Child, J. (1981). Culture, contingency and capitalism in the cross-national study of organisations. In Staw, B.M. and Cummings, L.L. (eds.), *Research in Organisational Behaviour*, Vol. 3. JAI Press, pp. 303–56.

Chitiris, L. (1988). Herzberg's proposals and their applicability to the hotel industry. *Hospitality Education and Research Journal*, 12, 67–79.

Chon, K. and Sparrowe, R. (2000). *Welcome to Hospitality: An Introduction*, 2nd edn. Delmar.

Clarke, A. (1997). *Managing in Sports*. National Coaching Foundation.

Comen, T. (1989). Making quality assurance work for you. *Cornell Hotel and Restaurant Quarterly*, November, 23–9.

Cornell (2005). *McDonald's Corporation – A Case Study*. Cornell Centre of Hospitality Research.

Coulter, M. (2003). *Entrepreneurship in Action*, 2nd edn. Prentice Hall.

Crotts, J. (2004). The effect of cultural distance on overseas travel behaviour. *Journal of Travel Research*, 42(2), 186–90.

Crotts, J. and Erdmann, R. (2000). Does national culture influence consumers' evaluation of travel services? A test of Hofstede's model of cross cultural differences. *Managing Service Quality*, 10(6), 410–19.

Crotts, J. and Pizam, A. (2003). The effect of national culture on consumers' evaluation of travel services. *Journal of Tourism, Culture and Communications*, 4(1). 17–28.

Crotts, J. and Litvin, S. (2004). Avoiding a potential pitfall in cross-cultural research: Are researchers better served by knowing respondents' culture of birth, culture of residence, or culture of citizenship? *Journal of Travel Research*, 6(1), 29–37.

Cunill, O.M. (2006). *The Growth Strategies of Hotel Chains: Best Business Practices by Leading Companies*. Haworth Press.

Czinkota, M. and Ronkainen, I. (2002). *International Marketing*. Harcourt College Publishers.

D

D'Aveni, R.A. (1994). *Hypercompetition*. The Free Press.

Daniels, J.D. and Radebaugh, L.H. (1998). *International Business*, 8th edn. Addison.

Daniels, J.D. and Radebaugh, L.H. (2001). *International Business: Environments and Operations*, 9th edn. Prentice Hall.

Daniels, J.D. Radebaugh, L.H. and Sullivan, D.P. (2004). *International Business: Environments and Operations*, 10th edn. New Jersey, Pearson Education.

DataMonitor (2004). *The Walt Disney Company*. [Online] Last accessed on 23 March 2005 at www.datamonitor.com

de Wit, B. and Meyer, R.M. (2004). *Strategy: An International Perspective*, 3rd edn. Thomson Business Press.

Dewald, B. (2001). Tipping by foreign tourists. *Pacific Tourism Review*, 5, 41–8.

Dibb, S., Simkin, L., Pride, W. and Ferrell, O. (2004). *Marketing Concepts and Strategies*, 4th edn. Houghton Mifflin.

Dicken, P. *et al.* (eds.) (1998). *The Logic of Globalisation*. Routledge.

DiFranco, S. (2002). *Marketing the Disney Way*. [Online] Last accessed on 23 March 2005 at www.saidmaterial.com

Dimitratos, P. and Plakoyiannaki, E. (2003). Theoretical foundations of an international entrepreneurial culture. *Journal of International Entrepreneurship*, 1, 187–215.

Disney Online. (2005). *Disney Official Website*. [online] Last accessed on 19th April 2006 at URL: http://disney.go.com/home

Doole, I. and Lowe, R. (2001). *International Marketing Strategy: Analysis, Development and implementation*, 3rd ed., Thomson Learning, London.

Doole, I. and Lowe, R. (2004). *International Marketing Strategy: Analysis, Development and Implementation*, 4th edn. Thomson Learning.

Douglas, S.P. and Craig, C.S. (1997). The changing dynamic of consumer behavior: implications for cross-cultural research. *International Journal of Research in Marketing*, 14, 378–95.

Dunning, J. (1993). *The Globalisation of Business*. Routledge.

Dunning, J.H. and McQueen, M. (1982). Multinational corporation in the international hotel industry. *Annals of Tourism Research*, 9, 48–63.

E

Economist (1993). America's little fellows surge ahead, 3 July, 69–70.

Elkington, J. (2001). Value Versus Values: Penetrating the Values and Value Barriers in Elkington, J. (2001). *The Chrysalis Economy: How citizen ceos and corporations can fuse values and value creation*. Capstone.

Ellis, D. (2004). Cost-conscious travellers will soon have more choice. *Business Wireless*, October.

Ellis, P. and Pecotich, A. (2001). Social factors influencing export initiation in SMEs. *Journal of Marketing Research*, 38, 119–30.

Erstad, M. (1997). Empowerment and organisational change. *International Journal of Contemporary Hospitality Management*, 9(7), 325–33.

Euro Disney, S.C.A. (2005). *Euro Disney in Figures, the Top European Destination*. [Online] Last accessed on 28 February 2005 at www.eurodisney.com/en/0120.php

Eyster, J.J. (1997). Hotel management contracts in the US, 12 areas of concern. *Cornell Hotel and Restaurant Administration Quarterly*, 38(3), 21–33.

F

Faulkner, B. (1997). A model for the evaluation of national tourism destination marketing programs. *Journal of Travel Research*, 35(3), 23–32.

Fisher, C. and Lovell, A. (2003). *Business Ethics and Values*. Prentice Hall.

Forman, J. (1998). Corporate Image and the Establishment of Euro Disney: Mickey Mouse and the French Press. *Technical Communication Quarterly*, Summer 7(3). P247–258.

Freeman, R.E. (1984). *Strategic Management: A Stakeholder Approach*. Pitman Publishing Company.

Frooman, J. (1999). Stakeholder influence strategies. *The Academy of Management Review*, 24(2), 191–205.

G

Gardenswartz, L. and Rowe, A. (2003). *US Coast Guard*. [Online] Last accessed on 31 March 2005 at www.uscg.mil/hq/g-w/g-wtl/divdef.htm

Getz, D. and Carlsen, J. (2005). Family business in tourism: state of the art. *Annals of Tourism Research*, 32(1), 237–46.

Go, M.F. and Pine, R. (1995). *Globalization Strategy in the Hotel Industry*. Routledge.

Gray, J.L. and Starke, F.A. (1988). *Organisational Behaviour: Concepts and Applications*. Charles E. Merrill.

Greiner, L. (1972). Evolution and revolution as organisations grow. *Harvard Business Review*, 50, 37–46.

Griffin, R.W. and Pustay, M.W. (2005). *International Business*. Pearson Education International.

H

Habermas, J. (1975). *Legitimation Crisis*. Beacon Press.

Hackman, J.R. and Oldham, G.R. (1980). *Work Design*. Addison-Wesley.

Hamill, J. (1997). The Internet and International Marketing. *International Marketing Review*, 14(5), 300–21.

Handy, C. (1993). *Understanding Organisations*. Penguin.

Harrison, J.S and Enz, C.A. (2005). *Hospitality Strategic Management: Concepts and Cases*. John Wiley & Sons.

Hatch, M.J. (1997). *Organisational Theory, Modern Symbolic and Postmodern Perspectives*. Oxford University Press.

HCITB–Ellis, P. (1981). *The Image of Hotel and Catering Work*. HCITB Research Report.

HCTC (1990). *Employee Relations for the Hotel and Catering Industry*. HCTC.

Hedley, B. (1977). Strategy and the Business Portfolio. *Long Range Planning*, February, 12.

Hellriegel, D., Slocum, D. and Woodman, R.W. (1992). *Organisational Behaviour*. John Wiley.

Hendry, J. (2004). *Between Enterprise and Ethics: Business and Management in a Bimoral Society.* Oxford University Press.

Henshall, B. and Roberts, R. (1985). Comparative assessment of tourist generating markets for New Zealand. *Annals of Tourism Research*, 12(2), 219–38.

Hill, C. and Jones, G. (2004). *Strategic Management: An Integrated Approach*, 6th edn. Houghton Mifflin.

Hirst, P. and Thompson, G. (1995). *Globalisation in Question.* Cambridge Polity Press.

Hitt, M.A., Ireland, R.D. and Hoskisson, R.E. (2005). *Strategic Management: Competitiveness and Globalization*, 6th edn. Thomson.

Hofstede, G.H. (1991). *Cultures and Organisations: Software of the Mind.* McGraw-Hill.

Hofstede, G.H. and Bond, M.H. (1988). The confucius connection: from cultural roots to economic growth. *Organisational Dynamics*, 16(4), 4–21.

Hoogevelt, A. (1997). *Globalisation and the Postcolonial World.* Macmillan.

Huyton, J.R. and Ingold, A. (1995). The Cultural Implications of Total Quality Management – the Case of Ritz Carlton Hotel in Hong Kong in Teare, R. and Armistead, C. (eds) (1995) *Services Management: New Directions, New Perspectives.* Cassell.

HVG (2007) *Heti Világ Gazdasági* 13 117 30th of March, 2007 Budapest.

Hwang, L. and Lockword, A. (2006). Understanding the challenges of implementing best practices in hospitality and tourism SMEs. *Benchmarking: An International Journal*, 13(3), P337–54.

Hyatt Hotels and Resorts (2004). *Melange: Hyatt Diversity Newsletter*, **5**(2). Hyatt Corporation.

I

InterContinental Hotels Group. *Explore the Most Global Hotel Company.* [Online] Last accessed on 19 April 2005 at www.ihgplc.com/index.asp

International Society of Hospitality Consultants (2005). *Top Ten Global Issues and Challenges in the Hospitality Industry*, www.hospitalitynet.org

J

Jameson, F. and Miyoshi, M. (eds.) (1998). *The Cultures of Globalisation.* Duke University Press.

Johanson, J. and Vahlne, J.E. (1990). The mechanism of internationalization. *International Marketing Review*, 7(4), 11–24.

Johns, N., Chan, A. and Yeung, H. (2003). The Impact of Chinese Culture upon Service Predisposition *Service Industries Journal*, 23(5), 107–122.

Jones, P. (ed.) (2002). *Introduction to Hospitality Operations: An Indispensable Guide to the Industry*, 2nd edn. Continuum.

Jones, P. (2004). Finding the hospitality industry? Or finding hospitality schools of thought? *Journal of Hospitality, Leisure, Sport and Tourism Education*, 3(1), 33–45.

Jones, P. and Pizam, A. (eds.) (1993). *The International Hospitality Industry: Organisational and Operational Issues.* Pitman.

Just Disney (2005). *Disneyland's History.* [Online] Last accessed on 1 March 2005 at www.justdisney.com/disneyland/history.html

K

Kelly, I. and Nankervis, T. (2001). *Visitor Destinations*. John Wiley & Sons.

Kim, B.Y. and Oh, H. (2004). How do firms obtain a competitive advantage? *International Journal of Contemporary Hospitality Management*, 16(1), 65–71.

Kincheloe, J. (2002). *The Sign of the Burger; McDonalds and the Culture of Power.* Temple University Press.

Knight, K.G. (2001). Entrepreneurship and strategy in the international SME. *Journal of International Management*, 7(3), Autumn, 155–71.

Knowles, T., Dimitrios, D. and El-Mourhabi, J.B. (2001). *The Globalization of Tourism and Hospitality: A Strategic Perspective*. Continuum.

Knowles, T. and Egan, D. (2002). The Changing Structure of UK Brewing and Pub Retailing *International Journal of Contemporary Hospitality Management*, 14(2), 65–71.

Kotas, R. *et al.* (1996). *The International Hospitality Business*. Cassell.

Kotler, P. (2000). *Marketing Management*. Millennium edition. Prentice Hall.

Kotler, P. (2003). *Marketing Management*, 11th edn. Prentice Hall.

Kotler, P., Bowen, J. and Makens, J. (2003). *Marketing for Hospitality and Tourism*, 3rd edn. Prentice Hall.

Krech, D., Crutchfield, R.S. and Ballachey, E.I. (1962). *Individual in Society*. McGraw-Hill.

L

Larry, Y. (1999). *The International Hospitality Business. Management and Operations.* The Haworth Hospitality Press.

Lashley, C. (2002). Emotional harmony, dissonance and deviance at work. *International Journal of Contemporary Hospitality Management*, 14(5), 255–7.

Lashley, C. and Morrison, A. (2000). *Franchising Hospitality Services: Hospitality, Leisure and Tourism.* Butterworth-Heinemann.

Lashley, C. and Lee-Ross, D. (2003). *Organisation Behaviour for Leisure Services*. Butterworth-Heinemann.

Lashley, C. and Upchurch, R. (2006). *Vacation Ownership: The International Timeshare Business.* Butterworth-Heinemann.

Lasserre, P. (2003). *Global Strategic Management*. Palgrave Macmillan.

Lawrence, P.R. and Lorsch, J.W. (1969). *Organization and Environment*. Richard D. Irwin.

Laws, E. (1995). *Tourist Destination Management – Issues, Analysis and Policies*. Routledge.

Levitt, T. (1960). Marketing myopia. *Harvard Business Review*, 38, 45–56.

Levy, D. (2005). *Old Europe, New Europe, Core Europe: Transatlantic Relations After the Iraq War*. Verso.

Lindstrom, M. (2005). *Your True Competitors*. [Online] Last accessed on 16 April 2005 at www.brandchannel.com/brand_speak.asp?id=41

Lines, D., Marcouse, I. and Martin, B. (2000). *Complete A–Z Business Studies Handbook*. Hodder & Stoughton.

Locke, E.A. (1968). Towards a theory of task motivation and incentives. *Organisational Behaviour and Human Performance*, 3, 457–80.

Luthans, F. (1989). *Organizational Behavior*, 5th edn. McGraw-Hill.

Lydecker, T. (1994). Men and women: two different markets sharing a table. *Restaurant USA*, August, 26–30.

Lynch, R. (2003). *Corporate Strategy*, 3rd edn. Prentice Hall.

M

Mack, D. and Ronald, M. (2003). *VHS Cassette Off Air Recording*. BBC Radio Four, 11 April.

Maddaus, G. (2005). *Disney's Flashy Campaigning Sets Precedent for Rose Parade Potential.* Disneylandreports, Disney Corporation.

Marvel, M. (2004). *Hotel Chain Expansion – Europe*. Mintel International Group Limited.

Marx, K. (1973). *Grundrisse.* Penguin.

Marx, K. (1975). *Capital: A Critique of Political Economy*, Vols. 1–3. Penguin.

Mc Spotlight Website. *Issues within McDonalds*. [Online] Last Accessed on 20 March 2005 at www.mcspotlight.org/issues/advertising/

McDonalds (2002). *Annual Report.* McDonalds Corporation.

McDonalds (2003). *Annual Report.* McDonalds Corporation.

McDonalds (2005). *Annual Report.* McDonalds Corporation.

McDougall, P.P. and Oviatt, B.M. (2000). International entrepreneurship: the intersection of two research paths. *The Academy of Management Journal*, 43(5), 902–6.

McKercher, B. (1995). The destination market matrix: a tourism market portfolio analysis model. *Journal of Travel Research*, 4(2), 23–40.

McKercher, B. and Chow, S.B. (2001). Cultural distance and participation in cultural tourism. *Pacific Tourism Review*, 5, 21–30.

Merrett, A. and Hill, I. (2005). *Corporate Social Responsibility in the Hospitality Industry.*

Middleton, V.T.C. and Clarke, J. (2000). *Marketing in Travel and Tourism.* Butterworth-Heinemann, published by Cassel.

Mintel (2005a). *International Hotel Industry*, Mintel International Group Limited.

Mintel (2005b). *Eating Out Review 2005*, Mintel International Group Limited.

Mintel (2003a). *International Hotel Industry*, Oct. Mintel International Group Limited.

Mintel (2003b). *Impact of Terrorism International*. [Online] Last accessed on 18th January 2007, at URL: http://www.mintel.co.uk.

Mintel (2006). *Condo Hotels – International*, Mintel International Group Limited.

Mintzberg, H. and Quinn, J.B. (1992). *The Strategy Process Concepts and Contexts.* Prentice Hall.

Mitchell, R., Agle, B. and Wood, D. (1997). Toward a theory of stakeholder identification and salience: defining the principle of who and what really counts. *Academy of Management Review*, 22(4), 853–886.

Moon, C. and Bonny, C. (2001). *Business Ethics, Attitudes and Approaches.* Profile Books.

Morrison, A. and Thomas, R. (1999). The future of small firms in the hospitality industry, *International Journal of Contemporary Hospitality Management*, 11(4), P148–154.

Mullins, L. (2002). *Management and Organisational Behaviour*, 6th edn. Prentice Hall.

Mullins, L.J. (1993). The hotel and open systems model of organisational analysis. *The Service Industries Journal*, 13(1), 1–16.

Mullins, L.J. (2001). *Hospitality Management and Organisational Behaviour*, 4th edn. Longman.

Murphy, P.E. and Price, G.G. (2005). Tourism and Sustainable Development in Theobald, W.F. (ed) *Global Tourism* 3rd edition. Elsevier, Oxford, 167–193.

N

Nield, K. (2003). *International Hospitality Management*, 2nd edn. DL Postgraduate Course Materials for Sheffield Hallam University.

Nyheim, P.D., McFadden, F.M. and Connolly, D.J. (2005). *Technology Strategies for the Hospitality Industry.* Pearson.

O

O'Connor, C. (2000). *Hospitality Management: A Strategic Approach.* Blackhall.

O'Connor, P. (2004). *Using Computers in Hospitality,* 3rd edn. Thomson.

OECD (1997). *Globalization and Small and Medium Enterprises (SMEs).* Organisation for Economic Cooperation and Development, Paris.

Ohmae, K. (1989). Managing in a borderless world. *Harvard Business Review,* May/June, 152–61.

Okumus, F. and Hemmington, N. (1998). Barriers and resistance to change in hotel firms: an investigation at unit level. *International Journal of Contemporary Hospitality Management,* 10(7), 283–8.

Oslen, M., West, J. and Tse, E.C. (1998). *Strategic Management in the Hospitality Industry,* 2nd edn. John Wiley & Sons.

Otto, A. (1993). On the Internationalization Process of Firms: A Crtical Analysis. *Journal of Internatoinal Business Studies,* Vol. 24. Issue 3, 211–25.

Oviatt, B.M. and McDougall, P. (1994). Toward a theory of international new ventures. *Journal of International Business Studies,* 25, 45–64.

Oviatt, B.M. and McDougall, P. (1995). Global start-ups: entrepreneurs on a worldwide stage. *Academy of Management Executive* 9(2), 30–44.

Oviatt, B.M. and McDougall, P. (2005). The internationalization of entrepreneurship. *Journal of International Business Studies,* 36, 2–8.

P

Papadopoulos, S. (1989). Strategy development and implementation of tourist marketing plans. *European Journal of Marketing,* 23(3), 37–47.

Park-Smith, A. (2004). *Innovations for our Customers* British Airways.

Pavesic, D.V. and Brymer, R.A. (1990). Job satisfaction: what is happening to young managers. *Cornell HRA Quarterly,* 30(4), 90–96.

Pavord, W.C. and Bogart, R.G. (1975). The dynamics of the decision to export. *Akron Business and Economic Review,* 6, 6–11.

Pearce, P. (1982). *The Social Psychology of Tourist Behaviour.* Pergamon.

Peet, R. (1991). *Global Capitalism: Theories of Societal Development.* Routledge.

Peisley, T. (2005). *Cruise International 2005.* Mintel International Group Limited.

Perdue, R. (1996). Target market selection and marketing strategy. *Journal of Travel Research,* 34(4), 39–46.

Pérez Moriones (1998). El contrato de gestion hotelera, Editoiral irant Lo Blanch.

Peters, T. and Waterman, R. (1982). *In Search of Excellence.* Harper and Row.

Poon, A. (2003). *The Berlin Report: A New Tourism Scenario – Key Future Trends* Tourism Intelligency International, Bielefeld and Port of Spain.

Porter, M.E. (1980). *Competitive Strategy: Techniques for Analyzing Industries and Competitors.* Free Press.

Porter, M.E. (1985). *Competitive Advantage*, The Free Press.

Porter, M.E. (1988). *Wettbewerbsstrategie. Methoden zur Analyse von Branchen und Konkurrenten*, 5th, Frankfurt.

Potter, C. (1989). What is culture and can it be useful for organisation change agents? *Leadership and Organisation Development Journal*, 10(3), 17–24.

Porter, M.E. (1998). *The Competitive Advantage to Nations*, Macmillan Press Ltd. London.

PricewaterhouseCoopers (2001a). *Hospitality Directions* – Europe Edition, July.

PricewaterhouseCoopers (2001b). *New Europe and the Hospitality Industry.*

R

Radhakerishnan, B. (2006). A lawsuit against KFC raises issues about foods that aren't good for us. *ABC News*, 14 June.

Radomski, J.K. (date unknown). *Guestology – Marketing Research Disney Style.* [Online] Last accessed on 23 March 2005 at www.saidmaterial.com

Randall, G. (2000). *Branding: A Practical Guide to Planning Your Strategy*, 2nd edn. Kogan Page.

Reid, T.R. (1990). Japan's No-Tell Hotel. *Washington Post*, 13 August.

Rennie, M. (1993). Born global. *McKinsey Quarterly*, 4, 45–52.

Ritzer, G. (1993). *The McDonaldisation of Society*. Pine Forge Press.

Ritzer, G. (1998). *The McDonaldization Thesis: Explorations and Extensions*. Sage Publications.

Ritzer, G. (1999). *The McDonaldization Theses*. Sage Publications.

Robbins, S.F. (2001). *Organisational Behaviour*. Prentice Hall.

Robertson, R. (1992). *Globalisation: Social Theory and Global Culture*. Sage Publications.

Roper, A. (1997). The emergence of hotel consortia as transorganizational forms. *International Journal of Contemporary Hospitality Management*, 7(1), 4–9.

Rowley, J. (2004). Online branding; the case of McDonald's. *British Food Journal*, 106(3), 228–37.

Rugman, A. and Rodgetts, R. (2003). *International Business*, 3rd edn. Pearson.

Rugman, A.M. and Collinson, S. (2006). *International Business*, 4th edn. Pearson.

S

Sangster, A. (2002). *Boutique Hotels – Global – April 2002*. Mintel International Group Limited.

Sassen, S. (1998). *Globalisation and Its Discontents*. The New Press.

Schaffer, J.D. (1990). Structure and strategy: two sides of success. In Rutherford, D.G. (ed.) *Hotel Management and Operations*. Van Nostrand Reinhold.

Schein, E.H. (1985). *Organizational Culture and Leadership: A Dynamic View*. Jossey-Bass.

Schofield, K. (2005). Celebrity chef Ramsay 'humbled' as Scots are recognised by Queen. *The Scotsman*, 31 December 2005.

Sexton, D.L. and Kasarda, J.D. (eds.) (1992). *State of the Art of Entrepreneurship*. PWS-Kent Publishing Co.

Sharma, I.J. (1984). The culture context of Indian managers. *Management and Labour Studies*, 9(2), 72–80.

Smeral, E. and Witt, S. (2002). Destination country portfolio analysis. *Journal of Travel Research*, 40(February), 287–94.

Smith, V.L. (ed) (1977). *Hosts and Guests: the Anthropology of Tourism*. University of Pennsylvania Press.

Smith, S.D. (2001). Tourism. *Money*, 30(12), 93–4

Styles, C. and Seymour, R.G. (2006). Opportunities for marketing researchers in international entrepreneurship. *International Marketing Review*, 23(2), 126–45.

T

Teare, R. and Boer, A. (1991). *Strategic Hospitality Management: Theory and Practice for the 1990s*. Cassell Education Limited.

Teare, R. and Olsen, M. (1992). *International Hospitality Management, Corporate Strategy in Practice*. Pitman Publishing.

Teare, R. and Olsen, M. (1999). *International Hospitality Management, Corporate Strategy in Practice*, Sixth Impression. Longman.

Teare, R. *et al.* (1996). *The International Hospitality Business*. Cassell Education Limited.

Texas Instruments (2001). *Ethics Matters: How to Implement Values-Driven Management*.

Thomas, C. (2005). *Disney Sets Sail On a Marketing Voyage*. [Online] Last accessed on 23 March 2005 at www.baltimoresun.com/sports

Thompson, J.L. (1997). *Strategic Management – Awareness and Change*, 3rd edn. International Thompson Business Press.

Tomlinson, A.L., Parker, L. and Dixon, A.C. (1994). NHSME Patient Charter Fellowship. *Review of Out-Patient Services*, Pontefract Hospitals NHS Trust, Unpublished Report.

Torrington, D. (1994). *International Human Resource Management, Think Globally, Act Locally*. Pearson.

Travel Trade Gazette (TTG) (2006). *25 Million People Taking Cruise in 2015*, Issue of 10-03-2006, London.

Trevino, L.K. and Nelson, K.A. (1999). *Managing Business Ethics: Straight Talk About How to Do It Right*. Wiley.

Triandris, H.C. (ed.) (1972). *The Analysis of Subjective Culture*. John Wiley.

Tribe, J. (1997). *Corporate Strategy for Tourism*. International Thomson Business Press.

Turley, L.W. and Moore, P. (1995). Brand name strategies in the service sector. *Journal of Consumer Marketing*, 12(4), 42–50.

Turner, B. (1994). *Orientalism, Post-Modernism and Globalism*. Routledge.

U

Ucbasaran, D., Westhead, P.H. and Wright, M. (2001). The focus of entrepreneurial research: contextual and process issues. *Entrepreneurship Theory and Practice*, Summer, 57–80.

Urwick, L. (1952). *Notes On the Theory of Organisation*. American Management Association.

Usunier, J.C. (2000). *Marketing Across Cultures*. Prentice Hall.

V

Vaghefi, R. and Huellmantel, A.B. (1998). Strategic leadership at General Electric. *Long Range Planning*, 31(2), 280–94.

Van Sister, L. (2004). *The Secret of Multi-Branding*. November, Issue 455.

Venison, P. (1983). *Managing Hotels*. Heinemann.

Verity, J. (1994). The information revolution. *Business Week*, 18 May, 12–18.

Vestergaard (2006). *Macau to Overtake Las Vegas Strip as World Largest Casino Market by 2007*. World Markets Research Limited online.

Vroom, V.H. (1964). *Work and Motivation*. Wiley.

W

Walker, J. (1999). *Introduction to Hospitality*, 2nd edn. Prentice Hall.

Walker, J. (2004a). *Introduction to Hospitality Management*, 2nd edn. Pearson.

Walker, J. (2004b). *Introduction to Hospitality Management*, 3rd edn. Pearson.

Walker, R.G. (1986). Wellsprings of managerial leadership. *Cornell HRA Quarterly*, 27(2), 14–16.

Walt Disney (2006). Annual report. [online] Last accessed on 19th Feb. 2007, http://corporate.disney.go.com/investors/annual_reports.html

Wearne, N. and Baker, K. (2002). *Hospitality Marketing in the e-Commerce Age*, 2nd edn. Hospitality Press Pearson Education.

Weaver, T. (1988). Theory M: motivating with money. *Cornell HRA Quarterly*, 29(3), 40–5.

Weber, M. (1964). *The Theory of Social and Economic Organization*. Free Press.

Weihrich, H. (1982). The TOWS matrix – a tool for situational analysis. *Long-Range Planning*, April, 60–8.

Wheelen, T. and Hunger, D. (2004). *Strategic Management and Business Policy*, 19th edn. London: Pearson.

Wheelen, T. and Hunger, D. (2006). *Strategic Management and Business Policy: Concept*. Pearson.

Williams, J.R. (1992). How sustainable is your competitive advantage? *California Management Review* (Spring 1992), 33.

Woods, R.H. (1997). *Managing Hospitality Human Resources*, 2nd edn. Educational Institute of the America Hotel and Motel Association.

Wood, L. (2000). Brands and brand equity: definition and management, *Management Decision*, 38(9), 662–9.

Woodward, J. (1980). *Industrial Organisation: Theory and Practice*. Oxford University Press.

World Tourism Organization (1998). *2002: Climbing Towards Recovery?* 1(9), 31 December.

World Tourism Organization (2003). *World Accommodation Capacity*.

Worldwide Hotel Industry Study (2003). *Horwath International and Smith Travel Research*, New York.

Wright, R.W. and Ricks, D.A. (1994). Trends in international business research: twenty-five years later. *Journal of International Business Studies*, 25, 687–701.

X

Xiaoyao, T. (2005). *The Future of the Shangri-la* www.shangri-la.com

Y

Yu, L. (1999). *The Hospitality Business: Management and Operations.* The Haworth Hospitality Press.

Z

Zhao, J.L. and Merna, K.M. (1992). Impact analysis and the international environment, in Teare, R. and Olsen, M., *International Hospitality Management Corporate Strategy in Practice*, Pitman New York, NY.

Zhou, Z. (2004). *E-commerce and Information Technology in Hospitality and Tourism.* Thomson/Delmar Learning.

Zongqing, Z. (2004). 'E-commerce and Information Technology in Hospitality and Tourism' *Journal of Teaching in Travel and Tourism*, 5(4), 71–73.

Websites

ABC News Website — www.abcnews.go.com/
Accor Group Website — www.accor.com
AFX International Focus Website — www.afxnews.com/
Answers.com Website — www.answers.com
Associated Press Website — www.ap.org/
Bangkok Post Website — www.bangkokpost.com
Best Western Official Website — www.bestwestern.com
Business Week Website — www.businessweek.com/
Business Wire Website — www.businesswire.com/
Business Wireless Website — www.topix.net/business
Carlson Hotel Worldwide: — www.carlsonhotelsmedia.tekgroup.com/
Carlson Official Website — www.carlson.com
Caterer Online Website — www.caterer-online.com/www.caterer.com/
Cendant Hospitality Worldwide Website — www.wyndhamworldwide.com/
CIA, The World Factbook Website — https://www.cia.gov/cia/publications/factbook/
Club 18-30 Official Website — www.club18-30.com
CNN Official Website — www.cnn.com
Daily Telegraph Website — www.telegraph.co.uk
Disney Ambassador Hotel Website — www.disneyambassadorhotel.com
Disneyland HK Official Website — www.disney.com.hk
Disneyland Official Website — www.disneyland.com
Disneyland Paris Official Website — www.disneylandparis.com
Disneyland Tokyo Official Website — www.tokyodisneyresort.co.jp
Distinguished hotels — www.distinguishedhotels.com
Dubai Tourism Online Website — www.dubaitourism.co.ae
E-hotelier Website — www.ehotelier.com/
EastJet Official Website — www.easyJet.com
Easy Group Official Website — www.easy.com
Emerald Library Website — www.emerald-library.com
Fairmont Hotels and Resorts (FHR) Website — www.fairmont.com
FEE Expatriots Website — www.expatica.com/
First Choice Holiday Website — www.firstchoice.co.uk
Four Season Hotel Website — www.fourseasons.com
FHI (Furama Hotels International) Website — www.furama.com/
Gordon Ramsay Official Website — www.gordonramsay.com
Guardian Unlimited Website — www.guardian.co.uk/
Hand Picked Hotels Website — www.handpicked.co.uk/
Hard Rock Café Official Website — www.hardrockcafe.com
Hilton Official Website — www.hilton.com
HSMAI (Hospitality Sales and Marketing Association International) Website — www.hsmai.org/
InterContinental Hotel Group Website — www.intercontinental.com

KFC Official Website	www.kfc.com
Kimpton Hotel Website	www.kimptonhotels.com
Le Meridien Official Website	www.lemeridien.com
London 2012 Olympic Game Official Website	www.london2012.org
Magna Hospitality Group Website	www.magnahospitality.com/
Malaysian Association of Hotels Website	www.hotels.org.my/
Marriott Official Website	www.marriott.com
McDonald's Official Website	www.mcdonalds.com/
MICE Online Dubai Website	www.miceonline.net/dubai
Mintel Online/Official Website	www.mintel.com
National Statistics Online Website	www.statistics.gov.uk
PR Newswire Website	www.prnewswire.com/
QSR Magazine Website	www.qsrmagazine.com
Raffles Hotel Website	www.raffles.com
Rediff Website	www.in.rediff.com
Rezidor SAS Hotel Website	www.rezidorsas.com
Rosewood Hotel Website	www.rosewoodhotels.com
SAGA Holidays Website	www.saga.co.uk/travel/general3/home.asp
Sandals Resorts Website	www.sandals.com/
Shangri-La Hotel Group Website	www.shangri-la.com/en/home.aspx
Shangri–La Hotel in London Bridge Tower	www.shangri-la.com/london/shangri-la/en/
Singapore Government Website	www.topix.net/business
Starbucks Official Website	www.starbucks.com
Starwood Official Website	www.starwood.com
Subway's Official Website	www.subway.com
Technomic Information Services (2006)	https://technomic.securelook.com/ cgi-bin/store_v3/commerce.cgi
TEDA Travel Group, Inc. Website	www.prnewswire.com/
The Conference Board Website	www.conference-board.org/
The Independent Website	www.independent.co.uk/
The Manager Online Website	www.themanager.org
Travel Daily News Online Website	www.traveldailynews.com
Travel Weekly Website	www.travelweekly.co.uk
TTG (Travel Trade Gazette) Online Website	www.ttglive.com
TTI (Tourism Technology Institution) Website	www.tti.org/
UAE Interact Online Website	www.uaeinteract.com
UNWTO Official Website	www.world-tourism.org
USA Today Website	www.usatoday.com/
Villa Feltrinelli Webstie	www.villafeltrinelli.com/
Washington Post Website	www.washingtonpost.com/
Wikipedia, The Free Encyclopedia Website	www.en.wikipedia.org/wiki/Main_Page
Xinhua News Website	www.news.xinhuanet.com
YHA Official Website	www.yha.org.uk/

Author Index

Subject Index

social factor, 328–9
technology factor, 329
Optimizers, 274
Orbis, 179
Organisation for Economic
Cooperation and Development
(OECD), 272, 278
Organizational culture, 45–8
elements of, 46
Schein's levels of, 47
Organizational mission, 205–6
Oriental Land Company, 338
Orlando, 83, 85, 103, 327, 339, 343
Outsourcing, 218, 330
advantages, 219
food and beverage facilities, 62
risk of, 219

Pacific Asia Travel Association
(PATA), 135
Pakistan, 148
Palazzo Versace, 210
Pan American World Airways, 191
Papa John, 277–8
Paris, 84, 109, 160, 231, 322, 339, 351
People for Ethical Treatment of
Animals (PETA), 118
Personal Video Recorders (PVRs), 130
PEST analysis, 105, 106–7
of Disney Theme Parks, 327–9
economic factors, 327, 328
political factors, 327, 328
social factors, 328–9
technology factors, 329
outcomes, 124–5
Philippines, 135, 136, 170, 294, 295
Philippines Amusement and Gaming
Corporation (PAGCOR), 295
Phoenix, 170, 172, 315, 348
Phuket, 161, 208, 295, 315
Pizza Hut, 68, 166, 239
Poland, 179
Politeness, 35
Polycentric predisposition, 240–1
Portfolio analysis, 234–6
Positive action, drivers for, 310
Power distance, 40, 42
cultural dimension scoring, 41–2
Predispositions, 225–6
PricewaterhouseCoopers research,
310, 312
Pricing
decisions, 159

difficulties in policy, 159
in marketing mix, 158–9
penetration, 159
strategy and status management,
223–4
Priority Club websites
functions, 129
Private automatic branch exchanges
(PABXs), 130
Production orientation, 144–5
Products, in marketing mix
alterations, 157
global product, 156–7
local product, 156
Promotion, 162–3
Pub catering, 69–70

Quality hotel, 66
Quality services, in marketing mix,
157–8
Question marks, 234
Quick service restaurant (QSR), 61,
122, 205
Quiet revolution, 302

Recreational facilities, 72
in country resort hotel, 76–7
in Shangri-La Hotels and Resorts,
134
in ski resort hotel, 75
Regiocentric predisposition, 225, 241
Relationship marketing, 137, 333
Renovations, 137
Research and Development Strategy,
of Disney, 334
Residence Inn brand, 82
Resistances to change
individual, 250
managerial, 250
Resort hotels, 75
Responsibility, question of, 304–5
Restaurant sector, 68, 69, 103, 112
Return of investment (ROI), 131
Rituals, 27, 39
Ritz Development Company, 185
Roadside catering, 65–6, 112
Rosewood Hotels & Resorts, 75–6
Royal Caribbean Cruises (RCC), 88, 231
Royalty fee, 86, 184, 186
Russia, 59, 153, 196–7

Sales orientation, 145
San Francisco, 77, 78, 180